Grow the Pie

What is a responsible business? Common wisdom is that it's one that sacrifices profit for social outcomes. But while it's crucial for companies to serve society, they also have a duty to generate profit for investors – savers, retirees and pension funds. Based on the highest-quality evidence and real-life examples spanning industries and countries, Alex Edmans shows that it's not an either-or choice – companies can create both profit and social value. The most successful companies don't target profit directly, but are driven by purpose – the desire to serve a societal need and contribute to human betterment. The book explains how to embed purpose into practice so that it's more than just a mission statement, and discusses the critical role of working collaboratively with a company's investors, employees and customers. Rigorous research also uncovers surprising results on how executive pay, shareholder activism and share buybacks can be used for the common good.

Alex Edmans is Professor of Finance at London Business School and a leading authority on reforming business to serve the common good – but using solutions based on rigorous evidence. He has spoken at Davos and in the UK House of Commons, and gave the TED talk 'What to Trust in a Post-Truth World' and the TEDx talk 'The Social Responsibility of Business'.

'I do not know whether capitalism is in crisis. But I do know Alex Edmans's superb book makes the case, compellingly and comprehensively, for a radical rethink of how companies operate, and indeed why they exist. It is the definitive account of the analytical case for responsible business, but is at the same time practical and grounded in real business experience. It is a *tour de force*.'
—*Andy Haldane, Chief Economist, Bank of England*

'This is an original and important book that will help transform how business sees itself – and how we see business. Alex Edmans, in his passionate advocacy of 'Pieconomics', challenges us all to adopt a mindset and unity of purpose in which all business actions contribute to pie-growing. The implications are radical and far-reaching. Read it: it will challenge how you think.'
—*Will Hutton, former editor-in-chief*, The Observer, *and author of* The State We're In

'Politicians are calling for large companies to be regulated or split up. In this compelling book, Alex Edmans argues that there is indeed a problem with corporate behaviour, but that the solution may be simpler: change corporate purpose so that companies focus on growing the pie rather than grabbing more of it. Edmans's arguments are a powerful and persuasive antidote to much of the conventional wisdom about the corporate world.'
—*Oliver Hart, 2016 Nobel Laureate in Economics*

'This is a brilliant and timely book, taking the business case for responsible capitalism to a whole new level. Edmans provides a rigorous, evidence-based approach, exploring numerous angles around how businesses can (and, as he shows, must) combine profit-seeking with purpose, as well as the role investors and other stakeholders can play in driving a genuine win-win approach. He tackles counter-arguments head on and has the courage to expose examples of virtue-signalling that falsely discredit responsible businesses. Citing case studies collated over decades, it's a great read, too, offering fascinating examples well beyond the usual suspects. *Grow the Pie* really has the power to convince the sceptics as well as to encourage advocates to consider new ways to embed the approach further in their businesses.'

—Dame Helena Morrissey, financier and founder of the 30% Club

'Alex Edmans has produced rigorous evidence that the choice between people and profits is a false dichotomy. Now he makes his work accessible to a broader audience and explains how it's possible to overcome the trade-offs that hold so many leaders and companies back.'

—Adam Grant, author of Originals *and* Give and
Take *and host of the TED podcast WorkLife*

'This is a must-read book for anyone interested in reforming capitalism – particularly in its role of serving wider society. The book is grounded in academic evidence, but the ideas are highly practical, and recognise the need for business to be profitable as well as purposeful. Most companies have inspiring mission statements; Edmans provides a concrete framework for translating them into actual practice. He does not shy away from acknowledging the challenges with running a purpose-driven company. Instead, he tackles them head-on, giving clear guidelines on how to navigate tough decisions, which he illustrates with powerful examples.'

—Dominic Barton, former Global Managing Partner of McKinsey

'In *Grow the Pie*, Alex Edmans has provided us with a valuable contribution to contemporary thinking about how business can be a force for good in society. I have long advocated seeing the mutuality of interests between business, the workforce, suppliers, communities, the government and other stakeholders, and Alex employs a solid evidence base to back up this belief so many of us intuitively share: that generating social value is good business. His thought-provoking, often contrarian, ideas are rigorously logical, delving beneath the superficial analyses we often see, which assume correlation implies causation. And Alex's engaging storytelling brings the principles of "Pieconomics" to life with examples of prominent businesspeople – not just those who understand the benefits of growing the pie, but also those who don't.

I'm pleased to see this impressive piece of work come out at a time when we in the business world need to raise our game in building trust with stakeholders. This means not just arguing for the benefits of business for society, but actually delivering on those benefits. It means an underlying shift in attitude away from "us versus them", towards mutual efforts to grow and share the pie of business value.'

—*Sir James G. M. Wates, Chairman of Wates Group*

'Alex Edmans provides robust evidence against the claim that businesses must choose between shareholder value and social responsibility. Although there are trade-offs, there is no single trade-off. What is good for shareholders can be good for society: evidence matters.'

—*Baroness Onora O'Neill, philosopher and former President of the British Academy*

'Alex Edmans has done a great service to society by showing that business doesn't have to be a zero-sum game if we focus more on growing the pie rather than maximising our slice of it. This is capitalism with a human face.'

—*Andrew Lo, MIT Sloan School of Management*

'As someone who believes passionately in the power of business to contribute powerfully to the broader well-being of society, I'd thoroughly recommend this important, timely and evidence-rich book. For me, three things jump out from its pages: healthy businesses help to make healthy societies; business and society should see each other as partners, not adversaries; and it is an act of enlightened self-interest for business to be driven by its long-term social purpose, not short-term profit maximisation.'

—*Liv Garfield, CEO, Severn Trent*

'Just as *Freakonomics* encouraged readers to look beyond the conventional wisdom that underlies many public policies, now Professor Alex Edmans introduces the concept of Pieconomics. In *Grow the Pie*, he challenges popular rhetoric that the free enterprise system is broadly detracting from society. Instead, through many and varied examples, he offers an alternate lens through which we can interpret what constitutes responsible business. In this thoroughly readable book, Edmans debunks mythologies about corporate behaviour and offers a new vocabulary by which we can have principled discussions about the role of business in society. A "must-read" for leaders in government, business and the media that reports on both.'

—*Paula Rosput Reynolds, Director of GE, BP and BAE*

'Contemporary discussion tends to focus on the exercise of power by investors, boards and executives, often involving confrontation and dispute. But while strong decisions will often be required and critically important to the success of a business, the overarching need is for the embedding of pervasive influence geared to the purpose of promoting long-term sustainable growth. A fundamental ingredient is the way in which shareholders discharge the obligations that inexorably go alongside their privilege and rights as owners. This book is a must-read for asset owners, fund managers and the boards and executives who lead business enterprise. It provides evidence-based analysis and guidance on how the influence of well-designed stewardship can yield benefit in terms of both financial returns for savers and investors and returns for all stakeholders in a way that benefits society as a whole.'

—*Sir David Walker, former Chairman of Barclays and Morgan Stanley International, author of the Walker Review*

'This uplifting book provides powerful examples, as well as evidence, that socially responsible businesses generate even higher long-term profits than corporations focused on short-term profit maximisation. Value is created particularly in new-economy enterprises by employee purpose, creation of brand and reputation, which drives customer preference. The findings reflect my own real-world experiences of striving for business excellence across the global Life Sciences industry.'

—*David Pyott, former Chairman and CEO of Allergan*

'Finance Professor Alex Edmans defines his purpose in life as "to use rigorous research to influence the practice of business". This book, *Growing the Pie*, demonstrates his manifest success in fulfilling that purpose. Edmans mobilises evidence – not anecdotes – to make a case, both accessible and compelling, for policies and practices that increase the value available for all stakeholders, versus simply and simplistically maximising profit. Edmans's critical contribution is to reframe arguments about business and capitalism from an all too prevalent short-term zero-sum game to collaborative games where, over time, all can benefit.'

—*Bill Janeway, Warburg Pincus*

'An important, thoughtful and timely book. The conflicts surrounding business, and its effects on society, are the subject of a heated debate. With clarity and insight, Alex Edmans makes a valuable contribution to this key debate. Anyone interested in this important subject would find much to learn from, or wrestle with, in this book.'

—*Lucian Bebchuk, Harvard Law School*

GROW THE PIE

How Great Companies Deliver Both Purpose and Profit

ALEX EDMANS

CAMBRIDGE
UNIVERSITY PRESS

CAMBRIDGE
UNIVERSITY PRESS

University Printing House, Cambridge CB2 8BS, United Kingdom

One Liberty Plaza, 20th Floor, New York, NY 10006, USA

477 Williamstown Road, Port Melbourne, VIC 3207, Australia

314–321, 3rd Floor, Plot 3, Splendor Forum, Jasola District Centre, New Delhi – 110025, India

79 Anson Road, #06–04/06, Singapore 079906

Cambridge University Press is part of the University of Cambridge.

It furthers the University's mission by disseminating knowledge in the pursuit of education, learning, and research at the highest international levels of excellence.

www.cambridge.org
Information on this title: www.cambridge.org/9781108494854
DOI: 10.1017/9781108860093

First published 2020

Printed in the United Kingdom by TJ International Ltd. Padstow Cornwall

A catalogue record for this publication is available from the British Library.

Library of Congress Cataloging-in-Publication Data
NAMES: Edmans, Alex, author.
TITLE: Grow the pie : how great companies deliver both purpose and profit / Alex Edmans, London Business School.
DESCRIPTION: New York, NY : Cambridge University Press, 2020. | Includes bibliographical references and index.
IDENTIFIERS: LCCN 2019042027 (print) | LCCN 2019042028 (ebook) | ISBN 9781108494854 (hardback) | ISBN 9781108816434 (paperback) | ISBN 9781108860093 (epub)
SUBJECTS: LCSH: Social responsibility of business–United States. | Corporations–United States. | Wealth–United States. | Income distribution–United States.
CLASSIFICATION: LCC HD60.5.U5 E33 2020 (print) | LCC HD60.5.U5 (ebook) | DDC 658.4/08–dc23
LC record available at https://lccn.loc.gov/2019042027
LC ebook record available at https://lccn.loc.gov/2019042028

ISBN 978-1-108-49485-4 Hardback

CONTENTS

INTRODUCTION

There is one and only one social responsibility of business – to ... increase its profits.

> Milton Friedman, Nobel Laureate in Economics

The public expectations of your company have never been greater. Society is demanding that companies ... serve a social purpose.

> Larry Fink, CEO of BlackRock

The most effective way to improve board performance is to increase the power of shareholders.

> Lucian Bebchuk, Harvard Law School

Shareholder activists ... are more like terrorists who manage through fear and strip the company of its underlying crucial assets ... extracting cash out of everything that would otherwise generate long-term value.

> Peter Georgescu, author

There's something wrong when the average American CEO makes 300 times more than the typical American worker.

> Hillary Clinton, 2016 US Presidential Candidate

Air France will disappear if it does not make the necessary efforts to be competitive ... I call on everyone to be responsible: crew, ground staff, and pilots who are asking for unjustified pay hikes.

> Bruno Le Maire, French Economy Minister

Capitalism is in crisis.

The consensus among politicians, citizens and even executives themselves – on both sides of the political spectrum and throughout the world – is that business just isn't working for ordinary people.

The 2007 financial crisis cost 9 million Americans their jobs and 10 million their homes. Even though the economy has recovered since then, the gains have largely gone to bosses and shareholders, while worker wages have stagnated. In 2018, just twenty-six tycoons owned the same wealth as the 3.8 billion poorest citizens in the world. Corporations impact not only people's livelihoods, but also their lives. In a single year, fourteen Chinese workers were allegedly driven to suicide by unbearable working practices at the Foxconn City industrial park, where they made electronics for US giants.

The damage isn't just to people, but to the planet too. In 2010, the explosion of BP's Deepwater Horizon drilling rig saw 4.9 million barrels of oil spill into the sea, threatening eight US national parks, endangering 400 species and spoiling 1,000 miles of coastline. Five years later, Volkswagen admitted installing a 'defeat device' in its cars, which cut emissions by up to forty times when it detected a test was being conducted. As a result, citizens were exposed to far higher pollution than Volkswagen claimed, causing approximately 1,200 deaths in Europe alone. Over and above these individual cases, the environmental costs created by business are estimated at $4.7 trillion per year.

Citizens, and the politicians that represent them, are fighting back. On 15 April 2019, the activist group Extinction Rebellion organised demonstrations in eighty cities across thirty-three countries, blockading roads, bridges and buildings in protest at climate change. US Presidential Candidate Elizabeth Warren has pledged, if elected, to break up tech giants Facebook, Google and Amazon, and to impose a wealth tax on the elites. Myriad other responses include Occupy movements, Brexit, the election of populist leaders, restrictions on trade and immigration and revolts on CEO pay. But while the precise reaction varies, the sentiment's the same. 'They' are benefiting at the expense of 'us'.

Even though the conflict between business and society is now at a peak, it's been around for centuries. In the mid-nineteenth century, Karl Marx wrote about the struggle between capital and labour. Since then, we've seen a pendulum swing back and forth between executives and shareholders on the one hand, and workers and customers on the other. Think of the late-nineteenth-century robber barons who created giant monopolies such as Standard Oil; policymakers responded by breaking some up. Or the peak of trade unions in the 1970s, followed by legislation that caused their decline. Or the rise of big banks in the early twentieth century, which culminated in the 1929 financial crisis and their regulation by the Glass-Steagall Act – itself partially reversed since the 1980s, contributing to another crisis in 2007. Unless we can come up with another way, this movie will keep on being replayed.

But the good news is that there is another way.

By applying a radically different approach to business, enterprises can create *both* profit for investors and value for society. So in the face of all these conflicts, this is a fundamentally optimistic book. Yet this optimism is not based on blind hope, but on rigorous evidence that this approach to business works – across industries and for all stakeholders – and an actionable framework to turn it into reality.

The heart of this new approach is a shift in thinking. Conflict arises from what this book calls the *pie-splitting mentality*. The value that a company creates is seen as a fixed pie. Then, the only way to get a larger slice of pie for 'us' is to reduce the slice given to 'them'. Business is seen as a zero-sum game. If a company serves society, this is at the expense of profits; if it pays its CEO more, this takes from worker wages. As a result, business and society are enemies. Some businesses view citizens as a sitting duck, to be exploited by hiking prices or cutting wages; some citizens seek to straitjacket business through regulation. When the pie is fixed, executives and policymakers face a dilemma: Should companies serve shareholders or society?

This book advocates a new approach: Companies can serve both. The *pie-growing mentality* stresses that the pie is not fixed. When all members of an organisation work together, bound by a common purpose and focused on the long term, they create shared value in a way that enlarges the slices of everyone – shareholders, workers, customers, suppliers, the environment, communities and taxpayers. Evidence suggests that visionary leaders can transform a company, growing the pie for the benefit of all. Engaged shareholders can intervene in a failing firm, growing the pie for the benefit of all. A motivated workforce can innovate from the bottom up, growing the pie for the benefit of all.

Crucially, the pie represents social value, not profits – profits are only one slice of the pie. Thus, under the pie-growing mentality, a company's primary objective is social value rather than profits. Surprisingly, this approach typically ends up *more* profitable than if profits were the end goal. That's because it enables many investments to be made that end up delivering substantial long-term pay-offs. But since these pay-offs couldn't have been forecast from the outset, the projects would have never been approved under a traditional shareholder value framework.

This positive effect on profits is critical. While other advocates of business reform correctly stress the importance of serving society, they often encourage the pie-splitting mentality – viewing investors as the enemy and profits as extracting value. Yet without profits, shareholders wouldn't finance companies, companies couldn't finance investments and investments couldn't finance shareholders' needs (citizens' retirements, insurance companies' claims or pension funds' liabilities). Thus, ideas to reform business that ignore profits' crucial role in society are unlikely to be implemented – enterprises aren't charities. The positive effect on profits also means that it's in companies' own interests to transform the way they do business and take very seriously their impact on society. In fact, it's urgent that they do. Otherwise, the promised regulations will be passed, and customers and workers will switch to competitors whose values they share.

That the pie can be grown means not only that purpose isn't at the expense of profit, as some executives and investors believe, but also that profit need not be at the expense of purpose, as some business critics argue. The implications are profound. High profits – and even high CEO pay – aren't automatically a reason to 'name and shame' a company, if earned in the right way. Profits are often the by-product of taking some things and making them better, the root of human progress across the ages. Investors shouldn't always be suppressed; they're allies in reforming capitalism to a more purposeful and more sustainable form. Companies, investors and citizens aren't adversaries; they can play for the same team. Because it needn't be a question of either-or – serving either investors or society. It's both-and.

This win-win thinking is what the book is about. We'll start in Part I with the *why* – why businesses exist and why they should focus on creating social value rather than just profit. It explains the pie-growing mentality and how it differs from not only pie-splitting, but also broader views of business such as 'enlightened shareholder value'. Part I also addresses potential objections to the pie-growing mentality and nuances in its implementation. Growing the pie doesn't mean ignoring profits, nor carefree investment with scant attention to the cost – it's focused and disciplined. Indeed, I'll provide an actionable framework to guide when to turn down a project and how to deal with uncomfortable trade-offs.

I then present evidence that generating profit as a result of serving society is not a too-good-to-be-true pipe dream, but realistic and achievable. It *is* possible for investors and society to simultaneously benefit. So creating value for stakeholders isn't just a worthy ideal – it's good business sense. When I speak to practitioners on the importance of purpose, I'm introduced as a Professor of Finance and the audience often thinks they've misheard. A company's finance department is frequently the enemy of mission-led initiatives, believing that they're simply a distraction from creating profits. This might be true in the short term, where trade-offs particularly bite. But the long-term evidence shows that any finance department with this mindset is failing at its job.

Part II discusses *what* grows the pie. It shows that many common reform proposals don't actually work, because they're based on splitting a fixed pie. We'll turn conventional views on some of the most controversial aspects of business on their head, by looking at them through a pie-growing rather than a pie-splitting lens. We'll see that executive pay, shareholder activism and share repurchases – often thought to serve CEOs and investors at the expense of stakeholders – can grow the pie for all. But the important word is 'can'. As currently practised, they're often failing to do so, and I'll discuss how to improve them.

Part III turns to the practical question of *how* to grow the pie. It highlights the power of purpose – an enterprise's reason for being and the role it plays in the world. Purpose answers the question 'How is the world a better place by your company being here?' But when the rubber hits the road and a CEO faces short-term profit targets, how can she put purpose into practice? This part highlights the ability and responsibility of companies, investors, regulators and citizens – individually and working together – to achieve this.

The pie-splitting mentality is widespread, and doesn't just apply to the relationship between business and society. The tale of Robin Hood, who robbed from the rich to give to the poor, is much more celebrated than the Elves and the Shoemaker, where the elves help the cobbler make shoes without taking from anyone else. We'll end in Part IV by discussing how the idea of pie-growing can be applied to wider contexts, such as international trade, interpersonal dynamics, serving others and personal leadership.

What underpins this shift in mentality? It's a careful study of the *evidence* for what drives long-term value creation within enterprise.

This evidence-based approach contradicts common views on business. Some views are based on quotes. But when giving a quote, you have the incentive to make it as one-sided as possible. To become famous for arguing that business needs to be reformed, you might portray companies as evil and call activists 'terrorists', like the Georgescu quote earlier. To become famous for supporting a profit focus, you might claim that extracting profits is the only socially responsible activity a business can do, like the Friedman quote earlier. An extreme quote reduces the need to back it up with evidence, by giving the impression that the point is so obvious that no proof is needed. And an extreme quote is more likely to be tweeted, shared and cited by others since it makes the strongest possible case. Because one-sided quotes advocate for only one slice of the pie – 'us', but not 'them' – they fuel the pie-splitting mentality.

Other views on business are based on case studies or stories. Stories are vivid, bring a topic to life and get retold. So they've been used successfully in business schools, books and TED talks. But as explained in my own TED talk, 'What to Trust in a Post-Truth World', stories tell you little, because you can always hand-pick a story to support any viewpoint. Supporters of an exclusive focus on profit might use the story of GE under Jack Welch to show it can succeed. Opponents might use the story of Enron to show it can fail. Indeed, both GE and Enron are major business school case studies, but neither story tells us whether running a company for profit works in general.

Evidence, instead, draws insights from thousands of companies, across dozens of industries, over several years. It tries to distinguish correlation from causation and address alternative explanations. Just as diagnosis precedes treatment in medicine, it's critical to use the best evidence to accurately assess the problems with capitalism before proposing reform.

Now there's substantial variation in the quality of evidence. One of the most dangerous phrases is 'research shows that …', because research can be hand-picked to show nearly anything you'd like it to show. For example, in the UK House of Commons' 2016 inquiry into corporate governance, the witness before me quoted research which 'found that firm productivity is negatively correlated with pay disparity between top executive and lower level employees', referencing a January 2010 work-in-progress draft. The finished version had actually been published three years prior to the inquiry. Having gone through peer review and tightened up its methodology, it found the opposite result:

- 'We do not find a negative relation between relative pay and employee productivity.'
- 'We find that firm value and operating performance both increase with relative pay.'

The danger of hand-picking studies is especially severe given confirmation bias – the temptation to accept any evidence that supports one's pre-existing view on business, regardless of its quality. So an evidence-based view gleans particularly from studies published in the most stringent peer-reviewed journals. These journals reject up to 95% of papers, such is the toughness of their standards. The above example shows that the rigour of a study isn't just an 'academic' issue, but can fully reverse its implications for real-world practice.

The evidence in this book will uncover many surprising results which contradict common myths about business, and suggest different solutions from those frequently advocated. We'll see how reducing the jaw-dropping levels of CEO salaries isn't actually the most effective way to reform pay for the benefit of society. We'll understand how an investor selling his shares in the short term can actually encourage businesses to act more for the long term. We'll learn how a company using cash to buy back shares rather than investing it may create long-run value, not just for its shareholders, but also the economy as a whole.

Now an evidence-based approach doesn't mean that there's only one right answer. Even if we agree on the facts, different people might have different opinions. So I expect you to disagree with some of my stances in this book. In fact, I hope you'll disagree, because I'd like this book to provide fresh – and potentially controversial – perspectives, rather than being an echo chamber that simply reinforces what you already think. Even if we all agree on the price and characteristics of a range of cars, different people will buy different cars depending on how important they view price versus emissions, safety and performance. Similarly, even if high pay ratios are linked to better productivity, citizens might argue they're still undesirable because they see inequality as more important than productivity. The role of evidence is to put the facts on the table so that policymakers, practitioners and voters can make informed decisions, fully aware of any trade-offs – just as accurate information on car characteristics allows customers to make informed purchasing decisions, even though they won't all make the same choice.

Critically, we'll present evidence *against* the book's key propositions. We'll acknowledge that the average socially responsible investing fund underperforms, and how 'sin' industries such as tobacco and alcohol have been highly profitable. We'll take seriously common concerns about responsible business and arguments for shareholder value maximisation, and recognise that the latter is far more nuanced than commonly caricatured. We'll emphasise that, even in the long run, there are externalities that affect society, but don't feed back into a company's profits.

When I started my academic career as a green PhD student at MIT Sloan, I had no clear views. I was lucky to attend a private school in London on financial aid, yet some of my comments were so left wing that my Economics teacher, the wonderfully named Mr Toy, would sing the Labour Party anthem 'The Red Flag' after I expressed them. Outside of school, I was First Division Young Football Journalist of the Year and wrote forcefully against the commercialisation of football and players' excessive wages, yet ended up working for investment bank Morgan Stanley after university. I started the PhD not only confused, but also ignorant. My first week showed me how far behind my class-mates I was academically, and caused me to hastily enrol in a remedial maths course.

The silver lining to knowing almost nothing was that I formed my views based on the strength of the evidence, rather than whether it supported a preconceived opinion. Doing so taught me that there are two sides to almost any debate and the importance of considering the whole pie together, not just one slice. It was through exploring the evidence that the idea of this book – growing the pie – was born.

In addition to balancing the need to serve both investors and society, this book will also balance academic and practitioner insights. As a professor at London Business School and Wharton, and as a PhD student at MIT, I've spent nearly two decades studying what catalyses and constrains long-term value creation by companies. The book will draw from not only my own studies, but also those by many other researchers, while employing the stringent standards for rigour I've learned while running a leading academic journal. Even though this vast body of knowledge contains many profound insights for practi-tioners, it often remains buried in academia. My goal is to share this collective wisdom with a wider audience. I hope to show that, even though the statistical tools that researchers use to nail a result may be complex, the insights themselves are simple.

These large-scale academic studies will be complemented by practical examples from forward-thinking companies and investors, across different industries and countries. And we'll learn from failures as well as successes. These examples are carefully selected to be representative of the large-scale evidence and bring it to life, so that no general conclusion is drawn from an individual case without it also being supported by the data.

I'll also glean from my experience working with and learning from directors, executives, investors, policymakers and stakeholders on embedding purpose into business. This experience has taught me the many practical obstacles in doing so. But these difficulties don't arise because the concepts themselves are difficult. In fact – just like the insights from academic research – they're surprisingly simple. Instead, complexity often has its roots in the pie-splitting mentality. The misguided belief that the sole purpose of business is to generate profits can lead to the need to justify every major investment by a giant spreadsheet calculating its profit impact. We'll see that a pie-growing approach to business is best implemented through judgment than calculation. Yet this judgment isn't arbitrary or a licence that anything goes, but one that's underpinned by rigorous principles.

Indeed, the combination of academic and practitioner insights aims to make the book not only rigorous, but also implementable. Many great academic ideas are truly 'academic' and difficult to put into practice. Serving society might seem a nice ideal, but too nebulous to implement compared to the frameworks currently used to maximise profits. This book shows that a pie-growing approach to business can be just as actionable, operational and concrete as one based on maximising profits – and ultimately lead to more profit in the long run.

By presenting this case for both purpose *and* profit, the intended audience is varied. It includes readers who view profit as important even if not the only goal, such as investors and executives, as well as those who emphasise the need to serve society, such as trade unions or stakeholder representatives. The ideas can be put into practice not only by senior executives, but also middle managers who can instil a social orientation into their teams, and employees who can spark ideas and manage upwards. It's also intended for readers outside business, who wish to learn both sides of the controversy surrounding business – the good and the bad – and understand the interesting, complex and nuanced shades of grey in issues often portrayed as black and white.

Before we start, a brief discussion on terminology. The words that are used to describe businesses can already convey a preconception that they don't or don't need to contribute to society.

- A writer suggesting that companies are exploitative monopolies may use the word *corporation*. We sometimes use the word *enterprise* to highlight how companies, both old and young, can grow the pie by being enterprising – come up with new products, services and ways to engage their employees.
- A company's managers are often referred to as *executives* who passively execute routine activities. It's little wonder that the public objects to CEO pay if millions are given to managers who simply execute. We sometimes use the word *leaders* to highlight how they can pursue new strategic directions and inspire their workforce.
- Executives receive *compensation*. They're assumed to have no intrinsic motivation to serve society by working hard; instead, they demand to be compensated for doing so. You get compensation for an injury, for something unpleasant. Leaders receive *reward*. Reward is earned for something intrinsically desirable, like finding a missing person.
- *Employees* suggest that workers are at the behest of the employer, employed as factors of production on a contractual basis. *Colleagues* are partners in the enterprise, contributing to its growth and sharing in its success.
- *Consumers* imply a one-time transaction: once you've consumed a good, it disappears. *Customers* provide an enterprise with their custom over the long term.
- *Shareholders* imply passive holding of an enterprise's stock. *Investors* highlight their responsibility to invest in the long-term success of a firm through active monitoring or engagement.

Enterprise, leaders, reward, colleagues, customers and investors. These words all emphasise the humanity of business and the relationships that underpin it, which we'll see are crucial in growing the pie to benefit all of society.

HOW TO READ THIS BOOK

Given the broad intended audience, this book contains a variety of material, some of which will be of most interest to particular types of readers. As a result, there are different paths through this book. The best approach, naturally, is to read all chapters in order. They're designed to be an integrated whole – each chapter builds on the next, there are multiple cross-references between chapters and some examples run throughout the book. However, readers short on time may choose to focus on particular chapters, depending on their objectives.

Chapter 1, which introduces the pie-growing mentality, and Chapter 4, which presents the evidence that growing the pie creates value for both investors and society, should be of interest to all readers. In addition to those chapters:

- The general interest reader, which includes those outside business wanting an introduction to how capitalism works and its role in society, as well as business sceptics, will likely find Chapters 3, 8, 10 and 11 of value.
- Leaders of businesses, who seek a framework to put these ideas into practice, and navigate difficult issues such as which projects to turn down and how to resolve trade-offs, should also read Chapters 2, 3 and 8.
- Investors or boards, interested in how shareholders should engage with companies and how to design governance structures to lay the grounds for long-term thinking, should find value in Chapters 5, 6, 7 and 9. Chapter 9 is especially useful for those interested in responsible investing.

- Policymakers, business leaders, academics and others interested in the highest-quality research on what creates long-term value, and how to apply this research to practice, should pay particular attention to Chapters 5, 6, 7 and the 'Policymakers' section of Chapter 10.
- Readers interested in real-world case studies, such as business students, professors or speakers seeking anecdotes for talks, and practitioners wanting examples to follow, should read Chapters 2, 3 and 8, as well as the opening examples of Chapters 5, 6 and 7.

PART I

WHY GROW THE PIE? INTRODUCING THE IDEA

1 THE PIE-GROWING MENTALITY
A NEW APPROACH TO BUSINESS THAT WORKS FOR BOTH INVESTORS AND SOCIETY

Judith Aberg stepped out of the subway station and looked ahead to an ordinary day at work. Her office building stretched across six blocks of Fifth Avenue in New York City and overlooked Central Park. But her employer wasn't the white-shoe investment bank that you'd expect to occupy such coveted real estate. It was Mount Sinai, one of the largest teaching hospitals in the US.

Judith's job was tough. She not only treated patients herself, but also served as Chief of the Division of Infectious Diseases, leading hundreds of researchers, clinicians and staff. Yet her job was also rewarding. In 2014, she oversaw the opening of the Institute for Advanced Medicine, which united physicians across multiple disciplines to provide care to over 10,000 HIV patients in New York City.

But 25 August 2015 was no ordinary day. A patient in Mount Sinai was being given Daraprim to treat toxoplasmosis, a parasitic infection that leads to fever, aching muscles and fatigue. Supplies of Daraprim were running low, so the Mount Sinai pharmacy tried to order some more. This reorder should have been routine. But the pharmacy staff were told that Mount Sinai's credit limit wasn't high enough, and brought this to Judith's attention.

'There must be some mistake!' she thought. Mount Sinai's credit limit was $40,000, surely enough to buy a single bottle of 100 pills. But when she called up Daraprim's supplier, Turing Pharmaceuticals, she was shocked to learn that the price had just been hiked from $13.50 to $750 per pill – a 5,500% increase. So a 100-pill bottle cost $75,000, nearly double the limit.

Turing had been founded in February 2015 and named after Alan Turing, who famously broke the code of the Enigma machines used by Germany in the Second World War. But while Turing the scientist was driven to innovate and break new ground, Turing the company wasn't driven by innovation at all. Rather than developing new drugs, like most pharma companies, its strategy was to buy existing drugs and hike their prices.

Such a strategy might seem like outrageous greed, but it was second nature to Martin Shkreli, Turing's 32-year-old CEO. Shkreli, the son of immigrant janitors, caught a break aged 17 when he landed an internship at Cramer, Berkowitz & Co., the hedge fund founded by CNBC's Mad Money host Jim Cramer. Shkreli started in the post room, but quickly made a name for himself when, in early 2003, he spotted a stock he thought was over-hyped – Regeneron, a biotech company developing a weight-loss drug. He advised his bosses to execute a short-sale, a trade which bet that the price would drop. On 31 March, Regeneron conceded that a clinical trial found that the drug had little effect. That day, its stock halved in value, making millions for Cramer, Berkowitz & Co.

But making millions for others wasn't satisfying for Shkreli. He wanted to make millions for himself. So in 2006, aged just 23, he started his own hedge fund, Elea Capital Management, which also bet on stock prices collapsing. After one of these bets went wrong and Elea itself collapsed, Shkreli was undeterred. He simply started afresh in 2009 by setting up another hedge fund with childhood friend Marek Biestek, named MSMB Capital Management after their initials.

MSMB was just as much of a failure as Elea – despite Shkreli's attempts to cover it up. In July 2010, Shkreli told investors that his fund had earned 36% since inception, when it had actually lost 18%. That December, he claimed that MSMB had $35 million of assets; in fact, it owned less than $1,000. MSMB was a Ponzi scheme similar to Bernie Madoff's, but thankfully Shkreli wasn't as adept at it. So under the guise that 'there wasn't enough money in hedge funds', and in an ironic U-turn, he transformed himself from an anti-biotech speculator into a biotech CEO. He first founded Retrophin in March 2011 and then Turing.

Shkreli saw more money to be made in biotech than hedge funds, not through the risky and expensive process of developing new medicines, but through buying existing medicines on the cheap, hiking their prices and restricting their supply. Turing started out with three drugs – ketamine for depression, oxytocin to induce labour and a ganglionic blocker for hypertension – all acquired from Retrophin. On 10 August 2015, Turing bought Daraprim from Impax Laboratories for $55 million. The very next day, it executed the 5,500% price increase.

This was a boon for profits, but a disaster for society. Toxoplasmosis is a dangerous disease, particularly for pregnant women, the elderly and AIDS patients. Left untreated, it can lead to seizures, paralysis, blindness, birth defects and even death. Such was the seriousness of toxoplasmosis that the World Health Organization included pyrimethamine (the chemical name for Daraprim) on its 'List of Essential Medicines'. But the price hikes meant that this essential medicine was no longer affordable. Judith had to cut its usage from five times a month to a maximum of one and, as she told the *New York Times*, switch to 'alternative therapies that may not have the same efficacy'. These substitutes were less tested, with unknown side effects. 'That doesn't make patients feel confident. It doesn't make us feel confident', she said to CNN.

Just as damaging as the extortionate prices was the restricted access. Despite Daraprim being a critical medicine, Turing distributed it only through one pharmacy, Walgreens, and only then through its 'specialty' rather than regular stores. This stopped potential competitors from getting their hands on it to test and develop cheaper alternatives. So widespread were these barriers that the HIV Medicine Association set up a web page where physicians could share their experience. One reported that it took four and a half days to get a medicine that, under Daraprim's former producer Impax, had been available immediately.

The Pie: The Value Created for Society

We can illustrate Shkreli's strategy using a pie. The pie represents the value an enterprise creates for society – for Turing, this value is generated from its drugs. *Society*, in turn, consists of many different members, as illustrated in Figure 1.1. These different members may

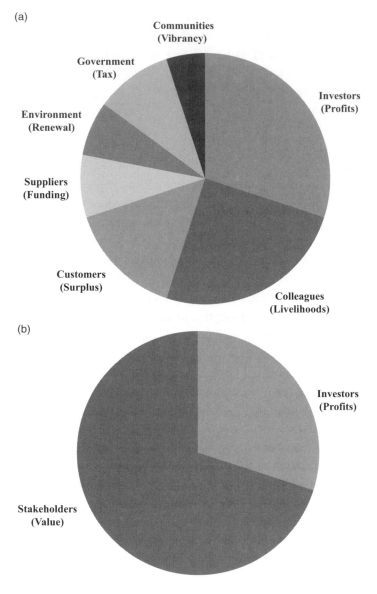

Figure 1.1

capture wildly different slices of the pie, depending on what strategy Shkreli chooses to adopt.

The member Shkreli focused on was *investors*, who enjoy *profits*. It's important to stress that investors aren't nameless, faceless capitalists, but include parents saving for their children's education, pension schemes investing for their retirees and insurance companies funding future claims. Investors are not 'them'; they are 'us'. The failure to serve investors can have wider societal implications. A reported £17.5 billion funding deficit led to the Universities Superannuation Scheme (the pension fund for UK university staff) announcing cuts to pension benefits in 2018. This caused 42,000 staff to strike. The missed lectures led over 126,000 students to sign petitions demanding tuition fee refunds, and forced some universities to remove the skipped content from their exams. So profits are important, and investors are an important member of society. But they're not the only member.

Because the pie includes more than just profits.

The pie includes the value an enterprise gives to its *colleagues*. This comprises their pay, but also training, advancement opportunities, job security, and the ability to pursue a vocation and make a profound impact on the world. We'll call this value *livelihoods*, to reflect both the workplace environment and the company's impact on its employees' home life. This includes parental leave policy, flexible working hours and the expectation to be on email outside the office.

The pie includes the value that *customers* enjoy over and above the price they pay, which we'll call *surplus*. This incorporates a product's effect on customers' long-term welfare. An enterprise can create surplus by using better ingredients in a food product, providing free after-sales service or not offering a loan that the customer can't afford.

The pie includes the value accruing to *suppliers* through a stable source of revenue. We'll call this value *funding*, because what matters is not only how much money suppliers receive, but how promptly they're paid.

The pie includes the value provided to the *environment*, by a company reducing its resource consumption and carbon emissions, and undertaking positive actions like planting new trees and encouraging recycling. We'll call this value *renewal*.*

The pie includes the value enjoyed by *communities*, by an enterprise providing employment opportunities, contributing to

---

* A common term is environmental 'conservation' or 'preservation'. We use 'renewal' to highlight that maintaining the status quo, for example not increasing pollution levels, is not sufficient.

schools, improving access to water and sanitation, and donating its knowledge or products to local initiatives. We'll call this value *vibrancy*.

Finally, the pie includes the value given to the *government* through *tax* revenues.

A company thus serves not only investors, but also colleagues, customers, suppliers, the environment, communities and the government. Together, these other constituencies are known as an enterprise's *stakeholders* who, collectively, enjoy *value*.* *Members* refer to either investors or stakeholders,** and *citizens* are the people who live in society.

The Pie-Splitting Mentality

Shkreli was a pie-splitter: He had the *pie-splitting mentality*. The pie-splitting mentality views the pie as being fixed in size. Then, the only way to increase one member's share of the pie is to split it differently, by reducing the shares of others. These other members are your rivals, whom you fight to grab as much of the pie as possible.

The member whose slice Shkreli wanted to increase was investors. He was a substantial shareholder in Turing himself, and he might come under pressure from other investors if he didn't generate enough earnings. He saw his objective as single-minded: 'My investors expect me to maximise profits.' Since he viewed the pie as fixed, at least in the short-term, the only way he could maximise profits was by taking from stakeholders, as shown in Figure 1.2.

By far the main stakeholder that Shkreli took from was customers – patients and health insurance companies. But Shkreli also took from his colleagues, who may have joined a biotech start-up excited about inventing new drugs, but instead spent their days instructed to reap higher profits from existing drugs. He took from suppliers, because the

---

* Some writers include 'investors' within 'stakeholders'. For clarity, we use 'stakeholders' to include only non-investor members, and 'society' to refer to investors and stakeholders combined. We don't have leaders as a separate category, since leaders are also colleagues and (often) investors.

** When we refer to a member affecting (e.g. taking value from) society, this refers to it affecting (e.g. taking value from) members other than itself – from *wider* society. Note that 'members' is sometimes used to refer exclusively to investors, such as in the UK Companies Act. We use a broader definition, since it's unclear why, say, a colleague is any less a member of an enterprise than an investor.

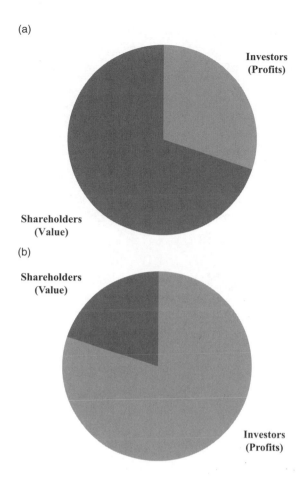

(a)

Investors
(Profits)

Shareholders
(Value)

(b)

Shareholders
(Value)

Investors
(Profits)

Figure 1.2

restricted sale and thus production of Daraprim decreased the demand for its inputs. And he took from communities, due to the impact of reduced access to Daraprim on patients, their families and their friends.

In Shkreli's relentless pursuit of capturing as much of the pie as possible, he paid little heed to growing the pie by developing new drugs. Worse still, his actions shrunk the pie. By restricting access to Daraprim, there was less Daraprim around to benefit society. But if investors' share of the pie increases enough, their slice rises even if the pie shrinks, as shown in Figure 1.3.*

---

* We use *share* to refer to relative value, the percentage of a pie that a member receives, and *slice* to refer to absolute value, the share multiplied by the overall size of the pie.

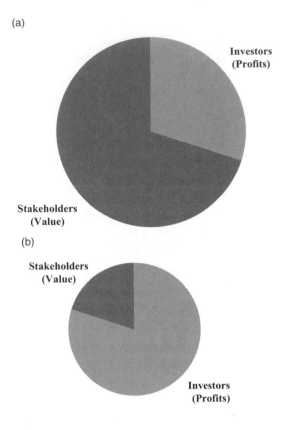

Figure 1.3

The pie-splitting mentality is attractive. Pie-splitting can be done almost immediately and at zero cost. In a single day, Shkreli increased the price of Daraprim by 5,500% without spending a dollar. Pie-splitting didn't require the substantial expense, time and risk of developing a new medicine, getting approval from the US Food and Drug Administration and marketing it. And it was entirely legal. As Shkreli brazenly declared, 'Everything we've done is legal' and 'I liken myself to the robber barons' – late-nineteenth-century American businessmen who used similarly unscrupulous, yet legal, strategies to get rich. Even though Shkreli was later sentenced to seven years in prison, this was for securities fraud at his hedge funds and unrelated to price-gouging at Turing.

In the Introduction, we discussed how you can always find a story to illustrate a point. Unfortunately, Turing appears to be far from an outlier. Enterprises can take surplus from customers not only by price-gouging, but also by pushing products that customers don't need or don't understand. From 1990 until the mid-2010s, UK banks sold payment protection insurance to customers who took out mortgages, loans and credit cards. This insurance had the potential to create value by repaying customers' debts if they lost their jobs or became ill. But it was mis-sold – 1.3 million customers were falsely told they'd only be approved for a loan if they bought the insurance, and 2 million were sold a policy they'd never be able to claim on (e.g. due to being self-employed). The price of the insurance was rarely disclosed, even though it typically added 20% to the cost of a loan, and sometimes as much as 50%.

Enterprises can also exploit colleagues. UK retailer Sports Direct allegedly paid workers below the minimum wage, fired them if they took sick leave and gave them 'zero-hours' contracts with no guarantee of work. It forced zero-hours employees to work overtime for free by threatening them with no work the next day. And companies can squeeze suppliers by paying them as late as possible or using their sheer size to demand rock-bottom prices, such as for cocoa, coffee and fruit from developing countries.

In all these instances, enterprises see society as there for the taking. Even if they don't actively exploit stakeholders, they may simply ignore them and focus on maximising profits, not caring whether stakeholders benefit as well. As mentioned in the Introduction, Jack Welch of GE is one of the most revered CEOs in history for his successful, and relentless, pursuit of profit maximisation. Welch had one goal – to make GE the world's largest company by shareholder value. He viewed serving stakeholders as a distraction that leads to inefficiency.

When businesses exploit society, citizens pressure policymakers to protect their share of the pie with regulation. Companies then respond by trying to bypass the laws. And the conflict continues.

But there is another way.

Roy Vagelos urgently needed money.

In 1978, William Campbell, a research scientist at Merck, had made a potentially breakthrough observation. Ivermectin, a drug that Merck had developed to treat parasitic infections in livestock, might also cure onchocerciasis in humans.

Onchocerciasis was a cruel disease. It was transmitted by blackflies which bred along river banks – banks where citizens of developing countries lived, played and worked because the soil was fertile and water was plentiful. A blackfly's bite injected the *onchocerca volvulus* larva, which matured into worms that lived under the skin and grew up to two feet long. Their larva caused itching so severe that it drove some sufferers to suicide. Once the larva invaded the eyes, it frequently caused blindness – hence the common name for onchocerciasis, river blindness.

River blindness was a serious epidemic. 18 million people were already infected with *onchocerca volvulus*, with over 100 million more at risk. River blindness would soon become endemic in thirty-four of the poorest countries in the world, mainly in West Africa, but also in Latin America. In the most affected villages, the entire population was infected by age 15 and went completely blind by age 30. Once blind, adults would need to be led to their farms by young children – who, as a result, believed blindness was an inevitable part of growing up. Families who tried to reduce their infection risk by moving away from the fertile river banks instead couldn't grow enough food. Having to choose between blindness and hunger reduced communities to empty shells, devoid of any real economic development.

William's hypothesis, therefore, was momentous, and would later see him jointly awarded the 2015 Nobel Prize in Medicine. But in 1978, it was still only an idea; it needed to be rigorously tested. Antiparasitic drugs didn't usually succeed across species. Following William's lab work, another Merck researcher, Mohammed Aziz, launched the first human clinical trial of ivermectin, in Senegal in 1981. It proved so successful – a single tablet completely cured the disease, without any of the side effects common in anti-parasitic drugs – that the WHO thought the data must have been recorded incorrectly. But Merck conducted trials in other African countries over the next few years, which found similar success. In 1987, ivermectin was approved for human use under the brand name Mectizan.

But there was one final challenge – money. It would cost Merck $2 million to set up a distribution channel to West Africa and an extra $20 million per year to produce it, even ignoring the millions that Merck had already spent on development. The West Africans suffering from river blindness were some of the poorest people in the world. They lived in huts caked together from mud and wore skirts woven from grass. They couldn't afford to pay for Mectizan, nor could their governments, which were riddled with debt. Roy Vagelos, Merck's CEO at the time, asked the WHO to fund Mectizan, but the answer was no. He pleaded with the US Agency for International Development and the US Department of State. Still no. That's why Roy urgently needed money.

Roy then went to one final, and radical, source of funding – Merck itself. On 21 October 1987, Roy announced that Merck would give Mectizan away for free, 'as much as needed, for as long as needed', to anyone anywhere in the world who needed it. Merck established the Mectizan Donation Program (MDP), which brought together the WHO, the World Bank, UNICEF, dozens of Ministries of Health and over thirty non-governmental organisations to oversee and fund the distribution of Mectizan.

On the face of it, donating a drug was a crazy idea. The MDP would cost millions to Merck's investors, mostly institutions with responsibilities to their clients – savers. These investors might sell their stock and drive down the stock price, or pressure Merck's board to fire Roy.

But this seemingly difficult decision was easy for Roy. He was driven not by profits, but by the desire to use science to serve society. The son of Greek immigrants, Roy grew up peeling potatoes, cleaning tables and washing dishes at Estelle's Luncheonette, his family's diner. Estelle's main customers were scientists and engineers from the nearby Merck laboratories, and Roy heard them talk excitedly about the drugs they were developing to improve people's health. As he recounted: 'They had great ideas and loved what they were doing. They were passionate about their work, and that infected me ... they encouraged me to pursue chemistry.' Roy's primary concern wasn't the millions of dollars the MDP would cost, but the millions of lives it would transform.

The MDP proved wildly successful. It's currently the longest-running disease-specific drug donation programme of its kind. It's delivered 2.7 billion treatments to twenty-nine African countries, six Latin American countries and Yemen in the Middle East, and now reaches 300 million people per year. Thanks to the MDP, the WHO has certified four Latin American countries (Colombia, Ecuador, Mexico and Guatemala) as having eliminated river blindness. It's no longer a major public health issue in the savannah areas of West Africa.

The decision to donate Mectizan grew the pie. Initially, most of the increase went to West African and Latin American countries, communities and citizens. But Merck subsequently benefited as well, even though such benefits were never the primary reason for Merck's decision. The MDP was a major contributor to Merck's reputation as a highly responsible enterprise. In January 1988, *Business Week* described Merck as one of 'the best in public service' and called the MDP 'an unusual humanitarian gesture'. *Fortune* named Merck America's most admired company for seven years in a row between 1987 and 1993, a record never equalled before or since.

This reputation for serving society in turn attracted both investors and stakeholders. Even though investors bear the financial costs of the MDP, many investors care about social as well as financial returns, as I'll discuss in Chapter 2. Ten years after launching the MDP, Roy reported that he hadn't heard any complaints from shareholders – but he did receive numerous letters from colleagues saying they'd joined Merck because of the MDP. They were excited by the potential to solve the world's most serious health problems through a career at Merck. Today, thanks in part to this reputation, Merck is one of the largest pharmaceuticals companies in the world, worth over $200 billion. It remains an extremely sought-after employer, and it's still on *Fortune*'s list of most admired companies. Investors have benefited too. Since 1978, they've enjoyed an average annual return of 13%, nearly one and a half times the 9% delivered by the S&P 500.

The Pie-Growing Mentality

Roy was a pie-grower: He had the *pie-growing mentality*. The pie-growing mentality views the pie as expandable. It aspires to grow the pie – to create value for society – because doing so benefits both investors and stakeholders alike. Profits, then, are no longer the end goal, but instead arise as a by-product of creating value, as shown in Figure 1.4. Since business is a positive-sum game, investors aren't trying to take from stakeholders, and stakeholders don't need to defend themselves from investors. They're on the same team.

Indeed, 'investor profits' are closely related to the common term 'shareholder value', which includes future as well as current profits.*

---

* A second difference is that shareholder value includes some stakeholder value if shareholders are also stakeholders. We'll come to this in Chapter 2 – for now, to keep things simple, we'll assume that shareholders and stakeholders are distinct.

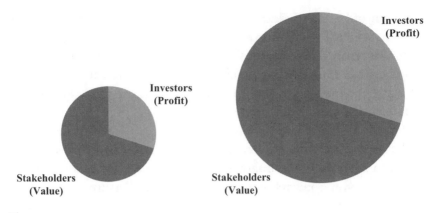

Figure 1.4

Profits are just another form of value, highlighting the alignment: creating value for society yields both stakeholder and shareholder value.

We'll use the term *Pieconomics* ('pike-onomics') to capture the pie-growing behaviour that this book is about. *Pieconomics is an approach to business that seeks to create profits only through creating value for society.* Pieconomics most definitely sees investors as important. But an enterprise serves them not by giving them a larger slice of what already exists, but through growing the pie.

Under Pieconomics, a leader constantly asks herself whether she's increasing profits through creating value or instead redistributing it from stakeholders. Do new products genuinely improve customer welfare or instead cause addiction? Are higher prices due to superior product quality or market power? Is the company committed to providing a healthy workplace, even if there are inevitably job losses in certain areas as technology evolves? Are profits being enhanced through ignoring the company's impact on the environment?

Pieconomics in turn leads to a shift in thinking about what leaders' and enterprises' responsibilities are, and how both should be held accountable by citizens. Its views differ from the traditional term Corporate Social Responsibility (CSR) in two fundamental ways. First, CSR typically refers to activities that are siloed in a CSR department, often to offset the harm created by a company's core business, such as charitable contributions. Pieconomics is embedded into the core business and ensures that its primary mission is to serve society. We'll thus frequently refer to an enterprise's social performance or purpose rather than its CSR. Second, a common dictum of CSR is 'do no harm' – not to take from other stakeholders. But Pieconomics stresses that it's even more important for a company to positively do good by creating value. Being a responsible business isn't so much about sacrificing profits to reduce carbon emissions (splitting the pie differently), but innovating and being excellent at its core business (growing the pie) – like Merck developing ivermectin for human use. Conversely, the main way that enterprises fail to serve society is not by *errors of commission* (giving too large a slice to leaders or investors), but by *errors of omission* (failing to grow the pie by coasting and sticking to the status quo).

In 1981, Sony released the Sony Mavica, a prototype of the electronic camera. Kodak had every ability to respond – after all, it had invented the digital camera in 1975 and held patents for it. But it was too tempting to stick with the status quo, film. Kodak was the clear market leader and its sales crossed $10 billion that year, nearly all from film. Why change? A study by Kodak's head of market intelligence, Vince Barabba, predicted that digital would replace film. But this displacement would take ten years, far too long to bother doing anything about. Kodak thus took no action, unlike its rival Agfa, which sold its film business, and Fuji, which made digital a strategic priority. Kodak's inertia was an error of omission that led to its bankruptcy in 2012 – a huge fall from grace, as Kodak had been worth $31 billion at its peak and employed 150,000 people at one point. Yet Kodak was never subjected to the media backlash that high CEO pay or share repurchases, supposed errors of commission, currently receive. Most people don't view Kodak as an example of corporate irresponsibility or socially destructive leadership, because neither executives nor shareholders lined their pockets. Yet the fact that investors also lost is of no comfort to the workers made redundant. Kodak's executives were pie-shrinkers who harmed everyone. Their complacency and inaction saw a once-great company fail.

While Pieconomics views coasting as destroying substantial value for society, it also stresses that high profits need not be at society's expense. Indeed, in Chapter 2, we'll explain how Pieconomics often generates more long-term profit than pursuing profits directly. Headlines sometimes highlight how much profit an enterprise makes in a single day – even a single minute – as if this requires an apology. *Time* magazine ran an op-ed entitled 'Every 60 Seconds, Apple Makes More Money than You Do in a Year'.

That's the pie-splitting mentality. Crucially, this mentality is sometimes practised by not only executives who exploit stakeholders, but also citizens and policymakers who evaluate companies. It indeed might be that high profits are at the expense of society. But before we criticise high profits, we have to first investigate where they came from. Particularly in the long term, they're much more likely to result from growing the pie – making products that transform customers' lives for the better, providing colleagues with a healthy and enriching place to work, and renewing the environment for future generations. If society has the pie-splitting mentality, then a leader's prime goal is no longer to be excellent at her business. Indeed, success is a liability if profits become large enough to be deemed excessive. She might earn more praise for cutting her own pay or making a large philanthropic donation than for being innovative or customer-centric. Yet delivering high profits need not be shameful. Failing to deliver profits and social value is.

Similarly, with the pie-splitting mentality, a policymaker's goal is to ensure that companies don't make what they see as too high profits. In February 2019, Amazon reversed its decision to build half of its second North American headquarters in Queens, New York City. This new headquarters would have created between 25,000 and 40,000 jobs, with an average salary of $150,000, and provided $27.5 billion of tax revenues. It would also have boosted local companies, generating 100,000 further jobs, and economic development with knock-on benefits such as reduced crime. But Amazon pulled out due to strong opposition from some local politicians and residents, based on the pie-splitting mentality. They objected to Amazon being offered $3 billion of tax breaks to come to Queens, thinking that this came at the expense of the community. Congresswoman Alexandria Ocasio-Cortez celebrated Amazon's withdrawal, saying that the $3 billion could now be used for subway repairs and teacher salaries.

This simply wasn't true. The tax breaks were not an upfront donation that would have diverted funds away from other uses, and thus potentially split the pie. Instead, they were reductions from future taxes that Amazon would have had to pay only if it had grown the pie. Queens would still have enjoyed a vastly increased slice, including taxes of over nine times the foregone revenue. Ocasio-Cortez tweeted: 'Anything is possible: today was the day a group of dedicated, everyday New Yorkers & their neighbors defeated Amazon's corporate greed.' But defeating Amazon didn't mean that Queens won. Everyone lost because the pie shrank.

The division of the pie is certainly important, and we'll turn to this shortly, but the spoils can be shared only if there are spoils to begin with. A well-paid leader is sometimes accused of stealing from the enterprise, but a leader steals more by coasting. Similarly, high pay is sometimes referred to as value extraction, but value destruction is a far worse problem. Average CEO pay in a S&P 500 firm is $14 million. That's substantial compared to average wages, but tiny compared to the median firm size of $22 billion. Even if an executive is overpaid by 100%, that's only $14 million. If the executive fails to create just 1% of firm value, that's $220 million lost to society.

The importance of the size of the pie, rather than just its division, is linked to another important distinction in this book – the difference between ex ante (before the event) incentives and ex post (after the event) outcomes. Merck's anti-cancer drug Keytruda generates value for patients who take it, colleagues who produce and market it, and suppliers who provide the inputs. But Merck's investors and leaders also benefit significantly – Keytruda generated $7.2 billion of sales in 2018. That's because a patent prevents other companies from making similar drugs until 2028. Perhaps ex post, after Keytruda was invented and approved, any company should be allowed to make it. That would ensure a more equal distribution of the gains – other companies' investors, employees and suppliers would share in the pie, and patients (and their insurance companies) would enjoy lower prices. But doing so would erode ex ante incentives to develop the drugs in the first place.

Just like Mectizan, Keytruda was developed to treat a serious disease rather than only to earn monopoly profits. But the reality is that developing and gaining approval for new drugs is extremely expensive – one study estimated an average cost of $2.87 billion. The vast majority of drug ideas fail. Without the prospect of profits in the rare case of success, enterprises could never justify exploring a new idea to begin with. As Merck's current CEO, Kenneth Frazier, points out: 'The price of [a] successful drug is paying for the 90%-plus projects that fail. We can't have winners if we can't pay for losers.'

The contrast between ex ante and ex post applies far beyond patents. Providing ex ante incentives to grow the pie may require giving ex post rewards to those who do so. Perhaps even a disproportionate share is necessary if growing the pie is uncertain and risks huge losses. As I'll stress in Chapter 5, this share should go to all members responsible for pie growth – colleagues as well as leaders. But without the prospect of rewards upon success to balance the risk of failure, leaders may coast and settle for the status quo – an error of omission. An unequal distribution of something is almost always better than an equal distribution of nothing.

Dealing with Trade-Offs

A key attraction of Pieconomics is that growing the pie can increase every member's slice. But the important word is 'can'. One member's slice might shrink even if the pie grows, because value creation often involves trade-offs. New technology might lead to better products for customers, higher profits for investors and easier jobs for colleagues that remain – but also many other workers being made redundant.

The famous Coase theorem, thanks to the Nobel Prize-winning economist Ronald Coase, shows that when the pie grows, it's always possible to find a way of compensating those whose slices would otherwise fall, so that no member ends up losing and at least one benefits. This harmonious outcome is known as a Pareto improvement, after Italian economist and political scientist Vilfredo Pareto.

Pareto improvements won't happen automatically, and so leaders must take active steps to ensure that a theorem becomes reality. While this book stresses the criticality of growing the pie, the distribution of gains is also important, otherwise losing members may oppose pie-growing actions. When trade-offs arise, Pieconomics aims to ensure fairness in the distribution of costs and benefits so that, to the extent possible, no member's slice shrinks. An enterprise that implements new technology may invest in outplacement and retraining to reduce the impact of layoffs, even if doing so lowers the profit boost from the technology. A business that builds a new factory may spend money on reducing emissions and noise pollution. Importantly, the members whose slice shouldn't shrink include investors. While Pieconomics stresses a firm's responsibility to stakeholders, it doesn't imply unfettered pursuit of societal goals, cheerfully ignoring profits. If a company delivers value to stakeholders entirely as a result of sacrificing profits, this splits the pie differently rather than growing it.

The Coase theorem is why a pie-growing enterprise *first* ensures that it increases the size of the pie and *second* tries to ensure that no member's slice shrinks. Now it may not be able to fulfil the second criterion, despite its best efforts. Even with outplacing and retraining, some displaced workers may not be able to find other jobs. Many trade-offs are real and can't be managed around.

How does Pieconomics deal with such situations? While enterprises should create Pareto improvements wherever possible, Pieconomics doesn't argue that they should only take actions where no one loses. As the French philosopher Voltaire noted, perfect is the enemy of good. Often, business critics highlight the damage caused by particular actions. But taking only perfect decisions would lead to serious errors of omission, where many good decisions aren't taken. Pieconomics does involve actions that grow the overall pie, even though some members lose.

Chapter 3 will stress the importance of a leader's *judgment* in evaluating trade-offs between investors and stakeholders. It introduces three principles to guide this judgment. Chapter 8 will emphasise how an enterprise's *purpose* – its reason for being and the members that it particularly aspires to serve – can guide trade-offs between different stakeholders. While CSR instructs a company to 'do no harm', nearly every significant activity hurts at least one stakeholder. If a firm closes a polluting plant, helping the environment, but laying off workers, does this grow the pie? Purpose helps a leader navigate these complex dilemmas.

Just as a pie-growing enterprise shares the gains from pie growth, it also shares the losses from pie shrinkage. In early 2009, as the financial crisis hit, manufacturer Barry-Wehmiller lost 40% of its orders in a few days. To avoid bankruptcy, the board concluded it needed to save $10 million and started to discuss layoffs. Typically, rank-and-file employees bear the pain and executives get off unscathed. But CEO Bob Chapman had something else in mind – to split the burden. Each colleague, from secretary to CEO, was required to take four weeks of unpaid vacation. Leaders took an extra hit as executive bonuses were suspended. As Bob said: 'It's better that we should all suffer a little than any of us should have to suffer a lot.'

By the next year, Barry-Wehmiller still hadn't laid off a single colleague. Not only did it safeguard its workers' jobs, but it also tried to ensure that their free time was used productively by putting on classes at its corporate university. Others used their furlough for volunteer work or to spend more time with their children over the summer. Barry-

Wehmiller ended up saving $20 million, double its original target, and morale soared.

In contrast, the consequences from not sharing the losses can be severe, as Sandra Sucher and Shalene Gupta describe in a *Harvard Business Review* article about Finnish telecoms firm Nokia. In 2008, Nokia faced stiff competition from low-cost Asian rivals, which had driven prices down by 35% in a few years. Over the same period, labour costs in Nokia's plant in Bochum, Germany, had risen by 20%. Nokia decided to close Bochum. The closure may well have grown the pie – without it, Nokia's long-term viability may have been jeopardised. But 2,300 workers lost their jobs. Nokia failed to minimise these colleagues' losses, and this failure ultimately cost investors. A week after the shut-down was announced, 15,000 people protested at Bochum, German government officials demanded that Nokia repay the subsidies it had received for the plant and unions called for a boycott of Nokia phones. Photos of crying employees and protesters crushing Nokia phones spread through the news and social media. As a result of the negative publicity, Nokia lost an estimated €700 million of sales and €100 million in profits over 2008 to 2010.

So in 2011, when Nokia needed to lay off 18,000 employees due to difficulties in its mobile phone business, it had learned its lesson. It launched the Bridge programme, giving these workers five potential paths forward: finding another job within Nokia, finding another job outside Nokia through outplacement, starting a new business, taking business or trade courses, or building a new path such as volunteering – the last three funded by grants from Nokia. Bridge cost €50 million, a drop in the ocean compared to its €1.35 billion restructuring budget from 2011 to 2013. As a result, 60% of the 18,000 workers knew their next step the day their jobs ended, and there were no protests in any of the thirteen countries where the layoffs occurred.

Collective Responsibility

We've talked about *enterprises* with pie-growing and pie-splitting mentalities. But an enterprise isn't a disembodied entity. It's the collection of investors, leaders and stakeholders. Pie-growing isn't the responsibility of only leaders – crucially, *every stakeholder can help grow the pie*. Sure, Roy Vagelos had the power to decide to give ivermectin away for free. But colleagues have the power to go the extra mile even if not explicitly required or rewarded by the employment contract. Indeed, when Barry-Wehmiller announced four weeks of unpaid leave across the firm, some employees took a double load in place of a colleague who couldn't afford to lose four weeks' pay. Customers have the power to risk buying from a new entrant rather than the safety of the market leader, provide feedback to improve a company's products or contribute to review sites to help other customers. Communities have the power to constructively express their concerns to an enterprise looking to enter the area, rather than engage in a 'not-in-my-back-yard' protest.

And pie-splitting is committed not only by investors and leaders. There are certainly investors who pressure CEOs to cut wages to boost short-term profit, or CEOs who voluntarily do so to hit bonus targets. But colleagues may resist a change in working practices that would safeguard the firm's long-term viability. Customers may boycott a firm if the CEO is being paid well, even if it's the result of creating value, or not bother to return products for recycling. Growing the pie may primarily be the responsibility of leaders, but it can't be done without all citizens playing their part. We'll come back to this in Chapter 10.

Why Is Pieconomics So Urgent Now?

The urgency of business recognising its responsibility to society is arguably greater today than ever before. The sheer size of firms, the vast workforces they employ and the billions of dollars that flow through them give them the power to solve social problems, provide fulfilling careers to colleagues and generate returns for all of society. But there are serious concerns that they're instead using this power to exacerbate social problems, exploit colleagues and generate returns only for the elites. Rapidly increasing sections of the population feel cut out of the benefits of economic growth. Incomes of ordinary people have stagnated, while profits and executive pay have soared.

Not only has business's power to affect social problems grown, but so have the problems themselves. As a society, we're facing challenges of a scale and complexity that capitalism as we know it is struggling to address. Some of these challenges, such as a growing and ageing population, aren't the fault of business – but society looks to business to address these problems rather than focusing on profit with little regard to them. Other challenges, such as resource usage, climate change and the displacement of workers through automation, are ones that business can both exacerbate and alleviate.

The consequences that enterprises exert on society, but don't feed back into their profits, are known as *externalities*. Externalities can be either positive or negative – donating ivermectin to cure river blindness creates a positive externality, and hiking the price of Daraprim a negative one. If companies don't recognise the value that they can create for, and take from, society, they'll lose their social licence to operate – as the increasing level of populism shows they may already be doing. This in turn may lead to anti-business regulation being passed that will damage their long-run productivity.

Both types of externality are ignored by traditional profit maximisation. But both types are taken into account by Pieconomics. By committing to create profits only by creating value for society, pie-growing firms help rebuild trust in capitalism. They do so by developing products that truly benefit customers, addressing societal challenges and sharing the fruits with colleagues. As the ivermectin example shows, businesses can solve some of the world's most serious problems. The benefits spilled over to not only West African communities suffering from river blindness, but also employees inspired by making a difference to the world and investors who saw their capital generate social as well as financial value.

Newer generations view serving society as particularly important. A recent survey found that 62% of millennials (born between 1980 and 1996) agreed that 'it is important for me to be known for making a positive difference in the world', versus 52% of Generation X (born between 1965 and 1979). Yet millennials also recognise the importance of profits – 58% agree that 'the successful business of the future will maximise shareholder value/profits', versus 51% of Generation X. Similarly, a joint study by PwC and the international student organisation AIESEC combined the responses of a PwC survey of CEOs with an AIESEC study of young leaders. Only 32% of CEOs view shareholders as more important than stakeholders, while 67% believe the opposite. In contrast, the responses were almost identical for young leaders (46% and 48%, respectively). Thus, to inspire a new generation of workers and provide them with vocations rather than just jobs, it's important for the business of the future to create value for society – but in a pie-growing way that also delivers profit.

Even if we accept that growing the pie is important, and that all members of an enterprise have a responsibility to help it create value, the idea seems general and vague. How do we know if an action grows the pie? What does it actually mean for a particular company to serve society? An oil firm does so in a very different way from a pharmaceuticals firm. We'll come to these questions in Chapter 3 and reprise them in Chapter 8. But first, in Chapter 2, we'll discuss how Pieconomics differs from other approaches to business that recognise its responsibility to society.

In a Nutshell

- The pie represents the value an enterprise creates for society. Society includes not only investors, but also colleagues, customers, suppliers, the environment, the government and communities. If companies consider only investors and ignore stakeholders, they'll lose their social licence to operate – as they may already be doing.
- *Pie-splitting* aims to increase one member's slice by reducing others'. Most commonly, enterprises may try to increase profits by price-gouging customers or exploiting workers. But the pie-splitting mentality may also be held by stakeholders, who think that cutting profits is the best way to increase their own slice.
- *Pie-growing* aims to increase the value that an enterprise creates for society – by inventing new and better products, developing and nurturing its workforce, or renewing the environment.
- *Pieconomics* is an approach to business that seeks to create profits only through creating value for society. Doing so may generate more profits than pursuing profits directly, and more value for stakeholders than reducing the slice taken by investors would.
- The biggest way that companies fail to serve society is not through *errors of commission* (such as overpaying their leaders), but *errors of omission* – failing to create value by coasting rather than innovating.

- Growing the pie involves trade-offs. A pie-growing company first aims to increase the size of the pie and second tries to ensure that, to the extent possible, no member's slice shrinks. The second goal may not always be possible, and a leader's judgment and an enterprise's purpose are important to navigate such trade-offs.

2 GROWING THE PIE DOESN'T AIM TO MAXIMISE PROFITS – BUT OFTEN DOES
FREEING A COMPANY TO TAKE MORE INVESTMENTS, ULTIMATELY DRIVING ITS SUCCESS

The idea that businesses should be driven by social value first and profits second sounds attractive. But it's also controversial. Milton Friedman is arguably the second most influential economist of all time, after John Maynard Keynes, and he advised the likes of Richard Nixon, Ronald Reagan and Margaret Thatcher. He won the Nobel Prize in Economics in 1976, mainly for his contributions to monetary policy, which form the bedrock of central banks' thinking worldwide.

Yet Friedman's most cited article isn't on monetary policy, nor even a research-based study, but a 1970 *New York Times Magazine* opinion piece entitled 'The Social Responsibility of Business Is to Increase Its Profits'. It's been quoted 17,000 times, over four times as frequently as any of his academic papers. It's particularly impactful because it argues that a company should care only about making as much money as possible. Some leaders thus use it to defend their profit-focused approach; critics reference it to highlight the narrow-mindedness of capitalism.

Many people may have cited Friedman's article without reading further than the title, since the title already seems to make his stance clear. But Friedman's argument is far more nuanced than it sounds – and as it's frequently quoted for being – for two reasons. First, it doesn't assume that investors only care about profits. Let Andrea and Miguel both be investors in Apple. Andrea cares about cancer prevention,

Miguel about environmental renewal. If Apple gave a large donation to the American Cancer Society, this would please Andrea, but not Miguel. Instead, Apple should make as high profits as possible, allowing it to pay as high dividends as possible. Then, Andrea can donate some of her dividends to the American Cancer Society, and Miguel his to Greenpeace.*

So Friedman does recognise that *individuals* have social responsibilities beyond profits. He argued that the social responsibility of *business* is to increase profits because doing so gives individuals – Andrea and Miguel – maximum flexibility to choose which social responsibilities they wish to fulfil. It's not the CEO's prerogative to take this decision away from them. As Friedman writes: 'if he does this, he is in effect imposing taxes, on the one hand, and deciding how the tax proceeds shall be spent, on the other'.

But Friedman's argument is founded on pie-splitting. It assumes that a dollar that Apple takes from investors creates only a dollar of value to society. That may be true for charitable donations. A dollar is worth the same to the American Cancer Society regardless of whether it's given by Apple or Andrea (ignoring taxes), and so Apple doesn't have a *comparative advantage* in donating to charity. But the assumption isn't true for most actions that directly affect society, which are pie-enlarging. If Apple invests a dollar in designing a reduction in its plastic packaging, it helps the environment much more than if it paid out that dollar as dividends and Miguel donated it to Greenpeace to lobby for a tax on plastic bags.

The second, and more powerful, defence of profit maximisation is that the only way an enterprise can make profits – at least in the long term – is if it serves society. So profit maximisation is socially desirable as it leads companies to invest in their stakeholders. Friedman acknowledged the importance of such investments: he pointed out that 'it may well be in the long-run interest of a corporation that is a major employer in a small community to devote resources to providing amenities to that community or to improving its government. That may make it easier to attract desirable employees'.

---

* Friedman argues that the same logic holds if Andrea and Miguel are colleagues, suppliers or customers. If Apple donates to charity, this reduces the wages or prices it can pay, or increases the prices it must charge, leaving less for Andrea and Miguel to donate.

Why is Apple one of the most valuable companies in the world, breaking the $1 trillion mark in August 2018? Because it serves *customers* by offering the highest-quality products. We take for granted the iPhone X's Face ID and camera. But they're the culmination of Apple spending over $400 million acquiring PrimeSense (3D sensors), LinX (multi-aperture camera models), Faceshift (facial motion capture software), Emotient (facial expression recognition) and RealFace (facial recognition technology). Apple's after-sales service is renowned – a customer can make a free appointment at an Apple store's Genius bar to fix a problem.

Apple nurtures its *colleagues*, who report numerous attractions of Apple as an employer on Glassdoor, a workplace review website. They can make a positive impact on the world, learn from and be inspired by smart colleagues, enjoy a start-up culture despite Apple's size, and have opportunities to grow and develop. Now, as with any large enterprise, Apple won't be perfect across every dimension, and we'll return to criticisms of its working practices in Chapter 4. Taking into account both the good and the bad, a 2018 LinkedIn survey ranked Apple the sixth-most sought-after employer in the US. Apple is one of only three US companies that have made Glassdoor's list of top-100 employers for all ten years since the list was started. This allows Apple to attract the employees who provide the innovation, strategic thinking and customer focus that drive its success.

Apple invests in long-term *supplier* relationships. It has a $5 billion Advanced Manufacturing Fund to support innovation in its suppliers. The Fund invested $200 million in the glass supplier Corning to keep its glass processing technologies state-of-the-art, and $390 million in Finisar to help it develop Face ID's lasers.

Apple has a strong *environmental* record, with 100% renewable energy in offices, stores and data centres. It's helping suppliers also transition to renewable energy, with twenty-three having committed to date. In 2017, it achieved its goal of obtaining 100% of its paper packaging from sustainable sources. Its new robot, Daisy, can disassemble nine versions of the iPhone and sort their components for recycling.

Apple contributes to local *communities* by running the Global Volunteer Program to equip colleagues in organising volunteer events, and partnering with (RED) to launch (RED) products, whose sales support HIV/AIDS programmes.

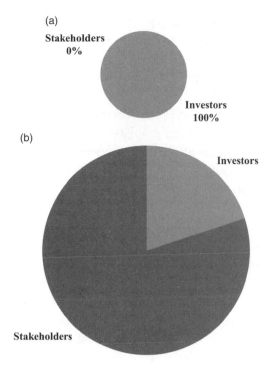

Figure 2.1

As a result of being profitable, Apple is the largest taxpayer in the world, remitting over $35 billion to *governments* between 2015 and 2017. Its effective tax rate was 25% in 2017 and 26% in the previous four years.* All these actions grow the pie.

It's true that the fastest way to increase profits is to split the pie differently. Shkreli did so overnight by hiking the price of Daraprim. But there's a limit to how much profit pie-splitting can generate in the long term. Even if Turing could hypothetically take the entire slice from stakeholders, it could never increase its profits higher than the size of the original pie. But if it grows the pie, the potential profits are much higher, as shown in Figure 2.1.

---

* As with most global enterprises, some critics argue that Apple locates activities in certain countries to reduce its tax burden. For Apple's response, see 'The Facts about Apple's Tax Payments' on its website. We don't take a stance on what the 'fair' tax rate is. Instead, our point is that, for any given tax rate, higher profits increase the tax payment.

Friedman's second argument is the foundation for a broader approach to profit maximisation called *enlightened shareholder value* (ESV). Enlightened shareholder value agrees with the pie-splitting mentality that an enterprise's goal is to maximise profits. But it's enlightened because it recognises that doing so in the long run requires it to grow the pie and thus serve stakeholders. As renowned economist Michael Jensen, a leading ESV advocate, emphasised: 'we cannot maximize the long-term market value of an organization if we ignore or mistreat any important constituency. We cannot create value without good relations with customers, employees, financial backers, suppliers, regulators, and communities'. Indeed, a stakeholder-focused company is often described as 'sustainable', but 'sustainable' simply means 'long-term'. ESV takes a long-term approach, albeit to maximise profits rather than social value, and so could be argued to be sustainable. We'll thus not use 'sustainable' in this book to describe a pie-growing enterprise, but we'll refer to it as 'purposeful' or 'responsible'.*

It's important to recognise that (enlightened) shareholder value takes stakeholders seriously. Some critics of shareholder value present it as a caricature – one that disregards stakeholders and only seeks to feed investors' greed – and then easily destroy the caricature. They then push their own theory of how an enterprise should operate, and it's not difficult to argue that theirs is superior when the alternative has been presented as a straw man. Such a one-sided presentation of shareholder value is not only inaccurate, but also unhelpful, as it fuels the pie-splitting mentality. It views investors as enemies of stakeholders, leading to proposals to restrain them, when they're partners in growing the pie.

ESV has many similarities with Pieconomics. Both highlight the criticality of companies investing in their stakeholders. Both argue that investor value and stakeholder value are highly correlated in the long run, as the evidence in Chapter 4 will show. Both stress the importance of profits – Chapter 3 will emphasise that a pie-growing enterprise must serve investors. Pieconomics isn't a licence to pander to stakeholders whatever the cost.

But there's a key difference. ESV argues that an enterprise's ultimate goal is to increase long-term profits – and by doing so, it will

---

* We'll only use 'sustainable' in Chapter 5 when referring to reward schemes, where long-term is indeed the dimension that matters.

create value for society as a by-product. Pieconomics argues that an enterprise's ultimate goal is to create value for society – and by doing so, it will increase profits as a by-product. *Profits are an outcome, not a goal.*

This difference is fundamental. It's not just about switching around words in a sentence. It's about why the enterprise exists, what drives its daily decisions and what it should be held accountable for. ESV advocates also acknowledge that there's a difference. Indeed, they'd argue that it's why ESV is better than Pieconomics. ESV has a single, measurable objective – long-term profit. Pieconomics seems to have a pretty fundamental problem – you can't measure the pie. It consists of several different slices, many of which, such as community vibrancy and environmental renewal, can't be quantified. Even if they could be, there's no clear formula to weight them. Pieconomics has multiple, unmeasurable objectives. ESV's single objective then leads, at least in theory, to two overlapping advantages.

First, ESV is *concrete*. Because there's a single, clear objective, there's a single, clear way to take a decision – will it increase long-term profit? With multiple objectives, there's no unambiguous way to take a decision. If an action improves vibrancy and reduces renewal, does it help or hurt society overall? By trying to be everything to everybody, a pie-growing enterprise can end up being nothing to nobody.

Second, ESV is *focused*. A company practising ESV has a single goal – increasing long-term profits. It will only take an action if it boosts profits. It won't spend millions on reducing emissions if they're already below the level that would lead to a fine. But a pie-growing enterprise might do so, simply to help the environment. Such actions may reduce profits.

I agree with both objections. But I'd argue that the same two reasons are why the pie-growing mentality is fundamentally superior – not only for society as a whole, but also, perhaps surprisingly, for investors themselves. I'd turn both reasons on their head. The pie-growing mentality may be less *concrete*, but it's *intrinsic* rather than *instrumental*. The pie-growing mentality may be less *focused*, but it considers *externalities* rather than just *profits*.

Being intrinsic is desirable because pursuing social value is often more profitable in the long term than pursuing profits directly. Considering externalities is desirable because investor welfare is affected not only by profits, but also by a company's social impact.

	Enlightened Shareholder Value	Pieconomics
Motivation	Instrumental	Intrinsic
Objective	Profits	Social value

Let's discuss each of these differences in turn.

Instrumental vs Intrinsic

Enlightened shareholder value believes an enterprise should be *instrumentally* motivated to create profits, whereas Pieconomics believes it should be *intrinsically* motivated to create social value.

Under ESV, a company should only create value for stakeholders if they'll pay it back by increasing profits in the long term. Every action is a trade, an exchange. Jensen states this motivation very clearly: 'change efforts should be guided by the sole purpose of increasing shareholder value'.

Under this view, Apple leaders and colleagues should be driven each day to think about how to make Apple's profits as high as possible. Increasing profit is what spurs its designers to innovate, its retail staff to provide excellent customer service and its leaders to develop new strategic partnerships. While this view may seem narrow, it has a key attraction. It provides a concrete way to evaluate the trade-offs that exist in nearly every decision. Paying to attract the best employees, giving free consultations at a Genius bar and developing the Daisy robot are all costly.

How does Apple evaluate each decision? In theory, it can set up an Excel spreadsheet to calculate all the effects on current and future profits. The spreadsheet then converts each future profit to an equivalent profit today, using a *discount rate* that takes into account the fact that $1 in the future is worth less than $1 today. Summing up all current and future profits, the spreadsheet spits out a final answer, known as the 'Net Present Value' (NPV) of the decision. If, and only if, the NPV is positive should Apple go ahead.

The idea of instrumental profit maximisation sounds sensible in theory. And it sometimes works in practice. Leaders use NPV analysis for major corporate decisions when it's possible to estimate, even very roughly, their costs and benefits. But it often doesn't work in practice, because it's very difficult to estimate the costs and benefits of most actions.

Let's see the trouble ESV has with even simple choices. Consider Apple's decision whether to provide colleagues with a free gym. The first step is to calculate the cost of the gym. The direct cost of building the gym, installing equipment and hiring instructors (or outsourcing this) is relatively simple to quantify. Much harder are the indirect costs – the number of hours employees will spend at the gym, how much this will reduce hours at their desk (rather than coming out of leisure time) and how much these lost hours will lower Apple's profits.

Even harder still are the benefits. Will the gym attract and retain workers, and what's their value to Apple? How many lost days due to sickness will the gym avoid, and how much would they have cost Apple? How many interactions between colleagues in different departments will the gym foster? These questions are almost impossible to answer. So you can't calculate the NPV of the gym, and without it, you can't justify the gym under ESV.

When decisions are instrumental – driven by the desire to achieve outcomes – they'll be made only on the basis of outcomes that can be quantified with some degree of accuracy. But most important outcomes can't be quantified. The gym example highlights the flaw in the argument that ESV is concrete because there's a single criterion (profits) which can be measured. Profits can only be measured looking backwards; it's very hard to estimate them looking forwards. The fact that you can measure profits years after taking a decision doesn't help you at the time that you take it.

This limitation is particularly problematic in a world where intangible assets are key. As Jonathan Haskel and Stian Westlake explain in their book *Capitalism without Capital: The Rise of the Intangible Economy*, an enterprise's most important assets have shifted from tangible capital (physical assets, such as factories) to intangible capital (non-physical assets, such as patents, brand and knowledge). Intangible assets accounted for 84% of the value of the S&P 500 in 2015, compared to 17% in 1975. One of the most important intangibles is *stakeholder capital*, the strength of an enterprise's relationships with its stakeholders. This includes the trust customers place in a company's brand, the reputation it has with regulators and the commitment of colleagues to its mission.

For a tangible asset like a machine, you can estimate its returns – how many widgets the machine will produce and how much you can sell them for. That's much harder for intangible assets, such as stake-holder capital. The returns to intangibles aren't only *uncertain*, but also *distant* – even if they do arise, they will be far into the future. A machine can start churning out widgets almost immediately, but if the gym helps prevent a colleague from developing diabetes in ten years' time, the financial benefit to Apple doesn't manifest for a decade. Evidence shows that leaders use a much higher *discount rate* for long-term benefits than they should. So NPV calculations are driven by short-term effects.

A maximisation mindset is problematic due to the mindset it engenders – *maximisation of one slice involves minimisation of another*. Even if an enterprise practises ESV and recognises the need to invest in stakeholders, it will do so to the minimum extent needed to generate profits. ESV would thus have led Apple to forsake many investments in its employees. Not only larger investments such as building the gym, but also – and especially – smaller investments such as upgrading the gym equipment, adding extra classes or extending the opening hours. And many other decisions beyond the gym, such as granting workers days off for volunteering or extending parental leave beyond the statutory minimum. Each of these smaller actions alone is likely to have a negli-gible effect on a worker's productivity. But the collective effect of taking none of them will be to significantly reduce productivity. Profits come from unpredictable sources, and so a mindset of maximising profits will rarely maximise profits.

That's where Pieconomics comes in. A pie-growing enterprise makes decisions for *intrinsic* reasons – to create value for society – rather than to instrumentally increase profits. Stakeholders are the end itself, rather than a means to an end. Apple invests in the gym simply because it cares about employee health. By doing so, it will recruit, retain and motivate great workers, likely increasing profits as a by-product, even if this increase couldn't be quantified at the outset. More broadly, Apple never set out to be worth $1 trillion, but to push the boundaries in innovation and design – and doing so led to its substan-tial value. While some executives draw a distinction between financial and non-financial value, Pieconomics argues that, *in the long run, almost all value becomes financial value.**

---

* When we use the term 'non-financial' in this book, it means 'non-financial in the short term'.

Growing the pie provides clearer practical guidance than growing profits, and leads to more investments, because it's much easier to see how an investment will affect stakeholders than profits. 'Maximise shareholder value' is a futile objective, since you can't predict how most actions will affect long-term shareholder value. But, using the gym as an example, the effect on colleagues is less *uncertain* – they clearly benefit from superior health, while the profit impact is harder to calculate. And the effect on colleagues is less *distant* – the health benefits arise within a few months, while the impact of health on future sick leave and productivity may not manifest for several years.

Because of the pie-growing mentality, Apple decided not only to build a gym in its head office, but to build a top-quality one. It's 100,000 square feet in size, with exercise physiologists monitoring data and three climate-controlled temperature chambers to mimic both Arctic and Saharan conditions. Did it justify such a substantial investment on NPV grounds? No. As Apple's current CEO, Tim Cook, said: 'I'm a big believer in people staying active. It's something that makes them feel better and more energetic. It's all about the fixation on the customer, and the customers here are our people, our employees.'

The gym is a deliberately simple example because it's well known that gyms improve employee health. But sometimes the best way to create value for society is unknown, and so an added advantage of the pie-growing mentality is to spur innovation. While these innovations primarily aim to benefit society, the benefits may spill over unexpectedly to investors.

Walkers Crisps wanted to reduce its carbon footprint out of environmental concerns. In 2007, it partnered with the Carbon Trust to study the carbon footprint of a packet of crisps across its life cycle, from the planting of a potato tuber to the disposal of a bag. The investigation found that much of the footprint came from drying the potatoes. Digging deeper, Walkers learned that the drying cost was so high because it bought potatoes by gross weight, incentivising farmers to keep potatoes humidified to increase their water content. So Walkers switched to purchasing by dry weight, not only lowering their own drying costs, but also discouraging farmers from using energy to humidify potatoes. In two years, Walkers reduced the carbon footprint of a packet of crisps by 7%, saving 4,800 tonnes of carbon dioxide emissions and cutting Walkers' energy bill by £400,000 per year. An exploration undertaken to benefit the environment ultimately helped investors.

Indeed, some of the greatest innovations in history have arisen despite dizzying odds – a profit calculation wouldn't have justified the investment, so they were instead spurred by the desire to address society's challenges. Even after William Campbell's hypothesis regarding ivermectin, it was highly unlikely that it would ever become effective and safe for humans. Only 1 in 1,000 compounds tested in a preclinical setting makes it to human trials, and only one in five of these ends up being approved. Reducing decisions to a profit forecast will stifle risk-taking, because many benefits either can't be foreseen or are so unlikely that the decision can't be justified on paper. But when social value, not profit, is the objective, the prize from successful innovation is much higher, which motivates exploration even if the odds are stacked against you. The effect ivermectin could have on citizens' lives, if developed successfully for human use, vastly outstripped its potential impact on profits, and so spurred Merck to invest in researching it.

Thus far, we've discussed how pie-growing actions often ultimately increase profits. On the flipside, pie-splitting actions that boost short-term profits often shrink the pie and reduce long-term returns. One channel through which investor losses arise is that pie-splitting activity is sometimes caught by regulators. While it might seem obvious that companies shouldn't engage in illegal activity, such occurrences are unfortunately not rare, and the penalties are often substantially higher than the perpetrators predicted. In September 2015, VW had to admit to the US Environmental Protection Agency that half a million cars contained the 'defeat device' mentioned in the Introduction. Within two business days, the value of VW stock fell by €28 billion, and on the third day CEO Martin Winterkorn resigned. Nine months later, VW paid $14.7 billion to settle a US class action lawsuit for the scandal. As mentioned in Chapter 1, UK banks mis-sold payment protection insurance, forcing them to set aside £48.5 billion to cover compensation costs.

A second channel is that people's buying behaviour may depend on how much they believe a company contributes to society. A review of multiple academic studies found that 60% of customers are willing to pay a premium for socially responsible products and the average customer will pay 17% more. On the other hand, enterprises that harm society may suffer boycotts, which can quickly spread via social media. Within days of the VW emissions scandal leaking, #boycottvolkswagen was trending on Twitter. Over the next twelve months, VW's light vehicle sales fell by 3,000 per month compared to an industry average increase of 7,000.

In addition to these examples of errors of commission, errors of omission – boosting short-term profit by not investing in stakeholders – also harm investors in the long run. Summing up, if a company only takes actions to get something in return, it won't take actions where it expects nothing in return, even if these actions unexpectedly lead to profits down the line. To create value that none of its competitors creates, a company must make investments that none of its competitors is making. In a world where investment decisions are frequently reduced to a mathematical calculation, these are investments that can't be reduced to a mathematical calculation.

Profits vs Externalities

Enlightened shareholder value believes an enterprise should be instrumentally motivated to create *profits*, whereas Pieconomics believes it should be intrinsically motivated to create *social value*.

We've just argued that many actions that enhance social value also improve long-term profit as a by-product. But it would be too naïve and unrealistic to assume that every single action that grows the pie also increases investors' slice. Although many consequences that leaders think of as externalities are eventually internalised, 'true' externalities still exist. Many pie-growing actions don't enhance profits, even in the very long term. Some are invisible, and so won't lead to customer boycotts, such as the nutritional content of a restaurant's food. Even for visible actions, many likely have a much smaller profit impact than their expense. The Mectizan Donation Program certainly improved Merck's reputation, but there's no way to calculate if this boost exceeded the cost. Several enterprises are investing in alternatives to plastic packaging. While some customers might change what they buy based on a company's environmental record, the extra sales may not be enough to cover the investment. With online shopping, customers often don't know how much plastic a product is packaged in when making purchase decisions.

Similarly, many pie-shrinking actions don't reduce profits, even in the very long term. Hypothetically, the Daraprim price hike could worsen Turing's reputation, and reduce future purchases of Turing's drugs. But, when a physician prescribes a medicine, or a patient buys one over the counter, their primary concern is the medicine's effectiveness – not the ethicality of the manufacturer. Or market power and lobbying may allow profits to be earned despite pie-shrinking behaviour. Despite the first evidence linking smoking to cancer being published in 1954, tobacco companies have continued to earn outsized profits. Margins rose 77% between 2007 and 2016, and the five largest firms made a combined $35 billion in profit in 2016.

While ESV considers only profits, Pieconomics also takes externalities into account. A pie-growing enterprise focuses on creating social value with the assurance that most value-creating actions will, sometimes unexpectedly, increase long-run profits – but also with the recognition that a few won't. So even if the profit effects of every action were perfectly predictable (which, as discussed, is almost never the case), Pieconomics might prefer an action that grows the pie even if it doesn't maximise profits.

Consider the trade-off illustrated in Figure 2.2. The pie at the top represents the status quo. The firm has the choice between two strategies. Strategy A grows the pie moderately and investors capture the entire gain. Stakeholders' slice is unchanged – they capture a smaller share of a larger pie. Strategy B grows the pie significantly, while keeping the shares unchanged, so both investors and stakeholders gain. However, investors gain less than under Strategy A.

As the evidence of Chapter 4 will show, in the long run these trade-offs are the exception rather than the rule. However, it's important for Pieconomics to acknowledge the exceptions and address how to deal with them.

Which strategy should leaders choose? At first glance, it seems to depend on who the law says they should run the company for. The most common view is that directors' primary responsibility is to investors, with a secondary responsibility to stakeholders, and so they should choose Strategy A. This is embedded in the UK Companies Act, is a common interpretation of US corporate law and is the approach taken by nearly all economic models. The manager maximises shareholder value subject to stakeholders obtaining a minimum level of welfare, which represents their outside option. Note that this approach isn't exploitative, as many business critics argue; it ensures that every stakeholder does at least as well from being a member of the firm as if they went elsewhere. Moving from the status quo to Strategy A is a Pareto improvement, because one member gains and no one loses.

Even though a Pareto improvement seems the ideal outcome, Pieconomics argues that leaders should go even further. Pieconomics

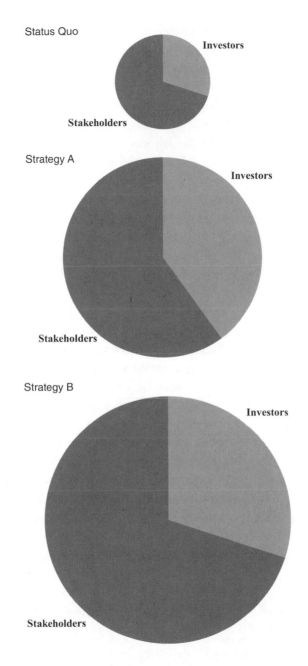

Figure 2.2

isn't about win-not lose, it's about win-win. Importantly, this approach is not driven by the law. It's true that directors' duties in some countries, particularly in Europe, are towards the company as a whole and that, even in the US, shareholder primacy has been successfully challenged in court.* But this stresses the futility of an approach based on the legal regime – the law varies across countries, making general guidelines impossible, and is ever-changing and open to interpretation.

Pieconomics isn't about simply complying with the law – it's about creating social value. It stresses that the legal regime doesn't matter for the trade-off in Figure 2.2. *Even if* investors have legal primacy, an enterprise should still care about externalities and may choose Strategy B, despite the lower profits.

Because investors are never just investors. They're often colleagues, customers and community members. They're affected by the environment, they pay taxes and they may own stakes in suppliers. So investors care about the livelihoods, stewardship, funding, vibrancy, renewal and taxes that a firm provides – not just profits.

Why do people invest in a company? To provide for their own or their children's future. A basic finance principle is that people care about the real value of money (what they can buy with their dollars), not the nominal value (how many dollars). They might prefer a lower salary in Montana to a higher salary in New York because the cost of living is lower. Similarly, people invest to provide a higher quality of life, rather than just a higher bank balance, for themselves in old age or for their children. If a company increases profits, but also pollution, investors' monetary returns may be higher, but their standard of living lower. The effect of externalities on investors may even be in financial terms. If a company farms unsustainably and raises food prices, investors lose financially in the long run because they're also customers.

And investors may care about externalities not only due to being stakeholders themselves, but also for altruistic reasons. Even if they're not the stakeholders affected by the externalities, they're concerned for those that are. Investors may care about noise and local air

---

* Thirty-five US states have 'constituency statutes' which allow directors to consider the interests of stakeholders as well as shareholders. However, in nearly all cases, constituency statutes are permissive rather than mandatory – directors may consider stakeholder interests, but don't have to, offering limited guidance. Moreover, even in states without constituency statutes, shareholder primacy has been successfully challenged. In Shlensky vs Wrigley, the Illinois Court of Appeal upheld a decision that took stakeholder interests into account, even though Illinois didn't have a constituency statute at the time. The Chicago Cubs baseball team decided not to install lights at Wrigley Field and play night games, despite the potential higher revenues, due to the negative impact on the local community.

pollution from a factory, even if they don't live in the vicinity; how a company treats its workforce, even if they don't work for that firm; and how global warming devastates coral reefs, even if they don't intend to visit these reefs in the future. As economists Oliver Hart and Luigi Zingales stress, shareholder welfare includes not only shareholder value, but also externalities, and so even if shareholders have primacy, companies should consider both.

These externalities are becoming increasingly important to investors. In 2018, $1 in every $4 under professional management in the US ($12 trillion) was invested in Socially Responsible Investing (SRI) strategies, which choose stocks on social rather than purely financial criteria. That's 38% higher than in 2016, and eighteen times as high as in 1995. This isn't just a US phenomenon. In 2018, Japan's Government Pension Investment Fund, the world's largest pension fund, increased its SRI investments from 3% to 10% of its equity portfolio – a rise of $9 billion. Moreover, many mainstream investors, which aren't classified as 'socially responsible', take externalities very seriously. Across all investors, 2,372, representing $86.3 trillion of assets, had signed the UN Principles for Responsible Investment – a commitment to incorporate environmental, social and governance (ESG) issues into investment decisions – by March 2019. That's substantially higher than the 63 investors and $6.5 trillion of assets when the principles were founded in 2006.

Moreover, even if a firm thinks that its decisions create 'externalities' that don't feed into profits, they may eventually be internalised in unexpected ways. The previous section discussed actions that ultimately affect the firm undertaking them, such as investing in employee health, but these consequences are difficult to predict. The effects are even harder to forecast – and so a leader may be even more tempted to think of them as externalities – if they affect business in general. Environmental externalities, which increase the likelihood of extreme weather, affect the food and natural resources industries. Chevron lost $1.4 billion in the second half of 2006 partly because Hurricanes Katrina and Rita reduced oil and gas production. Less obviously, weather can affect the manufacturing industry by disrupting supply chains. Floods in Thailand submerged Honda's assembly plants, costing it over $250 million. More broadly, a survey by the Carbon Disclosure Project found that 215 of the world's largest companies estimated a total potential value loss from climate change of $1 trillion.

Now the free-rider problem might suggest that an enterprise should ignore externalities even if they may ultimately feed back into profits. An individual firm is only one of thousands, so has little effect on the environment. But individual cases can have widespread effects, like the Deepwater Horizon disaster discussed in the Introduction.

A second feedback channel is that, if citizens don't view businesses as serving society, they may pressure policymakers to pass regulations to constrain them, or be less supportive of business subsidies such as R&D credits or legal protections such as limited liability. Again, an individual firm may be tempted to adopt the free-rider mentality, but that's not how things work in practice. As discussed in the Introduction, public perceptions are affected by individual anecdotes, not by the average firm. A single company's actions can have a substantial effect on the public perception of business.

Shortly after the Daraprim price hike, US Presidential Candidate Hillary Clinton tweeted that 'price gouging like this in the specialty drug market is outrageous' and proposed a $250 monthly cap on prescription drug costs if elected. This Tweet wiped $15 billion off the Nasdaq biotech index overnight. The damage from the VW scandal spilled over to the entire German auto industry, harming its international reputation. The US sales of BMW, Mercedes-Benz and Smart fell by $3.7 billion in the following year. German authorities are currently discussing increased regulation that will likely lower the profitability of the whole industry. More generally, in their book *Connect: How Companies Succeed by Engaging Radically with Society*, John Browne, Robin Nuttall and Tommy Stadlen cite McKinsey research finding that 30% of a company's value is at stake from regulation. This includes downside risk from punitive regulation if the company is seen as failing to serve stakeholders, and upside gain from deregulation if it positively contributes to society.

The effect of externalities on public perception is crucial. In many countries, investors call the shots – directors are elected by them and directors' legal responsibilities are primarily to them. Investors might object to Pieconomics because it's upfront that it doesn't always maximise profits. But if they don't urgently embrace a form of business that works for all of society, citizens will push for regulatory change and investors will no longer be calling the shots.

Since policymakers' responses to trust-eroding actions may ultimately reduce profits, you may wonder if these actions indeed create 'externalities' because they're eventually internalised. But that's more a semantic distinction. Regardless of whether we label trust-eroding actions as externalities, companies should be very serious about earning the public's trust. Even if externalities are eventually internalised, this internalisation is very difficult to predict, and so ESV will ignore them. And it remains the case that there are true externalities unlikely to affect future regulation, which Pieconomics will consider, but ESV won't.

Note that the significance of externalities doesn't mean that they have equal importance to profits, so that leaders can lump them together and focus entirely on the size of the pie, ignoring how it's divided. An enterprise that generates a large pie, but gives investors a tiny slice, would be unlikely to be funded in the first place. Chapter 3 will provide three principles to guide CEOs through difficult trade-offs between investors and stakeholders. These principles will show that, in some cases, leaders should indeed sacrifice profits to create a bigger pie – choose Strategy B in Figure 2.2. But in other cases, the stakeholder gains aren't sufficient to outweigh the investor losses, and so the trade-off shouldn't be made.

Triple Bottom Line

While this chapter has contrasted Pieconomics with ESV, we close by briefly comparing it to the Triple Bottom Line framework (TBL). Unlike ESV, which assumes that a company has a single financial 'bottom line' or objective, TBL argues that it also has social and environmental bottom lines. These three goals are often referred to as people, planet and profit.

To compare Pieconomics with TBL, let's use the same two dimensions that we used to contrast Pieconomics and ESV – objective and motivation. The objective is where there's greatest similarity. Both Pieconomics and TBL target social value, unlike ESV, which focuses on profits. Indeed, since the term was first coined by John Elkington in 1994, TBL has been successful in encouraging companies to think seriously about, and measure, their contribution to society. The motivation is where they differ. While Pieconomics' motivation is intrinsic, TBL – at least as commonly practised – is instrumental.

In a 2018 *Harvard Business Review* article, Elkington proposed a recall of the TBL concept. He argued that it's mainly been used as an accounting framework to measure an enterprise's social and environmental contribution, rather than to engineer a mindset change as originally intended. This leads to an instrumental motivation. A leader takes actions if they have a quantifiable impact on the social or environmental bottom line. This may skew investments to ones with a short-term pay-off, so that they have a faster bottom-line impact, or ones with quantitative outcomes as they're easier to report. A company might create more jobs, rather than improving the quality of existing jobs, as the former is more measurable. Stakeholders remain a means to an end – a non-financial end, but a short-term and quantitative one nonetheless. Pieconomics frees a leader to create value for stakeholders without being constrained by whether or how fast the outcomes can be accounted for. It's a mindset and an approach to business, rather than an accounting framework.

Now in Chapter 8 I'll stress how it's critical for enterprises to report on the value that they create for society. But improved stakeholder metrics, like improved profits, are a by-product rather than the end goal. An enterprise should invest in stakeholders and report on any outcomes after the fact, rather than make investments based on whether they'll improve metrics that can be reported.

The biggest difference between Pieconomics and TBL is the pie-growing mentality that's the heart of Pieconomics. It stresses the importance of the size of the pie, and avoiding errors of omission from missed opportunities to grow the pie. In contrast, Elkington points out that 'many early adopters [of TBL] understood the concept as a balancing act, adopting a trade-off mentality'. TBL is often used to ensure that an enterprise achieves a balance between purpose, planet and profit, consistent with the pie being fixed. It might view a high financial score, but modest social and environmental scores, as an error of commission – as if profits were achieved at the expense of planet and people. In contrast, Pieconomics stresses that the size of the pie is not fixed, and prioritises growth over balance. While it's important to ensure that, to the extent possible, no one's slice shrinks as the pie grows, growth that's unevenly distributed is often better than no growth at all.

In a Nutshell

- Milton Friedman's argument, that the social responsibility of business is to increase its profits, is much more nuanced than commonly portrayed. *Enlightened shareholder value* acknowledges that businesses should invest in stakeholders because they can't be profitable in the long run without doing so.

- ESV agrees with Pieconomics that profits and social value are linked, but argues that enterprises should put profits first and society second. Pieconomics argues the reverse. This leads to two key differences.
  - ESV believes that an enterprise should be *instrumental* – only create value for society if doing so will ultimately increase profits. Stakeholders are a means to an end. Pieconomics believes that an enterprise should serve society for *intrinsic* reasons, even if it can't calculate the profit increase from doing so. This approach actually often generates more profit in the long run by freeing up a company to make investments, particularly intangible ones, that it otherwise wouldn't. This is because the effect of investments on stakeholders is typically less *uncertain* and *distant* than the effect on profits.
  - ESV focuses on *profits*. Pieconomics focuses on *social value*, which includes externalities. Even if investors have primacy, they're never just investors – they're often colleagues, customers and community members, and thus affected by externalities. In addition, if companies persistently generate negative externalities, they will be regulated or lose customer trust.
- Profits and externalities are much more aligned than commonly believed – actions to create value for society often ultimately increase profits through unexpected ways. But true externalities still exist. Even if increasing stakeholder value reduces profits, investors may be willing to make the trade-off.
- The Triple Bottom Line framework agrees with Pieconomics that a company's primary goal should be social value. However, it's mainly an accounting framework and its motivation is more instrumental – encouraging activities where the social benefit can be reported – than intrinsic.

3 GROWING THE PIE DOESN'T MEAN GROWING THE ENTERPRISE
THREE PRINCIPLES TO GUIDE TRADE-OFFS AND WHICH PROJECTS TO TURN DOWN

Pieconomics is about creating value for society. While investors are far from the only member of society, they're still an important member. This chapter thus discusses two important caveats that must be heeded when practising Pieconomics – growing the pie doesn't mean ignoring profits, and growing the pie doesn't mean growing the enterprise. We then provide three principles to guide leaders in navigating these caveats.

Growing the Pie Does Not Mean Ignoring Profits

Investors are often seen as the least deserving members of an enterprise, particularly compared to stakeholders such as employees or the environment. But just as Chapter 2 stressed that investors are never just investors, stakeholders are rarely just stakeholders – many are investors themselves. Colleagues and customers hold shares, either directly or indirectly, through mutual funds or pension funds. Even hedge funds, often maligned as greedy capitalists, are often held by pension funds or university endowments.

Profits are a key element of a well-functioning society. Without profits, citizens can't fund their retirement, insurance companies can't pay out claims, and endowments and pension funds can't provide for their beneficiaries. And profits are important not only for investors, but also for stakeholders. Without profits, an enterprise can't fund future investment in new products for customers or training for workers; eventually, it will go out of business and create zero value for society. As Merck's Kenneth Frazier argues: 'We try to balance [affordable prices for customers] with the goal of ultimately providing a good return to our shareholders – because they keep financing the research that will produce tomorrow's drugs.' Without Merck's profits from its other drugs, including ivermectin for animal use, it would have been unable to launch the Mectizan Donation Program.

Not only is generating profits important after a company has already been established (ex post), but also the prospect of generating profits is important to get a company established in the first place (ex ante). Profits are what shareholders receive for risking their money in the firm, which they could have otherwise spent or invested elsewhere – just as wages are paid to employees for their time and effort, and revenues are remitted to suppliers for their inputs. If investors feared that a company would subsequently ignore them, they wouldn't fund it in the first place. Then, an idea could never attract start-up capital and embody itself into an enterprise; an established firm could never attract additional funding to grow and move from good to great.

And taking profits into account helps ensure that companies allocate resources in ways that satisfy stakeholders' needs. Profits are valuable *signals* for what society wants.* Customers increasingly value the convenience of online shopping, and so retail websites are more profitable than physical stores. This in turn encourages retailers to invest in their e-commerce offerings, exactly as many customers desire. Retailers may finance this investment by closing some high-street stores, allowing prime locations to be reallocated to other purposes, such as restaurants, coffee shops and health clubs, where there's increasing demand.

The importance of profits is why we defined Pieconomics as 'an approach to business that seeks to *create profits only through* creating value for society'. Creating value for society is the primary goal and so Pieconomics still represents a radical departure from ESV. But creating profits remains an important secondary goal.

---

* However, they're not perfect signals. As discussed in Chapter 2, a pie-growing enterprise should also take externalities into account, as these are benefits or costs to society that aren't captured in profits.

A definition that omits profits, such as 'an approach to business that seeks to create value for society', would be even more radical and get much greater support from some quarters. But to ignore profits completely would be unrealistic and undisciplined. It's unrealistic because it would be opposed by investors, as well as citizens who recognise profits' role in society, and thus be unlikely to be adopted. An enterprise that gives investors a tiny sliver of a large pie wouldn't be funded. It's undisciplined because it provides little guidance to leaders and prevents society from holding them accountable. Since almost every decision will benefit at least one stakeholder, a leader can argue that this stakeholder is the most important one and so the decision has grown the pie. Anything goes.

As we've stressed, an enterprise can't achieve the secondary goal of profits through calculation. Indeed, Pieconomics justifies many investments where there's no clear benefit to profits, such as the Mectizan Donation Program. Sometimes higher profits will manifest as an unexpected by-product, but other times they won't – that's the definition of profits being unexpected. A pie-growing company needs to be comfortable that not every single decision it takes will increase profits, even in the long term. But applying the pie-growing mentality across all its decisions will, in aggregate, likely lead to more profits than ESV. The three principles later in this chapter will guide whether an action is likely to ultimately increase profits, even if the source of the increase can't be predicted.

Growing the Pie Does Not Mean Growing the Enterprise

Pieconomics is about creating value for society. So it's tempting to think that the more an enterprise grows, the more value it creates. By reducing access to Daraprim, Turing shrank the pie. This might suggest that producing more of a drug, or inventing new drugs, always expands the pie. If Turing developed a new drug for hypertension, it would create value for customers (sufferers of hypertension), suppliers (of the inputs to the new drug), colleagues (through providing new jobs) and so on. Indeed, many policymakers argue that firms should invest as much as possible. Massachusetts Senator Elizabeth Warren proclaimed that 'the real way to boost the value of a corporation is to invest in the future'.

This argument isn't actually correct. Pieconomics is about *creating* value. Value is only created if the benefit of an investment exceeds its cost. The cost of investing resources is the next-best opportunity to which the resources could be deployed, known as the *opportunity cost*. Under ESV, a firm cares about private opportunity costs – its own alternative uses for the resources within the firm. Under Pieconomics, the lens isn't the firm, but society, and so the relevant opportunity costs are the alternative uses for the resources within society – social opportunity costs. If Turing built a new factory for the hypertension drug, it would use raw materials and workers, both of which could instead be deployed to build a school. Not investing could allow another firm within society to achieve more with the same resources.

Pieconomics stresses that *value is only created when an enterprise uses resources to deliver more value than they could elsewhere* – the social benefits exceed the social opportunity costs.* Simply investing resources may not create value. A baker can use a lot of flour, but if it falls on the floor rather than in the baking tray, it won't grow the pie.

This observation means that, contrary to common belief, an enterprise's responsibility isn't to provide jobs. It's to allow citizens to be assigned to careers where they can use their talents to serve society and flourish as humans. These careers may be outside the firm and require it to let certain workers go. In Japan, mass redundancies are a social taboo. So rather than laying off colleagues whose positions have been eliminated – for example, those who used to produce magnetic tapes for videos and cassettes – companies like Hitachi, Sony, Toshiba and Panasonic reportedly send them to 'banishment rooms'. There, they're made to do worthless tasks such as reviewing security footage or reading their undergraduate textbooks, and to file a daily report of what they've done.

Such jobs provide employees with neither meaningful work nor human dignity. Nor do they create value for society. The private opportunity cost of detaining employees in banishment rooms is low if there aren't other suitable jobs within the firm, but the social cost is

---

* This observation doesn't require a company to calculate how much value other companies could create with the same resources. In a competitive market, the price of the resources would reflect the value that other companies could create with them. Chapter 10 discusses the role of competition in helping the price system function effectively.

high since their talents could be used elsewhere. Job cuts can grow the pie by allowing citizens to flourish outside the firm. But as stressed in Chapter 1, firms can't just rely on market forces to do this reallocation, but should invest in outplacement and retraining – even at the expense of profits – to catalyse it.

The resources that an enterprise uses when it invests aren't just limited to real resources, such as raw materials and labour. It also uses up financial resources – money – which could instead fund other firms. Let's now fill in the missing dots from Senator Warren's quote earlier. Her full argument was that 'stock buybacks create a sugar high for the corporations. It boosts prices in the short run, but the real way to boost the value of a corporation is to invest in the future, and they are not doing that'. Stock buybacks, where a company returns profits to its investors in exchange for them returning their shares, will be covered in more detail in Chapter 7. For now, we note that, by choosing not to grow and instead paying out funds to investors, an enterprise can allow another company to be financed and grow.

Importantly, leaders have self-interested reasons to invest, even in projects that don't benefit society. This is known as empire-building. Bosses of larger firms earn significantly more and also enjoy prestige and status – the CEO of the market leader is most likely to keynote at industry conferences or speak at the World Economic Forum in Davos. This prestige may even outlast the CEO's tenure. Inside almost any large enterprise, legendary stories circulate about past leaders. Outside, the public knows about past CEOs of firms that are dominant today much more than CEOs of firms that have since been taken over. A leader may thus grow the firm to preserve her legacy.

CEO Angelo Mozilo was determined to make Countrywide Financial the market leader in US mortgages. He viewed the company as his 'baby' – not investors', nor society's. Aiming to become the market leader as a by-product of creating value is a worthy goal. But just like profit, market leadership shouldn't be the goal in itself.

Yet it was for Mozilo. In 2002, Countrywide was third with a 10% market share, with Wells Fargo number one at 13%. Getting Countrywide to 14% wouldn't be enough; he craved it to be so far ahead that it would remain the market leader for decades, guaranteeing his name in the history books. So Mozilo publicly announced that he'd at least triple Countrywide's market share to 30%, far higher than anyone in the industry had ever achieved. Nowhere did this personal ambition say that this growth had to create value for society (offering mortgages that customers could afford) or even investors (offering mortgages that would be repaid). Countrywide thus plunged recklessly into sub-prime mortgages, making it particularly vulnerable to the financial crisis. In January 2008, it was on the verge of bankruptcy and had to be bought out by Bank of America.

In addition to growing in one's own market, a CEO might expand into new markets, even if they're unrelated. This could be for empire-building or even escapism – exploring a new industry to avoid dealing with the problems in her core business. Rather than taking on the challenge to develop digital cameras, Kodak escaped into pharmaceuticals by paying $5.1 billion to buy Sterling Drug in 1988. But using chemicals to coat photo paper is very different from using them to make aspirin and Milk of Magnesia, Sterling's flagship products. A photography company has no comparative advantage in pharmaceuticals.

A prime example of unrelated empire-building is Daewoo, founded by former shipyard worker Woo Choong Kim in March 1967. Daewoo initially focused on labour-intensive clothing and textiles – a smart move given South Korea's large and affordable workforce. Before 1972, it bought only three businesses, two textile producers and one leather processor, which were related to its core business and helped cement its strengths.

But Kim soon wanted new toys to play with. In just one year, 1973, he bought eight companies in industries unrelated to textiles – machinery, shipbuilding and cars. It wasn't clear how Daewoo would create value compared to these firms remaining independent. By 1978, Kim now had forty-one businesses; twenty years later he'd added 589 international subsidiaries. Kim was an empire-grower, but a pie-shrinker – size was the only dimension in which Daewoo outperformed its peers. It lagged in product quality, technology, productivity and profitability, and was bottom of the table in valuation because the market realised that Daewoo had no business in owning many of its businesses.

In 1993, Daewoo entered the Vietnamese car market. Ten competitors entered soon after and the Asian financial crisis hit in 1997, so Daewoo could only sell 423 cars in the whole of 1998. But having invested $33 million in this venture, Daewoo refused to cut its losses and redeploy its resources. This attitude was replicated throughout the company. While other Korean conglomerates were cutting back after the financial crisis, Daewoo bought fourteen new businesses in 1998, despite losing $458 million that year.

The following year, with debts of $50 billion, Daewoo was about to go bankrupt and had to be broken up. This cost billions of dollars to both the South Korean banks which had lent to it and the government, which had injected money to soften the blow. 7,000 colleagues lost their jobs, and only five companies with the Daewoo brand name remain today.

Daewoo is far from an isolated example of how empire-building can destroy social value. A study by Sara Moeller, Frederik Schlingemann and René Stulz found that over just four years – between 1998 and 2001 – US firms lost their investors $240 billion through acquisitions. Buying those companies allowed CEOs to build their empires, but the opportunity cost was the substantial value that the purchased businesses were generating on their own beforehand.

Decision-Making under Pieconomics

Putting both caveats together, an enterprise should consider investors and six different stakeholders when making decisions. This seems an extremely tricky balancing act. It's difficult not only to forecast the effects on each stakeholder, but also to know how to weight the different stakeholders. So you can't measure overall social value and thus estimate how a decision will affect it.*

Yet nearly every real-life decision involves multiple criteria that can't be weighted. When a homeowner chooses which house to buy, she doesn't just maximise resale value. She also considers whether the house fits her family's needs, how close it is to her job and her kids' schools, and whether she likes the neighbourhood. When a worker chooses a job, he doesn't just maximise his income. He also considers his passion for the work, the amount and flexibility of the hours, and the camaraderie with his colleagues.

---

* Advocates of ESV argue that a single objective (profits) removes the need for weighting which arises with multiple objectives. As argued in Chapter 2, this is a poor argument for ESV. ESV would have to include the effects of, for example, employee health on profits – which effectively requires it to weight the importance of health for profits. But since ESV only considers what can be predicted, it simply ignores these effects, effectively assuming the weighting problem away.

There's no formula telling people how to weight each factor, nor a spreadsheet calculating how a decision will affect their welfare. Yet this doesn't matter. Citizens comfortably make decisions with multiple objectives every day, using not *calculation*, but *judgment* – their own internal assessment of the importance of each criterion.

But it seems a cop-out to sweep complex trade-offs under the carpet by saying that they're dealt with by a leader's judgment. Even though judgment *is* used in nearly every daily decision, it seems an unsatisfactory solution for companies. When a citizen chooses a job, he applies his own weighting criteria depending on how much he personally values salary, passion for the work, hours, flexibility and camaraderie. But leaders should serve society, not their own personal preferences on which stakeholders they favour. Appealing to judgment gives the leader freedom to do whatever she pleases. She can justify almost any decision as being based on her judgment, and because her judgment is a black box, she can't be held accountable.

The rest of this chapter provides three interrelated principles to guide a leader's judgment in these complex situations. The *principle of multiplication* ensures that the social benefits of an activity exceed its private costs, so that the activity delivers value to society. The *principle of comparative advantage*, combined with the principle of multiplication, ensures that the social benefits of an activity exceed its social costs, so that the activity creates value for society. The *principle of materiality*, combined with the first two principles, makes it likely that the social value created will ultimately increase profit. Then, the activity creates profits through creating value for society – the definition of Pieconomics. We'll sometimes use the word *discernment* to refer to judgment that leads to an enterprise being selective in the activities it undertakes.

Principle	Satisfied If	Consequence
Multiplication	Social Benefit > Private Cost	Activity Delivers Value
+ Comparative Advantage	Social Benefit > Social Cost	Activity Creates Value
+ Materiality	Social Benefit > Social Cost and Activity Benefits Material Stakeholders	Activity Creates Profits through Creating Value

Let's consider each principle in turn.

The Principle of Multiplication

The *principle of multiplication* asks the following: *If I spend $1 on a stakeholder, does it generate more than $1 of benefit to the stakeholder?* In other words, does the activity multiply the money I spend on it? If not, the social benefit of the activity is less than the private cost and so the activity doesn't deliver value. The enterprise could instead pay the dollar to the stakeholder (e.g. higher wages to colleagues or lower prices to customers), who can then use it more effectively.

Let's apply this principle to Apple's gym decision. How do we estimate the benefit to the relevant stakeholders (colleagues, in this example)? We could look at membership prices of local gyms and estimate how many workers would use the Apple one. Multiplying the two gives a lower bound to the benefit of the gym to the Apple workforce, to be compared to the cost. It's only a lower bound because employees will value an in-house gym more highly, due to the convenience and ability to socialise with co-workers. So as with all decisions, there's a limit to what can be quantified. But the calculation is still useful because it shows how big the non-quantifiable benefits must be to flip the decision. Say the cost of the Apple gym is $500 per employee per month, perhaps because few workers are likely to use it, and the highest-quality local gym costs $100. It's unlikely that the non-quantifiable benefits will be as much as $400, and so the principle of multiplication is violated. Rather than building the gym, Apple could pay higher wages, which some colleagues could spend on external gym memberships.

But haven't we just gone back to calculation? Yes and no. The principle of multiplication does provide a framework, so Pieconomics isn't nebulous. But the calculation is crucially different from ESV. ESV would ask: *If I spend $1 on a stakeholder, does it generate more than $1 of profit?* – not $1 of benefit to the stakeholder. This calculation is much harder due to the difficulty in estimating how the gym affects Apple's profits. But we can estimate the benefit of the gym to colleagues by looking at the cost of other gyms. Revisiting terminology introduced in Chapter 2, the cost of going to another gym is less *uncertain* (we can get data on it) and less *distant* (employees would bear it today if Apple didn't have a gym, so we don't need to come up with a discount rate).

For the gym, it's possible to calculate at least a lower bound on the stakeholder benefits by looking at prices of local gyms. But this isn't possible for many investments. If a company grants an employee days off for volunteering, it's impossible to calculate the value to either the colleague or the charity in financial terms. Again, the principle of multiplication offers a framework, not a calculation. The manager should think about whether the (non-financial) benefits to the employee and charity exceed the cost to the company of the day off. Such non-financial decisions are made all the time. The manager might contemplate spending a volunteer day herself, and weigh up similar benefits and costs. Even though the benefits are non-financial, they're still less uncertain and distant than the effect on long-term profits. The employee immediately benefits from the day out of the office, plus the fulfilment from contributing to a cause he cares about; the charity gains from his volunteering. On the other hand, it's almost impossible to estimate, even approximately, the effects of the volunteering day on the worker's productivity and likelihood of quitting.

Importantly, the principle of multiplication applies not only to undertaking activities that create social value, but also to reducing those that create social harm. As a particularly stark acknowledgement of multiplication, the Energy section of the New Belgium Brewing Company's website is entitled 'We're New Belgium and We Pollute'. It goes on to say: 'We make beer. And that means that we use energy and create greenhouse gas emissions.' Since New Belgium's core business has a multiplicative impact on the environment, investing $1 on reducing pollution likely generates far more than $1 of benefit to the environment. So New Belgium built 1,235 solar panels on the roof of the packaging hall in its Fort Collins, Colorado site, and provides its colleagues with bikes rather than motor vehicles to travel around the 50-acre Fort Collins site. It also took the radical step of introducing an energy tax on itself. For every kilowatt hour of energy it buys externally, it sets aside money to fund energy efficiency improvements and renewable energy projects – all of which have multiplicative effects, given how much energy New Belgium uses.

The Principle of Comparative Advantage

While the principle of multiplication helps a leader turn down some activities, it alone is rather weak and easy to satisfy. Donating to charity often satisfies that principle. If the American Cancer Society were cash-strapped and had a promising research project to fund, then $1 is worth more to the ACS than Apple. Thus, under the principle of multiplication alone, Apple should donate a substantial chunk of its profits to the ACS. Similarly, it should allow the homeless to eat in its staff canteen for free (outside of main meal times), since food likely benefits them more than it costs Apple. So leaders need additional principles to guide their decisions.

The *principle of comparative advantage*, which we've touched on before, asks the following: *Does my enterprise deliver more value through this activity than other enterprises?* If so, and only if so, undertaking the activity inside the firm grows the pie. It's tighter than the principle of multiplication because it requires the benefit to stakeholders to exceed not $1 (the private cost of $1 of investment), but the value that others could deliver with $1 (the social cost). In other words, the company needs to satisfy the principle of multiplication more than other companies. Only then does it create rather than merely deliver value. That enterprises may have a comparative advantage in serving society is what Friedman overlooked when he argued that they should focus on profits and leave it to investors to support social causes.

Let's apply this principle to whether Apple should let the homeless eat in its canteen. Food that costs Apple $1 might provide $1.50 of benefit to the homeless because they're hungry. But a soup kitchen might turn $1 into $3 of benefit because it has a comparative advantage in feeding the homeless. It knows exactly what food best addresses their nutritional needs and locates its kitchens close to where they sleep.

Apple thus doesn't have a comparative advantage in feeding the homeless, so it shouldn't do so. It could instead pay higher wages to colleagues or deliver higher profits to investors, who can then donate to soup kitchens. On the other hand, if Apple's canteen has surplus food which would otherwise be thrown out, then it does have a comparative advantage in donating that food. $1 of food now effectively costs $0 because it has no alternate use – there's no opportunity cost. If it costs Apple $0.30 to distribute it to the homeless (which gives them $1.50 of benefit), then spending $1 generates $5 of benefit, and so Apple should donate its surplus food. Indeed, the sandwich chain Pret a Manger does so at the end of each day.

Now apply the principle of comparative advantage to whether Apple should give to charity. Even if a $1 donation is worth $2 to the ACS, it's also worth $2 if given by investors or colleagues, so they can donate just as effectively. In fact, their donations would typically be more effective. The benefit of a charitable donation isn't just the instrumental use to which the charity can put the money, but also the intrinsic benefit of supporting a cause that the donor cares about.

Applying the principle of comparative advantage doesn't require a company to *calculate* the value it would create with a certain set of resources and compare it with the value every other company might create. Instead, it simply needs to *discern* what its comparative advantage is. There are two broad cases in which the principle is usually satisfied. First, a company typically has a comparative advantage in any activity it controls directly. While charities can fund cancer research and feed the homeless, only Apple affects the plastic packaging it uses for its products. Apple thus has a comparative advantage in reducing it, as mentioned in Chapter 1. Panasonic has a comparative advantage in shortening its colleagues' commute, since only it can decide the location of its offices. So it's built them closer to employees' homes, helping the environment by reducing car travel, communities by allowing colleagues to live close to schools, neighbours and activities, and the workers themselves by lowering travel time.

Second, a company may have a comparative advantage due to its expertise. Many charities are successful in getting medicines to the airports of developing countries, but the final challenge of transporting them to families or doctors in rural areas is much harder. That's where Coca-Cola steps in. One of its core competencies is distribution, which it's developed to sell its products in virtually every region in every country in the world. Coca-Cola's Project Last Mile initiative leverages this expertise for medicines, making them similarly available throughout several African countries – which includes navigating the onerous last mile to a rural household or hospital. Why doesn't Coca-Cola use its logistics knowledge to distribute books to schools, which would also be a worthy cause? Because its comparative advantage is specifically in refrigerated transportation since it sells drinks, and this expertise is critical for vaccines as they must be kept cool. Project Last Mile's mission statement makes its purpose clear: 'If you can find a Coca-Cola product almost anywhere in Africa, why not life-saving medicines?'*

---

* In addition to distribution, Project Last Mile also leverages Coca-Cola's marketing expertise to increase demand for healthcare services, such as HIV prevention, treatment and care.

Let's now apply the principle of comparative advantage to identify which activities an enterprise should undertake, when several satisfy the principle of multiplication. The food and drinks company Danone has a multiplicative effect on the environment through the waste created by its packaging. It also has a comparative advantage in improving its packaging material, since it directly controls this decision. Since both principles are satisfied, Danone has committed to make every piece of packaging reusable, recyclable or compostable by 2025.

But even making its packaging recyclable won't be enough for Danone to reduce its environmental impact. It has to ensure that the packaging is actually recycled. This involves two steps. The first is to encourage customers to play their part, and it has a comparative advantage in doing so due to its strong brand and customer engagement. For example, Danone's natural mineral water brand Evian launched a 'Flip it for Good' engagement campaign in April 2019, where customers post a video of themselves on social media 'flipping' a bottle into a recycling bin. The second is to build effective recycling systems to support customers' efforts. That's something that Danone doesn't have a comparative advantage in, because recycling systems are outside of its expertise and control. So it's established the Danone Ecosystem Fund, which works with local communities and governments to invest in recycling infrastructure and ensure that waste collectors work in a safe environment and are paid fairly.

The Principle of Materiality

Even the principle of comparative advantage could be too weak. As discussed, an enterprise has a comparative advantage in virtually every activity that it affects directly, so it might invest without limit in everything it controls, leaving few profits for investors. Recall how the second source of comparative advantage is expertise. Thus, if a company has high-quality workers and resources, it will have a comparative advantage in many external activities, and would undertake everything it does better than others. Apple might create value by asking its engineers to tutor local undergraduate students in design and innovation. Paraphrasing the definition of Pieconomics, it would be creating value for society, but wouldn't be creating profits as a by-product of doing so.

That's where the *principle of materiality* comes into play. It asks the following: *Are the stakeholders the activity benefits material to the enterprise?* Materiality stems from two sources. The first, which we'll call *business materiality*, is how material a stakeholder is to the enterprise's business. Suppliers such as Corning and Finisar are particularly important to Apple since they provide high-tech, bespoke inputs – so it supports them through the Advanced Manufacturing Fund. Suppliers are less important to a plastics or paints manufacturer that uses commodity chemicals as inputs. Local communities and the environment are critical to the Singaporean-headquartered agribusiness Olam, which grows cocoa, coffee, nuts, spices and rice. Communities provide workers and customers, and land and water are vital inputs for production. So Olam's core purpose of 'Growing Responsibly' aims to preserve the environment and regenerate the communities in which it operates. In contrast, communities and the environment are less material to an online services company, such as the flight aggregator Skyscanner. It can hire employees from all over the world, can sell all over the world and uses few natural resources.

The Sustainability Accounting Standards Board has devised a materiality map, which indicates how the (business) materiality of different stakeholders and stakeholder issues varies across industries. Figure 3.1 shows an excerpt.

Dimension	General Issue Category [①]	Consumer Goods	Extractives & Minerals Processing	Financials	Food & Beverage	Health Care
Environment	GHG Emissions		■		■	▨
	Air Quality		■			
	Energy Management	▨	▨		■	▨
	Water & Wastewater Management	▨	■		▨	▨
	Waste & Hazardous Materials Management		■			▨
	Ecological Impacts		■			
Social Capital	Human Rights & Community Relations		■			▨
	Customer Privacy	▨		■		
	Data Security	▨		■	▨	■
	Access & Affordability			▨	■	■
	Product Quality & Safety	■			■	■
	Customer Welfare				▨	▨
	Selling Practices & Product Labeling			■	▨	▨
Human Capital	Labor Practices	▨	▨			▨
	Employee Health & Safety	▨	■		▨	▨
	Employee Engagement, Diversity & Inclusion	▨		▨		▨

■ Issue is likely to be material for more than 50% of industries in sector
▨ Issue is likely to be material for fewer than 50% of industries in sector
□ Issue is not likely to be material for any of the industries in sector

Figure 3.1 The Sustainability Accounting Standards Board Materiality Map

While an enterprise has a responsibility to all members, it's important to prioritise the most material ones, because investing in them is more likely to ultimately improve profits. Indeed, as we'll show in Chapter 4, the evidence indicates that only investment in material stakeholders raises long-term stock returns. Pieconomics isn't about being all things to all people and investing in every stakeholder indiscriminately, but exercising discernment and showing restraint – knowing which stakeholders are material and which aren't.

Note that business materiality is subtly different from calculation. It doesn't require the firm to calculate how much investment will boost profits by, or even identify the channels through which it will do so – only to recognise that, if a stakeholder is material, creating value for that stakeholder is likely to flow back to profits. The Apple gym may ultimately improve profits given the materiality of colleagues. Apple doesn't need to scrutinise the financial effects of each health initiative; it simply understands that health is material to workers and that workers are material to Apple, which is why it considers health initiatives a pie-growing activity.

Combining these principles, creating profits through creating value for society requires a firm to undertake an activity that benefits stakeholders if and only if these benefits exceed the cost to the firm, it has a comparative advantage in that activity and these stakeholders have high business materiality. All three principles should be satisfied, because none of them automatically implies another. If a company creates $1.1 for every dollar spent on an activity, but another company creates $1.2, multiplication is satisfied, but comparative advantage isn't. If the numbers are $0.9 and $0.8, comparative advantage is satisfied, but multiplication isn't.* If an activity satisfies both multiplication and comparative advantage, the enterprise should only undertake it if it benefits material stakeholders. This increases the likelihood that creating value for stakeholders will enhance profits as a by-product.

The second dimension of materiality is *intrinsic materiality*. Stakeholders could be material to an enterprise simply because it cares for them, even if they don't contribute to its profits. For example, the homeless have low business materiality to Pret a Manger, but high intrinsic materiality, which is why Pret a Manger delivers surplus food to them. Separately, companies often perceive a responsibility towards a

---

* For example, there's currently no cost-effective way to recycle polystyrene, so firms shouldn't do it.

stakeholder harmed by their core business. Coca-Cola recognises that its substantial water consumption adversely affects the environment. Thus, in addition to lowering its water usage, it actively supports water projects. In 2009, it launched the Replenish Africa Initiative (RAIN), investing $30 million to improve access to safe drinking water for 2 million Africans by 2015.*

The role of intrinsic materiality in Pieconomics is subtly different from business materiality. Business materiality, when combined with multiplication and comparative advantage, helps ensure that actions to create social value also increase long-term profit. We thus obtain the outcome in Figure 1.4, where the pie grows and so does each member's slice. But Chapter 2 acknowledged that there are cases in which a larger pie lowers profits, even in the long run, as illustrated in Figure 2.2. Intrinsic materiality helps a leader discern when to opt for lower profits where a trade-off exists. In particular, if the gains go to stakeholders that an enterprise deeply cares for, these gains may outweigh any profit fall.**

Materiality is thus a two-way street. Even if a stakeholder doesn't help you, you may wish to help it. When Roy Vagelos donated ivermectin for free to West Africans, he did so out of concern for their livelihoods, even if they couldn't make a material difference to Merck's profits. Yet intrinsic materiality may unexpectedly translate into business materiality. Delivering value to intrinsically material stakeholders inspires investors, employees, customers and suppliers to join the enterprise, as we saw with the Mectizan Donation Program. Ultimately, this may enhance profits, even though profits were never the primary goal, and so we're back to Figure 1.4.

Given its different role, intrinsic materiality may sometimes be used in isolation, rather than combined with multiplication and comparative advantage. Those two principles affect how much value a company creates for a stakeholder, but intrinsic materiality gauges how much the company cares about that stakeholder. Apple engineers have a comparative advantage in teaching undergraduates compared to

---

* This goal was achieved. In 2016, the second phase of RAIN started, which pledged $35 million to help 4 million additional Africans by 2020.

** To account for these rare cases, one could redefine Pieconomics as 'an approach to business that seeks to create value for investors through creating value for society', since investor value is more than profits. We adopt the simpler definition throughout the book because, if investor value includes social value, it's tautological that the latter leads to the former, and so the alternative definition offers less practical guidance.

painting a local school or helping out with river conservation. But Apple might care more about local schools and rivers, and thus choose to support them in firm-sponsored volunteer programmes. An investment bank doesn't have a comparative advantage in reducing its carbon footprint compared to energy or manufacturing firms. Perhaps its executives should engage in air travel to win multi-million-dollar contracts, and invest the proceeds in social impact bonds that reduce other enterprises' emissions. But the bank may have a policy to cut down on air travel simply because it cares about the environment and believes that it should play its part, no matter how small.

Even though it's not necessary to combine intrinsic materiality with the first two principles, doing so can help an enterprise create even more stakeholder value. Coca-Cola recognises that it doesn't have a comparative advantage in improving water access. Thus, rather than investing $30 million to do so itself, RAIN partners with organisations such as the US Agency for International Development and the Worldwide Fund for Nature. Coca-Cola instead focuses on its comparative advantage – its convening power to bring together large organisations.

Who gets to choose which stakeholders a company should particularly care about – investors, leaders or colleagues? Ideally, it should be all three. As we'll discuss in Chapter 8, a CEO doesn't have a monopoly on purpose, but should form it in conjunction with employees. She can then seek investors' views through in-person discussions and a 'say-on-purpose' vote. Then, only investors with buy-in to the company's purpose will end up holding its stock. By engaging with investors, an enterprise gets the investors it deserves.

The principle of materiality seems similar to the 'materiality matrix' that many companies use today. This matrix classifies issues, such as climate change and data privacy, according to their materiality to the enterprise (analogous to business materiality) on one axis and their materiality to stakeholders (similar to the principles of multiplication and comparative advantage) on the other.* One important difference is that the materiality matrix doesn't consider intrinsic materiality. A company may care about a stakeholder even if it isn't critical to the business, and even if it has relatively little impact on it.

---

* If an issue is material to a stakeholder, a company delivers or creates significant value by investing in that issue, satisfying the principles of multiplication and comparative advantage.

A second difference is that the principle of materiality operates one level up and applies to stakeholders rather than issues. So it should be applied *before* drawing a materiality matrix. To assess how much an issue affects stakeholders, you must first ask which stakeholders you're particularly considering. To assess how much an issue affects the company, you must first ask how material the stakeholders impacted by the issue are to the company. Put differently, before asking *what* your enterprise is for – what issues it should or shouldn't focus on – you must first ask *who* it's for. While the principle of materiality helps construct a materiality matrix, it has independent value in guiding leaders through trade-offs – not only between investors and stakeholders, but also between different stakeholders.

In November 2016, the French electricity firm Engie announced the closure of its Hazelwood power station in the Latrobe Valley of Victoria, Australia. This decision involved very tough trade-offs, as 450 Engie employees and 300 contractors lost their jobs. Customers also suffered – since Hazelwood provided a fifth of the electricity generation capacity of Victoria, average household bills rose by 16% over the next year. But Engie took the decision because, earlier that year, it had announced a transformation plan to prioritise the environment. As new CEO Isabelle Kocher said: 'We want to focus our investments solely on generating low carbon energy . . . we are redesigning our entire portfolio.' Hazelwood was the most polluting plant in Australia, responsible for 3% of its greenhouse gas emissions (and 14% of Victoria's), and one of the most polluting plants in the world. In 2005, the World Wide Fund for Nature had named it the least carbon-efficient power station in the Organisation for Economic Cooperation and Development.

While Engie had decided that the environment was first among equals, an enterprise has a responsibility to all stakeholders. So Pieconomics *first* uses the principle of materiality to make a tough decision, and *then* compensates the members who lose from the decision, to the extent possible. As explained in Chapter 1, Pieconomics involves compensating the members who lose from a pie-growing action, to the extent possible. Engie set aside 150 million Australian dollars in severance payments, an average of $330,000 per colleague – nearly double the median house price in Morwell, the nearest town. It also participated in the Victorian Government's Latrobe Valley Worker Transfer Scheme, which helped 150 workers find jobs at other power generators in the Latrobe Valley.

The three principles in this chapter, and the importance of discernment, highlight that the pie is a framework, not a calculation tool. When making decisions, a leader shouldn't attempt to draw the pie, quantify how much each slice will grow, and weight the slices to assess whether the pie grows overall. As stressed in Chapter 2, many effects of a decision can't be predicted ex ante, regardless of whether the objective is profits or social value. Instead, growing the pie is a mental map for CEOs – and one based on evidence, as we're about to see. Leaders should seek to create profits only through creating value for society, and the principles help them assess whether a decision is likely to do so.

In a Nutshell

- Growing the pie doesn't mean ignoring profits, because profits play a critical role in society. Investors include pensioners and savers (or mutual funds who invest on their behalf), insurance companies and endowments. Without the prospect of profits, an enterprise could not attract funding; without having generated profits, an enterprise could not finance future investment.
- Growing the pie doesn't mean growing the enterprise. A company only creates value if it generates more value than the opportunity cost of the resources it uses. Investment shouldn't be unfettered and involves considering its costs as well as its benefits – but its social, rather than private, impact. Under Pieconomics, the lens is society. Not investing may allow another company within society to create more value with the same resources.
- Evaluating whether creating value for society will also create profits can't be done through calculation, but through judgment. We can provide three principles to guide leaders' judgment:
  - The principle of *multiplication* asks whether an activity creates more value to stakeholders (not more profit to investors) than it costs the enterprise.
  - The principle of *comparative advantage* asks whether the enterprise creates more value through the activity than other enterprises would.
  - The principle of *materiality* asks whether stakeholders are material to an enterprise, either through affecting its business (*business materiality*) or the enterprise having concern for them (*intrinsic materiality*).

4 DOES PIECONOMICS WORK?
DATA – NOT WISHFUL THINKING – SHOWS THAT COMPANIES CAN BOTH DO GOOD AND DO WELL

Even if Pieconomics makes sense as a concept, it sounds too good to be true in the real world. It would be convenient if firms that grew the pie became profitable as a by-product. But the fact that many companies seem to ignore stakeholders suggests that Pieconomics doesn't work in practice. Even if the pie can be grown, perhaps this requires so much investment that profits fall. Figure 2.2 could be the rule rather than the exception.

The Merck story in Chapter 1 might appear to be evidence in favour of Pieconomics. But it's not. It's only a single hand-picked story. Since I'm an advocate of Pieconomics, I could have researched thousands of companies, and then picked out the single best example of a pie-growing enterprise that's also profitable. As pointed out in the Introduction, you can always find a story to support any viewpoint, and a single story is not evidence. And perhaps Merck might have become even more profitable if it hadn't launched the Mectizan Donation Program.

So – as will be an occasional mantra throughout this book – let's look at the evidence. Does growing the pie ultimately benefit investors? In other words, does stakeholder value (also known as 'social performance') increase investor value (also known as 'financial performance')? That's what we'll explore in this chapter, using rigorous research from many disciplines – not just finance and economics, but also strategy, marketing, organisational behaviour and accounting.

The starting point for any study on Pieconomics is to measure social performance. Society includes many stakeholders, and so you typically choose one stakeholder to focus on, say, the environment. Then, you select either an *input* measure of performance (how much the firm spends on environmental initiatives, or whether it has an energy reduction policy) or an *output* measure (how much it's reduced energy consumption by, or an external agency's evaluation of its environmental record). The second step is to decide how to measure financial performance – such as market share, revenues or profits. Finally, you calculate the correlation between social and financial performance.

This correlation is of such importance that hundreds of studies have investigated it. Different studies will find different results, so how do you figure out the overall consensus? That's what a *meta-analysis* does. It's a 'study of studies', which aggregates the findings of individual papers. Joshua Margolis and James Walsh analysed 127 papers between 1972 and 2002 and concluded: 'A clear signal emerges . . . there is a positive association, and certainly very little evidence of a negative association, between a company's social performance and its financial performance.' An independent meta-analysis by Marc Orlitzky, Frank Schmidt and Sara Rynes reached the same conclusion.

But the studies covered by the meta-analyses document only correlation, not causation. There could be *reverse causality* – high market share, revenues or profits could cause social performance, because they give the firm resources to invest in stakeholders. Or there could be *omitted variables* – a third factor, such as good management, jointly improves both social and financial performance. And there are many other concerns in addition to correlation vs causation:

- Some studies use questionable measures of social performance. Early research asked management how much they care about particular stakeholders, but they might say they do even if the reality is the opposite. Others use a company's own disclosures, but companies can pretend to be virtuous when they actually aren't – a practice known as 'greenwashing'. Others still use input measures, such as expenditure on stakeholders, but this tells you little about the output of such expenditure. As discussed in Chapter 3, simply spending money doesn't grow the pie.

- Some studies use questionable measures of financial performance. Market share, revenues and profits all don't take risk into account. A strategy focused on building stakeholder capital is risky because, if the enterprise is in financial difficulty, it can't sell its environmental record to raise money. Investors care deeply about risk, which is why they require a higher return to invest in shares than save in the bank.
- Some studies consider short time periods and so could have got lucky. An advocate of bond investing could show that bonds beat stocks over 1999 to 2009, even if stocks beat bonds normally. Or, it could be that Pieconomics only pays off in economic upswings; in downturns, when money is tight, it's important to put profits first.
- Some studies only consider a single industry, and it's unclear whether the results are generalisable to other industries.

Digging Deeper

Since the jury was still out on the effect of social performance on financial performance, I decided to study it myself. My first decision was how to measure social performance. I chose employee satisfaction – how well a firm treats its colleagues – because there's a particularly good output measure available. That's the list of the 100 Best Companies to Work for in America, produced by the Great Place to Work Institute in California and, since 1998, published every year in *Fortune* magazine. This list is extremely thorough and the ultimate in grass-roots analysis. It surveys 250 employees at all levels, asking them fifty-seven questions on credibility, fairness, respect, pride and camaraderie. The Best Companies are spread across different types of industries – in 1998, the most-represented sectors were financial services (services), consumer goods (low-tech manufacturing) and pharmaceuticals (high-tech manufacturing). And the list is available since 1984, so my original study (which ran until 2009) had twenty-six years of data; I later extended it to 2011. Given the complexity in gauging social performance, most output measures have been developed only recently.

Data Mining and Spurious Correlation

There's a second reason for studying employee satisfaction – there's clear logic for why it might translate into financial performance. Employees are the most important asset in many modern firms – it's they who win client relationships and invent new products. Higher employee satisfaction allows an enterprise to recruit and retain top-quality colleagues, and leads to them being more motivated and productive. For other dimensions of social performance, the link to financial performance is less clear, particularly if the principle of materiality isn't satisfied. For example, animal rights may not be material in many industries.

Having a logical reason for why we can expect a link is important to avoid the problem of *data mining*. There's a large pay-off to finding a study that uncovers significant results. A professor who finds a variable that predicts stock returns will have a high chance of getting the paper published. A new mutual fund that claims to have done so in its launch prospectus will attract investors. So there's an incentive to mine the data. Run hundreds of regressions, correlating stock performance with many variables, and try to find something that's significant.

Some of these variables might be sensible, such as the CEO's incentives or education. But even if you ran 100 regressions on nonsense variables, such as the CEO's shoe size, the number of letters in her last name or her favourite colour, five will likely be significant at the 5% level by pure chance. These chance results are known as *spurious correlations*. You might find that CEOs who like red perform better – a spurious correlation because there's no reason for why red-liking should improve performance. But *after* uncovering a relationship, you can always spin a story to explain it. You could mine the psychological literature and find a study showing that red triggers dominance and thus can enhance performance – and indeed such a study exists, by Russell Hill and Robert Barton. Or if you found that CEOs who like red perform worse, you could search for a study showing that red is associated with the danger of failure and leads to fear – and indeed such a study exists, by Andrew Elliot, Markus Maier, Arlen Moller and Jorg Meinhardt. Several spurious correlations have become famous, such as the Superbowl Effect. If a team from the American Football Conference wins the Superbowl, the market tends to fall subsequently; if a team from the National Football Conference wins, the market rises. Some advisors even recommend investing on this effect. But there's no reason for why the Superbowl winner should affect the stock market.

The ability to mine the data is a particular concern in today's 'big-data' world, where data sources and computing power are becoming limitless. Finance professor Robert Novy-Marx parodied this ability when he was able to predict the performance of trading strategies using the identity of the US President, the weather in Manhattan, global warming, the El Niño phenomenon (the temperature in the Pacific Ocean), sunspots and the alignment of the planets. He noted wryly: 'It seems likely that others could replicate my success, especially given . . . the exponential growth in easily obtainable, machine readable data on candidate explanatory variables, and the ease of running these sorts of regressions.'

It's therefore important to choose a measure of social performance where there's a plausible link to financial performance, *before* looking at the data, to reduce the chance that any correlation is spurious.

The second decision is how to measure financial performance. Earlier studies had looked at market share, revenues or profits, which run into the causality problems described earlier. So I studied future stock returns. This helps because the stock return is the *change* in the stock price between now and next year (plus dividends). For the stock return to be high, the stock price must not only be high next year, but also low today. The stock market is pretty good at taking into account financial performance – indeed, a common criticism is that it focuses too much on financials. If the stock price is low today, it probably means that financial performance is also low today.

How does this get us closer to causality? Assume that the fictional enterprise Super Supermarkets is on this year's Best Companies list, and consider a world in which employee satisfaction causes higher future financial performance. Super's financial performance is unremarkable today, and so its stock price is only 100. Over the next year, Super's motivated colleagues improve its profits and push the stock price to 120. The stock return is 20%, and let's say that the market return is only 7%. Super beats the market.

Now consider a world in which reverse causality holds – employee satisfaction is simply the result of financial performance already being strong. Due to Super's high profits, its stock price is already 112 today. So the increase to 120 is a return of 7%, no different from the market. Thus, the Best Companies will beat the market only if employee satisfaction improves financial performance, not if financial performance improves employee satisfaction.

Looking at future stock returns thus reduces the problem of *reverse causality*. But we still have the problem of *omitted variables*. If Super's stock return was 20%, that could be due to many reasons other than motivated colleagues. Perhaps the entire supermarket industry performed well. Or perhaps Super is a small firm, and there's evidence that small stocks typically beat large stocks. Or perhaps Super *had* performed well recently, and the market was slow to recognise this. Maybe I'm too quick to assume that the stock market is good at incorporating profits – perhaps Super's stock price should have been 112 today, but the market got it wrong and was only charging 100.

To isolate the effect of employee satisfaction, I thus did two things. First, I studied not only Super, but every Best Company traded on the stock market. If Super beat the market, it could be due to its small size or strong recent performance. But if very many Best Companies – with different size and recent performance and in different industries – beat the market, then it's likely due to their one factor in common, employee satisfaction.

Second, I controlled for omitted variables. Studying hundreds of Best Companies only works if they're spread across different industries, are of different size and have different past performance. But if many Best Companies are tech firms, and the tech industry beat the market, then the Best Companies will also outperform even if employee satisfaction is irrelevant.

So I compared Super not only to the overall stock market, but also to other firms in the supermarket industry, or other small firms with good recent performance. I did the same for every Best Company. If Automatic Automobiles, a large car firm that performed badly recently, was also in the list, I compared it to other car firms, or other large firms with poor recent performance. Each enterprise thus had its own bespoke comparison group.* Importantly, I could also control for risk. There's no established way to adjust market shares, revenues or profits for risk, but decades of finance research have come up with tools to adjust stock returns. The most well-known is the Capital Asset Pricing Model; I used a more sophisticated version known as the Carhart model.

It took me four years to complete this study, to verify the robustness of the results and to rule out alternative explanations – including several more not considered here. After all that effort, studying 1,682 firm-years, what was the punchline?

I found that the 100 Best Companies to Work for in America delivered stock returns that beat their peers by an average of 2.3 to 3.8% *per year* over a twenty-eight-year period. That's 89% to 184% cumulative.

Are the Magnitudes Plausible?

Researchers typically want to find large results, as it makes their results more striking. 2.3% to 3.8% per year, for twenty-eight years, is not to be sniffed at. If a fund manager beats the market by 2% every year for five years in a row, he's considered highly skilled. Thus, even higher outperformance over a much longer horizon is striking.

But we must also check whether the results are too large to be plausible. A study which found a trading strategy that beat the market by 20% per year would cause any investor to drop his coffee cup, and would likely be tweeted and shared. But, while it's reasonable to believe that there are trading strategies that can generate returns of 2.3% to 3.8% – some shares are indeed under-priced by the stock market – it's much less likely that you can beat the market by 20% per year over any reasonable time period. Likely, the study has only considered a short time period or failed to control for other factors. A homebuyer should be sceptical of an apartment overlooking Central Park that costs just $1 million – an omitted variable from the advert is its state of repair.

---

* In addition to industry, size and recent performance, I controlled for several other factors, such as dividends, current valuation and stock trading volume.

This real-world sanity check is far too rarely done. Most people understand the need for caution with deals that seem 'too good to be true' – bargain holidays, cars or TV sets. But the same caution doesn't always apply to evidence. The more striking the finding – the higher the returns a trading strategy claims to yield, or the number of pounds that a dieting pill claims to shed – the more attention it grabs. But while there *are* opportunities to make money and lose weight, they're unlikely to make 20% per year or cure obesity overnight.

What Does It All Mean?

The study found that companies that treat their employees well also perform well. That seems a bit underwhelming. It's almost obvious that happier workers would be more productive than unhappy ones. Did I really need to waste four years showing something we could have guessed based on common sense?

Actually, the result is far less obvious than it sounds. Take the supermarket Costco. In 2014, Costco paid its colleagues $20 an hour, almost double the national average of $11.39 for a retail sales worker. It gave 90% of them health care – in part due to making part-time employees eligible after just six months of service, compared to two years at its rival Wal-Mart. Costco is shut on all major US public holidays, even though they may be particularly profitable days to open because customers are off work and free to go shopping. But Costco closes to allow its employees to spend these holidays with their families. All these policies are expensive, and drive some stock analysts and investors crazy. Indeed, an equity analyst, quoted in *Business Week*, lamented: '[Costco's] management is focused on . . . employees to the detriment of shareholders. To me, why would I want to buy a stock like that?'

That's the pie-splitting mentality. It assumes that the amount of value that Costco can generate is fixed, and so any slice that goes to colleagues is at the expense of investors. The title of a *Wall Street Journal* article also conveys this mentality: 'Costco's Dilemma: Be Kind to Its Workers, or Wall Street?' The crucial word is 'or'.

But the pie is not fixed. Giving a dollar to colleagues in the form of pay, health care or holidays improves their productivity and morale.

They may grow the pie by two dollars as a result, so investors gain rather than lose a dollar. Costco's Chief Financial Officer, Richard Galanti, said in the same *Wall Street Journal* article: 'From day one, we've run the company with the philosophy that if we pay better than average, provide a salary people can live on, have a positive environment and good benefits, we'll be able to hire better people, they'll stay longer and be more efficient.' Indeed, organisational behaviour scholars Ingrid Smithey Fulmer, Barry Gerhart and Kimberley Scott found that workers in a Best Company are more willing to remain with their employer. Daniel Simon and Jed DeVaro found that customer satisfaction is also higher, potentially because motivated employees design better products and are more positive in their customer interactions.

That might explain why I found that the returns to being a Best Company were similar across manufacturing and service industries, and high- and low-tech industries. Initially, I thought that employee satisfaction would be more important in companies like Apple, which hire highly skilled employees who are particularly scarce. However, it's equally valuable in sectors such as retail, even though the labour market is less tight, since colleagues are crucial for a positive customer experience.

So we can replace the word 'or' with 'and'. Treating colleagues as partners in the enterprise, rather than as a resource to be exploited or a cost to be minimised, benefits both workers and Wall Street.

Beyond Colleagues

My study showed that treating workers well benefits investors in the long run, but says nothing about other stakeholders. Fortunately, there are studies using similar methodology to examine other dimensions of social performance. Marketing researchers Claes Fornell, Sunil Mithas, Forrest Morgeson and M. S. Krishnan investigated the link between customer satisfaction and stock returns. Enterprises in the top 20% of the American Customer Satisfaction Index earned just under double the returns of the Dow Jones Industrial Average over 1997 to 2003. Again, this result isn't obvious. Customer satisfaction would improve if customers were offered lower prices, more tailored products and free after-sales service, but all these measures might reduce profits. Indeed, let's now fill in the dots in the *Business Week* quote earlier. The analyst's full complaint was that Costco's 'management is focused on *customers and* employees to the detriment of shareholders'.

Turning to the environment, a measure of 'eco-efficiency' from Innovest Strategic Value Advisors gauges the value of a company's goods and services relative to the waste it generates. Jeroen Derwall, Nadja Guenster, Rob Bauer and Kees Koedijk found that highly ranked stocks beat lowly ranked ones by 5% per year between 1995 and 2003.

Rather than focusing on one stakeholder group (colleagues, customers or the environment), another approach is to aggregate an enterprise's performance across multiple stakeholder dimensions. KLD, a leading environmental, social and governance (ESG) data provider (now owned by MSCI), scores firms on fifty-one stakeholder issues across seven themes: community, governance, diversity, employee relations, product, environment and human rights. Accounting professors Mozaffar Khan, George Serafeim and Aaron Yoon studied 2,396 enterprises between 1992 and 2013. They found that those with high KLD scores beat the market by only 1.5%, which isn't statistically significant (in other words, it's so small that it might be a product of chance). This study doesn't seem to be a ringing endorsement of Pieconomics.

But there's a twist. Recall the *principle of materiality*, that only delivering value to stakeholders with business materiality will ultimately benefit investors. The authors used the Sustainability Accounting Standards Board materiality map from Chapter 3 to stratify the fifty-one issues into material and immaterial ones, given each company's industry. Firms that score high on material issues and low on immaterial issues beat the market by a statistically significant 4.83%. So companies that do well on only a few items, and show restraint on others, actually perform better than those that do well across the board. Indiscriminately investing in stakeholders doesn't deliver long-run value to investors, but targeted investment in material stakeholders does.

Instead of studying the output of investment into stakeholders, an alternative approach is to examine the use of stakeholder-oriented policies, an input measure. Examples are protocols to support worker skills training, improve water efficiency or use human rights criteria when selecting suppliers. Bob Eccles, Ioannis Ioannou and George Serafeim investigated whether companies had genuinely adopted these policies (rather than simply announcing intentions), by scrutinising their annual reports and sustainability reports, and interviewing over 200 executives. They found that enterprises which had adopted a high number of these policies beat those which had adopted few by 2.2% to 4.5% over 1993 to 2010. What's most striking is that 1993 was well before the ESG movement became mainstream – even a decade later, only about a dozen Fortune 500 companies issued a sustainability report. Companies weren't forced to adopt stakeholder-oriented policies due to regulator, investor or public pressure. Instead, they did so voluntarily, because they wanted their businesses to serve society.

This observation is important. Currently, responsible business is still nascent in some countries – most investors ignore ESG factors, and there's little public scrutiny of social performance. These countries are similar today to the US in 1992. So those enterprises which are particularly forward-thinking, and adopt the pie-growing mindset voluntarily, may become the winners of tomorrow. Since most firms aren't focused on creating social value, those that do should enjoy a unique competitive advantage.

The above studies show how social value creation improves investor returns. But we can also study the flipside. There are numerous examples of how ignoring stakeholders damages the reputation of even world-leading companies that might have seemed untouchable, in turn hurting investors. Recall that Volkswagen lost €28 billion of value within two days of the emissions scandal breaking out. Similarly, news that Facebook shared users' data with Cambridge Analytica and Wells Fargo created fake bank accounts wiped $95 billion and $35 billion (respectively) off their market values. More generally, Philipp Krüger's large-scale analysis found that the average negative stakeholder event reduces the stock price by 1.31%, or $90 million. Negative events relating to the community or the environment have the biggest impact, with the decline exceeding 3%.

Armed with this evidence, let's revisit the discussion in Chapter 2 on whether an enterprise should pursue profits or social value (profits plus externalities). There are indeed some true externalities which are very unlikely to feed back into profits. But the results suggest that there are fewer true externalities than commonly believed. What firms typically think of as externalities actually come back to affect profits in the long term. Overall, the studies reach the following conclusion: To reach the land of profit, follow the road of purpose.

Thinking Long-Term

The first implication of my study is that growing the pie ultimately benefits investors – it's not just a pipe dream. But the second implication is more sobering and provides an important twist. Growing the pie benefits investors, but only in the long run.

All the measures used in the above studies are public information. For example, the Best Companies list is published in the February issue of *Fortune*, which has nearly 20 million print and online readers, to much fanfare. If the stock market were efficient – if it did a good job of taking information into account – the prices of all Best Companies should jump as soon as the issue hits the news-stands in mid-January. So they should already be high by 1 February, which is when I start calculating stock returns, and so the Best Companies shouldn't outperform going forwards. That they do suggests that the market doesn't fully respond to list publication. And the market's sluggishness doesn't last for just the two-week period between mid-January and 1 February. I found that it lasts for over four years.

If the market ignores the Best Companies list, what causes the stock price to eventually go up? Employee satisfaction improves recruitment, retention and motivation, all of which should eventually lead to higher profits.* But studying profits isn't enough. If a Best Company announces record profits, but the stock market already expected this, the stock price shouldn't change. I thus compared the Best Companies' quarterly profits to what stock analysts like Goldman Sachs and Credit Suisse forecast they'd be beforehand.** I found that the Best Companies systematically beat analyst expectations (known as a positive 'earnings surprise'), causing their prices to rise significantly. This suggests that employee satisfaction improved productivity, but the market didn't previously take this into account and so underpredicted their earnings.

This result shines a light on what the stock market does and doesn't value. For some intangible assets, the market values them not

---

* Analysing profits also addresses the alternative explanation that, after an enterprise enters the Best Companies list, socially responsible funds start buying it. While such buying would push up the stock price, it won't affect profits.
** Stock analysts, also known as equity research analysts, write evaluations of a stock. They typically include a recommendation on whether to buy, sell or hold it, and forecasts of future earnings.

directly, but only when they later show up in tangible outcomes such as profits. So a pie-growing mentality requires long horizons – treating other stakeholders well does benefit investors, but only in the long term. That's also true for other measures of social performance. Customer satisfaction, eco-efficiency and stakeholder-oriented policies are all public information, but take a long time to affect the stock price.

The market's slowness is frustrating for companies. A leader can grow the pie without any immediate reward from the stock market. But this slowness is attractive to smart investors. Good companies aren't always good investments. If an enterprise is good, and everybody knows it's good, then an investor pays for what he gets. It makes no sense to buy Facebook because it's a leader in social media. Everybody knows this, so its shares are expensive. A good investment is a company that's better than everyone else thinks. Stakeholder capital is a prime example of such hidden treasure: It ultimately leads to profits, but the market doesn't realise this. Some investors – like the analyst in *Business Week* – are stuck in the pie-splitting mentality, that stakeholder value is at the expense of returns. Or they understand the importance of stakeholder capital, but find it difficult to take into account. You might know that an enterprise has an engaged workforce, but not how this information should change cell C23 in your valuation spreadsheet.

This result is great news for Socially Responsible Investing (SRI). The traditional view is that social and financial criteria conflict. A socially responsible investor won't invest in companies that mistreat stakeholders. So they may be unable to buy stocks that are profitable in the short term, since splitting the pie is often the fastest route to profits. But the results suggest that there need be no long-term trade-off, because social performance eventually leads to financial performance. Investors can both do good and do well.

Take the Parnassus Endeavor Fund (formerly named the Parnassus Workplace Fund). It started in 2005 with a single investment criterion – employee satisfaction. One of its advisors was Milt Moskowitz, who co-authored the original 1984 and 1993 Best Companies lists. By 2017, it had returned 12.2% per year, compared with 8.5% for the S&P 500. The investment research provider Morningstar found that, out of all funds that invest in large growth stocks, the Endeavor Fund was the single best performer over every period, from one year to ten years.

Further Nailing Causality

Linking social performance to future stock returns, rather than market share, revenues or profits, takes us closer to causality. But it doesn't fully prove it. While I controlled for many other factors, such as industry, size and recent performance, I can only control for what's observable. Something unobservable, like management quality, can't be controlled for. Now the earnings surprise test helps. It's reasonable to assume that analysts take management quality into account when forecasting earnings. Since the Best Companies beat these forecasts, it must be something over and above management quality that's driving their profitability. But that's still an assumption, and there's no way to directly test it.

Strategy professor Caroline Flammer took a different approach to nail causality. She studied investor proposals, where a shareholder calls on an enterprise to take a specific course of action. This action might be a financial one – for example, to pay more dividends – but Caroline focuses on proposals related to social performance. In 2018, 43% of US shareholder resolutions concerned social and environmental issues. All investors vote on the proposal at the firm's annual general meeting. A proposal is non-binding, so the firm can choose to ignore it even if it passes, but 52% of those passed are eventually implemented.

Here are two recent examples. The following proposal was made to Lear, a supplier of car seats and electrical systems:

> [T]he shareholders request that the company commit itself to the implementation of a code of conduct based on the aforementioned ILO human rights standards and United Nations' Norms on the Responsibilities of Transnational Corporations with Regard to Human Rights, by its international suppliers and in its own international production facilities, and commit to a program of outside, independent monitoring of compliance with these standards.

Another was made to HCC Insurance:

> The Shareholders request that management implement equal employment opportunity policies based on the aforementioned principles prohibiting discrimination based on sexual orientation and gender identity.

The advantage of studying proposals is that they're a sudden change to an enterprise's social orientation, which is unlikely to coincide with (say) sudden changes to management quality. But this alone won't get around the causality issue. It could be the proposal came from a large engaged investor – and it's this investor's engagement more generally, over and above the proposal, that improves performance. So Caroline uses a methodology known as *regression discontinuity*. She compares proposals that narrowly pass (with just over 50% of the vote) to those that narrowly fail (with just under 50%). The Lear proposal failed with 49.8% of the votes and the HCC Insurance proposal passed with 52.2%. Whether a proposal narrowly passes or fails is virtually random. It's unlikely due to an engaged investor, because such an investor would have increased the vote from 49.8% to (say) 70%, not 52.2%.

Caroline pored through 2,729 proposals between 1997 and 2012. She found that narrowly passing one improves stock returns by 0.92% compared to a narrow rejection. Since an approved proposal is implemented 52% of the time, adoption improves shareholder value by an average of 0.92% / 52% = 1.77%. Importantly, the increase comes from pie-growing, not pie-splitting – operating performance, labour productivity and sales growth also rise, suggesting that a social orientation inspires both colleagues and customers.

The Other Side of the Coin

So why hasn't Pieconomics been more widely adopted? Because it's important to acknowledge the evidence isn't all one-way.

Earlier I mentioned the Parnassus Endeavor Fund as an example of the success of SRI. But that's a single fund – it's not evidence. One of the most challenging pieces of counterevidence is that SRI funds in general don't beat the market. Luc Renneboog, Jenke Ter Horst and Chendi Zhang found that, in the US, the UK, and several European and Asian countries, SRI funds underperform by 2.2% to 6.5% per year, although these differences become insignificant after controlling for risk. The same researchers conducted a separate meta-analysis which concluded that SRI funds perform similarly to non-SRI funds in the UK and the US, but underperform in Europe and Asia. Turning from public to private investing, 'impact funds' are those with social as well as financial objectives. Brad Barber, Adair Morse and Ayako Yasuda studied 159 such funds over twenty years and found that they underperform traditional venture capital funds by 3.4% per year.

Some SRI advocates sweep these findings under the carpet. One claimed in the *Financial Times* that: 'The outperformance of ESG strategies is beyond doubt.' Such a claim is unfortunately not true, but often accepted uncritically given confirmation bias. We'd like to live in a world in which ethical investing works – we want the good guys to win, and we can pretend that we don't need to deal with any of the awkward trade-offs discussed in Chapters 2 and 3.* A *Forbes* article heralded an unpublished meta-analysis which found that SRI outperforms,** explaining: 'That is the premise of a new report, and it is an accurate one, judging by many conversations with those interested in better business, better corporate governance and a sustainable future.' But whether a report 'is an accurate one' depends on its scientific rigour, rather than whether those who are predisposed to like its results deem it accurate. As Mandy Rice-Davis, who gave evidence in the 1963 trial that discredited the government of UK Prime Minister Harold Macmillan, is commonly paraphrased: 'They would say that, wouldn't they?'

So we must take seriously the fact that most SRI funds don't outperform. But most SRI funds may not actually be practising Pieconomics. Many funds use screens to assess whether a company creates value for society. They screen out a stock if it fails to tick a box (e.g. has insufficient board diversity) or ticks the wrong box (e.g. is in the oil and gas industry). This approach has three shortcomings, which may explain the average SRI fund's poor performance.

First, box-ticking measures are superficial, and thus incomplete at best or prone to manipulation at worst. As an example of incompleteness, the proportion of minorities on the board is sometimes used as a diversity measure, but says little about the board's diversity of thinking or culture of dissent, nor the extent to which these pervade the entire firm. As an example of manipulation, an enterprise could care little about diversity, but appoint a minority to the board to tick the box.

---

* Creditably, the *Financial Times* subsequently published a letter highlighting the ambiguity of the evidence: David Tuckwell, 'Case on ESG Investing is Far from Closed', *Financial Times* (28 November 2017).
** This meta-analysis studies the link between social performance and stock returns, unlike the meta-analyses by Margolis and Walsh (2003) and Orlitzky, Schmidt and Rynes (2003), mentioned earlier in this chapter, which study other measures of financial performance.

Second, box-ticking is one-size-fits-all. It assumes that better social performance is always beneficial to investors, but this ignores the principle of materiality that's central to Pieconomics. Which stakeholders are material vary from company to company, and the study by Khan, Serafeim and Yoon showed that investing in immaterial stakeholder issues doesn't improve returns.

Perhaps the most important drawback is that box-ticking is piecemeal rather than holistic. Most firms perform well on some dimensions, but not others. Apple does well on several aspects of employee satisfaction, but has been criticised for long hours and an intense working culture, paying minimum wage to its Genius bar workers and poor labour practices in its supplier factories at Foxconn City, which allegedly drove some employees to suicide. No enterprise will be perfect on every dimension – what may be a stretching and motivating culture to some colleagues may be a pressure cooker to others. The complexity of evaluating employee satisfaction means that it can't be whittled down to a single box that can be ticked, such as a measure of wages. As we'll discuss in Chapter 6, properly evaluating social performance involves getting your hands dirty – if the enterprise is a retail chain, you visit its stores. But some investors hold so many stocks that they don't have the capacity to do this, and instead make these judgments from their desk.

Not only is it hard to measure a company's contribution to one stakeholder, but also the pie contains many stakeholders. Is Amazon a pie-growing enterprise? It's a boon to customers by making thousands of products available at low prices, and its online platform allows them to compare products' specifications and customer reviews. It helps the environment by saving on physical stores in prime locations (instead, having warehouses where land is less scarce), and allows customers to resell rather than dump second-hand goods. But its treatment of colleagues is much more mixed. Amazon's warehouse working conditions are widely viewed as harsh, with long and intense hours, high injury frequency and little skill development. Some workers are allegedly afraid to use the toilet because it's far away and might lead to them being disciplined for idling, so they use bottles instead. Against that, a 2018 LinkedIn survey ranked Amazon the most sought-after employer in the US. Amazon's overall effect on the environment is similarly unclear as the above benefits must be weighed against the large usage of cardboard packaging and shipping resources.

Pieconomics involves trade-offs. Just as navigating them requires judgment from leaders, assessing them requires judgment from investors. Funds labelled as 'socially responsible' might underperform, not because social performance harms financial performance, but because they don't properly evaluate social performance. The performance of socially responsible *investors* tells us little about the performance of socially responsible *investing*.

And the performance of socially responsible *investors* tells us little about the performance of socially responsible *enterprises*. SRI funds don't just assess social performance. They also look at conventional criteria such as leadership and strategy, as they indeed should, but may get these assessments wrong, like conventional funds often do. Indeed, conventional funds also underperform the market, but that doesn't mean investors should ignore leadership and strategy when picking stocks.

Another inconvenient truth is the outperformance of 'sin' industries. Harrison Hong and Marcin Kacperczyk found that, over a forty-two-year period, alcohol, tobacco and gaming beat the most closely related non-sin industries (soda, food, entertainment and meals) by 3.2% per year. But this wasn't due to pie-splitting, i.e. these industries taking from customers by selling addictive products. If so, they should earn higher profits, which the authors didn't show. Instead, they found that sin stocks are shunned by institutional investors, such as pension funds and universities, who may be unable to hold them due to social norms. Since only a limited set of investors (not bound by social norms) can own sin stocks, the ones that do hold large risky positions. So the higher returns are simply compensation for risk.

Finally, even the studies supportive of Pieconomics may not generalise. All of the papers in this chapter study public companies since there's no reliable ESG data source for private companies. In addition, public companies have stock returns which reduce reverse causality concerns and can be risk-adjusted. That's why the vast majority of finance research is also on public companies. Most of the studies in this chapter also demonstrate significant improvements in profitability – the effects aren't only on the stock price – and so it's likely that the results also extend to private firms, which don't have stock prices. Moreover, the conceptual arguments for Pieconomics aren't specific to public firms, such as how it enables long-term investments that might otherwise be passed over. But the link between social and financial performance in private firms has not yet been rigorously shown, and hopefully future datasets will allow this.

In addition, the results may not extend to other countries. Together with Lucius Li and Chendi Zhang, I extended my study of the Best Companies to Work for in America to a global setting. The Best Companies list exists in forty-five countries worldwide. We found thirteen other countries with enough Best Companies that were locally headquartered and traded (i.e. weren't just subsidiaries of a US firm) for us to study them. The original US results did generally hold – in nine of the thirteen, the returns to the Best Companies were even higher than in the US.

But they didn't *always* hold. The Best Companies don't outperform in countries with heavily regulated labour markets, such as France and Germany. That makes sense. In those countries, the law already guarantees workers a decent level of well-being, for example by providing dismissal protection. When the average enterprise is already treating its colleagues well, a firm that's right at the very top may be investing in employee satisfaction excessively.

This result is important for two reasons. First, it highlights that even evidence – a cornerstone of this book – has limitations. Evidence is not proof. A proof is *universal*. When Archimedes showed that the area of a circle is pi times the square of its radius, he proved this not just for circles in Ancient Greece in the third century BC, but for circles in Modern Greece today and for circles throughout the world. But evidence may only apply to the country or industry in which it was gathered – evidence that the Best Companies outperform in the US doesn't mean they'll do so in France. And it may only apply to that time period. In the future, perhaps the stock market will be faster to recognise the benefits of employee satisfaction, and so investors can't earn higher returns by buying them after the list is announced. Second, the findings show how the pursuit of social value shouldn't be unfettered, as emphasised in Chapter 3. Investing beyond the point where the social benefit justifies its cost will shrink rather than grow the pie.

What's the conclusion from all this research? Pieconomics isn't a too-good-to-be-true pipe dream – serving stakeholders does in fact deliver higher long-term returns to investors. But it doesn't in every single situation. So while a company's primary goal should be to create value for society, it's important that it does so in a discerning way. Foundational to this approach are the concepts and principles introduced earlier in Part I, the evidence-based reforms we'll now discuss in Part II, and the action plan of Part III.

In a Nutshell

- Many studies find a positive correlation between social and financial performance. However, there could be *reverse causality* – the latter causes the former. Studying future changes in the stock price mitigates reverse causality, because financial performance should already be incorporated in the current stock price.
- The '100 Best Companies to Work for in America' delivered stock returns that beat their peers by 2.3% to 3.8% per year over a twenty-eight-year period (89% to 184% compounded). They also generated future profits that beat analysts' expectations.
- Customer satisfaction, eco-efficiency, stakeholder-oriented policies and performance on material stakeholder issues are also correlated with superior long-run stock returns. However, performing well on all stakeholder issues, regardless of materiality, is not.
- Even if the value an enterprise generates for stakeholders can be measured today, it takes several years for this value to show up in the stock price. As a result, investors and society should use long horizons when evaluating leaders.
- Socially responsible investment funds typically don't outperform the market, but this is likely because social performance is very difficult to measure, rather than it being a poor investment criterion. This highlights the dangers of a box-ticking approach to assessing social performance.
- Even if social performance is correlated with financial performance in one industry or country, this may not apply in others. Nor does it mean that increasing social performance without limit always increases financial performance.

PART II

WHAT GROWS THE PIE? EXPLORING THE EVIDENCE

This Part studies the evidence for what grows the pie. Now there's a virtually unlimited array of practices that increase the value an enterprise creates for society. Better leadership, state-of-the-art production techniques and incisive marketing are unambiguously beneficial. We won't study these mechanisms here because Pieconomics doesn't have a unique angle on them. You likely knew that good leadership, production and marketing were desirable before reading this book. Since they create value for both investors and stakeholders, you don't need the pie-growing mentality to understand their worth.

We'll instead focus on three determinants of the pie – executive pay, investor stewardship and share repurchases – that are particularly controversial as they're viewed as benefiting leaders and investors at the expense of stakeholders. That's why they're the subject of major reform proposals in several countries around the world. But we'll see that viewing these factors through a Pieconomics lens – recognising that the pie is not fixed – shifts our thinking on them. Gains to leaders and investors need not be at stakeholders' expense, but result from growing the pie for the benefit of all. This isn't just wishful thinking, but is borne out by rigorous, large-scale evidence. A careful scrutiny of the data will also show that many commonly held beliefs about pay, investors and repurchases, which are currently shaping influential reform proposals, aren't actually true.

Chapter 5 considers executive pay, which is seen as enriching managers at the expense of workers. Chapter 6 discusses stewardship – investor monitoring and engagement – which some argue pressures enterprises to prioritise short-term profit over long-run growth. Chapter 7 analyses share repurchases, which shareholders allegedly use to extract cash that could otherwise be invested in stakeholders.

I'll acknowledge that some of these concerns are founded and these mechanisms can be improperly used. But I'll also present evidence that, correctly designed and executed, they can grow the pie. The key words are 'correctly designed and executed' – which they're not always at present. I'll propose ways to significantly improve pay, stewardship and repurchases from current practices. So I'll agree with common wisdom that they need to be reformed. But the reforms that we should undertake are quite different when we realise that the pie can be grown.

5 INCENTIVES
REWARDING LONG-TERM VALUE CREATION
WHILE DETERRING SHORT-TERM GAMING

In April 2010, Bart Becht became the UK's public enemy number one. Not because of any fraud, customer harm or worker mistreatment he'd committed as CEO of Reckitt Benckiser. His crime was, in many people's eyes, far worse. News broke out that, last year, he'd been paid £92 million – shattering British records for executive pay.

The media were quick to express their outrage. One newspaper argued that Bart's pay was 'so shocking it may be necessary to take a lie-down'. If high pay makes you an alien, then 'Bart Becht is the Emperor Dalek'. Its trump card was to link Bart's pay to the banker bonuses that allegedly caused the 2007 financial crisis – something that would surely incite reader anger – expressing concern that the 'excess enjoyed by bankers ... is spreading to other sectors'. The newspaper suggested that bankers' pay might even be *more* justified than Bart's, because 'at least bankers do something that is hard to get your head around'. Reckitt didn't sell CDOs (collateralised debt obligations) or LYONs (liquid yield option notes), but household products that had actual names rather than acronyms – Dettol antiseptic, Strepsils cough sweets and Vanish stain remover. So running it 'is not rocket science'.

A publicity-shy workaholic, Bart loathed every ounce of shame. A year later, on 14 April 2011, he resigned without warning. Yet his departure didn't spark victory parades. The same journalists who'd slammed him a year ago for being an out-of-touch alien didn't claim credit for humiliating him into quitting. Nor did they celebrate a £92 million step towards greater income equality (less his successor's pay, of course).

Because the facts were indisputable. Bart's departure wiped £1.8 billion off Reckitt's market value, nearly twenty times his 2009 pay. The pie-shrinkage from losing Bart was orders of magnitude higher than any potential redistribution of his pay to other stakeholders. Some equity analysts now suggested selling Reckitt stock, with Investec calling the resignation a 'strongly negative event' because 'it's hard to overstate his impact and we think Reckitt now faces an uncertain future'.

The fears expressed explicitly by analysts and implicitly by the £1.8 billion fall don't prove Bart's worth. Perhaps Bart's huge pay duped the market into thinking he was special. But Reckitt's subsequent performance vindicated those fears. In the five years prior to 2011, sales, operating income and net income had grown by 14.0%, 21.4% and 21.0% per year, respectively. Over the next five years, these figures were 0.0%, –1.1% and –0.2%. From a human perspective, the slump was even more tangible – each year, the number of employees was lower than in 2011.

Bart lived and breathed Reckitt Benckiser. He'd been at its helm for fifteen years, becoming CEO of Benckiser in 1995 and leading the combined company after the 1999 merger with Reckitt & Colman. And he wasn't an ivory-tower CEO, but one who got his hands dirty – literally, as he still cleaned his own home, for which he was dubbed 'Becht the skivvy', and metaphorically, by engaging with customers at ground level. As Bart explained: 'I talk to shoppers in the store. I ask them why they're picking up the product, and then go into their house and find out why they do the laundry the way they do. If you don't like to do that you shouldn't be in this business.'

His leadership had been a clear success. Since the 1999 merger, Reckitt's shares had soared from £7 to over £36 on the day his pay-out was announced. This represented £22 billion of value created to investors, even excluding dividends, and made Reckitt the fourth-best-performing company in the FTSE 100 over the past decade. More importantly, Bart was a pie-grower. These shareholder gains weren't from price-gouging, but from creating value for all stakeholders.

Customers benefited under Bart. Even though household products might seem vanilla, Reckitt became widely recognised for innovation. It won *The Economist*'s Innovation Award in 2009 and is the subject of Harvard and INSEAD case studies on innovation. Reckitt didn't simply throw money around: it actually spent less on R&D than its rivals Henkel, Procter & Gamble and Unilever. Nor did it hype big new launches – Cillit Bang cleaning products were the only new brand launched during Bart's tenure. Bart instead preferred incremental, yet continuous, improvements to existing offerings. He compared his approach to baseball, where teams rarely win with just home runs, but instead by stringing together a series of hits.

Bart focused Reckitt's innovation on nineteen 'Powerbrands' – which included Dettol, Strepsils and Vanish – where growth potential was high, even if the market wasn't currently large. It would have been easy to coast along with tried-and-tested laundry detergent. But this market was already saturated and so there weren't unserved customer needs to be met. So Bart shifted to automatic dishwasher products and made advances to simplify customers' lives. They'd previously used three different products in their dishwashers – powder, salt, and a rinse agent. In 2000, Reckitt launched Finish Powerball 2-in-1 tabs, which integrated a rinse agent with powder. The next year, it unveiled Finish 3-in-1 Brilliant, which included salt. In 2005, it added a glass protector with Finish 4-in-1. None of these innovations cured river blindness like ivermectin. But they did make an everyday household chore, and thus millions of citizens' everyday lives, a little bit more pleasant.

While the output of innovation benefited customers, the process of innovation empowered colleagues. Reckitt's inventions came not only from the lab, but throughout the firm, due to the entrepreneurial culture and flat hierarchy that Bart created. As employees told the *Financial Times*, 'it's like running your own company'. Workers at all levels were encouraged to generate ideas, and required relatively few committee approvals to turn them into a reality. Bart wanted his colleagues to take risks and understood that this required tolerance of failure. The executive who spearheaded the failed Dettol Easy Mop still flourished at the company afterwards. Bart invested in his people through both headcount (which grew 50% over the 2000s) and skills (encouraging junior executives to switch countries and roles frequently, to develop an entrepreneurial mindset). In 2008, out of the top fifty global managers, 79% worked outside their home country and 95% had experienced at least one global transfer.

The environment benefited too. Reckitt launched the Vanish Eco Pack in 2008, which reduced plastic packaging by 70% by moving from a round tub to a resealable pouch. This reduction also helped customers, who now got 10% more Vanish for the same price. Between 2000 and 2011, Reckitt planted 5.4 million trees in Canada, reduced its greenhouse gas emissions by 48% and lowered energy use per unit of production by 43%. During Bart's leadership, Reckitt headed the UK's Business in the Community Corporate Responsibility Index and was awarded top status in the US Environmental Protection Agency's Safer Detergents Stewardship Initiative.

So Bart's slice wasn't at the expense of society. It was the by-product of more than a decade's worth of value creation. Yet few of the articles on Bart's pay mentioned how much he'd grown the pie. And the amount that went to Bart was far less than claimed. While headlines declared that he earned £92 million in a single year, only £5 million was 'compensation' for him working in 2009. The remaining £87 million came from selling shares and options that he'd received as early as 1999. They resulted from ten years of service, not a single year's graft – they'd have still been his even if he'd quit at the start of 2009. Bart simply sold what he already owned, just like withdrawing money from your bank account doesn't give you a windfall nor make you richer. In fact, Bart could have cashed out some of these awards as early as 2003. If he'd done so, he'd have avoided any large number in a single year. Instead, he held onto them far longer than he needed to, keeping himself accountable for Reckitt's long-run performance.

Out of the £87 million of cash-in value, £80 million arose because Reckitt's stock price soared after the shares and options were granted. Not only did Bart have to work for a decade to earn the shares and options, but that decade had to be an extremely successful one for them to be worth so much. Had Reckitt underperformed, Bart would have cashed in far less – avoiding any public outcry, but at the expense of society. Now the share price increase wasn't entirely due to Bart – colleagues contributed substantially to Reckitt's success, and the overall stock market also increased. We'll discuss these important complexities later. For now, the key point is that we can't label a leader's pay as excessive without assessing how much she's grown the pie.

At the same time as the cash-in, Bart actually gave an even greater amount (£110 million) to his charitable trust, which supported organisations such as Save the Children and Médecins Sans Frontières.

So even the slice that went to Bart was reinjected into society, but this was often excluded from the media coverage. (This isn't an isolated case: 204 individuals and couples have signed the Giving Pledge, a commitment to give more than half of their wealth away. The pledges currently total over $500 billion.)

Bart's departure was at the expense of both the enterprise and society. It's no wonder that during the public outcry, Bart 'was criticised by politicians but not by any of his major shareholders'. Even though it's investors who bore the £92 million cost, they recognised that Bart had helped create £22 billion of value. The heavy criticism, which may have contributed to his departure, is a prime example of how a pie-splitting mindset can obstruct pie growth.

Bart's story is consistent with many people's view of executive pay. The level of pay is perhaps the single most-cited piece of evidence that business is out of touch with society. In the US, the average (mean) S&P 500 CEO earned $14 million in 2017, 361 times the average employee – a ratio that's increased nine-fold since 1980, when it was forty-two. In the UK, the median FTSE 100 CEO earned £4 million in 2017, 137 times the median worker – a ratio that's also increased nine-fold since 1980, when it was fifteen. The High Pay Centre, a UK think tank, marks 4 January each year as 'Fat Cat Day' – the day by which a CEO has earned more than a typical colleague earns in a whole year. That high pay is a recent phenomenon seems to immediately rebut any argument that pay is justified given a CEO's talent. Leaders aren't obviously more talented now than in 1980, so why has the pay ratio increased nearly nine-fold?

No other enterprise decision, such as its product launches, pricing strategy or even its carbon footprint, attracts as much attention – and fury – as how much it rewards its executives. In the past, politicians sought voter approval by promising to reform health care and education. Now they also promise to reform executive pay. In the 2016 US Presidential election campaign, one of the few issues Donald Trump and Hillary Clinton agreed on was that pay was too high. Clinton lamented: 'There's something wrong when the average American CEO makes 300 times more than the typical American worker.' Trump, more bluntly, called high CEO pay 'a total and complete joke' and 'disgraceful'. In the same year, Theresa May launched her ultimately successful campaign to become UK Prime Minister with a speech that promised to curb executive pay. In January 2017, the leader of the opposing Labour Party, Jeremy Corbyn, proposed a maximum wage.

Reforms have not only been proposed, they've also been passed. In 2013, the Swiss public voted in favour of a reform to the Swiss Constitution 'gegen die Abzockerei' (against rip-off salaries). This banned sign-on bonuses and severance pay, and gave investors a binding say-on-pay vote (allowing them to veto an executive pay package). Violation is punishable by up to three years in prison. In 2014, the EU limited bonuses on senior bankers to twice their salary. In 2016, Israel made banker pay exceeding thirty-five times the salary of the lowest-paid worker (or 2.5 million shekels, if this is lower) non-tax-deductible.

There are many reasons why CEO pay is perceived as important. By paying herself millions, a leader takes resources that could instead be used to pay colleagues or invest in R&D. Even worse, the CEO may deliberately cut wages or investment to hit bonus targets. And the millions she receives directly contribute to income inequality, which has been rising almost constantly since the mid-1970s.

Each of these concerns is serious. So they need to be evaluated seriously, with the highest-quality evidence. Let's start with the first concern, that a leader's pay is at the expense of stakeholders. The AFL-CIO, the US's largest federation of trade unions, releases its Executive Paywatch data under the headline 'More for Them, Less for Us'. *Forbes* published an article arguing that 'CEOs are taking too much of the pie at the expense of workers'.

But this argument is founded on the pie-splitting mentality. The amount that can be reallocated through redistributing the pie is tiny. As pointed out in Chapter 1, the median equity value in the S&P 500 is $22 billion. Even if a CEO were willing to work for free, reallocating her $14 million would only release 0.06% of the pie. (In the UK, FTSE 100 CEO pay of £4 million is 0.04% of the median firm size of £9 billion.) Even if we multiplied this across all members of the executive team, and accounted for trickle-down effects on the level below, it would still be far smaller than the value increase from growing the pie by improving social performance, which runs into several percentage points, as discussed in the last chapter. As authors Yaron Brook and Don Watkins point out, the pie-splitting mentality may have made sense centuries ago when most wealth was in the form of land – there's a fixed amount of land to go round. But that's not true when most wealth is financial, because financial wealth can be created. A leader being paid more doesn't require colleagues to be paid less. Factors that affect citizens' welfare other than wealth can similarly be created. Curbing climate change benefits both CEOs and workers alike.

That's not to say that we should be indifferent to the level of pay. Almost any potential saving (such as reducing energy usage) becomes small when you divide it by $22 billion. Instead, it highlights that how much pay costs (its *level*) has a much smaller impact on society than how pay affects behaviour (which depends on its *structure*). Unlike Robin Hood, you don't need to rob from the rich to give to the poor. Like in the Elves and the Shoemaker, the best way to give to the poor is to directly create value.

Pay structures can either encourage or hinder value creation, so the second concern – that pay packages can distort CEO behaviour – is entirely valid. As Michael Jensen and Kevin Murphy titled their influential 1990 *Harvard Business Review* article, 'it's not how much you pay, but how'. So our bottom line is this: *The goal of pay reform should be to incentivise leaders to create long-run value for society, rather than reduce the level of pay.*

Three dimensions of pay structure are particularly important, and each leads to a desirable social outcome. *Sensitivity* leads to *accountability*, *simplicity* to *symmetry* and *horizon* to *sustainability*. We discuss each element in turn.

Pay Dimension	Pay Outcome
Sensitivity	Accountability
Simplicity	Symmetry
Horizon	Sustainability

Sensitivity

CEO pay should be *sensitive* to performance – leaders shouldn't be paid millions for simply showing up at the office. That's why we refer to pay as reward, rather than compensation. 'Compensation' implies that a leader finds hard work so unpleasant that she must be compensated for it. This difference isn't just semantic; it affects the philosophy behind pay design. Compensation is for *effort*. It's not clear that a CEO, whom some see as playing a few rounds of golf or flying in a private jet to a meeting, puts in more effort than (say) a warehouse worker. So a compensation criterion could never justify the level of CEO pay. In contrast, reward is for *value creation*. Pay should *reward value creation* rather than *compensating effort*.

Measuring value creation is difficult because the pie consists of many slices, and it's unclear how to weight them. The evidence of Chapter 4 shows that the *long-term* stock return captures not only investor value, but also various measures of stakeholder value. It's also reduced by pie-splitting, such as cutting R&D or employee training, even if these actions improve the short-term stock price. Consistent with the principle of (business) materiality, the long-term stock return puts highest weight on the most material stakeholders. For these reasons, it's the best available measure of the size of the pie, even though it's not a perfect one due to externalities.

The best way to make a leader *accountable* to the long-term stock return is to cut her salary, which she receives irrespective of performance, and pay her more in shares. Note that such a remedy would be ignored by the standard focus on the level of pay. A level of $14 million doesn't tell you whether this is $13 million of cash and $1 million of stock, or $13 million of stock and $1 million of cash. Yet these two schemes have substantially different effects on how accountable the CEO is for performance. Under the former, the CEO is a salaried bureaucrat. Under the latter, she's an owner, who's invested – literally – in its future success, just like how leaders of start-ups or family firms own substantial shares. She can't earn more unless she grows the pie; if the pie shrinks, her slice shrinks. *Sensitivity* leads to *accountability*.

Are leaders paid like owners in reality? Common wisdom is that they're not. A 2016 report by Chris Philp, a UK Member of Parliament, argued that 'there is clear evidence that high CEO pay is no longer strongly associated with performance, and two academic studies clearly show in fact high CEO pay negatively correlates with performance'. These studies use US data. The 2019 House of Commons Report on Executive Pay says that 'there is no perceivable link between corporate financial performance and the sums paid out to CEOs. There is academic evidence to suggest that this link is in any case statistically weak or non-existent', quoting a third paper using UK data. Outside of these influential reports, these three studies have attracted substantial independent attention, perhaps because they confirmed many people's prior beliefs that CEOs don't deserve their pay.

But as we discussed in the Introduction, that academic studies claim to find a result doesn't mean that it's true, because there's a huge range in the quality of evidence. Indeed, none of these three papers has been published because they all make a basic error. When calculating the link between pay and performance, they only consider the amount of *newly granted* cash and equity that a CEO receives in a particular year. These indeed don't change much from year to year – Steve Jobs was famously paid $1 a year at Apple, regardless of performance. But new grants ignore the main source of a leader's incentives – her *previously granted* equity, which can be substantial. Despite his fixed salary, Jobs did care about performance because, in addition to intrinsic motivation, he had a considerable chunk of his wealth invested in Apple stock – over $2 billion when he died in October 2011. More broadly, the average Fortune 500 CEO holds $67 million of equity, and so a 10% fall in the stock price costs her $6.7 million. That's equivalent to a $10 million pre-tax pay cut if the CEO doesn't have capital gains against which she can offset this loss. For the UK, these figures are £660,000 and £1.2 million. As noted by PwC: 'Analysing pay using only the amounts paid in a year but ignoring previously awarded equity is like analysing investment returns based on dividends but ignoring capital gains. In other words, it doesn't make sense.'

The omission is also inherent in many quotes. US Senator Bernie Sanders claimed: 'Wall Street CEOs who helped destroy the economy, they don't get police records. They get raises in their salaries.' While this quote creates shock value, it simply isn't true, and no evidence was cited in support. Bear Stearns CEO Jimmy Cayne once had a $1 billion stake in his firm, which he eventually sold for $60 million. Lehman CEO Dick Fuld owned over $900 million of stock, which ended up worthless when Lehman went bankrupt. Certainly, these CEOs still had substantial wealth despite these losses, and it's a fair question whether regulators should have the power to impose additional penalties (which we'll return to in Chapter 10). But the claim that they benefited from the financial crisis is false.

So most CEOs have large stakes in their firm. Do these stakes actually improve performance? Let's look at the evidence. Ulf von Lilienfeld-Toal and Stefan Ruenzi studied the relationship between CEO voluntary stock ownership and long-term stock returns over a twenty-three-year period. Firms with large CEO stakes beat those with small stakes by 4% to 10% per year, far higher than the maximum

0.06% gain from splitting the pie differently. They also enjoyed higher return on assets, labour productivity, cost efficiency and investment, all consistent with growing the pie.

Of course, correlation doesn't imply causation. One interpretation is that incentives work – high stock ownership today causes CEOs to improve the stock price tomorrow. But perhaps causality is the other way. When leaders expect tomorrow's stock price to be high, they ask the board to pay them in stock rather than cash, or buy shares on the open market. Either way, they hold more stock today.

To test if the first explanation is true, Ulf and Stefan studied whether the effect is greater where incentives are more likely to matter, because the leader would otherwise be unaccountable for poor performance. These are cases in which few institutions own the company's shares, there are few industry competitors, takeover defences are strong, the CEO was originally the founder and recent sales growth is high. (The last two make it less likely that the board will fire the CEO.) In all five cases, the link between stock ownership and long-run returns is stronger, suggesting that the former causes the latter.

That incentives improve performance isn't obvious. One common argument is that incentives are irrelevant because leaders should have sufficient intrinsic motivation. A pharmaceuticals CEO should invent new drugs to transform citizens' health, rather than to line her pocket. When John Cryan became Deutsche Bank CEO in July 2015, he said, 'I have no idea why I was offered a contract with a bonus in it because I promise you I will not work any harder or any less hard in any year, in any day because someone is going to pay me more or less.' This quote is widely cited to support the idea that incentives are unnecessary, but Cryan's claim that he'd work just as hard without financial accountability can't be verified by evidence. Despite his claim, Cryan initially accepted the bonus component of his contract, but Deutsche Bank ended up making losses each year of his tenure, so he felt pressure to waive it.

There's no doubt that intrinsic motivation is important. If you have a CEO for whom intrinsic motivation isn't enough, you've probably got the wrong CEO. The solution is to fire her, not to give her more equity. But Ulf and Stefan's results suggest that incentives can still have an incremental effect, beyond the intrinsic motivation that should already be abundant.

People act differently when they're owners. Tenants should take care of their landlords' property, but even an honest and conscientious tenant would look after a home even better if she owned it herself. Intrinsic motivation should drive a leader to ensure good performance. But great performance often involves very tough decisions, such as admitting a past mistake and reversing a strategy that the CEO herself came up with. Even honest leaders may not always take these difficult actions. Supplementing intrinsic motivation with a substantial amount of wealth at stake may shift performance from good to great, which is what Ulf and Stefan found.

Another argument against incentives isn't that they're irrelevant – they do affect performance, but in a negative way. Many prior studies show that incentives backfire, because a worker focuses only on the performance measure being rewarded. In 1902, the French colonial government ruling Vietnam wanted to incentivise rat hunters to kill more rats. So that it wouldn't be inundated with rat corpses, the government asked hunters to bring in rat tails to get paid. But this led to the hunters amputating tails from rats while keeping them alive, so that they could continue to breed and create more tails to be chopped off. In a more modern example, paying teachers based on test scores can lead to them teaching-to-the-test rather than instilling a love of learning and a respect for authority. All these problems are succinctly summarised in the title of Steven Kerr's classic article, 'On the folly of rewarding A, while hoping for B'.

But these studies typically investigate workers other than CEOs, for whom virtually all performance measures are incomplete. Test scores only capture a very small proportion of what society seeks from a teacher. But for CEOs, there's a good measure of performance – the long-term stock price, which incorporates stakeholder as well as investor value.

In addition to showing that incentives matter, Ulf and Stefan's study shows that CEOs also matter. A common criticism of high pay, even in successful enterprises, is that the leader only played a small role. There are thousands of other workers, and the company may have already been thriving before she took over. These other factors are clearly important – but Ulf and Stefan show that leaders are too. They compared firms only by their level of CEO stock ownership, and held as many other factors as possible constant. Higher CEO ownership alone led to higher long-term returns – just like changing the manager of a sports team can drastically improve performance, even if the players don't change.

Other evidence also points to the importance of CEOs. When Tidjane Thiam announced his departure from Prudential to Credit Suisse, Prudential's shares fell 3.1% (£1.3 billion) and Credit Suisse's rose 7.8% (£2 billion). But that's only an anecdote, and perhaps Prudential's stock fell not because Tidjane created value, but because his departure signalled hidden problems within the company (an *omitted variable*). To move from correlation to causation, Dirk Jenter, Egor Matveyev and Lukas Roth investigated what happens when CEOs die. Unlike a departure, death isn't voluntary, so it's unlikely to be due to problems within the firm. When younger CEOs die, the stock price falls by 4.2%, while deaths of older CEOs increase it by 3.6%. The key message for our purposes isn't that younger CEOs tend to be better than older CEOs, but that the choice of CEO matters. The difference between a good and bad CEO is around 7.8% (4.2% + 3.6%), which is far higher than the level of CEO pay. *It's costly to hire a good CEO – but it's even more costly to hire a bad one.*

You might still be sceptical. I said that it's unlikely that the CEO's death was due to problems within the firm. But maybe these problems caused her to have a heart attack. Then, poor performance causes death rather than death causing poor performance. So Morten Bennedsen, Francisco Pérez González and Daniel Wolfenzon investigated the deaths of a CEO's family members, which are likely not caused by stress from the firm's troubles. If the CEO's spouse, parents, children or siblings die, this diverts her attention. If she didn't matter, other executives could fill in. In contrast, the study found that profitability falls by 12% of its average level. The exception is that, if the CEO's mother-in-law dies, profits go up (although the effect is statistically insignificant).

Now even though the leader is a significant contributor, she isn't solely responsible for firm performance. Indeed, current pay schemes recognise this – CEOs in large US firms receive less than 0.4% of any increase in firm value. And colleagues should also be rewarded for performance improvements, as I'll soon emphasise.

Simplicity

In 2015, BP suffered the biggest loss in its history – $6.5 billion. This was a dramatic reversal of fortunes compared to the $3.8 billion profit it earned in 2014. BP argued that a different measure, 'underlying replacement cost profit', was more relevant as it excluded one-off items such as Deepwater Horizon and the fall in oil and gas prices. But even this halved from 66 to 32 cents per share. Investors suffered a 14% stock price fall, and 5,400 colleagues lost their jobs.

Yet BP increased the pay of CEO Bob Dudley from $16.4 million to $19.6 million. And investors could do nothing about it. Even though 59% voted against the pay package, this vote was only advisory rather than binding. BP went ahead with the pay-out, saying that it was simply following the pay policy that 96% of investors had approved in a binding vote the previous year.* And BP was right.

It seemed pretty simple to see that Dudley had underperformed, so how did the policy come up with a 20% pay increase? Because his pay package wasn't simple, but extremely complex. There were six components to Dudley's total pay; for brevity we'll focus on just two. One is *performance shares*. Unlike the standard shares considered thus far, here the amount of shares that 'vested' – that Dudley received – depended on several different measures of performance: total shareholder return (TSR – stock price growth with dividends reinvested), operating cash flow, safety and operational risk, relative reserves replacement ratio and major project delivery. Each performance measure had its own target, and the different measures were combined and weighted by a formula. This formula churned out a figure of $7.1 million of shares, 78% of the maximum that Dudley was entitled to – despite his failure on key dimensions.

The second was Dudley's cash bonus, which depended on even more measures. Figure 5.1 shows a table from BP's 2015 Annual Report which explained why he was awarded $1.4 million.

Confused? Well, you're in good company. Society, the media and even large investors couldn't figure out why Dudley was being paid so much. Ashley Hamilton Claxton, Head of Responsible Investment at

---

* In the UK, investors have two say-on-pay votes. One is on the forward-looking policy report, which stipulates how the firm will determine pay in the future – for example, how pay will be linked to performance metrics, and the existence of any exit payments. Here, companies are required to adopt a binding vote at least once every three years. This is the report for which BP had 96% support in 2014. The second is on the backward-looking implementation report that describes how the board determined realised pay over the past year, for which the vote is annual and advisory. This is the report for which BP had 59% opposition in 2015.

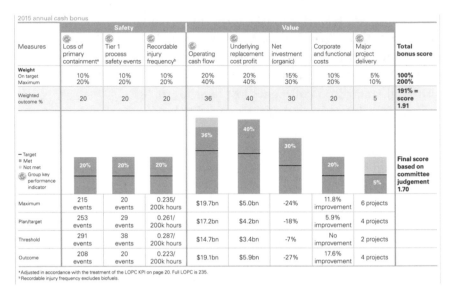

2015 annual cash bonus									
	Safety			**Value**					
Measures	Loss of primary containment[a]	Tier 1 process safety events	Recordable injury frequency[b]	Operating cash flow	Underlying replacement cost profit	Net investment (organic)	Corporate and functional costs	Major project delivery	**Total bonus score**
Weight On target Maximum	10% 20%	10% 20%	10% 20%	20% 40%	20% 40%	15% 30%	10% 20%	5% 10%	**100% 200%**
Weighted outcome %	20	20	20	36	40	30	20	5	**191% = score 1.91**
− Target ▪ Met ▫ Not met ◉ Group key performance indicator	20%	20%	20%	36%	40%	30%	20%	5%	**Final score based on committee judgement 1.70**
Maximum	215 events	20 events	0.235/ 200k hours	$19.7bn	$5.0bn	-24%	11.8% improvement	6 projects	
Plan/target	253 events	29 events	0.261/ 200k hours	$17.2bn	$4.2bn	-18%	5.9% improvement	4 projects	
Threshold	291 events	38 events	0.287/ 200k hours	$14.7bn	$3.4bn	-7%	No improvement	2 projects	
Outcome	208 events	20 events	0.223/ 200k hours	$19.1bn	$5.9bn	-27%	17.6% improvement	4 projects	

[a] Adjusted in accordance with the treatment of the LOPC KPI on page 20. Full LOPC is 235.
[b] Recordable injury frequency excludes biofuels.

Figure 5.1 Executive Directors' Cash Bonus Calculation, BP Annual Report and Form 20-F 2015

Royal London Asset Management, was one such investor. As she explained: 'This proposed increase is both unreasonable and insensitive. In a year in which BP has reported its worst ever annual loss, it has decided to sharply boost Mr. Dudley's remuneration ... It shows that the board is out of touch.'

But as with many issues, the arguments aren't all one way. While BP underperformed on some dimensions, it outperformed on others. Worker injuries fell by 23% per hour worked, and safety was a key strategic priority after Deepwater Horizon. BP's 14% stock price decline actually outperformed its peer group, which dropped 18%. This illustrates that much of BP's slump was due to the failing oil price, which was outside Dudley's control.

So reasonable people might disagree on whether Dudley's $19.6 million was justified. Instead, we'll focus here on the complexity of his pay structure – which is standard practice rather than specific to BP. Let's look at it more closely. A bonus typically pays the CEO according to several performance measures. Sometimes these measures may be calculated over multiple years, in which case the bonus is known as a *long-term incentive plan* (LTIP). For each measure (say profits), there's a lower threshold (say £4 billion) that the leader must beat to receive any bonus at all; if she does,

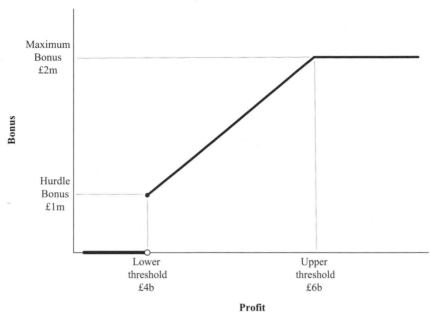

Bonuses / Long-Term Incentive Plans

Figure 5.2

let's assume she gets £1 million. Since we want performance to be great, not just good, the bonus increases if profits rise above £4 billion. But we don't want her to be paid too much, so we cap the bonus at £2 million once profits reach £6 billion. Figure 5.2 illustrates this.*

Performance shares work in a similar way. In Figure 5.3, the CEO receives 100,000 shares, worth £1 million at a share price of £10, if profits are £4 billion. As profits rise, she gets more shares, until a maximum of 280,000 if profits are £6 billion. Above £6 billion, the number of shares doesn't rise, but their value does (since higher profits increase the share price).

The complexity of the above structures seems justifiable because they need to balance several considerations. A lower threshold seems critical for providing incentives, as it ensures that the CEO is rewarded only for great performance. The threshold is also necessary for fairness – ordinary employees don't get a bonus for average results, so leaders shouldn't either. We need to precisely fine-tune the lower target so that

---

* The horizontal axis is not to scale.

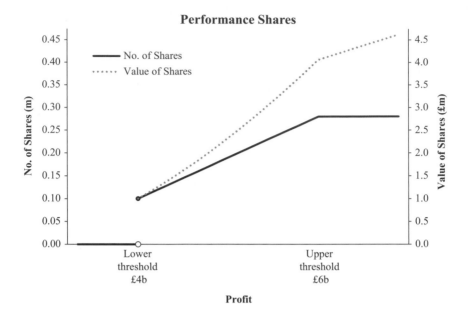

Figure 5.3

it's stretching, but also achievable, otherwise it would provide no motivation. For Dudley, was a 23% fall in injuries a good enough improvement to merit a bonus? It's not clear, so perhaps we need a detailed calibration.

The slope of the line after the £4 billion target must be high enough to encourage further improvement, but not too steep, otherwise the CEO will capture too much of the gains. And we also require an upper threshold to prevent pay becoming unbounded. Thus, given a single performance dimension, we need to decide two thresholds and a slope.

But the complexity doesn't stop there. Since the CEO's job is multifaceted, her performance can't be whittled down to a single measure such as profits. Profits can be inflated through short-term actions, so we want long-term financial measures such as the relative reserves replacement ratio. A pie-growing company should serve wider society, so we need non-financial metrics such as safety. Then, once we've decided on a comprehensive set of financial and non-financial measures, we need to weight them. Should it be 52% on profits, 27% on safety and 21% on the replacement ratio, or some other formula? Again, perhaps a large spreadsheet might tell us the answer.

This problem is so intricate that boards have a dedicated 'remuneration committee' to come up with the solution. These committees in turn hire specialist compensation consultants to advise them, costing the typical Fortune 100 firm $250,000 a year. As we've discussed, the effect of incentives on firm value is so large that this time and money is well spent if complexity indeed improves their efficacy. And the above arguments suggest that it should.

But does it actually? Let's look at the evidence. Ben Bennett, Carr Bettis, Radha Gopalan and Todd Milbourn studied 974 firms over fifteen years and found that companies were significantly more likely to just meet the lower threshold than just miss it. This seems to suggest that incentives work – perhaps unsurprisingly, performance targets encourage leaders to hit performance targets.

But they don't encourage them to create value. To paraphrase Steven Kerr, they reward A, but society and long-term-oriented investors want B. The researchers studied what actions CEOs took to hit the targets. They found that leaders that just hit the target undertake significantly less R&D than those who just missed it, suggesting that they reached their goal by cutting R&D. They also have more discretionary accruals, a way of using accounting policies to increase reported earnings.* So 'long-term' incentive plans actually lead to short-termism as the end of the evaluation period approaches. This highlights a fundamental problem with any target-based approach – non-targeted dimensions get deprioritised. Even if a bonus includes non-financial factors such as safety, it may encourage underperformance in other non-financial areas, such as climate change.

Another problem is that the CEO might take excessive risk. Let's say profits are just below £4 billion, so she expects no bonus. If she takes a risky project, there's a 50-50 chance of profits instead being £3 billion or £4.5 billion. Expected profits with the project are £3.75 billion, compared to just below £4 billion without it, so the project is bad for the firm. But it's good for the leader. If the project succeeds and profits are £4.5 billion, she gets a bonus of £1.25 million. If it fails, she gets nothing, but she'd have received nothing by not taking the project.

---

* Accruals arise when there's a timing difference between earnings and cash – for example, a magazine company receiving subscription money upfront, but only 'earning' the money when it sends out future monthly issues of the magazine. There are many legitimate reasons for accruals, but these reasons won't explain why accruals should be significantly higher for firms that just meet profitability targets than firms that just miss them.

The bonus gives her a one-way bet – encouraging risk-taking even if it's pie-shrinking. It leads to *asymmetry*.

And the problems aren't limited to the bottom end. If profits are just above £6 billion, there's no further upside. Rather than innovating, the CEO may coast and be excessively conservative. If the leader has a risky project with a 50-50 chance of profits being either £7 billion or £5.5 billion, expected profits are £6.25 billion, so the project is good. If it succeeds, she gets the maximum bonus (£2 million), but she'd have received that anyway. If it fails, her bonus falls. So she has a one-way bet in the other direction – discouraging risk-taking even if it's pie-growing. Indeed, Ben, Carr, Radha and Todd find that, where pay-outs taper off beyond a given target, leaders deliver results at or just above the target rather than beyond it.

These thresholds make no sense. Society loses if firm performance is bad (£3 billion) rather than mediocre (£4 billion). And society gains if firm performance is great (£7 billion) rather than good (£6 billion). But for the bonus, there's no difference between bad and mediocre, or between great and good.

All of the above problems arise even if a bonus has a single performance measure. But further complexity arises from companies having multiple performance measures, because it's unclear how to weight them. Adair Morse, Vikram Nanda and Amit Seru found that the weightings sometimes change after the fact, to overweight the dimension that the leader performs best on. The more complex a system is, the easier it is to game because you have more dimensions to play with.

What's the solution? It's simplicity – to replace formula-driven bonuses with standard shares that the CEO can't sell for several years (known as 'restricted shares'). The value of these shares is *automatically* sensitive to performance. It depends on the stock price in several years' time, so there's no need to lay on complex performance conditions or choose particular measures, weightings or thresholds.

Restricted shares lead to *symmetry* along three dimensions. First, the effect of performance on pay is consistent for all performance levels. This is shown by the constant slope of the dotted line in Figure 5.4, which illustrates what happens if we remove the £4 billion profit target and instead halve the number of shares. The leader gains from increasing profits at all levels and loses from all decreases in profits. There are no jumps in pay when hitting a target,

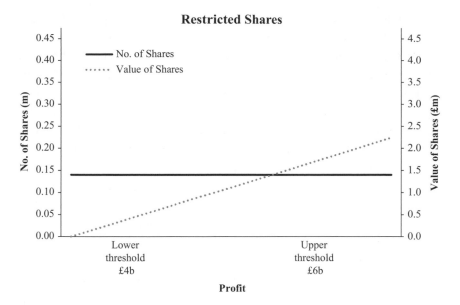

Restricted Shares

Figure 5.4

removing incentives to cut R&D or take risks to do so. She's rewarded for delivering a performance flow, rather than meeting performance goals.

Second, restricted shares avoid the asymmetries associated with emphasising particular performance measures. The long-term stock return captures almost all actions that affect firm value, including those impacting stakeholders, and weights them according to their materiality, so we don't need an arbitrary weighting scheme. Judgment is still needed to determine how much stock to give, and it's here that the board might factor in externalities that even the long-term stock return doesn't take into account. Judgment is also needed to determine how long the stock should be locked up for, as we'll discuss shortly. But an otherwise complex problem is reduced to two dimensions – how much stock to give and how long to lock it up for.

A third dimension of symmetry is that restricted shares can be awarded to employees as well. This ensures that they share in the firm's success that they helped create. When engineering firm The Weir Group introduced restricted stock for its executives in 2018, it simultaneously launched an All-Employee Share Ownership Plan for its colleagues. If a company is successful, it's never just down to the CEO. While Bart Becht created an innovative culture, it was employees who designed the new Finish products and reduced the plastic packaging in Vanish. If both leaders and workers are given shares, leaders can't gain without workers gaining also. But if leaders get bonuses and workers get shares, the bonus might pay off even if the stock price falls, leading to concerns of 'one rule for them, another rule for us'.

Indeed, evidence shows that non-executive equity schemes are generally associated with higher firm performance. Han Kim and Paige Ouimet show that this link is higher when the scheme is motivated by the desire to share success with colleagues, rather than to defend the firm against takeovers or to preserve cash (since shares can be used in place of wages). Yael Hochberg and Laura Lindsey find that the effect is stronger in enterprises with more growth opportunities, where a worker's new ideas or efforts can have a particularly large effect. Importantly, the benefits only arise when equity is broadly shared throughout the firm, rather than targeted to particular groups (such as the R&D team). This is consistent with the idea that giving an employee shares encourages him not only to work hard on his own tasks, but also help out his colleagues, hold them to high standards and foster a performance culture throughout the organisation. Also supporting this idea, the effects of broad-based equity are stronger in small companies, where both individual effort and helping or monitoring others has a larger effect on overall performance.

Broad-based equity schemes allow employees to share in not only the fruits of their own labour, but also the windfalls arising from external forces. For example, technology can generate substantial cost savings, but at some workers' expense. We'll discuss in Chapter 11 how a pie-growing firm has the responsibility to redeploy displaced colleagues, to the extent possible. But this won't always be feasible, and all-employee ownership programmes will ensure the gains from technology are widely distributed, partially softening the blow to colleagues made redundant.

There are potential concerns with paying executives in shares. Indeed, no reward plan will be perfect – but we shouldn't let perfect get in the way of good. And many of the concerns frequently voiced are actually much milder than they seem. Let's discuss some of them:

- *Even the long-term stock return depends on factors outside the executive's control, such as a rise in the stock market. So the executive gets a windfall.*

General stock market upswings also benefit investors and stake-holders. Companies buy more inputs from suppliers and hire new workers; existing workers benefit if they've been given shares. The high value of leaders' shares isn't due to taking slices from stakeholders, since the entire pie grows in an upturn. If a CEO were given salary instead of incentives, she'd likely invest most of it in the stock market and thus still benefit from any upswing. It's much better for a CEO to be invested in her own firm, whose value is partly under her control, than other firms whose values are not.

Crucially, the effect works both ways. If there's a stock market decline, investors and stakeholders suffer – and the leader will also if she has substantial wealth tied up in her firm. But she won't if she's been paid in cash.

Despite the above arguments, windfalls might still be a concern due to the optics. In December 2017, UK house-builder Persimmon announced that CEO Jeff Fairburn's share options were worth £110 million – causing chair Nicholas Wrigley to resign as he was blamed for Jeff's high pay. While Persimmon's market value had risen by £8 billion since the options were granted in February 2012, much of it was because low interest rates and the UK government's 'Help to Buy' scheme had boosted the housing market. It's true that, had Jeff been given cash instead of options in 2012 and invested it in Persimmon, he'd have earned a similar amount. It's also true that, if interest rates had risen and the housing market collapsed, these options would have been worth nothing. But these arguments fell on deaf ears – what might have happened under different circumstances is far less salient than what actually happened.

If optics are a major concern, another solution is to pay leaders not with standard shares, but with indexed shares whose value depends on TSR relative to industry peers. This ensures that the CEO isn't rewarded for favourable industry conditions outside her control. But a downside is that she'll be insulated from bad luck, which may seem unfair if colleagues are losing their jobs and investors their savings in a downturn. Ingolf Dittmann, Ernst Maug and Oliver Spalt estimated that full indexation would increase the cost of incentives by 50% for most US firms; even applying the optimal amount of (partial) index-ation would only lead to modest savings.

- *With bonuses, it's clear what the executive should do to get paid – hit a profit target of £4 billion, or a sales growth target of 5%. The long-*

term stock return is so far off that the executive doesn't know how to hit it.

This is true – *and is precisely the point*. It's clear how to meet short-term targets, which is why they encourage manipulation. It's much harder to improve the long-term stock return in instrumental ways – instead, it's a by-product of growing the pie. Removing targets frees the leader from trying to hit them and instead frees her to create value. She does so with the reassurance that she'll be rewarded after the fact, since value creation typically improves long-run stock returns. With shares, the CEO is an owner of the firm, who thinks and acts like an owner, rather than a hired outsider who's focused on maximising her bonus.

- *With stock-based pay, the pay-outs to an executive are unbounded. Since firm value can rise without limit, the value of an executive's shares can rise without limit.*

Pieconomics stresses that the main problem isn't paying a leader generously – giving her a large slice of the pie – but not growing the pie in the first place. With stock-based pay, the leader can *only* be paid more if value has been created. Her gain isn't at the expense of society; it's a result of creating value. If there's an upper bound, the CEO may coast as she approaches it – as the study by Ben Bennett and co-authors found.

- *If we removed the threshold in performance shares, the executive would receive her shares regardless of performance and the link between wealth and performance would be substantially weaker. She effectively receives shares for free.*

Paying an executive in shares isn't giving them for free – the firm can lower the CEO's salary so that her total package is unchanged. This observation is commonly overlooked. Bart Becht's pay was criticised for arising 'from cheap and free share schemes handed to him since the company was created in 1999'. But the shares given to Bart weren't a free handout. Instead of paying Bart purely in cash in 1999, Reckitt Benckiser reduced his cash and paid him partly in equity. Indeed, doing so is like paying a CEO entirely with salary and then requiring her to buy shares – a frequently suggested reform. But this alternative reform allows the leader to time her share purchases to coincide with troughs in the stock price. Such manipulation isn't possible if the CEO is simply paid stock in the first place.

And targets aren't needed to tie wealth to performance. Without them, the number of shares the CEO receives won't depend on performance, but their value will. Recall that a US CEO suffers the equivalent of a $6.7 to $10 million pay cut for a 10% stock price fall, even without performance conditions. Targets only make her accountable for performance measures that long-term-oriented investors shouldn't care about. Creating a sudden drop if the CEO misses a threshold simply gives short-term incentives to hit it.

Indeed, shares without performance conditions are exactly what investors hold – another dimension of *symmetry* – and so fully align a CEO with investors. She's paid in exactly the same way investors are paid. Investor returns rise and fall with the stock price, rather than depending on complicated formulas. Investors don't suddenly receive more shares if profits cross an arbitrary threshold, or forfeit their shares if they fall below, so the CEO shouldn't either.

Just like shares aren't free, targets won't be removed for free. Since removal eliminates the risk of forfeiting shares, CEOs should accept fewer shares in return. When The Weir Group moved from LTIPs to restricted stock in 2018, it applied a 50% discount. But a better alternative would be to *increase* shares and significantly cut salary. In Figure 5.5, the solid line represents a package consisting of £1.2 million of salary plus the performance shares in Figure 5.3. The dotted line represents a new package consisting of £0.5 million of salary plus an increased level of the straight equity in Figure 5.4.

Would a CEO accept this? She should – particularly over alternative reforms to slash total pay. First, expected pay won't fall because the lower salary is balanced by more shares and no performance conditions. The line is higher in some places and lower in others. Second, her overall wealth-at-risk (the slope of the line) won't rise. The substantial risk that the CEO used to bear at a single arbitrary threshold (£4 billion) is spread out over all levels of performance.

Restricted Shares with Underpins

If targets are removed, the CEO still receives shares upon poor performance. The shares are worth little, and Figure 5.5 shows that

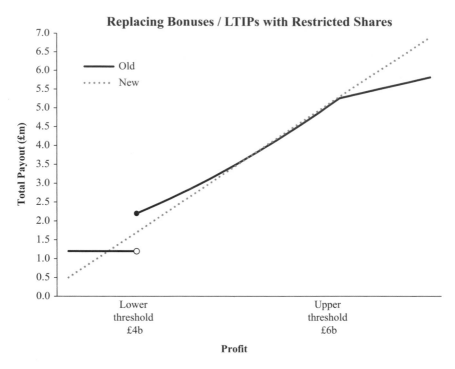

Figure 5.5

total pay is lower than if she'd been given performance conditions and a higher salary instead. But the optics, of a CEO keeping her shares upon poor performance, may be a concern. Critics may not recognise that she'd have received a higher salary had performance conditions been imposed. Just like with windfalls, the alternative of what might have otherwise happened is far less salient.

If these optics are a concern, share awards can be combined with an 'underpin', where they're forfeited upon a severe performance failure. An underpin is like a target, but much lower. Targets should be stretching and only reward good performance, but this encourages manipulation to hit them if performance is average. Underpins should be met except if performance is poor and so there should be no need for manipulation. For example, The Weir Group's underpins include no material governance failures and not breaching a debt covenant. Of course, because an underpin is easy to meet, a CEO should accept a lower salary if given underpins rather than targets.

The idea of rewarding executives with restricted stock, rather than bonuses or LTIPs, is increasing in popularity. The April 2017 corporate governance report of the UK House of Commons concluded that 'LTIPs' impact on incentivising performance is unproven at best, and, at worst, they can create perverse incentives and encourage short-term decision making'. It recommended that they be replaced with 'shares which can only be sold after set periods of time'. In the same month, the Norwegian Sovereign Wealth Fund issued a position paper on CEO pay, proposing that 'a substantial proportion of total annual remuneration should be provided as shares … Allotted shares should not have performance conditions … The performance conditions of so-called long-term incentive plans are often ineffective and may result in unbalanced outcomes. Long-term incentive plans tend to have complex and opaque metrics that are open to discretion, and boards often adjust, supplement or rebalance metrics during the measurement period'. In September 2019, the US Council of Institutional Investors overhauled its policy on executive pay, highlighting the merits of simple shares. Several UK companies have recently adopted restricted stock.

But most still have not. Throughout this book, and particularly in Chapters 6 and 9, I emphasise that investors are allies of stakeholders in growing the pie – and this is particularly the case for pay reform given their 'say-on-pay' vote. They can vote against complex bonuses that evidence has shown to encourage short-sighted gaming, and for simple equity that both supports far-sighted thinking and matches what investors themselves hold. I've heard some investors argue against restricted shares by calling them fixed pay, because the number doesn't depend on performance. This doesn't make sense, because the value depends substantially on performance. Indeed, these shareholders would likely object to being classified as fixed income investors, a term reserved for debtholders.

Despite the widespread misunderstandings of both the conceptual arguments and evidence for restricted stock, these implementation challenges are not insurmountable. When Clare Chapman, the remuneration committee chair of The Weir Group, began consultations to replace LTIPs with restricted stock in 2018, she knew that many investors would be sceptical. So she met or had conference calls with almost all of Weir's anchor investors, plus ISS and Glass Lewis (proxy advisors who counsel investors on how to vote), to explain the rationale, which she always grounded in evidence. As a Harvard Business School case study explains: 'Throughout the discussions, Chapman emphasised the importance of data and evidence: "We could not afford to be working off people's opinions – we really did need to be working off a pretty solid fact base, otherwise we would have little chance of being strategically coherent to our shareholders."'

But these meetings weren't just to persuade, but also to listen. Clare and her Weir colleagues heard investors' concerns and revised their initial proposal. Then they brought a new reward package to a second round of investor consultations, listened to the feedback and modified it further. As a result, Weir became the first UK firm to obtain a positive vote recommendation for restricted stock from both proxy advisors. The proposal passed in April 2018 with 92% support.

Horizon

The key argument for stock-based pay is that, in the long run, the stock price incorporates value to stakeholders as well as investors. The critical words are 'in the long run'. In the short run, the stock price can be gamed – cutting R&D increases short-term profit and thus the stock price. Shouldn't the market see through such behaviour and not take profits at face value? In fact, Sanjeev Bhojraj, Paul Hribar, Marc Picconi and John McInnis compared firms that just beat analyst forecasts due to low R&D, low advertising or high accruals, with those who just missed due to high R&D, high advertising or low accruals. Beaters outperformed missers by 2% to 4% in the short term, suggesting that the market took the earnings increase at face value. However, over the next three years, they underperformed by 15% to 41%, suggesting that these tricks harm long-run value.

To deter such errors of commission and ensure *sustainability* of performance, any granted shares must be locked up for several years. Recall Angelo Mozilo from Chapter 3, who oversaw Countrywide's plunge into subprime loans. This expansion not only helped achieve Mozilo's market share objectives, but it also generated short-term revenue, boosting the stock price and thus his wealth. He then cashed out $140 million of equity in the nine months to August 2007, the start of the financial crisis. Countrywide's stock price fell 70% over the next five months and it had to be taken over by Bank of America. Even though Mozilo privately acknowledged that these loans might eventually become delinquent, he also knew that he could cash out before they did.

Locking up equity should also deter errors of omission – leaders failing to take long-term investments because the benefits won't arise for many years. In Chapter 4, we saw that improving employee satisfaction boosts the stock price, but it may take five years for the full improvement to show up. A CEO who knows that she can sell her shares in three years may not bother to do so.

The optimal lock-up period isn't one-size-fits-all, but depends on the enterprise. It should be higher in industries, such as pharmaceuticals, where a CEO's actions have particularly long-term effects. It should also last at least one industry cycle, so that a leader can't cash out when the stock price is temporarily high. Shares given to Exxon's executives vest half after five years and the other half after ten, requiring them to hold shares through the oil price cycle.

Importantly, deterring errors of both commission and omission requires companies to lock up a leader's shares beyond her departure. Otherwise, she may take short-term actions whose damage will be her successor's problem or won't make investments whose fruit will be her successor's windfall. Jim Collins, in his book *Good to Great*, distinguishes between good leaders, where the enterprise is successful only under their control (e.g. Stanley Gault of Rubbermaid) and great leaders, whom we don't miss because the enterprise continues to be successful long after they're gone (e.g. George Merck). Requiring a leader to hold equity after she's left encourages greatness. Now an objection might be that this imposes too much risk on the leader. But this encourages one of the most important long-term actions that a leader can undertake: succession planning. Moreover, if the CEO were allowed to cash out, she'd likely invest most of the proceeds in the stock market, whose performance is fully out of her control.

Companies are increasingly introducing post-exit holding requirements. Former Unilever CEO Paul Polman has to hold stock worth five times his annual base salary for the first year after his departure – a shareholding requirement exceeding £5 million – and 2.5 times for the second year. The 2018 revision of the UK Corporate Governance Code requires companies to develop a formal policy for post-departure shareholding requirements.

Clawbacks

Another way to hold a leader accountable for the long term is to impose clawbacks. Perhaps we can pay leaders for hitting short-term targets – and if we later find out that they did so with bad actions, we claw back the bonus. The first settlement in the US forced former UnitedHealth CEO William McGuire to repay his company $468 million in 2007, for inflating his pay through a process known as backdating. In the UK, Barclays clawed back £300 million in staff bonuses following fines for interest rate fixing and mis-selling of payment protection insurance.

Now the rhetoric of clawbacks is attractive – it sounds like we're punishing leaders for bad actions. But it's like shutting the barn door after the horse has bolted. Clawbacks involve paying the leader prematurely – for good short-term performance without waiting to see what caused it – and then trying to take money back if you learn it was due to manipulation. It's far better not to open the door in the first place: not to allow the leader to sell her equity for several years. A clawback is costly to implement because it requires legal action. And a far bigger problem is that its scope is very limited. It can be applied in clear cases of fraud, such as backdating, but the lines are much greyer for short-termist actions, such as cutting R&D, which are far from fraudulent: as discussed in Chapter 3, reducing investment sometimes grows the pie. And it almost certainly can't be applied to errors of omission, such as failing to improve workplace culture.

What's the evidence that short-term equity causes leaders to take short-term actions? Finding convincing evidence is difficult because of the common causation vs correlation challenge. You might show that, when an executive sells shares, she cuts investment. But an *omitted variable* may drive both. If prospects are looking bleak, this might cause the CEO to rationally scale back investment, and separately to sell her shares.

Vivian Fang, Katharina Lewellen and I thus took a different approach. We measured short-term incentives not by the amount of shares the CEO actually sells, but the amount that's scheduled to vest (i.e. whose lock-ups are about to expire). Upon expiry, CEOs typically sell their shares to diversify. So just before vesting, a CEO may boost the stock price so that she can sell her shares for more. Importantly, the amount of equity that vests today depends on how much equity was given several years ago, and so isn't correlated with current prospects.

Studying over 2,000 firms, we found that the more equity is vesting in a quarter, the more slowly investment grows. This result was remarkably robust – it held for five different measures of investment, and also if we excluded performance shares, where vesting depends on hitting performance targets rather than the passage of time.

What do the results mean? One interpretation is that the CEO inefficiently cuts good projects to inflate short-term earnings. But a second is that she efficiently cuts bad projects. It takes effort to identify wasteful projects and shut them down, and doing so may make the CEO unpopular. When she's about to sell her shares, she's willing to take tough decisions. If true, then short-term pressures are motivating, rather than distracting – a bit like how an impending essay deadline forces students to stop procrastinating.

If vesting causes the CEO to get her act together, you'd expect her to improve performance not just by cutting bad investment, but also by cutting other expenses or increasing sales growth. We found no evidence of this, suggesting that the investment declines are myopic, rather than part of an overall efficiency programme. Also supporting the myopia interpretation, the leader reduces investment more when she's more likely to get away with it – for example if she's closer to retirement and so is less concerned with the reputational damage from scrapping good investments.

Tomislav Ladika and Zach Sautner found independent corroboration that short-term equity causes short-term behaviour in a different setting. To identify causality, they studied the effect of the US accounting standard FAS 123R. This accounting change, effective from June 2005, reduced firms' profits by the value of unvested executive options. To avoid this, many firms allowed their options to vest early, giving the CEO incentives to boost the stock price by cutting invest-ment. One potential concern is that other events in 2005 may have affected companies' incentives to invest. So Tomislav and Zach com-pared companies with fiscal years ending between June and December, which had to comply with the new standard in 2005, with those with fiscal years ending between January and May, which didn't need to comply until 2006. They found that option vesting led firms to significantly cut investment.

We can demonstrate the importance of pay horizons by documenting not only the costs of short-term equity, as in the above two papers, but also the benefits of long-term equity. Caroline Flammer, who wrote the paper on shareholder proposals to improve social performance discussed in Chapter 4, teamed up with Tima Bansal to study a related subject – shareholder proposals to increase long-term incentives. They used a similar 'regression discontinuity' approach, comparing proposals that passed with just over 50% of the vote to those that just failed. Investigating over 800 proposals between 1997 and 2012, they found that proposals that just passed improve long-term return on assets, net profit margin and sales growth. Interestingly, performance decreases slightly in the short run, highlighting that long-term thinking requires short-run sacrifices. But the benefits outweigh the sacrifices – firm value rises overall.

So far, we've used the long-term stock return as a proxy for the size of the pie. However, it doesn't take true externalities into account, and so it's only correlated with the pie, not identical to it. Caroline and Tima explicitly investigated measures of stakeholder value. KLD ratings for the environment, customers, communities and especially colleagues improve. They also study innovation, which benefits both stakeholders and investors. After a proposal to increase long-term incentives passes, firms generate more patents, higher-quality patents and more innovative patents.

These three studies highlight the importance of pay horizons. Cutting pay in half will win more headlines than extending the horizon, but the latter has a much greater effect on society as it affects the CEO's incentives to invest in stakeholders – provide employees with meaningful work and development opportunities, forge long-term relationships with suppliers and build customer trust. Indeed, the 2018 UK Corporate Governance Code extended the minimum horizon from three to five years. Recall the Norwegian Sovereign Wealth Fund's pay principles, which argue that CEOs should hold significant equity in their firms. These principles also recommend that these 'shares are locked in for at least five and preferably ten years, regardless of resignation or retirement'.

Pay Ratios

We've discussed three pie-growing ways to reform reward: make the leader a significant owner; simplify pay by removing complex bonuses; and increase the horizon of pay. We close this chapter by examining a frequently proposed reform to pay which, while well-intentioned, may backfire because it's based on pie-splitting.

This remedy concerns the pay ratio: the ratio of CEO pay to average worker pay. The basic form of the remedy is to force firms to disclose this ratio, as the US and the UK have required from 2018 and 2019, respectively. Some investors take this further by using the pay ratio as an investment criterion or actively trying to lower it. In 2017, Black-Rock wrote to over 300 UK companies to say it would only approve salary increases for CEOs if worker wages increase by a similar amount. The media has frequently shamed enterprises for having a high pay ratio, and policymakers have started to penalise it too. In 2016, the Portland City Council in Oregon imposed an extra 10% city business licence tax on companies with pay ratios exceeding 100, and 25% if they exceed 250.

The idea behind pay ratio disclosure is that a high ratio is unfair. Indeed, Chapter 4 highlights the importance of treating colleagues fairly. Surely, paying them 361 times less than the leader is the antithesis of fairness? And an unfair split of the pie may in turn shrink the size of the pie, by demotivating the workforce and damaging the corporate culture. So it seems prudent for not only governments but also investors to closely monitor the pay ratio.

But fairness isn't the same as equality. Fairness is in relation to performance. If I gave all my students the same grade, regardless of their performance, that would be equal, but unfair. A comprehensive meta-analysis by Yale psychologists Christina Starmans, Mark Sheskin and Paul Bloom, entitled 'Why People Prefer Unequal Societies', concluded that citizens dislike not inequality, but unfairness. In a reward context, fairness is pay that's proportionate to the leader's contribution – pay should *reward value creation*. That's what giving long-term equity achieves. The correct benchmark isn't how much a CEO's colleagues are being paid, but how much she's grown the pie. Indeed, the frequent shaming of high-ratio firms typically doesn't ask whether the leader's high pay is merited (or not merited) by performance. JP Morgan CEO Jamie Dimon was lambasted for a ratio of 364 in 2017 – but the stock price had risen 62% over the past two years.

The pay ratio measures how the pie is split between the CEO and colleagues. It ignores stakeholders, but more importantly the size of the pie and thus the main way leaders can create value for society – growing the pie. The ratio can appear worse even if there's a Pareto improvement where everyone's better off. If an enterprise generates £8 billion of value, the CEO gets £4 million and the average worker earns £32,000, the ratio is 125:1. If the CEO innovates so that the enterprise generates £12 billion of value, she gets £6 million and workers earn £40,000 – everyone benefits – but the ratio increases to 150:1. Pieco-nomics holds a leader accountable for creating value, but a pay ratio instead holds her accountable for being paid not too much more than her colleagues.

This isn't just a hypothetical example. Sabrina Howell and David Brown find that when US firms win government R&D grants, they share a significant amount of this success with workers. Employees enjoy an average 16% pay increase, but the founder gains more – since she has a larger effect on the firm, her pay is more sensitive to both increases and decreases in performance. So the pay ratio rises, even though everyone gains. Indeed, in the Introduction, we mentioned US research which finds that, when the pay ratio is higher, firms are more valuable and perform better. A separate study by Holger Mueller, Paige Ouimet and Elena Simintzi found that, in the UK, higher ratios are associated with higher valuations, operating performance, long-run stock returns and earnings surprises. For example, firms with a pay ratio in the top third outperform those in the bottom third by 9.7% to 11.8% per year, after controlling for several other determinants of stock returns.

A separate issue is that the pay ratio is incomparable across firms. It's lower in Goldman Sachs (163:1 for 2017) than Wal-Mart (1,188:1) – not because Goldman's CEO is modestly paid, but because his colleagues are richly paid. Even within an industry, it will depend on an enterprise's business model. It's lower in Goldman Sachs than JP Morgan (364:1) because the latter employs bank tellers. It's lower in Dunkin' Brands (48:1) than Chipotle (814:1) because Dunkin' fran-chises out all its Dunkin' Donuts and Baskin-Robbins restaurants; Chipotle franchises none and so directly employs lower-paid service staff. A company that hires more part-time workers, outsources or automates low-paid jobs, or pays more in salary rather than training, vacation days and working conditions will report a higher average pay for full-time employees and thus a lower ratio. Indeed, leaders may take such actions to manipulate the ratio.

What about inequality? Social welfare depends not only on the size of the pie, but its distribution. But the pay of the 500 CEOs in the S&P 500 has very little effect on inequality across the 250 million adults in the US. Steve Kaplan and Josh Rauh show that pay in private equity, venture capital, hedge funds and law has risen faster than for CEOs. The *Forbes* 400 list of the wealthiest American residents contains far more hedge fund, private equity and real estate investors than public company leaders.

Pay has risen even in non-corporate settings. Take Alexis Sánchez, the Chile and Manchester United footballer. Even though Sánchez is a great player, it's hard to agree that he's better than Johan Cruyff. Cruyff is widely regarded as one of the greatest footballers of all time, and won the Ballon D'Or for the world's best player three times in the 1970s. Yet Sánchez earned £26 million in 2018, even excluding endorsements. His salary is far more than the $600,000 per year Cruyff earned in his heyday. Even adjusting for inflation, that's £2.2 million in 2018. This difference is because football is now a multi-billion-dollar industry, due to TV advertising and a global marketplace, unlike in Cruyff's time. Even if Sánchez is only a tiny bit better than the next-best midfielder, these tiny differences in talent could have a huge effect on Manchester United's profits. If Sánchez's goals get Manchester United into the Champions League, that's worth hundreds of millions. So it's worth it paying top dollar for top talent. Indeed, we see pay rising in almost every scalable profession. J. K. Rowling isn't clearly more talented than Jane Austen, but is paid far more since her books can be sold worldwide, adapted into movies and used to create merchandise. Actors, musicians and even reality TV stars have a much greater reach, and thus command much higher pay, than in the past.

This observation can explain why pay has risen so much for CEOs. It's hard to argue that CEOs are more talented now than in the past – but talent has become more important. Just as the football industry has become much bigger, so have enterprises. They also compete in a global marketplace, and technology changes so rapidly that the inability to keep up can render firms virtually extinct – contrast Blackberry with Apple. Thus, just like in football, it's worth paying top dollar for top talent. Average firm size in the S&P 500 is $22 billion. So even if a CEO is only slightly more talented than the next-best alternative, and contributes only 1% more to firm value, that's $220 million. Suddenly, her $14 million salary doesn't seem so out of line.

That's the argument in one of the most influential finance papers so far this century, by economists Xavier Gabaix and Augustin Landier. It was cited as a reason for Xavier being awarded the Fischer Black Prize for outstanding research by a financial economist under 40 (similar to a Fields Medal for mathematics). Moreover, it's not just an abstract theory; you can test it. The authors show that the increase in US CEO pay between 1980 and 2003 can be fully explained by the rise in firm size over that time. An update with Julien Sauvagnat, studying 2004 to 2011, shows that subsequent changes were also linked to firm size – in 2007 to 2009, firm size fell by 17% and CEO pay by 28%.

Why doesn't this logic apply to employees? Because a CEO's actions are scalable. If she implements a new production technology, or improves corporate culture, this can be rolled out firm-wide, and thus has a larger effect in a larger firm. 1% amounts to $22 million in a $2.2 billion firm, but $220 million in a $22 billion firm. In contrast, most employees' actions are less scalable. An engineer who has the capacity to service ten machines creates $80,000 of value regardless of whether the firm has 100 or 1,000 machines.

We can draw two takeaways from this observation. On the one hand, it means that high pay for CEOs is part of a general trend throughout society. It need not imply that rising executive pay is an inside job, rubber-stamped by boards who are in the leader's pocket – no matter how attractive this story sounds. On the other hand, it suggests that the problem of inequality is much more serious and widespread than implied by skyrocketing CEO pay. Pay has been rising in any scalable profession, so addressing income inequality *within firms* is an ineffective way of addressing income inequality *within society*. The latter should be addressed in a more systematic manner, such as a higher rate of income tax above £1 million, or higher inheritance tax (while recognising the trade-off between ex post redistribution and ex ante incentives). Doing so will address income inequality from all highly paid professions, not just public company CEOs.

Summing up all the evidence, what does it mean for executive pay reform? Current reforms try to crack down on the level of pay, but doing so will only split the pie differently and I know of no evidence that such changes improve either investor or stakeholder value. The structure of pay – its sensitivity, simplicity and horizon – is more important and ensures that a leader is rewarded only for growing the pie for the benefit of both investors and stakeholders alike. Rather than bringing the CEO's slice down, reforms should encourage the CEO to bring other stakeholders' slices up.

In a Nutshell

- Common criticisms of, and proposed remedies to, leader reward focus on the level of pay. This is based on pie-splitting. The amount of value that could be redistributed to other stakeholders by reducing pay is very small: CEO pay, while large compared to average wages, is tiny compared to enterprise value.
- Far more important than how much pay costs (its *level*) is its effects – whether it incentivises leaders to grow the pie by creating long-term value or shrink it by pursuing short-term targets. The goal of pay reform should be to encourage value creation rather than reduce the level of pay.
- The effects of pay depend on its *structure*, which comprises three dimensions:
  - The *sensitivity* of wealth to performance leads to *accountability*. Sensitivity is much higher than commonly believed, due to a leader's sizable shareholdings. These shareholdings are significantly correlated with future stock returns and the relationship is likely causal.
  - The *simplicity* of pay leads to *symmetry*. Complex target-based bonuses encourage a leader to focus only on the targeted performance measures, and may encourage excessive risk-taking close to the lower threshold or coasting close to the upper threshold.
  - The *horizon* of pay leads to *sustainability*. Lengthening the leader's horizon can deter both errors of commission (taking short-term actions that destroy value) and errors of omission (failing to invest for the long term).
- The pay ratio is based on pie-splitting and compares two incomparable quantities. A leader's pay should be tied to her performance, not worker pay. Colleagues should be paid fairly irrespective of executive pay. The pay ratio is incomparable across enterprises, even within the same industry, and a focus on the ratio can encourage manipulation.

- Fairness can be addressed by giving stock to all colleagues, not just executives, allowing them to share in any value increase that they help create.
- Pay has increased substantially across all scalable professions, not just CEOs, and for arguably justifiable reasons – their potential value creation has grown. Thus, inequality should be addressed in a systematic way, such as a high income tax on earnings above £1 million, rather than trying to regulate the pay of CEOs only.

6 STEWARDSHIP
THE VALUE OF ENGAGED INVESTORS THAT BOTH SUPPORT AND CHALLENGE MANAGEMENT

In 1995, the Fidelity Value Fund was a prime place for Americans to invest their money. Its performance had outstripped its peers over the five years since manager Jeff Ubben took the reins, attracting hordes of new savers who wanted in on the action. This new money should have been an unmitigated blessing to Jeff, as it boosted the fund to $5 billion.

But there's a catch. A fund can't hold too large a position in any one stock, otherwise it bears too much risk. Also, if your stake exceeds 10%, US law classifies you as an 'insider', which restricts you from selling your shares – so you're stuck if your own investors need to withdraw. This new money thus had to be invested in other stocks, which spread Jeff and his team too thinly. Jeff recounted: 'Every day, I ended up having new money coming in which would dilute my fund and I would end up with 120 positions, instead of concentrating on my best ideas. And every time I would get it back down, the fund would grow and I would end up again with 120 positions.'

To focus on his best ideas, Jeff co-founded the activist fund ValueAct, which holds a concentrated portfolio of only ten to fifteen stocks. An *activist* fund doesn't simply buy a stock and wait for it to go up. Instead, it tries to influence how the enterprise is run, known as *engagement* or *activism*.* Investor activism is widely misportrayed, based on individual anecdotes. The best-selling book and movie *Barbarians at the Gate* dramatises investor KKR's takeover of RJR Nabisco as a bloodthirsty battle, like barbaric invaders seizing control of a civilised city. Stories like these promote a popular image of activists as callous pie-splitters, leading to deep distrust by society. Just as raiders plunder a city by taking spoils from its inhabitants, activist investors allegedly plunder other stakeholders by firing workers, price-gouging customers and cutting R&D.

In response, executives and policymakers push for defences against these barbarians. In 2014, France enacted the Loi Florange, a law that halves an investor's voting rights until he's held his stake for at least two years. Some enterprises, particularly young tech firms such as Facebook, Google and Snap, feature 'dual class shares', where the shares sold to outside investors confer only a tenth of the voting rights of those held by leaders – or, in the case of Snap, no voting rights at all.

Certain instances of activism are indeed bruising battles, but these battles often create value rather than stealing it. In *Barbarians at the Gate*, the real barbarians were inside the gate – RJR Nabisco executives who wasted money on pie-in-the-sky projects like the Premier smokeless cigarette, a venture hidden from the board for several years that wasted over $800 million. Particularly egregious was their perk consumption. The firm had ten private jets and thirty-six pilots which flew not only executives, but also the CEO's dog (listed as passenger 'G Shepherd') to golf tournaments, and were housed by a hangar containing $600,000 of furniture and surrounded by $250,000 of landscaping. KKR created substantial value simply by ending such abuse of investors' – and society's – resources.

But most engagements are far more boring, and far more collaborative, than commonly believed. As Pieconomics stresses, investors and leaders are on the same team. Jeff and his colleagues at ValueAct are pie-growers. The ten to fifteen stocks they choose to own are ones where they believe the pie is much smaller than its potential. They then engage with each company to help it realise this potential.

A prime example is how ValueAct helped turn around Adobe. Ex-Xerox colleagues John Warnock and Charles Gerschke founded

---

* The latter term is more commonly used for more confrontational engagement, but we'll use the two interchangeably.

Adobe in 1982 to develop PostScript, a way for printers to handle different fonts and geometric objects. Such was its promise that Apple CEO Steve Jobs offered $5 million to buy Adobe after just a year. John and Charles turned him down, instead selling Apple a 19% stake and a five-year licence for PostScript. Thanks in part to Apple using it in its LaserWriter printers, by 1987, PostScript became the first industry standard for computer printing. Two years later, Adobe launched Photoshop, an image editing software, and in 1993 its Portable Document Format (PDF) which converts spreadsheets, presentations and documents into a universal format for easy sharing. The momentum continued, and a crowning moment was its 2005 purchase of rival Macromedia. That gave it a suite of new products, such as Dreamweaver for website design and Flash for video and audio streaming. Its stock price soared 584% from the start of 1999 to the end of 2007.

But then Adobe started to lose its way. It suffered poor sales on its Creative Suite products, into which it had integrated Macromedia. Apple, which had earlier catalysed PostScript's growth, hit Adobe with a hammer blow in 2010 by refusing to allow Flash on its products – instead preferring its rival HTML5. As a result, Adobe had to fire 2,000 employees across three rounds of cuts in 2008, 2009 and 2011.

ValueAct was well aware of all these problems, and more. It saw Adobe as an outdated company that focused too much on desktop products, had missed the mobile revolution and clung to the archaic revenue model of selling its software rather than licensing it on subscription. But it also saw potential in Adobe that the rest of the market didn't, and so invested in it. Between September and December 2011, ValueAct went from a zero to a 5% stake. Adobe management stated that they 'talked frequently' with ValueAct after it became a large investor, and found 'their input on our business and our strategy to be helpful'. In December 2012, with ValueAct now owning 6.3%, Adobe appointed ValueAct partner Kelly Barlow to its board.

With a ringside seat, ValueAct started to do what its name promised – act to create value. Far from the common portrayal of going for the quick buck, this was a long-term game. As Jeff said, 'I don't need the quick hit . . . You can't just keep throwing stuff at the wall, you need to get in there, get the information and work on a long-term plan that is going to be sustainable.'

Left alone, Adobe might have tried to revive Flash. Having paid $3.4 billion for Macromedia, it was reluctant to cut its losses. That would be admitting that buying Macromedia was a mistake, so Adobe might have thrown good money after bad – just as Daewoo refused to exit from the Vietnamese car market. ValueAct hadn't been involved in the Macromedia purchase, wasn't emotionally tied to it and so could provide an outside perspective. It encouraged Adobe to move away from Flash and embrace HTML5 rather than viewing it as the enemy. So Adobe started to create content using HTML5 and other open technologies, and plans to end Flash for good in 2020.

The transformations extended well beyond Flash. Having fallen behind in the mobile revolution, Adobe started developing new and better mobile apps. It transitioned to a subscription-based revenue model, reducing piracy and giving Adobe more stable revenues than one-off purchases. This not only pleased Adobe's finance department, but also encouraged innovation, like the long-term equity incentives discussed in Chapter 5. Photoshop creator Thomas Knoll explained: 'Engineers were very much in favour of the transition. Previously, they had to come up with new features every two years, and these features had to demo well, because you had to convince someone to buy a new version based on those features . . . Now the incentive is to create features people actually use and don't want to do without. I think it's a better incentive to have engineers making a product more valuable to its users than to make eye candy for a demo.'

Adobe's revenue grew from $4.2 billion in 2011 to $7.3 billion in 2017. As Figure 6.1 shows, after seven years of stagnation, its stock price more than tripled between ValueAct's initial entry in December 2011 and its exit in March 2016. Stakeholders benefited too. The expansion into HTML5 allowed customers to integrate Adobe's products with Apple's, and the mobile apps let them use Adobe's products across different devices. Between 2011 and 2017, Adobe's headcount grew from 10,000 to 18,000 and its tax payments soared from $202 million to $443 million.

And ValueAct didn't just focus on turnarounds that would pay off during its own investment horizon, but also beyond – Adobe's stock price doubled in the two years since its exit. Why did ValueAct sell out? Because it had already set Adobe back on track, and found pie-growing opportunities in other companies. In September 2016, it bought 4% of Seagate Technology. Contrary to the common view that investors are the enemy, Seagate approached ValueAct to buy a stake and granted it an 'observer' seat on the board (allowing participation in all

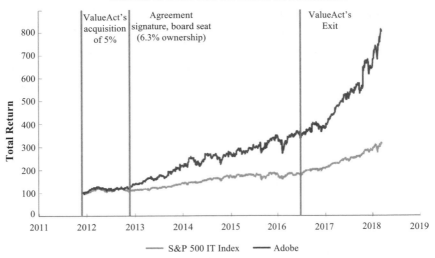

Figure 6.1

discussions, but no vote). As CEO Steve Luczo explained, 'Seagate approached ValueAct to . . . become an investor in our company, given their commitment to and success in creating long-term value for the companies in which they invest.'

ValueAct's turnaround of Adobe is only a hand-picked anecdote. There are other cases where activists boost short-term profits at the expense of long-term value. Carl Icahn took a 20% stake in Trans World Airlines and sold its profitable assets to competitors, causing it to go bankrupt. So what usually happens – is ValueAct an exception or the rule? Why do some investors succeed in improving the companies they own, but others fail? And can shareholders enhance a firm's performance even without influencing how it's run? These are some of the questions we'll explore in this chapter.

The Long-Term Benefits of Hedge Fund Activism

Let's start with the first question – is ValueAct an outlier? To answer that, we first need to understand in more detail the type of investor that ValueAct is. It's a particular type of activist investor – an activist hedge fund. A *hedge fund* can short-sell stocks as well as buy them, whereas *mutual funds* can typically only do the latter. But while hedge funds are most known – and most notorious – for short-selling, that's not their most critical feature for Pieconomics. Two other features are more important. First, while a mutual fund charges its clients around 1% of the money it manages each year, a hedge fund charges 2% plus – importantly – a performance fee of 20% of the fund's profits. Second, while mutual funds aim to beat the market, hedge funds aren't evaluated against the market, but in isolation. They thus endeavour to generate positive returns even in a down market.

If activist investors are seen as the worst species of shareholder, activist hedge funds are a particularly maligned breed. Perhaps their strong performance incentives and need to generate returns in all conditions spur them to boost short-term profits through slashing wages, cutting investment and selling a company's prime assets.

As Peter Georgescu argued in the Introduction, 'Shareholder activists . . . are more like terrorists who manage through fear and strip the company of its underlying crucial assets . . . extracting cash out of everything that would otherwise generate long-term value.' In 2016, US Senators Tammy Baldwin and Jeff Merkley proposed the Brokaw Act to crack down on activist hedge funds, claiming: 'Activist hedge funds are leading the short-term charge in our economy. They abuse lax securities laws to gain large stakes in public companies . . . We cannot allow our economy to be hijacked by a small group of investors who only seek to enrich themselves at the expense of workers, communities and taxpayers.' These concerns are very serious, and if true, should be urgently addressed.

But are they actually true? Let's look at the evidence. Finance professors Alon Brav and Wei Jiang have spent over a decade studying the effects of hedge fund activism, in a series of papers with various co-authors. This research is particularly striking even though activist hedge funds are only a small part of the investment industry, and thus far from the only focus of this chapter, because they're viewed as the epitome of a pie-splitting investor. But the evidence actually shows they often grow the pie.

When any investor buys a 5% stake in a US firm and intends to affect how it's run, it must file a 'Schedule 13D' form, stating the changes it wishes to pursue in Item 4 of that form. Alon, Wei and legal scholars Frank Partnoy and Randall Thomas analysed over 1,000 13D filings by activist hedge funds. They found that a 13D increases the stock price by an average of 7%, with no long-term reversal. Alon, Wei and Lucian Bebchuk discovered that even after the hedge fund exits, stock prices keep rising for the next three years – like the Adobe case, and contradicting common concerns that hedge funds 'pump and dump'. As Paul Singer, founder of the activist investor Elliott, argues: 'The benefits of fixing a broken strategy, getting rid of a bad acquisition, redeploying an underperforming asset, or replacing an ineffective management team or board may show up right away in a company's stock price, but that immediate result doesn't diminish the long-term benefits.' Moreover, hedge funds typically own a company for two years, attenuating concerns that they're not around long enough to implement long-term improvements.

Now rising stock prices could simply be due to hedge funds extracting dividends or piling on debt to save taxes, rather than improving actual performance. So together with Hyunseob Kim, Alon and Way investigated hedge funds' impact on profitability. Figure 6.2 tells a thousand words.

The 'Event Year' is when the investor files the 13D, and the solid line is return-on-assets (ROA) relative to the industry. ROA falls significantly before hedge fund entry, suggesting that hedge funds aim to turn around underperforming firms. After the 13D, ROA rebounds – and it's not just a flash in the pan. The improvement becomes stronger

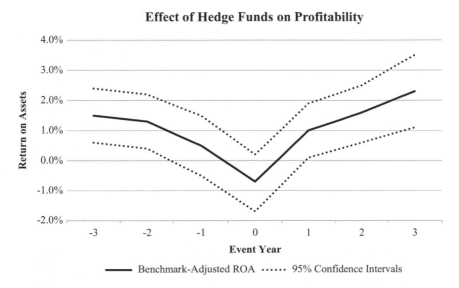

Figure 6.2

year after year, and the results continue to hold even if you look five years out.

Still, higher profitability isn't conclusive evidence of pie-growing – it might be at the expense of other stakeholders. Perhaps spurred on by the hedge fund's short-term demands, the enterprise now slave-drives employees, compromises product quality or squeezes suppliers. The way to dig deeper and find out the root causes of the higher profitability would be to obtain information on the productivity of each individual manufacturing establishment, or 'plant'. But this data isn't available in any annual report or public filing – it's confidential and housed by the US Census.

So Hyunseob jumped through many hoops in order to gain access to this data that would help him, Alon and Wei really nail the cause of the profit increases. He first needed to write a detailed proposal to the Census Bureau to convince them of the benefits of the research. This involved multiple rounds of revision and resubmission before it was finally approved. He then applied to become a special 'sworn status' researcher with the Census Bureau, which required background checks through his contacts and an interview with a federal government agent.

After finally obtaining access to the data, Alon, Wei and Hyunseob found that plants targeted by hedge funds enjoyed a rise in total factor productivity, but there was no recovery for similarly under-performing plants that weren't targeted. The recovery isn't just a bounce-back that would have happened anyway. In Figure 6.3, the solid line tracks the productivity of a targeted plant and the dotted line a similar non-targeted plant.*

You might still be sceptical. Total factor productivity measures output relative to wages (plus other inputs). Perhaps the hedge fund turns a plant into a sweatshop, cutting wages or increasing hours. So Alon, Wei and Hyunseob drilled deeper and studied labour productivity – output per labour hour. This rose by 8.4% to 9.2% over the three years after the 13D. Indeed, working hours didn't rise and wages didn't fall.

---

* The scale on the y-axis is 'standardised' total factor productivity, which standardises the productivity measure to have a standard deviation of 1. The actual standard deviation is 0.32. Thus, a y-axis value of 0.1 corresponds to a 3.2% (= 0.1 * 0.32 = 0.032) increase in total factor productivity.

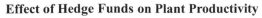

Effect of Hedge Funds on Plant Productivity

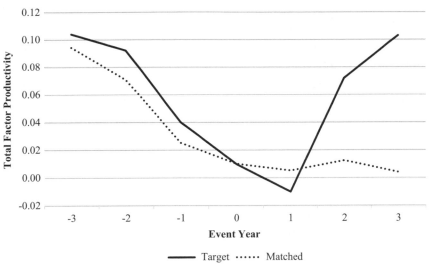

Figure 6.3

Surely, the common concerns about hedge funds can't all be false? Indeed, they're not. The researchers found that hedge funds do lead to companies selling plants. When it comes to the accusation of being asset strippers, they're guilty as charged.

But there's a twist. The Census data allows the researchers to track the productivity of the plants under their new owners. They find that productivity improves – but it doesn't improve when plants are divested without the involvement of hedge funds. So hedge-fund-led disposals aren't myopic, but reallocate assets to buyers who can make better use of them. This is consistent with the principle of comparative advantage and recognises the social opportunity costs of holding onto a plant – doing so prevents another enterprise using it to deliver value. It's well accepted that it's a waste of talent if a promising striker isn't getting into the starting line-up of his football club, so he should be sold to a club where he can – but this recognition is often not applied to selling assets or businesses.

What happens to investment? Inconsistent with concerns of short-termism, IT spending increases, which might be a reason for the productivity gains. But even more important for society is innovation because of its spillover effects. Alon, Wei, Song Ma and Xuan Tian found that, when a firm is targeted by a hedge fund, R&D falls by an average of 20% compared to non-targeted firms.

This appears to be a smoking gun. It confirms one of the worst fears about activism. Senators Baldwin and Merkley, when launching the Brokaw Act, claimed that 'firms targeted by activists experience lower investment and R&D'. While they didn't cite any studies, it turns out that they were spot on.

Yet here again there's a twist. Even though R&D expenditure falls, firms file 15% more patents, and each patent that it does file generates 15% more citations (a measure of patent quality). The firm produces more output for less input – the investor stops it throwing flour outside the baking tray.

This is an important point. Commentators often use the level of investment to measure short-termism. But investment only measures how much you spend (the *input*), not what you do with what you spend (the *output*). Sports fans are less impressed by teams that spend millions on players than those that deliver results on a shoestring, but we don't always recognise this distinction when analysing companies. As mentioned previously, it takes no skill to simply spend money. Recall from Chapter 5 that Bart Becht transformed Reckitt Benckiser's innovation not by throwing around cash – his R&D spend was lower than competitors' – but by focusing on the Powerbrands.

Just like the reallocation of plants, Alon, Wei, Song and Xuan find that engagement spurs the reallocation of patents and inventors. The firm sells patents, particularly those less related to its technological expertise – its comparative advantage. After the sale, the patent becomes more impactful, i.e. generates more citations. Inventors who leave produce more and better patents at their new employer. Those who stay also become more productive, compared to inventors who stay at firms not targeted by hedge funds.

How do these companies magically become more productive and innovative? The change starts at the top. Some CEOs leave; for those that stay, their share ownership increases significantly as recommended in Chapter 5. New directors added to boards have better credentials and more technology or industry expertise.*

---

* Is this correlation or causation? Perhaps the investor predicted that an enterprise would improve performance and so bought large stakes in anticipation. This is hard to reconcile with the breadth of the evidence – the investor would have had to predict improvements in labour productivity and innovation efficiency, the sale of underperforming plants and non-core patents, that some inventors would leave, but those that stay would become more productive, that the CEO would change and that new

And the wider societal benefits of activism are broader than just the firm in question. They spill over to its competitors – Hadiye Aslan and Praveen Kumar find that rivals take actions to remain competitive, and Nick Gantchev, Oleg Gredil and Pab Jotikasthira show that they do so to pre-empt hedge funds taking a stake in them. Peer firms improve their own productivity, cost efficiency and capital allocation, and cut prices and increase product differentiation to benefit customers.

The Value of Engagement

The studies by Alon, Wei and their co-authors turn the traditional view of investors on its head. Since investors need to generate profits for savers, the fear is that they'll do so by taking from stakeholders. Some investors may well have the pie-splitting mentality – but as Figure 2.1 showed, there's a limit to how much profit you can generate by pie-splitting. Investors who don't grow the pie will generate lower long-run returns, and savers will walk away. So investors and stakeholders are much more aligned than commonly believed.

But CEOs and their advisors often view hedge funds as enemies who attack the firm. Lawyer Marty Lipton, a prominent opponent of hedge funds, wrote a blueprint on how to deal with them, which uses the word 'attack' and its variants twenty times. Yet engagement improves long-run stock returns, profitability, productivity and innovation – exactly what leaders (and society) want to happen. Rather than viewing restructuring suggestions as an 'attack', and immediately going on the defensive and arguing they're wrong, executives' first reaction should be to entertain the possibility that they may be right. Activists' challenges may be tough to hear, but this

directors would be appointed. In addition, across their different papers, the researchers conduct a battery of additional tests to suggest causation. For example, the increases in productivity are stronger when the engagement is more confrontational or targets operational issues (such as strategy or asset sales) in Item 4 rather than undervaluation or capital structure. The improvements arise even when the investor owned a significant position prior to the 13D – so the fund didn't increase its stake much, but the 13D gave notice of its intent to engage. When the hedge fund exits, the market response is worse if it hasn't succeeded in implementing the Item 4 changes, suggesting that these changes would have added value.

shouldn't detract from their value. It seems the main target that activists are attacking is underperformance, and companies should ally with them in this attack.

In 2014, investors raised concerns to UK outsourcing firm Carillion about its high debt, widening pension deficit and weak cash flow generation, and suggested a change in strategy. But management viewed this as an attack and ignored them. Carillion went bankrupt in January 2018, hurting not only investors, but society – its failure caused 3,000 job losses, jeopardised the pensions of 27,000 retirees and pushed some of its own suppliers into bankruptcy. A UK government report found that 'had it been more receptive to the advice of key investors at an earlier stage it may have been able to avert the darkening clouds that subsequently presaged its collapse'.

How can investors provide useful perspectives when they're outsiders with far less knowledge of the business than leaders? By providing an independent sounding board, for example when brainstorming a new strategic idea or discussing competitive threats. While investors indeed don't work for the company day to day, this outsiders' view helps overcome a CEO's attachment to the status quo – a strategy she designed or a business she bought. As the fable goes, a frog placed in a jar of water won't notice if the water slowly starts to boil. But an outsider can, by seeing bubbles begin to form. Activist Bill Ackman explains: 'The value add of an activist . . . is that we can help prevent the next Kodak from disappearing, where tens of thousands of jobs are lost, by waking up a complacent company to the competitive threats it faces and the inefficiency that has crept into their business because of complacency.'

Policymakers are indeed realising the value of engaged investors. Since the early 1990s, Japan has suffered prolonged economic stagnation – initially referred to as the 'Lost Decade', but now dubbed the 'Lost 20 Years' due to its longevity. One symptom is Japan's very low returns on equity, which stems in part from companies taking the easy option of sitting on cash rather than finding innovative investment opportunities. Prime Minister Shinzo Abe sees greater investor engagement as a solution. His structural reforms – the third of his 'three arrows' of economic policy to revitalise the Japanese economy (the first two being monetary easing and fiscal stimulus) – thus include strengthening investor rights. One example is creating the Japanese Corporate Governance Code in 2015.

However, as with most issues, the evidence isn't all one-way. While Alon and Wei comprehensively study hedge funds, evidence is not *universal* as highlighted in Chapter 4. The results are more mixed for activism by non-hedge fund investors, such as pension funds and mutual funds. David Yermack's 2010 survey of the activism research to date (written before the hedge fund studies) found that 'the success of institutional investor activism to date appears limited'.

So, just as socially responsible investing doesn't always pay off, as discussed in Chapter 2, engagement doesn't always pay off. The reasons are similar. Socially Responsible Investing (SRI) can be implemented in a box-ticking fashion – for example, choosing stocks based on pay ratios without considering pay horizons. Similarly, engagement can also be implemented through box-ticking – pushing for quick wins on ratios rather than deeper issues such as horizons. What matters is engagement quality, rather than simply engagement activity.

What Strengthens Engagement?

There are three reasons why activist hedge funds are particularly effective at Adobe-like engagements. Importantly, none is unique to hedge funds and other investors can adopt them too. The first is their *portfolio concentration*. Since ValueAct only owns ten to fifteen stocks, it has a substantial stake in each one. This gives it incentives to get into the weeds of every enterprise that it owns.

This isn't the case for many mutual funds. There are two main types. *Index funds* hold an index – for example, the Russell 1000 Index of the thousand largest US companies. Since there's no fund manager who actively picks stocks, these funds are typically very cheap, with an annual fee of around 0.1% (in September 2018, Fidelity launched zero-fee index funds). The second type is *actively managed funds*, or *active funds*. An active fund specifies a benchmark index that it aims to beat by choosing different stocks from it. To pay the fund manager and his team of analysts, the fee might be 1%.

But even though active funds in theory are free to select whatever stocks they like, in reality many hold hundreds of stocks to be close to the benchmark, a practice known as 'closet indexing'. Such funds' primary concern is to avoid underperforming the index – doing so leads to client withdrawals and potentially the fund manager being fired. They may thus hold a stock simply because it's part of the index rather than because they believe in its long-term potential. They don't mind if it falls in value, because the benchmark they're evaluated against falls too. Morningstar found that 20% of European Large Cap funds could be classified as closet indexers. Such behaviour means that a fund is spread too thinly to engage meaningfully with each stock.

Similar problems arise for pension funds. In the US, pension funds must follow 'prudent man' rules that require them to diversify. Diversification may be prudent if all you care about is errors of commission – investing in bad stocks. But Pieconomics is more about avoiding errors of omission; from this perspective, excessive diversification is imprudent. If a fund holds hundreds of stocks, it's unlikely to have a deep understanding of each one and will miss many opportunities to create value. In few other areas of life is excessive diversification prudent. It's well understood that taking on hundreds of commitments prevents you from devoting sufficient time to each.

A hedge fund owns a concentrated portfolio because it isn't evaluated relative to an index. If it loses 10%, it can't use the fact that the index lost 15% as an excuse, because its stated mission is to generate positive returns regardless of market conditions. So every stock it owns is a *conviction holding* – a deliberate choice rather than a default, because it's part of the benchmark. This large stake then gives it the incentives to engage.

A second reason for activist hedge funds' effectiveness is their strong financial *incentives*. Consider a hedge fund and a mutual fund who both own a $100 million stake. If a hedge fund's engagement raises firm value by 5%, its stake goes up in value by $5 million. In the first year, the fund keeps $1.1 million of this increase: $1 million through the 20% performance fee and $0.1 million through the 2% annual fee. A mutual fund with a 1% annual fee will keep $50,000, so its incentives are twenty-two times less. These incentives are important because engagement costs money as well as time – Nick Gantchev estimated that the average activist campaign that ends in a proxy fight (a public battle for board seats) costs over $10 million. Engagements should start off collaborative, but confrontation is a useful – yet costly – escalation mechanism if management is intransigent.

Some savers might balk at a hedge fund's 20% performance fee, just like citizens may object to high CEO pay. But the performance fee isn't at the expense of anyone – it's only earned if the hedge fund has grown the pie. Moreover, consistent with the long-term incentives advocated in Chapter 5, pay to hedge fund employees is typically deferred for several years.

A third reason is the substantial *resources* activist hedge funds devote to engagement – it's a central part of the investment process. Some mutual funds market themselves primarily on cost and see engagement as a wasteful activity that simply adds expense. But engagement is a profit centre, not a cost centre.

The silver lining is that none of these three features is unique to hedge funds. Other investors can adopt the same practices – and many of the best do. As we'll discuss in Chapter 9, investors should pay their fund managers according to long-term performance and devote significant resources to engagement. Active funds should hold concentrated stakes rather than hugging the index. There's nothing special about hedge funds; they're just one example of a concentrated, incentivised and resourced investor.

Indeed, studies of non-hedge fund investors with the above features find more positive results. Private equity investors have the same characteristics. They're nearly as maligned by the public as hedge funds. But evidence shows that, when they take over a company, profits rise, total factor productivity increases, new products are launched and the quality of patents improves.

Turning to investors in public firms, the UK investor Hermes manages the British Telecom and Post Office pension funds, as well as client money. In 1998, it set up the UK Focus Fund, in response to concerns that its main funds were too diversified. As the name suggests, it held a small number of stocks – no more than thirteen at any time. It was dedicated to engagement, only buying underperforming stocks it believed it could turn around. Employees had a low base salary, but a strong incentive scheme that could yield seven-figure bonuses upon exceptional performance.

The fund's engagements aimed to apply the principle of comparative advantage and sell non-core assets. Marco Becht, Julian Franks, Colin Mayer and Stefano Rossi found that stock returns rose by an average of 5.3% if an engagement achieved its goal. The returns were higher for confrontational than for collaborative engagements, suggesting Hermes was overturning poor decisions by entrenched management. Profitability, which had declined in the two years before the engagement, rebounded over the next two.

A separate study by Elroy Dimson, Oğuzhan Karakaş and Xi Li investigated a large anonymous investor which had a major commitment to SRI, and thus developed specialist expertise in environmental and social engagement. While such activism aimed to benefit stakeholders, investors gained also – the pie grew. The stock price rose by 2.3% over the following year and 7.1% if the engagement achieved its stated goals. Profits improved as well.

Generalised Engagement

The activism that ValueAct undertook in Adobe, and that Alon, Wei and their co-authors researched, is *specialised engagement*. Here, the best course of action is situation-specific. ValueAct had to deeply understand Adobe's specific problems and evaluate tailored solutions, such as changing its revenue model.

But that's not the only type of engagement that creates value. Some improvements can be implemented across most firms, which we'll call *generalised engagement*. Increasing pay horizons or encouraging disclosure of carbon emissions is usually desirable, so investors can push for such changes without deep strategic analysis. While specialised engagement is 'bottom-up', starting from the enterprise's strategy and operations, generalised engagement is 'top-down', applying a broad issue across several firms.

Specialised engagement is harder for index funds, since they hold every stock in an index and may be spread too thinly to focus on one particular company. But they're well placed to undertake generalised engagement, because they're large and thus have strong voting power. In 2014, they held over a third of all US mutual fund assets, four times their share in 1998. The asset managers that offer these index funds, such as Vanguard, Blackrock, State Street and Legal & General, are often the largest shareholders in a firm.

Ian Appel, Todd Gormley and Don Keim use the regression discontinuity approach to study how index fund ownership affects governance. Here's how they showed causation. The Russell 1000 Index contains the largest 1,000 US public companies, and the Russell 2000 the next 2,000. Whether a stock is at the bottom of the Russell 1000 or the top of the Russell 2000 is essentially random – but has a big effect on its index fund ownership. The 1,000th largest firm will have little ownership by index funds that track the Russell 1000, because it's the smallest in its index. In contrast, the 1,001st largest firm will have high ownership by index funds that track the Russell 2000, because it's the largest in its index.

Ian, Todd and Don show that index fund ownership is 66% higher for stocks at the top of the Russell 2000 than those at the bottom of the Russell 1000. This increase is associated with several improvements in governance, higher profitability and enhanced valuations. It also leads to lower voting support for management proposals and higher support for governance-related shareholder proposals – consistent with the idea that index funds improve generalised engagement due to their voting power.

Investor Rights

We can shed light on the value of engagement by studying not only actual instances of activism, but also investor rights – shareholders' ability to engage with a company and influence how it's run.

Enterprises can put several mechanisms in place to reduce investors' influence. One is the staggered board. Let's say Paolo is the CEO. He's corrupt, spending the firm's cash on bad acquisitions, plush offices and, of course, a high salary for himself. He's also devious. He's chosen as his three directors Amit, Sarah and Delphine, all of whom are his buddies from business school and support his personal self-enrichment plan. And he's staggered their elections. Amit comes up for election this year, Sarah next year and Delphine in two years' time. An activist might try to get his own directors elected to the board to fire Paolo. But because only one-third of the board is up for election in any given year, the activist can't get a majority unless he waits another year and wins a second election. Paolo is protected from investors and can continue to destroy value.

But staggered boards might not be bad. Rather than entrenching a pie-splitting leader, they may protect a pie-growing leader from being fired for short-term losses, freeing her to focus on long-run investment.* So let's look at the evidence. A seminal paper by Paul Gompers, Joy Ishii and Andrew Metrick gathered data not only on staggered boards, but also on twenty-three other mechanisms to protect management from shareholder pressure. The results were striking. Companies with the fewest protection mechanisms and thus the strongest investor rights beat those with the opposite by 8.5% per year. They also had greater sales growth, suggesting they fulfil customers' needs, and higher profitability. While Paul, Joy and Andrew study investor rights in general, three more papers focus on staggered boards and find causal evidence that they reduce firm value.

Paul, Joy and Andrew conducted a separate analysis on the effects of dual-class shares, documenting a significant decline in firm value. Ron Masulis, Cong Wang and Fei Xie then uncovered the sources of this decline. Dual-class shares are associated with higher CEO pay, worse acquisitions and poorer investment decisions – suggesting that they entrench management and allow them to empire-build.

These findings are important and go against current thinking. There are many calls to restrict investor rights, based on the claim that shareholders extract value from stakeholders or interfere with the CEO's vision, particularly if she founded the enterprise, by pushing for short-term profit. This narrative is popular given the differing public perceptions of entrepreneurs and investors. Entrepreneurs create ideas; investors make money on the back of someone else's idea.

Entrepreneurs arguably grow the pie more than any other member of society. But Pieconomics stresses the importance of balance – between an entrepreneur's vision and investors' oversight, just as cars have both accelerator and brake pedals. This balance is crucial since there are several cautionary examples of once-promising businesses declining due to an untouchable founder. As *The Economist* described the Daewoo founder, 'Kim is used to making investment decisions on the spot, based on hunches', rather than consulting others. Jerry Yang of Yahoo rejected a $47.5 billion takeover bid from

---

* If insulation from short-term pressures is a concern, a better approach might be to have three-year terms, but have all directors come up for election in the same year – in years 3, 6, 9 and so on. Directors then become accountable for three-year, rather than one-year, performance, reducing short-term pressures. But if performance remains poor after three years, the whole board can be voted out.

Microsoft in February 2008 because he didn't want to cede control of what he saw as his company – but it was Yahoo shareholders' company as he'd sold out to them when Yahoo went public. By November, Yahoo's value had fallen to a third of Microsoft's offer, and two Detroit pension funds sued Yahoo for violating its fiduciary duty to investors by rejecting the Microsoft bid. Travis Kalanick's uncompromising, do-what-I-want leadership style was viewed as contributing to Uber's allegedly sexist workplace culture, departures of key executives, regulatory fines and poor public reputation. Groupon co-founder Andrew Mason turned down a $6 billion offer from Google in 2010. Poor sales growth, accounting restatements and unprofessional behaviour – such as wearing gorilla costumes in the office and giving a death stare when interviewed on why he didn't sell to Google – led to CNBC's Herb Greenberg naming him 'Worst CEO of the Year' in December 2012 and Groupon's value plummeting below $3 billion. He was fired on 28 February 2013, causing Groupon's value to jump by 4%; it ended the year at $7.9 billion.

The studies on investor rights are upfront that they identify correlations. Two subsequent papers make progress towards causation. Vicente Cuñat, Mireia Giné and Maria Guadalupe use the same regression discontinuity approach as Caroline Flammer's study in Chapter 4, but analyse proposals to strengthen governance rather than social performance. Implementing a proposal increases the share price by 2.8% on average. Acquisitions and investment fall, but long-term firm value rises – suggesting that the cuts are to empire-building rather than value-creating projects. Jonathan Cohn, Stu Gillan and Jay Hartzell investigated the proxy access rule, passed by the US Securities and Exchange Commission (SEC) in August 2010 (but struck down by the Court of Appeals in July 2011). This rule would have helped certain investors to propose their own directors for election. Stock prices rose after events that increased the likely strength of the rule and fell after events that reduced it. The reactions were stronger in poorly performing firms, suggesting that investor power helps discipline underperformance.

Let's now explore how investors affect wider society. Alan Ferrell, Hao Liang and Luc Renneboog studied thirty-seven countries and found that pro-investor laws were positively correlated with eleven different measures of stakeholder value, including labour relations, community involvement and environmental orientation. Alexander

Dyck, Karl Lins, Lukas Roth and Hannes Wagner analysed forty-one countries and concluded that institutional investor ownership is associated with improvements in various environmental and social measures, such as renewable energy use, employment quality, low carbon emissions and few human rights violations. The effect is larger when the institutional investors are from countries with strong social norms, such as Germany, the Netherlands and the Nordics, suggesting that they export their norms to investee companies.

But the evidence isn't all one-way. The above studies investigate what happens in general, but evidence isn't universal – limiting shareholder power may be valuable in particular instances. William Johnson, Jon Karpoff and Sangho Yi suggest that takeover defences can bond long-term stakeholder relationships when an enterprise goes public. When contract manufacturer Pemstar went public in 2000, IBM was its largest customer. IBM had teamed up with Pemstar to open a manufacturing operation in Brazil and share its manufacturing know-how. Such a relationship requires trust that Pemstar wouldn't abscond with the shared knowledge or suddenly increase prices.

After Pemstar went public, it ran the risk of being taken over. A rational new owner would understand the value of stakeholder relationships and preserve them – indeed, acquirers often pay a premium price for these relationships. But if the acquirer were irrational, it might break the relationship by charging IBM higher prices. Pemstar thus put five takeover defences in place when it went public. William, Jon and Sangho find that, if and only if an enterprise has a large customer, dependent supplier or strategic alliance, takeover defences increase its valuation when it goes public. Martijn Cremers, Lubo Litov and Simone Sepe show that, when a company adopts a staggered board, its value increases if and only if it has the above business relationships.

As we'll soon discuss, takeover defences aren't the only way to preserve long-term relationships. Still, these papers are consistent with the idea that uninformed investors may ignore the value of a company's stakeholder relationships and intervene destructively. So the optimal design of investor rights isn't one-size-fits-all, which explains the variety across firms and countries that we see. It may also vary over time for a particular firm, with defences preserving stakeholder relationships for a newly public enterprise, but leading to entrenchment when it matures. The challenge for regulators is to ensure that protections from investors, which might be justified in certain circumstances, aren't abused by underperforming leaders to entrench themselves at society's expense.

Monitoring

Engagement is a form of *stewardship*. The Merriam Dictionary definition of stewardship is 'the careful and responsible management of something entrusted to one's care'. An investor is entrusted with savers' money. Managing this money responsibly typically involves improving the long-term performance of the firms he invests in. We'll thus move from a stewardship definition that looks backwards at savers to one that looks forwards at companies, as Figure 6.4 illustrates. *Stewardship is an approach to investment that improves the value an enterprise creates for society*. It seeks to grow the pie and enhance a company's performance, rather than taking the pie as given and profiting from finding undervalued pies.

While engagement is the best-known form of stewardship, it's not the only one. Investors can also undertake stewardship by taking the time to deeply understand a company's long-term value – looking beyond its short-term profit to its intangible assets, strategy and purpose. We'll call such behaviour *monitoring*. As I'll soon explain, this analysis grows the pie even if the investor only uses it to decide whether to buy, retain or sell a company rather than influence how it's run.

Legendary investor Peter Lynch, one of Jeff Ubben's mentors, was an extremely successful monitor. He ran the Fidelity Magellan Fund between 1977 and 1990, posting an average annual return of 29% and beating the S&P 500 in eleven out of thirteen years. In his book *Beating the Street*, Peter wrote: 'behind every stock is a company, find out what it's doing . . . often, there is no correlation between the success of a company's operations and the success of its stock over a few months or even a few years. In the long term, there is a 100 percent correlation between the success of the company and the success of its stock'.

If Peter was thinking of buying a retail stock, he'd visit its stores to see first-hand how customers and colleagues were being treated. His

Figure 6.4 The Investment Chain

favourite source of investment ideas was the Burlington Mall, which featured 'more likely prospects than you could uncover in a month of investment conferences', and he'd meet with over 200 companies a year. On one visit, Peter's wife and kids dragged him to The Body Shop, a socially responsible cosmetics retailer. Peter was immediately impressed by how well it was managed, the enthusiasm of its colleagues and its large number of customers. This sparked months of further analysis that led to him purchasing a large stake.

Perhaps Peter's most famous investment was in Chrysler, and a shining example of his investment approach. In 1982, Peter decided to buy into the automotive industry – he wanted a cyclical sector as the US was recovering from a recession. There were three main players at the time. The table shows their financial statistics.

	General Motors	Ford	Chrysler
1982 US Market Share	44%	17%	9%
1981 Profit	$333 million	–$1.1 billion	–$476 million
1982 Profit	$963 million	–$658 million	–$69 million*

* Excluding one-off $239 million gain from asset sales.

Which would you choose? It seems a no-brainer – General Motors was the clear market leader, churning out profit even in the 1981 recession and tripling it as the recession ended. But GM was precisely the stock that Peter underweighted (although he still bought some shares, since he was bullish on the auto industry), while heavily overweighting the two loss-makers. Peter looked beyond the profits and to the strategy and leadership. He concluded that GM was 'arrogant, myopic, and resting on its laurels'.

While Peter purchased a large position in Ford, his top pick was Chrysler. He started buying it in spring 1982, even though the Wall Street consensus was that it would go bankrupt after its 1981 losses. In June, on what Peter later described as 'the most important day in my 21-year investment career', he visited Chrysler's headquarters and saw the new cars it was preparing to launch. One ended up becoming the first ever minivan with significant market presence. This potential convinced Peter to go all in, and by July, Chrysler represented 5% of Fidelity Magellan's assets – the maximum allowed by the SEC.

History proved Peter right. His industry bet paid off, with even GM tripling in price over the next five years. But his stock-specific bet paid off far, far more – Ford's stock price grew seventeen-fold over the same period, while Chrysler rose by almost fifty times.

How does monitoring help enterprises grow the pie? Didn't the Chrysler purchase just make money for Peter at the expense of shareholders who sold to him in 1982? In fact, monitoring is critical to Pieconomics. Without truly understanding a company's long-term value, an investor can't partner with it to grow the pie.

We've discussed the problem of short-termism several times in this book. Leaders may make errors of commission (cutting investment) or omission (not improving employee satisfaction) to increase immediate profits, because any value erosion only occurs in the long term. The heart of the problem is *information asymmetry*. Investors may value a company based on quantitative information because it's easy to gather. You can easily look up dividends, earnings and revenues on Yahoo Finance without even knowing what products the firm sells – and certainly without investing the substantial time and effort, as Peter did, in studying its customer relationships, corporate culture or product pipeline.

A non-monitoring investor may dump a stock that's suffered poor short-term earnings without asking whether these low earnings are due to long-term investment. This drives the stock price down, reducing the value of the CEO's shares and increasing her risk of being fired. Knowing that investors will assess her based on short-term profits and not long-term value, a leader will prioritise the former. A highly influential survey of 401 Chief Financial Officers, by John Graham, Cam Harvey and Shiva Rajgopal, found that 80% would cut discretionary expenditure (such as R&D and advertising) to meet an earnings benchmark. As one survey respondent pointed out, the market 'sells first and asks questions later'.

That's why monitoring is crucial. By taking the time to ask questions first – understand whether low earnings are due to mismanagement or investment – investors shield a leader from short-term pressures. Chrysler didn't worry that Wall Street doom-mongers were predicting its bankruptcy. They didn't own the stock – Peter did – and so what mattered to them was how he voted and whether he'd keep or sell his stake. They knew Peter cared about Chrysler's pipeline rather than its current losses. Similarly, when Kraft made a takeover bid for Unilever in February 2017, offering investors an 18% premium to the current value, most weren't interested. They'd deeply scrutinised Unilever's long-term strategy, including its Sustainable Living Plan to halve its environmental footprint and improve customer well-being, and realised that it wasn't yet captured in the stock price. Investors' response to Kraft was loud and clear. Mike Fox, Head of Sustainable Investments at Royal London Asset Management, said: 'For a lower quality business it would be acceptable, but for a business of Unilever's quality it is nowhere near the right price.' Kraft withdrew its bid two days later.

Patience Isn't Always a Virtue

The above discussion might suggest that the ideal investor is one who holds his shares for the long term and never sells. Such investors are known as 'patient capital' – loaded language, as patience is seen as a virtue, and so policies aim to encourage it. We've already discussed France's Loi Florange, which doubles the votes of investors who've held their shares for two years. Similarly, Toyota introduced a class of shares that gives investors 'loyalty dividends' if they hold onto them for five years. And Hillary Clinton, during her Presidential election campaign, proposed a sharply higher capital gains tax on shares sold within two years.

But patience isn't always desirable. The praise of patient investors is fundamentally flawed because it confuses the *holding period* of an investor with his *orientation*. The former is how long an investor holds shares before he sells. The latter is the basis – long-term value or short-term profits – that triggers an investor to sell.

Former Vanguard CEO Bill McNabb advocated patience, arguing: 'Our favourite holding period is forever. We're going to hold your stock when you hit your quarterly earnings target. And we'll hold it when you don't. We're going to hold your stock if we like you. And if we don't. We're going to hold your stock when everyone else is piling in. And when everyone else is running for the exits.' That makes sense for index funds, which Vanguard predominantly runs. But an active investor who holds onto his shares for the long term, regardless of how an enterprise is performing – whether it's creating value for society or exploiting it, or whether 'we like you' or 'we don't' – shouldn't be called a patient investor. He's an irresponsible investor who's failing to monitor the firm. Similarly, an investor shouldn't automatically 'hold your stock when you hit your quarterly earnings target'. It should investigate how the company hit the target, and take action if it did so by scrapping good investments.

For example, Volkswagen's 'patient' shareholders, such as the Porsche family and the State of Lower Saxony, were asleep at the wheel, doing nothing to stop it cheating emissions tests. Kodak's investors sat back and enjoyed its high profits in the 1980s and 1990s, oblivious to the fact that Kodak was failing to invest in digital photography. Indeed, its market value hit an all-time high of $31 billion in 1997, sixteen years after Sony had unveiled a prototype of the electronic camera in 1981, despite Kodak having done little to respond to the threat.* Just as one of the worst things a leader can do is coast and fail to grow the pie, one of the worst things an investor can do is coast and fail to monitor.

Most people agree that customers should walk away from a firm that's delivering low-quality products, polluting the environment or mistreating its workers. Similarly, most view divestment as a legitimate way for investors to hold companies to account, which is why the praise of patience doesn't make sense. *Generalised divestment* involves selling a company not because of its low profits, but due to the industry or country it's in, or another criterion that can be applied across all firms, such as insufficient board diversity. The predominantly US-led campaign, which peaked in the 1980s, to divest from South Africa aimed to influence its government to end apartheid. But there may be even greater need for investors to engage in *specialised divestment*, based on firm-specific factors, such as a company's contribution to society, intangible assets and strategic direction. Customers can easily assess a firm's industry or country and organise boycotts, but are less

---

* Instead, Kodak took many actions suggesting that it didn't view the threat from digital technology as serious. In 1989, when CEO Colby Chandler retired, it chose Kay Whitmore as his successor, who represented the traditional film business, rather than Phil Sampler, a strong believer in digital technology who later became President of Sun Microsystems. In 1996, it spent $500 million to launch the Advantix Preview film and camera system, which allowed users to preview their shots before printing them on regular film. While it used digital technology to do this, Kodak saw digital technology as a way of enhancing its traditional film business, rather than replacing it.

able to evaluate these more complex issues. Large investors have a comparative advantage in such evaluations, given their access to management and strong financial incentives to monitor.

Selling shares might thus not be an act of short-termism, but an act of discipline. Economists call this 'governance through exit' (while they label engagement 'governance through voice'). For exit to be effective, what matters is the information it's based on, which is what we mean by the investor's *orientation*. If he sells based on short-term earnings, this is indeed damaging, because the leader then prioritises short-term earnings. But if he sells based on long-term value, the CEO knows she'll be held to account for long-term value. Ford announced record profits in 2015, followed by its second-highest profits in 2016. Yet the stock price fell 21% over those two years due to concerns that Ford wasn't investing enough in electric cars or self-driving vehicles. The stock price decline, despite soaring profits, was a big contributor to CEO Mark Fields being fired in May 2017.

So the crucial question isn't whether investors hold for the long term, but whether they trade on long-term information. How can we ensure the latter? Through the same way as we promote engagement: investors taking large stakes. One of my papers demonstrated that large investors, also known as blockholders, have the incentive to look beyond earnings and invest the time and resources necessary to truly understand an enterprise. While stake size encourages monitoring, loyalty dividends and taxes on selling discourage it, by making it expensive for the investor to divest if he learns something negative.

Relatedly, we do want investors to be loyal. But *unconditional* loyalty – staying with a firm, regardless of whether it's creating long-run value – simply entrenches management. Much better is *conditional* loyalty: remaining with a company, despite low short-term earnings, if it's growing the pie. It's the combination of loyalty if the firm invests for the future, and exit if it doesn't, that represents good stewardship. That's also the key difference between blockholders and unconditional protections, such as dual-class shares, staggered boards and loyalty shares, which entrench a leader regardless of her performance. For example, the Loi Florange allowed Vincent Bolloré to grab control of the media company Vivendi, despite only holding a 14.5% stake, and engage in empire-building acquisitions.

The value of short-term decisions based on long-term concerns applies to engagement as well as trading. We'll use 'long-term-oriented' to describe investors who engage and trade based on long-term considerations, in contrast to 'long-term', which typically refers to investors who've held their shares for a long time. We'll instead refer to the latter as *low-turnover investors*.

Warren Buffett is a long-term-oriented investor. He buys a large stake to shield an enterprise from the short-term demands of uninformed shareholders, giving it freedom to build its brand. But he's not blindly loyal – he'll take tough decisions if a leader acts myopically. In 2000, Buffett's investment fund, Berkshire Hathaway, bought paint company Benjamin Moore, which sold almost exclusively through independent dealers. Since its founding in 1883, Moore had usually been run by a member of the Moore family. Buffett knew that Benjamin Moore's dealers were worried that he'd switch to selling through Home Depot and Lowe's – giant chains that offered higher profit potential. So he sent a video to thousands of independent dealers promising to stick with them.

Twelve years later, Benjamin Moore CEO Denis Abrams was nearing a distribution deal with Lowe's. Buffett fired him and stopped the deal, even though it would have increased short-term profits, and even though Abrams had delivered solid results in his five-year tenure and was praised by Buffett in Berkshire Hathaway's 2009 annual report. This shows how takeover defences aren't necessary to preserve long-term relationships – informed investors are often enough.

Policymakers should promote engagement by all investors, just as enterprises should encourage engagement by all employees. Excluding new hires from employee consultations would not only fail to tap a valuable source of ideas, but also deter creative minds from joining the firm to begin with. Similarly, requiring investors to wait several years before they have full voting rights will both hinder them from improving a company they already own and deter them from owning it in the first place. And monitoring and engagement aren't separate stewardship mechanisms, but complementary ones. The power of voice often depends on the threat of exit. Intransigent leaders will be more willing to listen to investors who'll sell if underperformance continues, just as companies will listen to customers' feedback if they'd otherwise walk away.

The Informational Role of Stock Prices

Investor trading, which causes stock prices to reflect long-term value rather than short-term earnings, has benefits beyond incentivising leaders to prioritise the former. When prices reflect long-term value, they're valuable *signals*, just like profits can be, as Chapter 3 discussed. High stock prices of Silicon Valley firms encourage bright undergraduates to learn computer science and go into tech rather than coal mining. Suppliers are willing to sink large investments to manufacture inputs for highly valued enterprises, as they're confident that they'll be around for decades. Boards can use forward-looking prices to guide whether to fire the CEO.

And leaders themselves may use stock prices to guide investment decisions – evidence shows that, when stock prices are high, CEOs infer that their investment opportunities are good and invest more. But when investors fail to gather and trade on long-term information, stock prices are poor signals and can lead to misguided decisions. By holding onto their shares despite Kodak not investing in digital cameras, investors kept the stock price high. This may have encouraged Kodak to continue with its film strategy, suppliers to continue manufacturing the inputs for film and employees to join or remain with the company. Had investors sold out and reduced the stock price, they may have shaken management out of their inertia.

We won't discuss this further here, because this is a vast topic in itself. Instead, I refer the interested reader to an article I wrote with Philip Bond and Itay Goldstein, entitled 'The Real Effects of Financial Markets', which surveys the extensive research on how financial market trading can improve company decisions.

The Value of Monitoring: The Evidence

Let's turn to the evidence. The criticism of short-term trading isn't new. An influential 1992 *Harvard Business Review* article by strategy guru Michael Porter heralded the Japanese ownership structure, in which investors hold long-term stakes that they rarely sell. But the 'Lost 20 Years' since then suggests that Japan isn't the model economy previously thought. Japan's mediocre performance could be for many reasons, but there's direct evidence on the benefits of liquidity – the ease with which investors can trade their shares. To identify causation, a series of studies uses the decimalisation of the major US stock exchanges.

Here's how decimalisation works. All stock markets have a 'tick size' – the minimum amount a stock price can move. Before 2000, all three US exchanges, the NYSE, AMEX and NASDAQ, had a minimum tick size of 1/16 of a dollar. If IBM's stock price is $20 and an investor sells, he might only fetch $19 15/16 ($19.9375), which makes selling costly. Between August 2000 and April 2001, the three exchanges reduced the minimum tick size to one cent. So a sale might now only lower the price to $19.99 – selling is less costly. Vivian Fang, Tom Noe and Sheri Tice showed that decimalisation improved firm value, and Sreedhar Bharath, Sudarshan Jayaraman and Venky Nagar documented that this improvement was stronger in firms with blockholders and where the CEO owns a larger stake – suggesting that governance through exit was a key driver of the gains. Vivian Fang, Emanuel Zur and I found that decimalisation also made it easier for investors to acquire large stakes in the first place.

Rather than studying liquidity, which makes trading easier, other researchers investigate actual trades. A key question is what drives them – are trades a knee-jerk reaction to public information, such as earnings, or are they based on a shareholder's own analysis? Sterling Yan and Zhe Zhang show that high-turnover investors trade on their own information and are actually better informed than low-turnover investors. While contrary to the common critique of high-turnover (or 'short-term') shareholders, these results make sense. High turnover could arise because a shareholder has many insights not captured by the market and is acting on them. Lubos Pastor, Luke Taylor and Rob Stambaugh find that mutual funds are more profitable in periods when they trade more, and numerous studies show that trades by large investors are particularly informed. Turning to the consequences of trading, David Gallagher, Peter Gardner and Peter Swan found that 'short-term "swing" trades . . . increase stock price informativeness . . . and improve market efficiency. This increase in stock price informativeness is associated with subsequent firm outperformance'.

A final strand of research investigates how companies act differently when they have blockholders. They manipulate earnings less and need to restate earnings less often, likely because leaders know that blockholders will see through earnings inflation. They also invest more in R&D and produce more patents. Blockholders deter firms from cutting R&D to meet analyst earnings forecasts, while fragmented investors encourage such behaviour.

The above results could be because blockholder stewardship allows firms to think long-term. But it might also be that long-term firms attract blockholders. Philippe Aghion, John Van Reenen and Luigi Zingales suggest that causality is in the first direction by investigating what happens when a company is added to the S&P 500 index. This causes institutions to hold more of a stock, which then leads to the firm generating more and better-quality patents.

While the studies in this chapter have their own individual findings, taken together we can draw two broad conclusions. First, while advocates of shareholder value claim that investors are unambiguously good, and opponents claim that they're unambiguously bad, you can't lump all investors together. A closet indexer who hogs the benchmark and holds onto his shares regardless of performance is a world away from an investor who deeply understands every holding and partners with management to create value. Second, while investors are often seen as the enemy of stakeholders, the evidence suggests that large, long-term-oriented investors grow the pie for the benefit of all. Rather than heralding patient investors, who may just passively hold shares, society should promote investors who take their stewardship roles seriously. By doing so, they help build the great enterprises of the future.

In a Nutshell

- Investors engage in *stewardship* – improve the value an enterprise creates for society – through either *engagement/activism* or *monitoring*.
- Common criticism of investor *engagement* is based on pie-splitting – the idea that investors enrich themselves at stakeholders' expense. Instead, large-scale evidence suggests that hedge fund activism grows the pie by ousting underperforming leaders, increasing labour productivity and improving innovation efficiency.
- Hedge funds are effective at *specialised engagement* because they own concentrated positions, have strong financial incentives and devote

substantial resources to engagement. These features can be adopted by other investors.

- Index funds are effective at *generalised engagement* since they typically have sizable voting power and can apply best practices across hundreds of stocks.
- Greater investor rights, which facilitate activism, are generally linked to higher long-term performance. Protection from investors may add value in specific situations, e.g. where stakeholder relationships are particularly important.
- Through *monitoring* – looking beyond short-term profits to understand an enterprise's potential – investors can insulate a leader from the pressure to hit earnings targets and free her to create long-term value. Monitoring involves a combination of loyalty if the firm invests for the future and exit if it pursues short-term profit or coasts.
- It's critical to distinguish the *holding period* of an investor from her *orientation*. Selling shares need not be short-termist if based on an analysis of long-term prospects. The ideal investor is *long-term-oriented*, rather than simply holding for the long term.
- The evidence suggests that greater stock liquidity, which facilitates investor trading, is associated with higher firm value and superior stewardship. Blockholders – large shareholders – are associated with higher investment and less earnings manipulation.

7 REPURCHASES
INVESTING WITH RESTRAINT, RELEASING RESOURCES TO CREATE VALUE ELSEWHERE IN SOCIETY

2014 was a disappointing year for the health insurer Humana. Without repurchases, its earnings per share (EPS) would have been $7.34, over 5% below the $7.73 earned in 2013. This was costly for not only investors, but especially CEO Bruce Broussard, who had an EPS target of $7.50 in his bonus. As we saw in Chapter 5, executives sometimes change accounting policies to try to hit bonus thresholds. And Broussard played this game. He claimed that expenses Humana had incurred to pay back debt early were one-off and should be excluded from the EPS calculation. But this was only enough to increase the EPS to $7.49, just shy of the target.

Broussard had one more trick up his sleeve – a share repurchase. Three months earlier, Humana announced that its earnings for the third quarter of 2014 had fallen 20% from the previous year. Perhaps fearing that he'd miss his EPS target, Broussard at the same time announced a plan to buy back $500 million shares. And this trick worked. By reducing the number of shares outstanding, it nudged EPS up two more cents to $7.51. This just beat the magic $7.50 number and netted Broussard a $1.68 million bonus – despite Humana's poor performance on what it was actually supposed to focus on, providing citizens with health insurance.

The Humana anecdote is most people's view of stock buybacks. If excessive CEO pay is seen as the pinnacle of pie-splitting behaviour, buybacks may well take second place. A buyback arises when an enterprise has spare cash, but rather than investing it or paying higher wages, it repurchases shares from existing investors.

CEOs have incentives to engage in buybacks even if they destroy value. Many bonus schemes include EPS as a performance metric because it's increased by many pie-growing actions, such as improving product quality to boost revenues or production efficiency to cut costs. But buybacks allow the leader to meet an EPS target artificially without actually raising firm performance, because they lower the number of shares outstanding – as we saw with Humana. As a result, until 1982, the SEC essentially prohibited buybacks by classifying them as stock price manipulation.

It seems that buybacks split the pie in favour of investors and executives, at the expense of stakeholders – like the price-gouging by Turing – and so have no place in Pieconomics. An influential 2014 *Harvard Business Review* article by William Lazonick argued that, even though profits surged as the US economy recovered from the 2007 financial crisis, ordinary citizens didn't benefit because these profits went to buybacks. S&P 500 firms spent $2.4 trillion on buybacks between 2003 and 2012; when adding in dividends, 91% of net income went to investors. According to Lazonick: 'That left very little for investments in productive capabilities or higher incomes for employees.' So buybacks might actually do worse than splitting the pie differently – they shrink it by preventing investment.

Now leaders often justify buybacks by claiming they've run out of good investment opportunities. But, surely, it's a CEO's job to come up with ideas? Not doing so seems an error of omission. If she can't think of anything better to do than buy back stock, you've probably got the wrong CEO.

For all the above reasons, politicians – surprisingly, from both sides of the political spectrum – are calling for restrictions on buybacks. In February 2019, Democratic Senators Chuck Schumer and Bernie Sanders published a plan to limit share repurchases, and a week later Republican Senator Marco Rubio announced his own proposal. In 2017, the UK government launched an inquiry into buybacks due to concerns that they 'may be crowding out the allocation of surplus capital to productive investment'. Even investors, who supposedly benefit from buybacks, seem to be feeling guilty about taking from other stakeholders. BlackRock leader Larry Fink wrote in a March 2014 open letter to company CEOs that: 'Too many companies have cut capital expenditure and even increased debt to boost dividends and increase share buybacks.'

This chapter will take a more nuanced view. We'll draw from rigorous academic research as usual, but also the 2018 inquiry into buybacks that the UK government appointed PwC and me to jointly conduct. I'm grateful for the many discussions I've had with PwC, the government officials who worked with us on the study and numerous others who also provided input. I'll acknowledge that buybacks can indeed be a pie-splitting device that fails to create or actively destroys value. And I'll argue that pie-growing enterprises should engage in far fewer buybacks than those that practise ESV. But I'll also stress that, properly executed, buybacks can grow the pie.

Of course, the critical words are 'properly executed' and 'can'. So we'll use large-scale evidence to show that, in most – but not all – cases, buybacks do create value. That still doesn't mean that policy-makers should take no action, and we'll close with suggestions for reform.

We'll explain how viewing buybacks through the lens of Pieconomics leads to a different conclusion from conventional wisdom. But we'll first see how some concerns come from a misunderstanding of how buybacks actually work and are independent of whether one has the pie-splitting or pie-growing mentality. This isn't to be an apologist for buybacks, but because we need to understand how they operate before suggesting how they can be reformed.

Buybacks: Correcting Some Misperceptions

Buybacks Are a Free Gift to Investors

Critics of buybacks view them as a free gift or windfall to investors that could otherwise have been paid to stakeholders or invested. One article on buybacks was titled 'Congress Could Give Bank Shareholders a $53 Billion Gift'; another had the headline 'Shell Kick-Starts £19bn Windfall for Patient Shareholders'. This perception may be partly shaped by terminology – buybacks are a form of 'payout'. But buybacks aren't a freebie where investors get something for nothing. Investors do get cash, but only in return for giving up their shares. This is like how an enterprise repaying debt gives cash to the bank today, in exchange for reducing the bank's future claim on the firm – and few would argue that repaying debt is a free gift to the bank.

Buybacks Are Needed for Investors to Cash Out

Other critics acknowledge that investors have to give up something (future claims) to get something (current cash). While they acknowledge that buybacks aren't a freebie, they'd claim that they're a cashing-out mechanism. A selling investor is no longer interested in the enterprise's long-term future. Perhaps the stock price has already gone up in the few months since he's bought the shares, and he demands a buyback to allow him to cash out.

This argument is also misguided since investors can sell their shares on the stock market at any time to new shareholders. They don't need the company to buy them back.*

Allocating Net Income to Buybacks Is at the Expense of Wages

The Lazonick statistic that 91% of net income is paid out to investors, which 'left very little for investments in productive capabilities or higher incomes for employees', is commonly taken at face value and widely quoted as a smoking gun. For example, when Senators Schumer and Sanders launched their anti-buyback proposal, they wrote: 'When more than 90 percent of corporate profits go to buybacks and dividends, there is reason to be concerned.'

But this statistic makes a very basic mistake. Net income is already *after* deducting wages, other expenditures on colleagues such as training or wellness programmes, and intangible investments such as R&D and advertising. Indeed, a major reason for Humana's lower 2014 profits was its investment in health-care exchanges, adding nuance to the anecdote.

---

* A more nuanced argument is that buybacks temporarily boost the stock price, allowing the investors to sell at a higher price. As we'll show, the evidence shows that buybacks increase the stock price even more in the long term than the short term. Thus, selling shareholders lose out on the long-term gain and it's continuing shareholders who benefit the most.

So the Lazonick argument makes no sense. It's like saying 'the kids can't have had much to eat because their plates are empty' – they already ate the food that was on the plates, which is why they're now empty. And as we'll soon see, wages and investments come before buybacks not only in accounting statements, but also in the priority with which leaders actually make decisions.

Buybacks Aren't an Investment

It's true that buybacks aren't a *real* investment – the money spent doesn't train staff, advertise a brand or build a factory. But an investment is anything that costs money today and delivers returns (or value to stakeholders) in the future. People invest for retirement not only by buying or renovating property, but also with *financial* investments such as a bank account or the stock market. A buyback is a financial investment. It reduces the amount of dividends an enterprise has to pay in the future,* leaving more cash for future real investment – just like paying down debt reduces its future interest payments.

When a citizen saves for his future, he'll consider both real and financial investments. If there are value-creating ways to renovate his house (a real investment), he should undertake them. After doing so, he'll then evaluate various financial investments – bank accounts, mutual funds and shares – and choose the one with the best risk–return trade-off.

The same is true for enterprises. After a leader has taken all value-adding real investments, she'll then evaluate various financial investments – bank accounts, mutual funds and even other companies' shares. The returns to those investments have nothing to do with the CEO's performance. So if she fully believes in her abilities as a CEO and her strategy for long-term value creation, the most attractive investment is her own shares.

Buying back shares is investing in your own enterprise's stock. It signals confidence in your strategy, which is why a CEO purchasing equity with her own money is typically a good sign.

---

* We'll shortly mention the survey by Brav, Graham, Harvey and Michaely (2005), which finds that companies use cash first to maintain dividends and then to invest. Thus, reducing dividends frees up cash for investment. If a company doesn't pay dividends, it needs to give a return to investors instead through capital gains.

Profits Should Go to Stakeholders, Not Investors

Another charge against buybacks is that, if the enterprise has made unexpectedly high profits, they should be given to stakeholders, not just investors. We've already explained how a buyback doesn't 'give' profits to investors. Moreover, the claim that colleagues are as entitled as investors to any profit increase is actually not correct.

Colleagues will have played a major role in the profit increase with their hard work. The same is true for suppliers who provided the inputs and customers who spent their cash. And it's also true for investors who risked their money, which they could have otherwise invested elsewhere.

Many members contribute to a company's profits, so they all should share in its success. And they do – just as investors receive returns, workers receive salaries, suppliers receive revenues, and customers receive goods and services. The difference between investors and stakeholders isn't that only the former are rewarded for their contributions. Both are rewarded, but investors' rewards are risky, while stakeholders' are generally safe.

Let's use the analogy of a house. A homeowner is thinking of selling her house, but decides first to re-roof it to increase the sale price. She hires a builder and pays him for his labour. The builder clearly contributes to the sale price of the house. By working harder, he'll improve the quality of the roof and thus the sale proceeds.

But the sale price depends on lots of factors outside his control – the state of the housing market and the homeowner ensuring the house is in good condition when potential buyers visit. Making the builder's payoff depend on the sale price subjects him to a lot of risk. So the builder normally receives a fixed price, independent of how much the house sells for, and the homeowner bears all the risk. This protects the builder from a collapse in the housing market – he still gets paid and the homeowner suffers the entire house price decline. But the flipside is that, if the housing market booms, it's the homeowner who gets the benefit.

And the same is true for enterprises. Colleagues work hard to design, manufacture and market goods. In return, they receive salaries. Importantly, these salaries aren't clawed back even if the economy takes a downturn and the goods fetch a lower price or can't be sold at all. Investors come right at the bottom of the food chain. Profits are what's left over after everyone else has been paid off first. In a downturn, workers and suppliers still get paid, so shareholders suffer lower profits – indeed, their returns are often negative. But the flipside is that they also enjoy the upside if the economy booms. This is just how the returns are divided up – stakeholders get safe claims and investors get risky claims.* Importantly, *any increased profits go to investors even without buybacks*. Even if the higher profits stayed within the firm, they're still owned by investors, just as the homeowner benefits from any house price increase, even if she doesn't immediately sell the house. So the buyback has nothing to do with how increases or decreases in profits are split.

Now giving stakeholders fixed claims isn't the only possible division. The roof could be so material to the sale price of the house that, to incentivise diligence, the homeowner lowers the builder's fixed pay and replaces it with a share of the sale price. Similarly, Chapter 5 advocated awarding colleagues shares. But while this division gives them a share of the upside, it also exposes them to risk on the downside.** They might still be willing to accept this risky division. But this division depends on whether workers are given shares, not whether enterprises buy back stock or instead reinvest spare cash within the firm.

---

* One might argue that employees still bear risk. If economic conditions are poor, the firm might go bankrupt, leading to job losses. Even in this case, employees will still be paid for their *past* contributions to the firm – the work they've already done – but investors won't get a return on the money they've already invested. Certainly, employees are better off if the firm remains afloat and their jobs are preserved because they can make *future* contributions and be paid for them. In this sense, they share in its upside, by enjoying continued employment, unlike the builder who engages in a one-time transaction.

** One might think that companies could give colleagues a share of the upside with no downside risk. A contract could pay a worker $50,000 per year plus a share in any profits above $1 billion; if profits fall below $1 billion, he still gets his $50,000. However, such a contract still bears downside risk. Let's say that half of the time profits will fall below $1 billion and so the worker gets nothing; around half of the time they'll exceed $1 billion and his profit share is $20,000. So the expected value of the profit share is $10,000 and the worker's total expected pay is $60,000. Instead of this contract, the companies could offer him a fixed salary of $60,000. Thus, the contract still bears downside risk, because if profits end up low, the worker is paid $50,000 rather than $60,000. This is similar to 'guaranteed investment plans', where a saver is guaranteed part of any increase in the stock market over a certain level, and her money back if the stock market falls. This scheme isn't risk-free, because if the stock market falls and the investor gets her money back, her return is zero, but it would have been positive had she put her money in the bank.

As we've stressed, Pieconomics isn't about a firm only fulfilling its minimum contractual obligations. Even if it's offering fixed salaries, it could choose to share the profits with colleagues through pay rises, training programmes and superior working conditions. Indeed, Pieconomics classifies such uses of cash as an 'investment', since investment includes actions that benefit stakeholders even if there's no clear link to profits. Throughout this chapter, we'll consider a company's choice between buybacks and this broad definition of investment.

That buybacks come out of profits addresses another concern. Buybacks are only possible if the firm has earned profits to begin with. So just like high CEO pay, buybacks are often a by-product of growing the pie rather than at the expense of stakeholders. Indeed, as we'll later discuss, when enterprises underperform, buybacks are one of the first things to be cut.

While this section addressed some misperceptions about buybacks, other concerns remain true. For example, it's indeed the case that the money spent on buybacks could have instead been invested (where investment includes giving workers pay rises). We now look through the lens of Pieconomics to show that, despite these valid concerns, buybacks can still be fully consistent with growing the pie.

A Pieconomics View of Buybacks

It's tempting to think that any profits left over, after stakeholders have been paid, should be reinvested. Recall Senator Warren's concern that 'stock buybacks create a sugar high for the corporations. It boosts prices in the short run, but the real way to boost the value of a corporation is to invest in the future, and they are not doing that'.

But as stressed in Chapter 3, *growing the pie does not mean growing the enterprise.* Any investment involves opportunity costs to society because it uses resources that could have been reallocated elsewhere. In their quest for growth, Daewoo and Countrywide both invested with little heed to the cost, causing substantial damage to society.

Importantly, the number of value-creating investment opportunities a company has will always be finite – no matter how hard a leader works or how many ideas she has. A homeowner wanting to increase her resale value might re-roof the house, build a conservatory and refurbish the kitchen. But after doing so, there may be no investments left that are worth the cost. So she invests her remaining cash in the stock market. An inspired film director may think of additional scenes to add to a film, or special effects to put into a particular scene – but there's a limit to how much he can do before further additions reduce value. So he uses his remaining cash to pay down debt.

The same is true for enterprises. A retail chain might build several new stores, choosing the most attractive locations first. But after a point, further shops would either be in unattractive locations or stretch management so thin that it couldn't properly run the initial additions. So the CEO uses her remaining cash to buy back shares.

Now there's a key difference between an enterprise that practises Pieconomics and one that practises enlightened shareholder value – and this difference is one reason why some critiques of buybacks are justified. Under ESV, a leader makes investments where she can, at least roughly, forecast an increase in profits. This approach might lead her to believe she only has a few good investments and so large buybacks are justifiable. But a pie-growing leader makes investments that she thinks will create value for society, even if she can't forecast an eventual increase in profits. She'll generally invest more, and buy back less, than a leader who pursues ESV. Therefore, a CEO who buys back stock, believing she has no more investment opportunities, *could* be accused of having run out of ideas. She's failed to notice that some projects would create value for society even though the link to profits isn't clear.

But even under Pieconomics, the list of value-creating investments is finite. There's only a limited number of projects that satisfy the principles of multiplication, comparative advantage and materiality. As a result, a buyback doesn't automatically mean that the CEO has run out of ideas or is narrowly maximising shareholder value. She may already be making many investments with no clear link to future returns – such as choosing to share profits with colleagues through pay rises, training programmes and superior working conditions. But she recognises that increasing pay even further may endanger the firm's future viability, particularly since it's very difficult to subsequently cut wages. A pie-growing leader can discern between projects that create value for society and those that don't, and she shows restraint and grows the pie by turning down the latter.

Yet many CEOs don't show such restraint. Recall from Chapter 3 that, even if growing the company destroys value, a leader may do so to increase her prestige and pay. Similarly, raising worker salaries may help the CEO justify higher pay for herself, if society is scrutinising pay ratios. So using cash for buybacks rather than investment may actually be against the CEO's personal interests, contrary to popular perception.

The Evidence

The above arguments for buybacks' role within Pieconomics are conceptual. *If* leaders have taken all value-creating investment opportunities, then buybacks may be optimal. But that's a big 'if'. How do we discern whether this condition is satisfied? It could be that CEOs are scrapping good investments to meet EPS targets.

Perhaps the biggest accusation against buybacks is that they lead to a temporary 'sugar high', which 'boosts prices in the short run', but destroys long-run value. That CEOs enrich themselves at the expense of society is a popular view, given the current mistrust in business. It's also a plausible one, given the evidence in Chapter 5 that executives sometimes take myopic actions to increase their own pay. But when it comes to buybacks, this claim is widely made without looking at the evidence.

So let's do so. Buybacks do increase the short-term stock price – but they increase the long-term stock return even more. A seminal paper by David Ikenberry, Josef Lakonishok and Theo Vermaelen found that firms that bought back stock beat their peers by 12.1% over the next four years. While this study was published in 1995 and analyses US firms, a 2018 investigation of 31 countries by Alberto Manconi, Urs Peyer, and Theo Vermaelen finds that this result generally holds worldwide.

One example is – surprisingly – Humana. Even though this story might seem like egregious manipulation, the reality is more nuanced. The $500 million buyback was announced on 7 November 2014 when the stock price was $130.56. It was completed on 16 March 2015 when the price was $174.31, and the average price Humana paid for its stock was only $146.21. So Broussard's confidence in his own enterprise was justified. The buyback did net Broussard a $1.68 million bonus, but continuing investors gained $96 million. The long-term gains are even higher – at the time of writing, the stock price is $290.

Broussard's bonus wasn't at the expense of continuing investors. The only losers were shareholders who cashed out because they didn't see potential in Humana.*

This example again illustrates the importance of the pie-growing mentality. In a *Financial Times* debate on 'should the US rein in share buybacks', where I was asked to take the 'No' side, the 'Yes' side argued that 'research shows the corporate insiders who *execute buybacks* often benefit personally from their use'. In evaluating such arguments, a useful rule of thumb is to substitute 'take good projects' in place of a contentious action. If 'research shows the corporate insiders who *take good projects* often benefit personally', that wouldn't be an argument to rein them in. What matters is whether the action grows or shrinks the pie, rather than whether leaders share in any pie growth. Indeed, a fair incentive scheme rewards a CEO for good actions and punishes her for bad ones.

Other research investigates the link between buybacks and investment. Gustavo Grullon and Roni Michaely show that enterprises repurchase more when growth opportunities are poor, and Amy Dittmar finds that they do so when they have excess capital. Now that's only a correlation. To get closer to causation, we need to get inside firms and see how they actually make repurchase decisions – do buybacks have higher or lower priority than investment?

An influential study by Alon Brav, John Graham, Cam Harvey and Roni Michaely does just this, surveying 384 US Chief Financial Officers (CFOs) on how they make buyback (and dividend) decisions. There's an obvious concern here – might the executives lie? Perhaps, but the CFOs admitted that they might cut investment to avoid cutting the dividend, attenuating concerns that they won't truthfully acknowledge short-termist behaviour. Strikingly, they reported no such pressure for buybacks. They only buy back stock if they have cash left over after taking all desirable investments. *It's low investment opportunities that lead to buybacks, rather than buybacks leading to low investment.* PwC

---

* Note that this doesn't mean that Humana was justified in giving Broussard a bonus with a $7.50 EPS target. If he had received long-term stock instead of the bonus, he'd also have benefited from the buyback. The correct amount of the buyback depended on the investment opportunity from the undervaluation of Humana's stock versus the investment opportunities from real projects. When deciding how many shares to buy back, a leader should trade off these two investment opportunities, rather than buying back just enough to meet an EPS target.

and I conducted a similar survey of seventy-four executives for the UK government study, which reached the same conclusions. Only a single respondent claimed that buybacks prevented the company from making all the investments it wanted to.

Now this evidence doesn't prove that firms are undertaking exactly the right level of buybacks. Perhaps executives are defining 'desirable' investments as ones that have a clear link to investor returns, and thus are investing too little. Even if true, the cause of underinvestment isn't buybacks – it's CEOs practising ESV rather than Pieconomics. If buybacks were prohibited, ESV managers would invest the same amount, and save the leftover cash within the firm or pay down debt – the fact that they chose a buyback means they think there are no good investment opportunities left.* So buybacks are a symptom of a deeper problem rather than the problem itself. The solution isn't to tackle the symptom – take any special action against buybacks – but the problem, which is enterprises failing to adopt the pie-growing mentality. That's what the earlier chapters in Part II, plus Part III, aim to do.

The Bigger Picture

The social opportunity costs of an investment are central to Pieconomics, since our lens is society rather than just the enterprise making the investment. If a firm doesn't use real resources such as labour and raw materials, other firms can use them to create value. And the same is true for financial resources. Even though a buyback involves money leaving the firm, that money doesn't leave the economy – it gets invested elsewhere. The main difference is that it's shareholders, not the firm's CEO, who decides where to invest the money, and they have a much wider range of investment opportunities to choose from, since they can invest outside the firm. Indeed, citizens who save for their retirement using a bank account or mutual funds aren't lambasted for not creating jobs by instead renovating their house. The money they save doesn't disappear – the bank or mutual fund invests it.

---

* Even if a government passed an absurd law forcing all enterprises to reinvest all of their profits, the leader would still choose investments by their profit rather than value-creation potential.

Investors are very unlikely to sell shares in a buyback to sit on cash, so they'll only sell if they have better investment opportunities elsewhere. Start-ups are financed by venture capitalists, who get much of their money from institutional investors that also own shares in public companies. It's mature firms showing restraint and buying back stock (or paying dividends) which allows these investors to put money into venture capital, financing the enterprises of tomorrow. By first generating profits as a by-product of creating value for society, then investing in all pie-growing projects and finally paying out the remaining cash to investors, an enterprise starts a virtuous circle that allows others to then create value. In contrast, when leaders hoard cash, thinking that it's theirs rather than investors', they prevent such redeployment. Such hoarding has contributed to Japan's low return on equity mentioned in Chapter 6. Capital is a scarce resource, and a capital allocation system that can deploy capital to its most effective use is a national competitive advantage.

The funds paid out in buybacks aren't recycled in only small private enterprises, but also medium-sized public ones. Huaizhi Chen follows the money and shows that, when a company pays out dividends or engages in a buyback, the cash is reallocated to other stocks held by its investors. This reallocation increases the prices of those stocks and makes them more likely to issue equity in the future. Jesse Fried and Charles Wang find that, even though US S&P 500 firms buy back more stock than they issue, non-S&P 500 firms (which are smaller and typically have better investment opportunities) do the opposite.

This observation addresses a concern beyond buybacks – that the financial industry creates little value for society. This industry is enormous and worth $1.45 trillion in the US in 2017. It pays some of the highest salaries, earns substantial profits and benefits from government bailouts, yet doesn't produce any goods. Finance apologists argue that they provide funding to allow other enterprises to do so. But in the US and (more recently) the UK, the amount raised on stock markets roughly equals the amount spent on buybacks. So the stock market isn't actually a net supplier of financing.

But looking at *net* financing flows is incorrect. The stock market's role is to allocate scarce funds to companies where they'll benefit society the most. This involves firms with poorer opportunities paying out their excess cash, allowing those with better opportunities to invest more. Zero net financing is consistent with some firms raising a lot of funds and others returning them, just as a zero net trade balance doesn't suggest that a country is failing to trade; some firms could be importing a lot and others exporting. Indeed, at a country level, Joseph Gruber and Steven Kamin find no evidence that economies with high repurchases (or dividend payments) invest less.

Buybacks vs Dividends

If an enterprise has taken all its pie-growing investments, buybacks aren't the only remaining option. It could hold onto the surplus cash as a buffer, to protect against adverse events, and to allow it to make future investments nimbly, without the time or cost of raising new funds. But cash balances have grown by 50% over 2007 to 2016, so firms likely already have a big enough buffer. This also contradicts the concern that buybacks have starved firms of cash for investment. As Warren Buffett wrote in Berkshire Hathaway's 2016 shareholder letter: 'Some people have come close to calling [buybacks] un-American – characterizing them as corporate misdeeds that divert funds needed for productive endeavours. That simply isn't the case: Both American corporations and private investors are today awash in funds looking to be sensibly deployed. I'm not aware of *any* enticing project that in recent years has died for lack of capital. (Call us if you have a candidate.)' (emphasis in the original).

Hoarding cash within the firm prevents investors from using it to finance start-up companies. Moreover, cash burning a hole in the leader's pocket may make her trigger happy and more willing to empire-build, just as having your phone on the table makes you more likely to check it. Throughout much of the 2010s, Yahoo was valued at below the sum of its parts, partially due to concerns that it would fritter away its cash on bad acquisitions. Amy Dittmar and Jan Mahrt-Smith found that, in poorly governed firms, $1 of cash is valued at only $0.42 to $0.88. This highlights the value that can be unlocked simply by paying out cash rather than wasting or even retaining it.

A third option is to pay out the funds as dividends to investors – in nearly all countries, dividend pay-outs substantially exceed buybacks. Like repurchases, and unlike hoarding cash, dividends allow the funds to be invested elsewhere. But repurchases have several advantages over dividends. First, they're more flexible. Once you've paid out a dividend, you're committed to maintaining it in the future – potentially restricting investment down the line. Wei Li and Erik Lie show that reversing course and cutting the dividend reduces the stock price by an average of 4%, which explains why the CFOs surveyed by Alon Brav and co-authors were so reluctant to do so. In contrast, an enterprise can chop and change its repurchase policy depending on its investment requirements and available cash. It can repurchase one year, yet cut repurchases to zero the next, if profits drop and it needs every dollar for investment. Indeed, Murali Jagannathan, Clifford Stephens and Mike Weisbach find that repurchases *are* cut when profits fall.

Second, repurchases are targeted. In a buyback, investors choose whether to sell. Those that do will be the ones with the best alternative investment opportunities or who value the stock the least. So buybacks get rid of investors with least buy-in to the company's long-term strategy and ensure the remaining investors are ones who believe in it. In contrast, dividends are paid to all investors, even those without good other uses for the cash and who may allow it to sit idle.

Third, repurchases – but not dividends – lead to more concentrated ownership. Both the CEO and continuing investors now have a greater share of the firm, increasing their incentives to create value (see Chapters 5 and 6). Indeed, in the 1980s, Warren Buffett used buybacks at GEICO to concentrate ownership in his own hands.

Finally, as discussed earlier, repurchases are a good investment if your stock is under-priced. Chapters 4 and 6 explained how the stock market may focus excessively on short-term earnings and fail to fully appreciate a company's long-term value. A solution is for a CEO to put her money where her mouth is and buy her own enterprise's stock. Not only is buying shares profitable if they're currently undervalued, but it also signals the undervaluation to the market and helps correct it. The possibility of using buybacks to correct undervaluation means that leaders don't have to worry about it as much – freeing them to pursue investments whose pay-offs arise in the long term.

How Buybacks Can Destroy Value – and How to Fix It

Even if the evidence suggests that most buybacks grow the pie, they may not do so in every single case. And the analogy between a leader and a homeowner isn't perfect. The homeowner owns the entire equity in the house and so has full incentives to increase value. But leaders often own only a fraction of their firm. They're partially paid with bonuses, which may have EPS targets that can be met using a buyback. So buybacks might be conducted to hit short-term targets rather than to create long-term value.

Does this actually happen? Let's look at the evidence. Recall from Chapter 5 the study by Ben Bennett and co-authors, which compared leaders who just hit bonus thresholds with those who just missed. The former do significantly less R&D than the latter, so CFOs are certainly willing to take certain actions to hit thresholds. But buybacks aren't one of them – the same study found no difference in buyback behaviour between the two groups. It seems that Humana was an exception. Similarly, in the government study with PwC, we found that not a single UK FTSE 350 firm undertook a repurchase to hit an EPS target between 2009 and 2016.

Chapter 5 also noted that short-term pay incentives stem not only from bonuses, but also from vesting equity, which Vivian Fang, Katharina Lewellen and I showed is linked to investment cuts. In a subsequent paper, Vivian, Allen Huang and I discovered that vesting equity increases the likelihood of stock buybacks and reduces the long-term returns to these buybacks. While buybacks in general are associated with higher long-term stock returns, those induced by vesting equity aren't. Yet even these buybacks aren't the problem itself, but a symptom of the underlying problem – short-term equity – which causes other short-term behaviours like investment cuts.

So the solution isn't to restrict buybacks. This would do nothing to deter investment cuts and may actually increase them, if CEOs switch from buybacks to investment cuts as a way to boost the stock price. Instead, we should address the underlying problem by lengthening the horizon of equity, or boards scrutinising firm decisions more closely when equity is vesting.

The study with Vivian and Allen uncovered a more serious practice. CEOs typically sell their vesting equity shortly after the buyback, taking advantage of the short-term price increase that it causes. This finding was independently corroborated by SEC Commissioner Robert Jackson. For example, Angelo Mozilo used Countrywide's money to buy back $2.4 billion of shares between November 2006 and August 2007 – yet sold $140 million of his own shares over the same period. I argued earlier that buybacks signal the CEO's confidence in her own firm. But if she's selling her own shares at the same time as buying shares with the company's money, this is duplicitous. If the CEO really were positive about her firm's prospects, she'd hold onto her equity when it vests rather than selling it. A potential remedy would be to prohibit executives from selling their own shares within a given window (e.g. six months) after undertaking a buyback.

Short-term incentives can stem not only from the CEO's contract, but also from the desire to meet analyst earnings forecasts. Heitor Almeida, Slava Fos and Mathias Kronlund compared firms that would have just met the EPS forecast without a buyback (and thus have no incentive to undertake one) with firms that would have just missed (and so have strong buyback incentives). The latter repurchase more shares, and over the next year they cut investment by an average of 10%, and reduce headcount by 5%. As discussed in Chapter 5, these cuts could be either efficient (the EPS forecast encourages the leader to scrap unprofitable projects) or myopic, and the tests don't distinguish between these cases. But the results are certainly consistent with the idea that EPS-induced buybacks can destroy long-term value.

Even if true, buybacks are again a symptom of an underlying problem, the desire to meet analyst EPS forecasts. Recall that Sanjeev Bhojraj and co-authors found that this desire causes managers to cut R&D and advertising. Buybacks may simply be a by-product, undertaken out of the cash left over. As I'll stress in Chapters 8 and 10, the solution is to address the root cause of the behaviour – companies' desire to meet EPS forecasts – by them ceasing to report quarterly earnings.

We've discussed how value-destroying buybacks should be addressed by general solutions to underinvestment. One final general solution may also be effective here: giving colleagues equity in the firm. This allows them to share in any value increase created not only by their hard work and ideas (as stressed in Chapter 5), but also by buybacks – and means that buybacks don't just benefit investors, but employees too. Buying out other investors, who don't value the firm and don't care about its long-run prospects, increases the stake of colleagues who do.

In a Nutshell

- Share buybacks are often viewed as splitting the pie in favour of leaders and investors. This can indeed be the case, but many common criticisms are based on misperceptions. Buybacks aren't a free gift to investors, nor do investors require them to cash out.

- Pie-growing enterprises should take projects that are likely to create value for society, even if they don't clearly increase long-run profits. They should invest more, and buy back less, than firms that pursue enlightened shareholder value.

- Pie-growing enterprises shouldn't invest all spare cash. They should only take investments that satisfy the principles of multiplication, comparative advantage and materiality. Once they have done so, buybacks are a legitimate alternative use, particularly if the stock is undervalued.

- The evidence is consistent with a pie-growing use of buybacks. While a buyback increases the short-term stock price, it increases the long-term stock price even more. Enterprises buy back more stock when their investment opportunities are low and they have surplus cash. They make investment decisions before repurchase decisions, so buybacks are the result of low investment, not the cause.

- Buybacks are a better way of returning surplus cash than dividends because they're flexible, targeted to the investors who have least buy-in to the firm's long-term strategy, and concentrate the stakes of continuing investors (including leaders). They also create value for the company if its stock is undervalued.

- There's evidence that buybacks may destroy value when driven by vesting equity or analyst forecasts, but they're not used to hit EPS targets in bonus plans.
  - Even where buybacks destroy value, they're symptoms of an underlying problem – short-term pressures – which lead to other symptoms such as investment cuts. Solutions should be targeted at the underlying problem.

PART III

HOW TO GROW THE PIE? PUTTING IT INTO PRACTICE

This Part discusses how to put the ideas in Parts I and II into practice. The concept of creating value for society might seem a nice ideal, but unrealistic. When the rubber hits the road on Monday morning and you've got short-term targets to hit, growing the pie may seem impossible. We now explore how it can be made real.

There are separate chapters for enterprises (Chapter 8), investors (Chapter 9) and citizens in their role as customers, influencers and voters who influence regulation (Chapter 10). Part III will loosely mirror the evidence in Part II. Chapter 5 discussed incentives, which are implemented by enterprises; Chapter 6 tackled stewardship, which is undertaken by investors; and Chapter 7 addressed buybacks, which government policy can facilitate or constrain. Knowing what we know from Part II, we'll see how enterprises, investors and citizens can grow the pie.

But the lines are blurred. Incentives may be implemented by boards, but are voted on by investors and legislated by governments. Stewardship depends on the willingness to engage of not only investors, but also enterprises, and may also be regulated. Policies may be imposed by legislators, but also voluntarily adopted by shareholders or companies themselves.

In addition, there won't be full congruence with Part II, since it focused on pie-growing practices that most people believe to be pie-splitting. There are many factors that are widely accepted to be pie-growing, such as an enterprise having a purpose (few citizens advocate that companies should be purposeless). Here, the main challenge isn't so much proving that these factors are beneficial, but putting them into practice – so they appear only in Part III.

Part III also broadens out the ideas of Part II. Chapter 5 gave evidence on the value of long-term CEO incentives; Chapter 8 will discuss how to embed long-term thinking in companies more generally. Chapter 6 illustrated the value of stewardship by asset managers; Chapter 9 (and the Appendix) will discuss how stewardship is a responsibility of the whole investment chain, which includes asset owners, equity analysts, proxy advisors and investment consultants. Chapter 7 highlighted how any value-destroying repurchases are typically a symptom of an underlying problem; Chapter 10 will highlight the wider market failures that regulation can address.

8 ENTERPRISES
THE POWER OF PURPOSE AND HOW TO MAKE IT REAL

Excellence

The Great Rift Valley stretches for 6,000 kilometres across two continents, from Lebanon in Asia to Mozambique in Africa. It's bordered by some of Africa's highest mountains, yet houses some of the world's deepest lakes. In Kenya, the lakes are shallower and have no outlet to the sea. So in the dry season when the water evaporates, they're particularly rich in minerals. In Lake Magadi, the southernmost lake in the Kenyan stretch of the Great Rift Valley, the salt can be up to forty metres thick.

Millions have seen Lake Magadi in the film *The Constant Gardener*, based on John Le Carré's book of the same name. But fewer than a thousand people call Magadi, the township lying on the lake's east shore, their home. One of these people is Emmanuel Sironga, who makes a living for himself and his family trading goats.

For Emmanuel – like millions of Africans – cash used to be king. It's cash that Emmanuel needed to buy goats and equipment. It's cash that Emmanuel received from selling goats, which he'd first check for forgery and then store at risk of robbery. When he'd amassed enough, he'd take it to the bank. But the nearest bank was hours away, so a round trip deprived him of nearly a day of trade, and Emmanuel was restricted in where he could graze his goats because he couldn't be too far from a bank. And if he wanted to send money to his relatives, it's cash that he'd put in an envelope, before hiring someone to travel on a country bus to deliver it. Sometimes the cash might not get there because the bus broke down; other times the courier might run off with it.

But all that changed with M-Pesa, a mobile money service that allows citizens to deposit, withdraw and send money using their phone. Emmanuel no longer suffers the risk and inconvenience of using cash. He buys goods and takes payments on his phone, and M-Pesa's electronic records help with his accounting. He can send money to anyone, regardless of where he is or where they are, which frees him to focus on his vocation – tending his flock. In Emmanuel's words: 'As pastoralists, we have to travel long distances in search of greener pasture. M-Pesa has made our lives easier because we do not have to travel long distances to give our relatives and friends money.'

How was this life-changing technology created? A seed was sown when researchers funded by the Department for International Development (DFID), the UK government's foreign aid arm, noticed that Kenyans were transferring mobile minutes to each other as an easier option than sending cash. While it was a government that sparked the initial idea, it took a pie-growing enterprise to transform this idea into reality. DFID introduced the researchers to Vodafone, the UK's largest telecoms company, which had been investigating how to use its mobile platform to improve Kenyans' access to finance since banking was limited. The ensuing conversations gave Nick Hughes, Vodafone's Head of Global Payments, the idea to use phones to transfer not mobile minutes, but cash. A vision was born and was named M-Pesa – M for mobile and Pesa being the Swahili word for money.

Vodafone was committed to making M-Pesa a success. It invested colleagues' time and £1 million of funding to overcome the substantial obstacles in their way before M-Pesa could go live. Nowadays, apps that transfer money through smartphones are plentiful, but M-Pesa needed to run on the basic mobile phones that Kenyans had back then (and many still do). Vodafone had to establish a nationwide network of retail outlets and train a team of agents to allow customers, anywhere in the country, to open accounts, make deposits and cash out. The freedom provided by mobile money also makes money laundering easier, so Vodafone designed processes to combat illegal use.

In 2007, Vodafone launched M-Pesa in Kenya – and since then, M-Pesa has transformed citizens' lives. Entrepreneurs like Emmanuel can buy and sell goods, parents can pay their children's school fees, grown children can fund their parents' health care and all can save for their future. Tavneet Suri and William Jack found that access to M-Pesa lifted 196,000 Kenyan households (2% of the population) out of poverty by 2014. The effect is stronger among households headed by women, largely due to the career shifts that M-Pesa allows – 186,000 women switched out of agriculture and into business and retail. M-Pesa has since been rolled out to several other countries, including Tanzania, Afghanistan, South Africa, India, Romania and Albania.

The success of M-Pesa highlights the main way in which enterprises can grow the pie – *excellence*. Companies can create even more value by having an uncompromising commitment to excellence in their core business than by pursuing ancillary activities with an explicitly social mission. The biggest way that Vodafone serves society isn't through reducing its carbon footprint, even though doing so is still important, but by being excellent in delivering its existing mobile services and constantly innovating new ones.

Recognising the importance of excellence is critical for many reasons. First, it stresses that 'serving' society goes far beyond making financial sacrifices, such as Merck giving ivermectin away for free or Apple building the gym without a calculation. Such actions are indeed valuable, and we've stressed them throughout this book. But, often, *excellence is the best form of service*. Most activities that an enterprise undertakes aren't ones of explicit service, but they're no less valuable. While many companies undertake significant philanthropic efforts, their most important contributions to society are often through excellence in their core activities.

For example, an R&D department may be driven by the excitement of making a scientific breakthrough rather than serving a known customer demand. Many innovations happen by accident and fill a need that never previously existed, and never previously asked to be served. When 3M scientist Spencer Silver tried to create a strong adhesive for plane manufacturing, he accidentally made a weak one, and called it a 'solution without a problem'. Colleague Art Fry realised that it could be used to prevent him losing his bookmark in his church hymn book, and the adhesive was developed into Post-It Notes. More generally, while many companies are good at problem-solving (noticing a market demand and figuring out how best to satisfy it), the most radical innovation typically involves problem-finding (creating a new market that didn't previously exist, such as a use for the weak adhesive) – an example of excellence rather than service. Even though successful problem-finding leads to profits, this doesn't detract from the value it creates.

This observation highlights the difference between Pieconomics and CSR which we introduced in Chapter 1. Pieconomics is about creating value for society through your core business. CSR is sometimes about a non-core CSR department undertaking activities to compensate for a pie-splitting core business. As Matt Peacock, Vodafone's former Group Director of Corporate Affairs, told my class, CSR is like a company cutting down an ancient forest to farm the land, and justifying it by using some of the logs to build a youth club in the nearby village.

Second, not every company has as clear an effect on society as Merck or Turing – but that doesn't mean that it's any less important. Instead of moving into pharmaceuticals, it should focus on fulfilling its role in the world in an excellent manner. Many Westerners consider a mobile phone as a commodity, but as Matt pointed out, 'if you're in a developing country and put a mobile phone into someone's hands, you change their life'. So a telecoms company can create tremendous social value through excellence in its core activity, as Vodafone did with M-Pesa. Commuting may seem just part of the daily grind, but a great transport company can connect citizens to jobs, allow families to live closer to communities rather than the office and enable new enterprises to start. A children's toy company might not seem obviously socially responsible. But high-quality toys can make a big difference to children's happiness (and their parents' peace), and educate as well as entertain them. Of course, there's a small handful of core activities that don't create social value, such as producing tobacco, but the set that does is much larger than commonly thought.

The importance of excellence in growing the pie is even more relevant for colleagues, because many jobs may not have an explicit social function – but these jobs are no less important to the company or to society. Keeping accurate financial budgets or meeting minutes allows others to take decisions in an informed manner; efficient procurement of goods or management of working capital enable a firm's resources to go further. A company often does value employees whose jobs are directly linked to its vision – and indeed Roy Vagelos was inspired by hearing the lunchtime conversations of Merck's scientists, not payroll clerks. But it's critical to acknowledge the extraordinary value that seemingly ordinary jobs can contribute simply by being performed with excellence, and recognise how every colleague is key to the business. Recall from Chapter 5 that shares for rank-and-file employees improve performance only if awarded throughout the organisation, rather than targeted at specific groups (e.g. the R&D department). Similarly, a company needs to ensure that its mission connects with everyday tasks and activities. Otherwise, even a visionary statement will fail to inspire a payroll or procurement worker.

While it might seem obvious that an enterprise should strive to be excellent, this goal is sometimes underweighted by firms who (correctly) recognise their need to serve society and (incorrectly) think this means they should focus on explicit 'serving' activities. In contrast, one of the biggest ways in which a company can destroy value is to tolerate mediocrity over excellence – an error of omission. If Vodafone hadn't strived for excellence and pushed itself to explore what initially seemed to be a crazy idea – banking without a bank – there would have been no media backlash, but 196,000 Kenyan households would have been worse off. Sometimes, the pursuit of excellence may involve tough decisions, such as letting go of an underperforming colleague. A leader may use social objectives, such as wishing not to hurt a particular stakeholder, to justify the failure to take tough decisions. But the damage done to society from accepting mediocrity can be far greater.

Purpose

Pursuing excellence is a useful principle, but is insufficient by itself. Companies undertake many activities, and it's impossible to be excellent in every one of them. A company's resources are limited, so it must choose which activities to be particularly excellent in; many decisions involve trade-offs, so it must choose which stakeholders to particularly serve. Relatedly, the central idea of this book – that companies should grow the pie – sounds aspirational, but also somewhat ambiguous. A pharmaceuticals firm grows the pie in very different ways from a transport firm. What does 'growing the pie' entail for a particular company's unique circumstances?

It means fulfilling its purpose. The impact of this simple yet powerful principle is clear from my work with The Purposeful

Company, a UK consortium that aims to inject purpose into the heart of business. This chapter will draw from lessons learned while serving on its five-person Steering Group, and the insights of various executives, investors, consultants, stakeholder representatives and policymakers who are part of our broader Task Force.

What is purpose? *Purpose is why an enterprise exists – who it serves, its reason for being and the role it plays in the world.* It's the answer to the question 'How is the world a better place by your company being here?' Purpose is the particular way in which an enterprise serves society and thus grows the pie. A purpose might be to develop medicines that transform citizens' health; to provide an efficient rail network that connects people with their jobs, family and friends; or to manufacture toys that entertain and educate children. Since profit is often a by-product of growing the pie, it's also a by-product of an enterprise fulfilling its purpose. As economist John Kay wrote: 'profit is no more the purpose of business than breathing is the purpose of living' . . . 'we must breathe to live but breathing is not the purpose of life'. BlackRock CEO Larry Fink stressed that 'purpose is not the sole pursuit of profits but the animating force for achieving them'.

Purpose is powerful because it glues different stakeholders together in a common mission. But some claim it's not the only way to achieve this glue. Economist Ronald Coase, whose Coase theorem we introduced in Chapter 2, viewed a firm as a nexus of contracts, where each member responds rationally to incentives provided by those contracts. For example, a salesperson works hard to close deals because he's paid on commission. But the view that stakeholders can be united purely through contracts is too simplistic. You can't quantify many ways in which a salesperson creates value, such as mentoring subordinates or helping colleagues, and so you can't enforce them with a contract. And even if enforcement were possible, leaders don't have all the relevant knowledge to tell the salesperson what to do in every situation – it may be better to let him decide. If a group of bikers tries to ride in lock-step, looking at the leader to ensure they follow her, they'll crash. If they look up and aim for the same destination, and are free to choose their speed and route, they'll get there safely.

But, most importantly, building an enterprise around contracts ignores the human side of business. A web of transactions is an empty shell, where members act out of compliance rather than commitment. In contrast, a shared purpose creates a sense of belonging, where members choose to be part of the company because they're inspired by its mission – even though they could obtain products, salaries and returns elsewhere. Purpose is what inspires an entrepreneur to launch a start-up, taking on substantial personal risk. It's what motivates colleagues to go above and beyond what's seen by their superiors, customers to choose the enterprise over cheaper rivals, investors to stay with it even when profits are low and suppliers to undertake multi-year commitments to resource it. They become stake-holders quite literally, holding stakes – although personal rather than financial ones – in the enterprise's success, and so contribute far more than any contract could enforce. By replacing contracts with trust, a company gives stakeholders discretion to take whatever action they believe best furthers its purpose.

As mentioned at the end of Chapter 1, purpose is a particularly important glue for millennials. The PwC/AIESEC study we mentioned back then concluded that 'millennials want to be proud of their employer, to feel that their company's values match their own, and that the work they do is worthwhile'. In a Deloitte survey, only 27% of millennials responded that they intended to stay with their current employer for five years, but 88% said that they would do so if they 'were satisfied with the company's sense of purpose'. The stakes are high – Gallup estimated that millennial turnover due to lack of engagement costs the US economy over $30 billion per year.

To see the value of purpose, let's return to Merck. We discussed how Roy Vagelos gave ivermectin away for free because he saw Merck's purpose as using science to transform livelihoods. But Merck wasn't just lucky in having an unusually purposeful CEO at the right time. This purpose had been instilled in Merck from the outset, ever since George Merck emigrated from Germany to the US in 1891 to establish Merck's US subsidiary.

The ivermectin story was far from unique, but simply the way Merck conducted business. Numerous other stories abound in Merck's history. In 1942, penicillin was still a new drug. It hadn't been made outside the lab before because it was too expensive. But George Merck, still serving as Merck's President, took a punt and Merck became the first company ever to manufacture penicillin on a large scale.

Ann Miller was a 33-year-old woman who lived in New Haven, Connecticut. She was married to Ogden Miller, the Athletics Director of Yale University. On 14 March 1942, Ann lay dying in a hospital bed, stricken with streptococcal septicaemia, which she contracted after suffering a miscarriage. Her fever had hit 104 to 106 Fahrenheit for eleven straight days, and everything the doctors had tried had failed.

Until penicillin. Thanks to Merck, Ann became the first American ever to be treated with penicillin and it saved her life. The very next day, her temperature was back down to normal. She went on to have three sons and lived until 90 years old.

Having discovered how to make a life-saving drug, Merck didn't use this discovery to make monopoly profits. Instead, it shared the secrets of how to manufacture penicillin with its rivals, so that they could produce it also. Together, as a team effort, these competitors treated 100,000 Allied soldiers in the Second World War. As George Merck said, 'We try never to forget that medicine is for the people. It is not for the profits. The profits follow, and if we have remembered that, they have never failed to appear.' Indeed, Merck's number one core value was that: 'Our business is preserving and improving human life.'

It was this commitment to using scientific breakthroughs to serve the people, rather than to generate profit, that attracted Roy to Merck. After receiving his medical degree from Columbia in 1954, Roy held various scientific research roles at the National Institute of Health, the Massachusetts General Hospital and the Washington University School of Medicine. There, he did research not to develop commercial products, but to advance the boundaries of science and generate insights that could be shared with the public. He published over 100 papers; his work would later see him elected to the American Academy of Arts and Sciences and the National Academy of Sciences. So if Roy were to move into the private sector, he'd only join an enterprise that was equally committed to using science to benefit society.

That enterprise was Merck. Inspired by the employees he met at his family's diner, and Merck's past record of growing the pie, he joined as Senior Vice President of Research in 1975, three years before William Campbell's discovery. The rest is history. And vital to that history is that William's vision to explore the use of ivermectin for humans and Roy's decision to give it away for free weren't an anomaly. They were the fruit of Merck's purpose which had been embedded throughout the organisation since the days of George Merck.

Defining Purpose

Purpose is far more than a statement. As we'll discuss in the next section, an enterprise must *live* purpose. But a statement of purpose is a necessary starting point, just like a hiker must decide which mountain to climb before figuring out the best path. So we'll first explore how a company can define its purpose.

A purpose should contain two related dimensions – *who* it exists for and *why* it exists.* The *why* explains the company's reason for being. Using earlier examples, this may be to develop medicines, connect citizens through transport or to entertain children. The *why* has rightly been receiving increased attention, for example in Simon Sinek's book *Start with Why*.

The *who* tends to receive less focus. The *who* highlights which members an enterprise particularly endeavours to serve. It's linked to the *why*, since a firm exists to serve these members. But the *who* is of independent value since many decisions involve trade-offs. An action may increase some slices of the pie and decrease others. The *who* helps weight these different slices and thus figure out whether the action grows or shrinks the pie overall. Effectively, the *who* asks which members are first among equals to navigate these difficult dilemmas – even though it doesn't mean completely ignoring others, nor prioritising these members in every decision.

Most statements of purpose focus on customers. Merck's current vision is: 'To make a difference in the lives of people globally through our innovative medicines, vaccines, and animal health products.' Network Rail 'connects people – with friends and family, and with jobs, underpinning a thriving economy.' The toy company Mattel's purpose is 'to inspire the wonder of childhood as the global leader in learning and development through play.' A statement of the *why* thus already sheds light on the *who* – sick people and animals, commuters and travellers, and children.**

---

 * Some enterprises may have a different definition of purpose, and instead have a 'mission' or 'vision' statement that corresponds more closely to our definition. When giving examples of company purposes, we use the statement that most closely fits our definition, even though some companies may use different terminology.
 ** Which comes first will vary across firms. Some will first decide why they exist, and who they serve naturally flows from this reason for being; others will decide first who they wish to serve, and then the way they can best serve them. Importantly, these

But customers aren't the only important stakeholder, so a purpose statement should go beyond customers. Agricultural firm Olam 'endeavours to generate economic prosperity, contribute positively to social well-being and manage our stewardship of the environment by providing sustainable agricultural products and food ingredients', which emphasises its responsibility to the environment. Southwest Airlines' purpose highlights colleagues, aiming 'to provide our Employees a stable work environment with equal opportunity for learning and personal growth. Creativity and innovation are encouraged for improving the effectiveness of Southwest Airlines. Above all, Employees will be provided the same concern, respect, and caring attitude within the organization that they are expected to share externally with every Southwest Customer'.

How does a company decide on the why and the who, and thus define its purpose? Three points can offer guidance. First, *a purpose is only meaningful if the converse would also be reasonable.* Many companies have broad purpose statements, thinking it's more aspirational to serve as many stakeholders as possible. But while a purpose 'to serve customers, colleagues, suppliers, the environment, and communities while generating returns to investors' might sound inspiring, it's meaningless, as no enterprise's purpose would be to exclude all of those members. Since the converse – serving nobody – is unreasonable to begin with, a purpose statement that rules this out doesn't tell you anything. In contrast, Southwest Airlines' purpose that emphasises employees is meaningful, because it would also be reasonable for it to highlight the environment or suppliers.* Moving to the why, Costco's purpose of providing 'quality goods and services at the lowest possible prices' is meaningful as it highlights that price is of primary importance, while keeping quality above a threshold. It would also be reasonable for a retailer's purpose to be to provide 'the highest quality goods and services at affordable prices'.

A purpose statement should therefore be focused and selective. This seems uncomfortable, because highlighting certain members or

---

statements don't contain the *how* – the specific goods and services that the company will offer, because these will change over time as customer preferences and tastes evolve.

* Note that the 'converse' need not mean literally the opposite (e.g. 'to provide our employees with an unstable work environment') but other stakeholders that an enterprise might instead prioritise.

activities suggests deprioritising others. But the trade-offs enterprises face are uncomfortable. A broad purpose statement ignores the reality of trade-offs, but an uncomfortable statement provides guidance in three important dilemmas. The first is whether to take actions that help some stakeholders and hurt others. Engie took the difficult decision to close the Hazelwood plant, even though it led to job losses, because its purpose prioritised the environment.

The second is where to allocate an enterprise's limited time and resources. What a company leaves out in its purpose can be as important as what it includes because omission helps guide trade-offs. To paraphrase leadership expert Craig Groeschel, 'to do things no-one else is doing, you have to not do things everyone else is doing'. This is similar to an effective strategy. Reckitt Benckiser could only concentrate on its nineteen Powerbrands by reducing investment in its other products.

The third is which business opportunities to turn down. The pharmacy CVS's purpose is 'helping people on their path to better health'. In 2014, CVS stopped selling cigarettes even though they generated $2 billion in sales, shortly before renaming itself CVS Health. What seemed a crazy business decision had a simple justification. As CEO Larry Merlo said, 'put simply, the sale of tobacco products is inconsistent with our purpose'. CVS's sales rose from $139 billion in 2014 to $185 billion three years later. While many factors could have caused this increase, it's consistent with purpose not being at the expense of profit. In 2013, Barclays closed a division that helped clients avoid tax, sacrificing £1 billion of revenue and contributing to the loss of 2,000 jobs. As CEO Antony Jenkins explained: 'There are some areas that relied on sophisticated and complex structures, where transactions were carried out with the primary objective of accessing the tax benefits. Although this was legal, going forward such activity is incompatible with our purpose. We will not engage in it again.'

We saw in Part I how pie-growing firms make decisions with judgment rather than calculation. The clearer the purpose, the easier it is to judge whether an action furthers it – such as whether selling cigarettes helps people on the path to better health. A large-scale study by Claudia Gartenberg, Andrea Prat and George Serafeim confirms the value of a clear purpose. Recall from Chapter 4 that I examined the publicly disclosed list of the 100 Best Companies to Work For. This new study obtained proprietary access to the half a million individual survey responses used to construct the list. The researchers used four of the fifty-seven survey questions to measure the strength of a company's purpose – 'My work has special meaning: this is "not just a job"', 'When I look at what we accomplish, I feel a sense of pride', 'I feel good about the ways we contribute to the community' and 'I'm proud to tell others I work here'. They found that these measures led to significantly higher profits and stock returns, but only when combined with clarity from management. Companies with a strong and clear purpose beat the market by 5.9% to 7.6% per year, controlling for risk.

While the first guideline highlights that a purpose statement should be focused, the second helps leaders decide this focus. *The why should be based on the principle of comparative advantage and the who on the principle of materiality.* Starting with the why, Chapter 3 explained that comparative advantage arises from what an enterprise is good at. Here, we also point out that it can also stem from what it's passionate about – *passion is a source of comparative advantage.* The passion of leaders, colleagues, investors and other stakeholders is a resource like expertise, land and capital, since it allows a company to get more out of these other resources.

After finishing my PhD at MIT, I started as an assistant professor at Wharton. There, several MBA students dream of launching a start-up. One of Wharton's most successful entrepreneurs in recent years is Will Shu, who founded the food delivery company Deliveroo. Over the two-year MBA, one of Will's classmates had about fifty different ideas for a start-up – he was certainly passionate about being an entrepreneur. After graduating, the one idea he ended up pursuing out of those fifty was to make high-quality pet toys, similar to an Etsy for pets. Only a few years later, Will caught up with his classmate and was surprised to find he'd packed it in. Will asked his classmate why. He replied, 'I realised that I just don't like dogs.' He pursued this idea because there was a market niche, a profit opportunity, not because he cared about the idea. In coming up with his fifty ideas, he was more passionate about being able to introduce himself as an entrepreneur at parties than the way his start-up would serve society.

Will founded Deliveroo because he was passionate about food delivery. What was that? You can be passionate about curing diseases, inventing smartphones, even entertaining kids, but delivering food? Indeed, you can. Will's passion came from his time as an analyst at

Morgan Stanley. Will joined Morgan Stanley in the same year as me, although he was in New York and I was in London; we didn't know each other until nine years later at Wharton. As an analyst, you might arrive in the morning after four hours' sleep and know that you'll work past midnight again. But there was one thing that you could look forward to – dinner. If you stayed after 8pm, which was almost always the case, you were entitled to free food. In New York, this was a treat, because you could order from Seamless, a web-based platform where you had your pick of hundreds of restaurants. And if you were particularly lucky, you might even be able to take a 15-minute break away from your desk, to eat it with fellow analysts in a meeting room, where you'd complain to each other about your bosses.

But when Will moved to London as a third-year analyst (just as I was leaving for MIT), he was dismayed to learn that all the stereotypes about the poor quality of English food were true. And importantly there was no shared platform. Analysts would pass around individual menus for Domino's Pizza, Chili's Bar and Grill, a Chinese restaurant called Good Friend and First Edition, a Mediterranean grill in the same building as Morgan Stanley – but those were your only options. The one small oasis in your day was dry.

That's how Will became passionate about food delivery. There were thousands of young professionals in London, working long hours and surviving on little sleep as they tried not to fall off the first rung of the ladder, but they couldn't even get a decent meal. This passion is what caused him to reject an offer from a leading hedge fund where he'd interned in the summer of his MBA. Instead, he started a career in delivering food. And this passion would be his comparative advantage. It made him willing, eager in fact, to spend five hours a day for the first nine months carrying the food himself – partly because Deliveroo was strapped for cash as it was getting off the ground, but more importantly because Will wanted to understand first-hand the challenges of being a rider. It also had unexpected side benefits, as Will's former Wharton classmates, now working as bankers and consultants in London, would order food from Deliveroo to have him deliver it to them. Even now as the CEO of a billion-dollar business, Will tries to do a shift a week as a Deliveroo rider. When I took my MBA students to visit Deliveroo, he made all of us (including me) do a shift as he said it was crucial for us to understand his enterprise.

Like most gig-economy firms, Deliveroo faces major challenges in ensuring that it treats its colleagues fairly. But passion, which translates into willingness to work as a rider, gives Will a comparative advantage in understanding these challenges – while he recognises that working the odd shift is a far cry from riding being your main source of income.

The *who* of an enterprise's purpose should be based on the *principle of materiality* – which stakeholders are material to the firm (business materiality), and which stakeholders the firm is particularly concerned about (intrinsic materiality). Recall from Chapter 4 that only companies that create value for stakeholders with high business materiality generate superior returns to investors. Just like comparative advantage, passion is a source of intrinsic materiality. Stakeholders can be material to a company simply because its leaders, colleagues and investors care about serving them.

The third guideline is that *a purpose is both deliberate and emergent.* Leaders should set the tone from the top, but also recognise that they don't have a monopoly in defining the enterprise's purpose. Purpose may bubble up from colleagues, and a purpose that emerges in this manner may be more likely to be embedded throughout the organisation than remaining in the C-suite. When workers have helped shape purpose, they feel ownership of it and are more likely to embed it. This requires viewing employees as a source of ideas rather than just a way to execute them. For example, the consulting firms McKinsey and the Disney Institute team up to help companies define their purpose. This involves interviewing colleagues at all levels on what inspires and matters to them, and holding workshops where employees from different departments share ideas together. Outside of formal consultations, leaders should be willing to allow purpose to evolve in response to changing conditions, such as shifting societal needs. Thus, while clarity of purpose is valuable, it shouldn't come at the expense of flexibility.

Purpose can also be shaped by input from an enterprise's key external stakeholders, so that outside perspectives are incorporated. The Constitution of the UK's National Health Service (NHS) includes a statement of its purpose and the rights and responsibilities of patients and staff. When it was initially drafted based on internal discussions, it focused on a purpose of helping people stay healthy and recover from illnesses. But the NHS then engaged in an extensive consultation with a variety of external stakeholders, such as citizen representatives, patients, clinicians and health charities, trade unions, public health

authorities and politicians. One of the many insights was the importance of a decent death when the time came – for a service so focused on
wellness, this need could have been easily overlooked without external
testing. This feedback materially changed the purpose stated in the
Constitution when it was eventually published: 'The NHS belongs to
the people. It is there to improve our health and well-being, supporting
us to keep mentally and physically well, to get better when we are ill
and, when we cannot fully recover, to stay as well as we can to the end
of our lives.' Similar to consultations with employees, outside input not
only sharpens the purpose statement, but also leads to stakeholders
rallying around it and taking ownership of it.

Once a purpose has been decided upon, it must go beyond a
statement and live in the enterprise. Living purpose means two things –
communicating purpose externally and embedding purpose internally.
Let's now look at how to do so.

Communicating Purpose – and Communicating beyond Purpose

Communication involves a company reporting its purpose statement,
and more importantly whether it's being put into practice. An enterprise
should set long-term targets for the value it delivers to each stakeholder
in the purpose statement, and then report whether it's on track. While
numbers are valuable to hold a leader accountable for purpose, they're
incomplete by themselves and should be supplemented by narratives.
One role of narratives is to provide the context behind the numbers. If a
company is on track to hit its targets, it can share success stories and the
milestones reached; if not, why it's off-track and what it's doing to get
back on. Similarly, an employee satisfaction score of 73% tells a reader
little. More informative are which areas of employee satisfaction are
strong and weak, the key successes, and plans for improvement. Second,
numbers only capture what's been achieved to date, while narratives
can be forward-looking. For innovation, in addition to reporting the
number of patents generated, a firm can describe its efforts to recruit
and train a top-quality R&D team, and create an innovative culture
that embraces risk-taking and tolerates failure.

Let's look at an example of reporting on purpose. The food and
clothing store Marks & Spencer has embodied its purpose into an
initiative called Plan A, 'because there is no Plan B'. Plan A aspires to

'build a sustainable future by being a business that enables our customers to have a positive impact on well-being, communities, and planet through all that we do'. Marks & Spencer made this concrete by setting itself 100 specific targets. For example, its environmental goals include ones for energy consumption, food waste and recyclability of packaging. Every year, it discloses whether a target had already been 'Achieved' or 'Achieved – Late'; for those still ongoing, it reports whether it is 'Progressing' or 'Behind'. Figure 8.1 shows an extract from the Energy Consumption and Sourcing section of Marks & Spencer's 2017 Plan A report.

The myriad of numbers in Figure 8.1 addresses the common concern that you can't measure social value, and so Pieconomics fails to hold leaders accountable. Many dimensions of social performance *can* be quantified. It's true that the wealth of information in Figure 8.1, which is only a small excerpt from the full Plan A report, can't be conveniently reduced to a single number, such as quarterly profits. But that's because a leader has responsibility for multiple stakeholders, which similarly can't be whittled down into a single objective.

While a purpose prioritises particular stakeholders, an enterprise has a responsibility to all stakeholders. It should therefore report how much value it delivers to them, with the extensiveness depending on a stakeholder's materiality. Currently, only 18% of UK FTSE 350 companies use materiality to determine what non-financial information to disclose, highlighting significant potential for improvement.

Communicating non-financial measures of stakeholder value goes beyond traditional reporting, which focuses on financial measures of shareholder value. This more complete model is known as *integrated reporting*, and is illustrated in Table 8.1.* The International Integrated Reporting Council provides a principles-based framework on how an integrated report can be structured, and the Sustainability Accounting

---

* Currently, most companies that disclose non-financial information do so through a stand-alone 'Sustainability Report', such as Marks & Spencer's Plan A report. This goes alongside the Annual Report which contains their financials. 'Integrated reporting' is sometimes reserved to refer to a single report which combines both financial and non-financial information. While most Sustainability Reports simply report non-financial information, an integrated report will also discuss what it implies for future financial profitability. Here, we use 'integrated reporting' to refer to the combination of financial and non-financial reporting, whether undertaken in a separate report or one single report.

Table 8.1 *Traditional vs Integrated Reporting*

Traditional Reporting		Integrated Reporting		
What?	How?	What?	How?	Format
Investor value	Financial	Investor value	Financial	Quantitative
		Stakeholder value	Financial	Quantitative
			Non-financial	Quantitative Narrative
		Purpose, strategy, competitive environment, etc.	Non-financial	Quantitative Narrative

---

ENERGY CONSUMPTION AND SOURCING

UK AND ROI ENERGY EFFICIENCY (1)

(AIM)
Improving energy efficiency in UK and ROI stores, offices and distribution centres by 35% per sq ft by 2015.
See 2015 Plan A Report

UK AND ROI ENERGY EFFICIENCY (2)**

(AIM)
Improving energy efficiency in UK and ROI stores, offices and distribution centres by 50% per sq ft by 2020.

(PROGRESS)
This year, we improved total energy efficiency across our stores, offices and warehouses by 39%, to 35.1 KWhs/sq ft compared with 2006/07 (57.4 KWhs/sq ft).

Store energy efficiency was +38% at 42.3 KWhs/sq ft, compared to (67.9 KWhs/sq ft) in 2006/07. Gas usage included in our calculation has been adjusted using standard degree days to reflect changes in the number of cold days (44.2 KWhs/sq ft before adjustment). This performance is slightly down on last year due to an increased proportion of new Food sales floor, which consumes more energy than Clothing & Home.

We improved energy efficiency in our warehouses by 41% at 15.7 KWhs/sq ft compared with 2006/07: 26.4 KWhs/sq ft.
We improved energy use in our offices by 36% at 31.8 KWhs/sq ft (2006/07: 49.4 KWhs/sq ft).

UK and ROI Energy Efficiency
Total store, office and warehouse energy usage in KWhs/sq ft

2006/07 Actual	2015/16 Actual	2016/17 Actual	2020 Target	Achievement on 2006/07
57.4	34.9	35.1	28.7	-39%

INTERNATIONAL ENERGY EFFICIENCY**

(AIM)
Improving energy efficiency in our international stores, offices and distribution centres outside of the ROI by 20% per sq ft by 2020 against a newly developed baseline.

(PROGRESS)
Last year we operated stores in 16 countries outside the UK and ROI, including a joint-venture business in India. Around a third of this international footage uses energy provided by a landlord and is outside our operational control. We've only included the energy and footage where we have operational control.

In 2016/17, we reduced our energy consumption by 9%, achieving 25.5 KWhs/sq ft compared to 2013/14 (27.9 KWhs/sq ft). Energy consumption in our International stores is much lower than in those in the UK and ROI as most don't sell chilled food and use heating and air-conditioning provided by a landlord.

We have four international warehouses. Their primary function is to support our UK business. These warehouses showed a 77% improvement in efficiency, due to changes in the way they use their footage.

International stores (outside of ROI)
Total store energy usage in KWhs/sq ft

2013/14 Actual	2015/16 Actual	2016/17 Actual	2020 Target	Achievement on 2013/14
27.9	27.5	25.5	22.4	-9%

Internationally located warehouses
Total warehouse energy usage in KWhs/sq ft

2013/14 Actual	2015/16 Actual	2016/17 Actual	2020 Target	Achievement on 2013/14
9	6.9	2.1^	7.2	-77%

^ The main reason for this improvement is the removal of a warehouse in Hong Kong from the data, due to its multi-user status.

STORE REFRIGERATION – DOORS**

(AIM)
By 2015, we will conduct a trial to retrofit doors on fridges in stores in the existing estate, then fully evaluate it, with recommendations for future roll-out.

(PROGRESS)
We are not reporting additional progress this year but plan to install further refrigeration energy efficiency measures during 2017/18.

Figure 8.1 Energy Targets and Outcomes, Marks & Spencer Plan A Report 2017

Standards Board and Global Reporting Initiative are examples of standards that guide companies on what ESG information to report. These frameworks are particularly valuable to increase reporting comparability across companies.

Since there are thousands of potential non-financial measures that enterprises might report, the Embankment Project for Inclusive Capitalism brought together thirty-one major companies and investors managing over $30 trillion of assets, to funnel the measures down to an initial set of sixty-three. These sixty-three metrics are ones where there's consensus from both CEOs and investors on their materiality to long-term performance, and so companies can disclose them knowing that investors will take them seriously. For environmental renewal, the measures include energy consumption, carbon emissions and water usage; for innovation, they include the number of patents produced and how many times they've been cited. Importantly, while financial metrics only capture the *input* into investment – how much money has been spent – non-financial metrics like patent numbers and citations can gauge the *output*.

There are numerous benefits of integrated reporting. One is to attract investors and stakeholders aligned with the firm's purpose. A second is to ensure that they evaluate the company on intangible rather than purely financial dimensions. Laura Starks, Parth Venkat and Qifei Zhu found that firms with higher ESG ratings (which are based on a company's disclosures) are less likely to experience investor selling after negative earnings surprises. This suggests that investors recognise that quarterly earnings are less relevant for companies that deliver and report strong stakeholder performance.

Arguably, *the greatest role of integrated reporting is to spark integrated thinking*. It triggers conversations about what the company's purpose is and whether it's delivering it, and leads to employees analysing major decisions in terms of their stakeholder as well as investor impact. As the saying goes, 'what gets measured gets done'. Recall in Chapter 2 that Walkers reduced the carbon footprint of its crisps, ultimately benefiting investors. This reduction was sparked by Walkers adopting carbon labelling, which made its carbon footprint visible and motivated Walkers to reduce it. *The Economist* noted: 'It's not so much the label itself that matters ... but the process that must be gone through to create it.' Just as purpose is the goal of an enterprise and profit the by-product, integrated thinking should be the way a company operates and integrated reporting the by-product.

Integrated reporting not only includes non-financial measures, but also excludes some financial ones. On his first day as Unilever CEO in 2009, Paul Polman decided to stop reporting quarterly earnings. As discussed in Chapter 6, 80% of Chief Financial Officers (CFOs) would cut investment to meet an earnings benchmark. While that's a survey of what CFOs say they'll do, two studies of what they actually do confirm that quarterly reporting reduces investment. Yet even though the EU has scrapped the requirement for firms to issue quarterly reports, many still choose to do so. Moving away from quarterly earnings will give them freedom to focus on long-term value. Indeed, during Paul's ten-year tenure, Unilever's shares rose 150%, double the returns of the FTSE 100.

Concerns with Integrated Reporting

Integrated reporting is often viewed as desirable in theory, but unrealistic in practice, because non-financial measures aren't comparable between companies. Employee satisfaction scores may be compiled using different methodologies across firms. But non-financial measures are *inherently* incomparable because they depend on an enterprise's unique purpose. Even if two firms prioritise colleagues, one may emphasise wages, another learning and personal growth (like Southwest Airlines). So comparability is a red herring. Peter Lynch would visit each store independently and assess it on the dimensions most relevant for its particular situation. He'd need to do a comparison to decide which enterprise to invest in, but based on his overall qualitative assessment rather than directly ranking individual metrics. As mentioned in Chapter 3, people make decisions all the time based on overall assessments that include many non-comparable dimensions. Homeowners choose a house on more than its square footage, parents select a school on more than its exam results and a citizen takes a job on more than its salary – even though these metrics are comparable.

Moreover, demanding predominantly comparable metrics may backfire for investors, as it makes them ripe for replacement by computers. 'Smart beta' funds, where an algorithm chooses stocks based on quantitative factors, have grown substantially in recent years and broke $1 trillion in December 2017. Some are starting to use non-financial as well as financial criteria. To prevent them from being replaced by artificial intelligence, investors should ask companies for non-comparable, narrative information that can only be understood within the context of the enterprise's purpose – an assessment that can only be done by humans.

From Reporting to Communication

Communication involves more than just reporting, but also engaging with a company's investors and stakeholders – in particular, those included in the *who* of its purpose statement. There are two main differences. First, *reporting is impersonal, while communication is personal*. Reporting occurs through documents such as annual reports; communication occurs best through face-to-face meetings – a significant amount takes place through non-verbal means. Investors and stakeholders can glean far more information from a meeting, where answers are from the heart and they can observe how a company's leaders interact, than a sanitised report. Focusing Capital on the Long Term, a global consortium of companies and investors, provides a roadmap of ten topics that such conversations can be centred around, to maximise their effectiveness.

Second, *reporting is one-way, while communication is two-way*. At employee 'town halls' or webinars, colleagues can ask questions, make suggestions and share their own experiences. Leaders can similarly learn from their investors in private meetings. Many only reach out when there's an emergency, such as a takeover bid or an upcoming vote, but they should do so as a matter of course. Companies pay consultants high fees for advice on issues such as strategy and capital allocation, but investors and stakeholders are happy to share their ideas and act as a sounding board for free. They're allies of enterprises in growing the pie, but too often are an untapped resource. Similarly, meeting investors on a routine basis is one of the best ways to pre-empt confrontational shareholder activism. Doing so allows leaders to notice simmering investor concerns and address them before they boil over.

One idea to improve two-way communication with investors is to give them an advisory 'say-on-purpose' vote. Similar to 'say-on-pay' in the EU, this could be split into two – a forward-looking 'policy vote'

on the enterprise's purpose statement, and a backward-looking 'implementation vote' on whether it's put it into practice. The policy vote
would ensure that investors have bought into an organisation's purpose, and are comfortable with any trade-offs it implies – such as
spending millions to donate a drug. The implementation vote then
requires investors to track relevant metrics and hold the company
accountable for putting it into practice.

As with all yes/no choices, the vote itself is a blunt tool. An
against vote doesn't tell the company which aspects the investor
is unhappy with; a for vote doesn't mean he's satisfied with all
dimensions. So the vote should only be one outcome of a broader
engagement process. Voting requires an investor to analyse the statement and delivery of purpose in detail. He can then not only use this
evaluation to decide how to vote, but also communicate it directly to
management.

Investors already have a 'say-on-pay' vote in most countries,
but a firm's purpose is more important than its pay policy. While a bad
pay policy can make a company bad, a great pay policy can't make it
great. But purpose can. Say-on-purpose would allow investors to vote
on perhaps the most important aspect of a firm to society. Obtaining
investor buy-in would then give leaders the confidence to act in line with
the enterprise's purpose, even if doing so sacrifices short-term profit.
These investors will then help ensure that purpose remains embedded
even if the current CEO leaves.

The value of moving from reporting to communication can be
substantial. When a company receives an unwanted takeover bid, it
typically has to go on the defensive and argue why the bid undervalues
the enterprise. But when Kraft bid for Unilever, it was Unilever's shareholders who led the defence and quickly rebuffed the bid, as mentioned
in Chapter 6. This is because Unilever had made substantial investment
into ensuring that its shares were held by investors that looked
beyond short-term measures and wouldn't be tempted by Kraft's 18%
premium – as we've discussed, a company gets the investors it deserves.
Not only did CEO Paul Polman stop reporting quarterly earnings, but
also Unilever spent time and effort in regularly meeting its major
investors, explaining how a substantial part of its value was its Sustainable Living Plan and keeping them appraised of progress. If Unilever
had waited until an emergency to reach out to its investors, it would
most likely have been too late.

The term *share capital* (or *shareholder capital*) is often used to describe how much money shareholders initially contributed to the firm. But *stakeholder capital* describes the value of a firm's relationship with its stakeholders, not the amount that stakeholders contributed. We thus define the term *investor capital* as the value of the relationship a company has with its investors. This goes far beyond the money they invested, and even the current value of this investment. It includes the extent to which the investors have bought into the enterprise's purpose, understand the metrics that matter and are willing to engage to ensure excellence.

One study documented the benefits of investing in this relationship. A company's stock price rises by an average of 2% after it presents at 'CEO Investor Forums' – events run by the US Strategic Investor Initiative for leaders to share their long-term plans with their anchor investors. Reactions were particularly positive when enterprises disclosed specific and actionable information around purpose.

Embedding Purpose

A purpose statement is meaningless unless it translates into action. We'll discuss five channels through which purpose can be embedded in an enterprise – strategy, operating model, culture, internal reporting and governance.

Let's start with strategy. A company's purpose should shape the activities it's involved in. Outdoor clothing company Patagonia's purpose is environmental renewal, as highlighted by its statement 'Patagonia is in business to save our home planet'. These aren't just aspirational words. On Black Friday – the biggest shopping day – in 2011, it placed a full-page advert in the *New York Times* which pictured a Patagonia fleece with the headline 'Don't Buy This Jacket'. The advert highlighted its Common Threads Initiative, encouraging customers to repair and reuse their clothes rather than buy new ones. The initiative repaired over 30,000 items in eighteen months – and ended up not being at the expense of sales, which rose 30% in 2012. In 2017, Patagonia created its Worn Wear online marketplace for used clothing, even though this would reduce its sales of new items. Similarly, we earlier saw how CVS didn't simply rename itself CVS Health, but made the strategic decision to stop selling cigarettes, and Barclays closed its tax avoidance division.

The potential to build credibility through strategy is another advantage of the focused purpose we advocated earlier. It's easier for stakeholders to verify whether a focused purpose statement is being put into practice than a vague one that tries to do everything, and so almost any strategy might be consistent with it.

A second way to embed purpose is to align the operating model – how an enterprise runs its core operations – with it. For example, when the UK supermarket Tesco defined its core purpose as 'to create value for customers to earn their lifetime loyalty', it needed to ensure that its processes were uncompromisingly geared towards customers. For example, it already had over 90% efficiency in getting products onto store shelves, but this wasn't enough for an aspirational purpose such as 'lifetime loyalty'. Thus, it redesigned its processes to ensure customers could always buy the products they wanted when they wanted them.* Similarly, it made a promise that all stores would have 'a manager who helped me', but didn't yet have a management or training system to deliver this promise. So it simplified its store routines and delayered its hierarchies to give managers freedom to serve customers rather than spending time in unnecessary upwards reporting. It also launched a major programme of leadership development.

You might think that an operating model with efficient processes and management training should be a feature of any good company, not just a purposeful one. Even ESV would advocate improving processes and upskilling managers if the benefits can be roughly estimated. But all enterprises face trade-offs. Even in the best companies, many dimensions of their operating model can be enhanced. Operating model alignment involves prioritising the dimensions that

---

* As an example of a process improvement, milk used to be first loaded onto pallets at the bottling plant, then wrapped in plastic, then loaded onto trucks and transported to stores. Once they reached the store, they were unwrapped from the plastic, taken off the pallets, put into cages and then brought to the shop floor. Based on colleague input (which Tesco actively sought), it scrapped this inefficient process. Now it puts milk straight into cages at the bottling plant. These are wheeled into the trucks, transported and wheeled off the trucks onto the shop floor, and the milk is sold off the cages. This significantly shortened the supply chain, increasing product availability, as well as saving on labour and packaging costs. In addition, Tesco was one of the first UK retailers to invest in hand-held computers for its in-store stock controllers. This improved stock control accuracy and thus product availability, as well as giving employees meaningful work, as they no longer needed to count products.

most urgently need to be improved to put purpose into practice – which again highlights the need for purpose to be focused.

Third, a CEO should ensure that integrated reporting occurs inside the enterprise as well as outside. This involves gathering a rich set of information on how employees, teams and projects are performing on purpose-related dimensions. One use for this information is performance evaluation. Sometimes a CEO gives a rallying speech about purpose, only for senior management just below the C-suite to tell their team to ignore her and focus on their division's financial targets. An executive described this senior management layer to me as the 'clay', which blocks purpose from flowing throughout the enterprise just as clay blocks water flow. Such blockage isn't deliberate sabotage, but arises from the reality of how senior managers are evaluated. One firm invited me to speak at a purpose offsite, but in their briefing admitted that their most important metric remained short-term profit per partner. In contrast, when Marks & Spencer launched Plan A, it evaluated business unit and store managers using a 'balanced scorecard'. This combined traditional financial metrics with several non-financial measures tailored to the Plan A goals most under their control.*

In addition to allowing bosses to evaluate them, integrated internal reporting also allows employees to evaluate themselves, so that they know how they're performing and can make more informed decisions. This requires breaking down company-wide targets into sufficient granularity that workers can affect them. Marks & Spencer reports its overall greenhouse gas emissions and breaks them down by region, activity (e.g. refrigeration vs heating) and department (e.g. food vs clothing). However, even that's not granular enough to guide an individual colleague, who may manage a single store rather than a region. So Marks & Spencer internally tracks information at an individual store level. It also measures the emitting activity (e.g. electricity, gas and refrigeration) rather than the emissions generated, because it's the former that employees have direct control over.

---

* How does this square with our recommendation in Chapter 5, that a CEO's reward should be primarily based on the long-term stock return and not additional factors? The CEO is responsible for the entire enterprise, for which the long-term stock return is a comprehensive measure – it incorporates many dimensions of stakeholder value. An individual division doesn't have its own stock price, and any one measure (such as divisional profits) will be very incomplete. In addition, CEOs are likely wealthier and thus more able to accept pay being deferred for many years.

A fourth way to embed purpose is by aligning the enterprise's culture with it. While purpose concerns why an enterprise exists and who it serves, culture captures how it operates – in simple terms, it's 'the way we do things around here'. Culture is critical to ensure that a purpose permeates throughout the company. Recall the study by Claudia Gartenberg, Andrea Prat and George Serafeim, which documents strong performance of companies perceived by their employees as having a clear purpose. This link was driven by the perceptions of middle managers rather than senior leaders, likely because the former are particularly important for ensuring that purpose translates into day-to-day actions. This highlights a further benefit of a focused purpose statement – the simpler it is, the less likely it will be lost in translation when passed down the organisation.

For purpose to live in the enterprise, the right culture needs to be promoted. For example, a purpose that prioritises innovation, such as Reckitt Benckiser's ('to create healthier lives and happier homes through our product innovations'), is best supported by a culture that emphasises autonomy, rewards risk-taking and tolerates constructive failure. In contrast, a purpose that emphasises cost (such as Wal-Mart's, 'to save people money so they can live better') should be accompanied by a culture that emphasises efficiency and clearly defines job roles.

Leaders shape culture through their strategic choices and own behaviours, but they can't do everything themselves. Some companies thus task selected employees with ground-level culture change. Danish biotech firm Novo Nordisk has developed a set of cultural principles, known as the 'Novo Nordisk Way', to support its purpose to 'drive change to defeat diabetes and other serious chronic diseases'. It has a team of 'facilitators' that visits business units to help them implement the Novo Nordisk Way. The team observes a unit in action, interviews managers and employees, examines its policies, and then reports overall findings and trends to company leadership. French personal care company L'Oréal has developed four ethical principles to support its purpose of 'cosmetic innovation for all',* and has a network of seventy-five ethics correspondents to embed them across the company and in every country. They adapt these principles to local customs, ensure that employees are

---

* For example, one of the ethical principles is courage, which supports its purpose of innovation. Another is transparency, which is particularly important for an enterprise that aims to serve all citizens.

trained on ethical behaviour and know how to raise ethics concerns, and act as a sounding board for ethics queries.

Another way to shape culture is by hiring colleagues with a strong cultural fit. Recall Patagonia's purpose is to 'save our home planet'. As founder and CEO Yvon Chouinard explains: 'whenever we have a job opening, all things being equal, hire the person who's committed to saving the planet no matter what the job is'. The shoe manufacturer Zappos gives new hires a month-long training programme, which includes an induction on the company's values, and offers them $2,000 to leave if they don't share them. (A similar programme has since been adopted by Amazon, which bought Zappos in 2009.) Herb Kelleher, the co-founder of Southwest, placed cultural fit over experience and education when recruiting – as exemplified by his motto 'Hire for attitude, train for skill'.

Finally, embedding purpose often requires changes not only below the CEO, but also at the board above her. A 2014 *Harvard Business Review* article reported that only 10% of US public firms had a board committee dedicated to corporate responsibility, and advocated that this practice become more widespread. But purpose should be a formal duty of the entire board – it's fundamental to a company's core business, rather than an ancillary activity that can be delegated to a subcommittee. The board shouldn't approve an M&A deal, strategic initiative or capital expenditure proposal without first verifying that it's consistent with the firm's purpose. Similarly, a board typically devotes two days per year to discussing and agreeing strategy; these sessions should be anchored to purpose. The board can also ensure that the company's non-financial targets are both appropriate and aspirational given its purpose, and monitor whether it's achieving these targets.

Since purpose can't be assessed purely with quantitative metrics, the UK's Financial Reporting Council recommends that non-executive directors "walk the shop floor" to truly understand an enterprise. At present, there are proposals in the UK and US to put workers in the boardroom, and some European countries already do. But a more effective approach is to bring the boardroom into the workforce – for it to spend time in the business and hear from colleagues first-hand, through structured site visits. I serve on London Business School's Governing Body (the equivalent of our board) as an elected faculty representative – loosely analogous to a worker director. Even though I try to talk to non-Finance faculty and non-academic staff, I'm unable to represent their views as accurately as I can those of other Finance faculty. At a Governing Body Away Day, a colleague thus challenged the external governors to spend time on campus and understand the "smell" of London Business School, to hear the voice of the broader workforce.

While purpose should be the responsibility of the full board, committees can be useful for monitoring specific dimensions of purpose. Most board structures focus exclusively on shareholder value, and thus have committees dedicated to remuneration, director nominations, risk and audit. The last two are geared towards downside protection. But Pieconomics stresses the importance of upside value creation, and so an Innovation Committee may be valuable for some firms. In addition, after an enterprise has decided on the *who*, it can create committees responsible for key stakeholders, such as a Human Capital Committee or an Environment Committee – or, alternatively, these issues should be major agenda items for the full board. Setting the tone at the top helps ensure that purpose flows throughout the organisation.

Stakeholders as Partners

Enlightened shareholder value views stakeholders as a means to an end – a company only invests in them if it can calculate, at least approximately, an effect on future profits. In contrast, a pie-growing enterprise acknowledges *stakeholder mutuality* – the long-term, two-way relationship it has with its stakeholders, who are partners in the company rather than factors of production. This recognition transforms the relationship in two ways. First, rather than seeing stakeholders as sources of only profit (customers, workers and suppliers providing revenues, labour and inputs), the enterprise views them as sources of ideas and collaborators in fulfilling its purpose. Second, instead of only taking from stakeholders – receiving their revenues, labour and inputs – it strives to deliver long-term value to them, beyond its contractual obligations.

This highlights the importance of purpose having a *who* as well as a *why*. An enterprise is a network of relationships, which it must nurture and grow, not just a nexus of contracts. This section discusses what a partnership approach to stakeholders entails. For brevity, we'll focus on colleagues rather than going through every stakeholder, but the principles extend to other stakeholders.

Many influential books have already been written about managing people, so my goal isn't to provide an encyclopaedia. Instead, we'll focus specifically on what Pieconomics teaches us about how to lead a workforce. We'll apply three tenets of Pieconomics to employees, each of which implies an attitudinal shift. One tenet is to avoid errors of omission rather than just commission by granting workers autonomy, the *attitude of empowerment*. A second is to invest in colleagues even if the link to profits is unclear, the *attitude of investment*. A third is to share the benefits of pie growth with employees, the *attitude of reward*. (As mentioned, these principles can be applied to other stakeholders – for example, a company can empower customers by viewing them as a source of ideas, ensure that its products improve their long-term welfare and share the benefits of success rather than extracting the highest possible price.)

The three attitudes are closely linked not only to Pieconomics, but also to what's measured by the Best Companies survey, which Chapter 4 showed is linked to long-term performance. Recall that the survey gauges workers' perceptions of credibility, fairness, respect, pride and camaraderie. These perceptions reflect, in part, whether leaders display the attitudes of empowerment, investment and reward, as can be seen by the sample questions in the table below.

Credibility	People here are given a lot of responsibility
Fairness	I feel I receive a fair share of the profits made by this organisation
Respect	I am offered training and development to further myself professionally
Pride	My work has special meaning: this is not 'just a job'
Camaraderie	People care about each other here

These sample questions highlight how improving employee satisfaction involves an attitudinal shift, rather than simply spending money, which makes it hard to replicate. Let's now see what underpins this competitive advantage.

The Attitude of Empowerment

The *attitude of empowerment* views employees as a source of ideas, inspiration and innovation. Failing to tap into this source is an error of omission, but traditional management practices are based on avoiding errors of commission.

Henry Ford is widely seen as one of history's most creative business leaders, often credited with the quote 'If I had asked people what they wanted, they would have said faster horses' – an example of the importance of problem-finding, not just problem-solving. He didn't invent the car, but he developed the first car that middle-class Americans could afford (the Model T) by introducing the assembly line into the manufacturing process.

The assembly line was based on Frederick Taylor's *Principles of Scientific Management*, published in 1911. Taylor viewed ground-level workers as having two characteristics. The first is that they're effort-averse and so, left alone, will shirk. The second is that they're unintelligent and unable to think for themselves, as vividly captured by his description of Schmidt, a pig iron handler at Bethlehem Steel:

> Now one of the very first requirements for a man who is fit to handle pig iron as a regular occupation is that he shall be so stupid and so phlegmatic that he more nearly resembles in his mental make-up the ox than any other type . . . He is so stupid that the word 'percentage' has no meaning to him, and he must consequently be trained by a man more intelligent than himself into the habit of working in accordance with the laws of this science before he can be successful.

Taylor believed that there was a single best way to carry out any task, and so leaders had two responsibilities. The first was to find out this best way through scientific experimentation – quantify how much pig iron to carry at a time, and how long to take breaks. The second was to ensure that workers followed this one best way. As Taylor told Schmidt:

> You will do exactly as this man tells you to do to-morrow, from morning till night. When he tells you to pick up a pig and walk, you pick it up and you walk, and when he tells you to sit down and rest, you sit down. You do that right straight through the day. And what's more, no back talk.

Taylor conceded that this was 'rather rough talk', but with a man of 'the mentally sluggish type as Schmidt', it was 'appropriate and not unkind'. And this leadership approach was effective, at least in the short term and for routine jobs – it quadrupled Schmidt's haulage from 12 to 47 tons of pig iron a day.

The assembly line was inspired by Taylor. It forced employees to keep up with the pace of production and took division of labour to the extreme – workers repeated a narrow set of tasks non-stop without thinking. While modern-day working conditions aren't so extreme, elements of scientific management still persist, aiming to prevent errors of commission from shirking or making mistakes.*

Some bosses assume that employees will naturally shirk, so good management involves squeezing as much as possible out of them, by creating a long-hours culture or shackling workers to targets. Just as Taylor gave Schmidt targets for pig iron haulage, Wells Fargo handed its bank employees daily sales goals, and any shortfall was added to the next day's target. Former CEO John Stumpf coined the term 'Going for Gr-Eight', encouraging employees to sell at least eight products to each customer, regardless of need or want. Why eight? Not because an analysis showed that eight products improve customer welfare. Simply because 'it rhymed with great'.

The desire to prevent mistakes is based on the assumption that, even if a worker won't shirk, he lacks the expertise to take the correct decisions himself. This assumption leads to micromanagement and hierarchy, which limit how much a worker can contribute. In my second year in investment banking, Abbey National, a client I'd worked with for many months, asked me to investigate a US situation. I called a US Associate (the level above Analyst, my rank) to inquire, and was told that Jeff, a US Managing Director, was the relevant person to ask. The Associate advised me 'you should call Jeff', before correcting himself to 'you should get your Associate to call Jeff'. The unspoken concern was that, as an Analyst, I was too junior to speak to a Managing Director. Perhaps my rank meant that I couldn't speak articulately and would waste Jeff's time, an error of commission. Even though I knew first-hand what the client wanted, the hierarchy required me to brief an Associate, the Associate to call Jeff and then report back to me – wasting her time and risking the message getting lost in translation. (I ended up calling Jeff anyway, who turned out to be very helpful.)

---

* One may wonder why shirking is not labelled as an 'error of omission' as it involves omitting to work. Throughout the book, we've used 'errors of omission' to refer to not launching new ideas, rather than the failure to perform routine tasks.

The *attitude of empowerment*, in contrast, argues that you don't need close supervision to avoid errors of commission. Colleagues are intrinsically motivated to work hard due to their 'seeking systems' – a term social psychologist Dan Cable uses to describe their innate desire to explore and create. They also have specialist expertise and ground-level information to come up with the best way of achieving a goal. The challenge for leaders is to activate and channel these seeking systems. Micromanagement and hierarchy suppress them, risking errors of omission by failing to tap into employees' skills and knowledge.

Empowerment was a key pillar behind Japan's success after the Second World War. In Ford's American assembly line, factory workers executed tasks designed by superiors, who then checked the quality of the final product. In contrast, under the Andon system used by Japanese manufacturers such as Toyota, factory workers were themselves responsible for quality, and had the authority to stop the production line whenever they saw a defect. A flashing light would come on to call for help – hence the name, Andon, taken from the Japanese word for a paper lantern. This attitudinal shift was radical, since stopping production was previously seen as management's call. Japanese factories became hubs of continuous improvement, since those closest to the action could contribute to innovation efforts. When I toured a Toyota factory in Tokyo, the Toyota employee proudly pointed out every feature of the production process that came from workers.

This attitude is now adopted by many Western enterprises, and is measured, in part, by the Best Companies survey question 'People here are given a lot of responsibility'. For example, Kim Jordan, New Belgium Brewing Company's co-founder, describes her firm's approach as follows: 'We have a high involvement culture. Everyone knows where the money goes and everyone is expected to participate and build strategy. It's created an environment not only with a level of transparency that fostered trust, but also a shared "we're in this together" feel.' We discussed in Chapter 3 how New Belgium acknowledged its environmental impact. It runs a crowdsourcing scheme, 'Bright Ideas', which asks colleagues for ideas on how to reduce it. One was to eliminate the cardboard dividers it had been using inside its boxes to separate bottles. This saved hundreds of trees, as well as $1 million per year in raw material costs. But there were several indirect benefits. It sped up production, which historically had been slowed down at the packaging phase. The smaller boxes meant that more could fit into a delivery truck, reducing fuel costs and carbon emissions. This is an example not only of the value of empowerment, but also the principles of Pieconomics – actions taken to benefit the environment ultimately benefiting investors.

Empowerment also involves tolerance of mistakes. As discussed in Chapter 5, Bart Becht entrusted Reckitt Benckiser managers to launch new ideas without requiring a stack of approvals. This increases the risk that initiatives fail, but such failures are less costly than stifling innovations. Financial software company Intuit and conglomerate Tata go further than tolerating mistakes – they actively celebrate them by giving awards for ideas that ultimately failed, but provided valuable learnings.

Large-scale evidence backs up the takeaways from these specific examples. A comprehensive meta-analysis of 142 studies by Scott Seibert, Gang Wang and Stephen Courtright found that individual empowerment is associated with higher performance along several dimensions – routine tasks, 'organisational citizenship behaviour' (going above and beyond regular duties) and innovation. They similarly found that, when teams are empowered, team performance is significantly better.

Before closing, it's important to acknowledge that, while empowerment can unleash untapped potential, it's also channelled effectively through purpose and training. Micromanagement and hierarchy aren't necessarily driven by the assumption that employees are lazy – leaders may worry that they'll work hard, but their efforts will be misdirected on immaterial issues. That's why purpose is powerful – captured, in part, by the survey question 'My work has special meaning: this is not "just a job"'. If colleagues are inspired by the company's mission, they'll contribute to it even if the shackles are released; if the purpose clarifies the priorities, they'll discern where to direct their energies. In a quote attributed to author Antoine de Saint-Exupéry: 'If you want to build a ship, don't drum up the men to gather wood, divide the work and give orders. Instead, teach them to yearn for the vast and endless sea.' Indeed, as discussed previously, Claudia Gartenberg, Andrea Prat and George Serafeim documented the benefits of a strong and clear purpose, particularly as perceived by middle managers rather than senior leaders.

Another way to ensure that employees make best use of their autonomy is by continually investing in their skills. This is the attitude of investment, to which we now turn.

The Attitude of Investment

The *attitude of investment* seeks to enhance a colleague's skills and well-being, not only because he'll become more productive, but also because you care about him as a person. This attitude is measured, in part, by the survey question 'People care about each other here'. The classic economic model of Nobel Laureate Gary Becker argues that a company should only invest in *firm-specific* training that's of value exclusively within the firm, such as how to use its databases. If it invests in *general* skills, which have value in other potential employers, the worker can command a higher salary – so he, not the company, captures the benefits of his increased productivity. These economic models aren't just abstract theory, but affect practice. Most general education is financed either by governments (e.g. public schools), workers themselves (e.g. Masters of Business Administration degrees) or a combination of both (e.g. public universities).

But the attitude of investment doesn't calculate how firm-specific or general the training is, or how much of the benefits the company will capture. Indeed, the survey question 'I am offered training and development to further myself professionally' doesn't make these distinctions. The attitude of investment views it as an enterprise's responsibility to develop its workers' skills, increasing not only their value to their current firm, but also their future employability if they are later displaced. In her book *Janesville*, Amy Goldstein relates how the 2009 closure of General Motors' factory in Janesville, Wisconsin led to chronic unemployment that seriously depressed the entire city. Since GM had focused on teaching its colleagues specialised skills, retraining efforts were largely unsuccessful. Many didn't know how to use a computer and so couldn't take the courses offered by local technical colleges.

As an example of the attitude of investment, in August 2016, the Singapore offices of Standard Chartered bank launched the Skills-Future@sc programme, giving employees paid study leave and free tuition to take one of fifty bank-sponsored courses. It particularly targets workers whose roles are at risk from changes in technology, and trains them in not only technology, but also human skills that technology is unlikely to replace, such as customer interaction. And investment in skills doesn't always require financial expenditure or official programmes, but management practices such as coaching.

Similarly, we've discussed how empowerment taps into colleagues' initiative today; a separate benefit is that it invests in their future potential by giving them the chance to step up.

Earlier, we referred to investment as 'enhancing a colleague's skills *and well-being*'. For a physical asset, investment expands its maximum capacity – if you upgrade an IT system, it can process more data. For colleagues, investment can similarly increase their maximum potential by enhancing their skills. However, many workers operate below their potential, for example due to poor mental or physical well-being. Thus, for employees, investment involves not only raising their potential, but also helping them achieve their current potential. However, while companies often know how much they're spending on IT, they're less aware of how much they're investing in employee wellness.

In 2015, the leaders of UBS Wealth Management recognised that their demanding culture might be harming employees. So they created a Health Matters Initiative, which they asked Claudia Oeken to lead. In this role she puts on major events to improve physical health, such as a '100 days, 1 million steps' initiative, encouraging employees to form teams and each take 10,000 steps per day, with each step leading to a charity donation. Quantifying the benefit of such initiatives, a meta-analysis by Harvard researchers Katherine Baicker, David Cutler and Zirui Song found that $1 spent on well-being programmes is associated with a $3.27 fall in medical costs and a $2.73 reduction in absenteeism costs.

We've discussed how the attitude of investment internalises the benefits of training for the employee even if the firm doesn't capture them. It also internalises the costs of additional work to the employee even if the firm doesn't need to pay him overtime. This contrasts with the attitude of *free disposal* – a boss views subordinates' time as hers, free to spend as she pleases 'just in case' the work ends up being useful, without considering the cost of time to the worker. She might request multiple analyses in a presentation appendix, just in case the client asks a technical question. Chapter 3 explained how the pie shrinks if the firm takes an action whose benefit is less than the social rather than private opportunity cost. An employee's time often has no private cost to the firm, but a significant social one, as he could use that time for recreation. Commissioning work ignoring this social cost shrinks the pie.

This consideration means that well-being initiatives should be expanded in two ways. First, from physical to mental wellness. While the importance of physical health has long been recognised, only more recently have enterprises – and society – acknowledged the criticality of mental well-being, which is severely harmed by both ever-increasing work expectations and the attitude of free disposal. Joel Goh, Jeffrey Pfeffer and Stefanos Zenios estimate that workplace stress in the US causes 120,000 extra deaths per year and increases healthcare costs by $190 billion – ultimately borne by companies themselves through higher insurance premiums. Second, well-being initiatives should expand from one-off programmes to ongoing culture change. In addition to major events, Claudia continuously educates employees on energy and stress management, and managers on the criticality of preserving their colleagues' mental wellness – for example, by not disturbing them during evenings and weekends. The attitudinal shift from free disposal to investment is often substantial. A leader's own time was viewed as a free good when she was junior, so she's used to viewing juniors' time similarly. This is why employee satisfaction can be a competitive differentiator that's hard to replicate – it requires a major culture change, rather than simply spending money.

Claudia told me her main challenge is measuring the success of an initiative, as it's impossible to know how many sickness and burnout days would have occurred without it. Indeed, the meta-analysis of Katherine Baicker and co-authors doesn't make strong causality claims because other factors, such as changing management practices, may have led to the benefits. This highlights the importance of the attitude of investment – investing in colleagues even without a calculation. Companies already recognise the importance of safety if their employees have physically dangerous jobs. As discussed in Chapter 5, BP made workplace injuries a strategic priority after the Deepwater Horizon disaster. Here, calculations are easier. Since on-the-job injuries stem exclusively from a company's working conditions, improving them is indeed likely to reduce the injury rate.

But workplace safety extends far beyond injuries to the physical sickness and mental burnout caused by an attitude of free disposal and a culture of long hours. If a colleague becomes physically or mentally ill, we don't know whether that's due to the workplace or factors outside work. But this doesn't matter to a company with the attitude of investment – it strives to provide a healthy, safe and fulfilling environment even if the benefits can't be quantified.

The Attitude of Reward

The *attitude of reward* shares the benefits of pie growth with colleagues. The most obvious way is to give employees *financial ownership* – equity in the company, as recommended in Chapter 5. Traditional economic theory argues that a rank-and-file employee should never be given shares. He has little effect on the firm's stock price, so equity shouldn't make him work harder. But humans don't act based on economic cost-benefit analyses. Giving a colleague shares treats him as a partner in the enterprise, who deserves to share in its success. This is captured, in part, by the survey question 'I feel I receive a fair share of the profits made by this organisation'.

Just like investment, rewarding employees doesn't just involve money. Due to their seeking systems, colleagues are also motivated by the desire to contribute. The attitude of reward thus involves sharing the intrinsic as well as financial benefits of pie growth by giving them *task ownership* – responsibility for a task, sometimes unconditionally. One benefit of task ownership is empowerment, as discussed earlier. But another is the fulfilment the colleague enjoys when he completes the task. Sometimes a senior might wish to rewrite part of a document that a junior has written. The changes might lead to a genuine improvement, but a minor one. The small cost of sticking with the original is outweighed by the reward the employee enjoys from having had full responsibility for the final product.

In my second year at Morgan Stanley, my Executive Director (William) often worked with me without either an Associate or Vice President in between. Usually, the executive summary of a presentation is the prerogative of senior bankers. But rather than leaving this page blank for William to fill in when he commented on my other slides, I dared to take first crack at it. The first few times, he'd suggest major changes – not only improving the presentation for the client, but also coaching me. Having learned from those changes, I slowly improved. I still remember the fulfilment when, for the first time, an executive summary came back to me unchanged. Almost certainly, William could have suggested incremental improvements, but chose not to. This cost to the final product was little, but the reward to me was significant, and remains vivid two decades later.

In a Nutshell

- The main way in which an enterprise can grow the pie is *excellence*. Serving society goes beyond taking actions that are explicitly 'serving'. Almost all firms and colleagues make a major contribution to society by being excellent at their specific role, regardless of whether it directly affects stakeholders.
- An enterprise's *purpose* is its reason for being – how it seeks to serve society.
  - A purpose defines *who* the enterprise is for and *why* it exists. The *who* is based on the *principle of materiality* and the *why* on the *principle of comparative advantage*.
  - Such a definition involves uncomfortable prioritisations. But a purpose is only meaningful if the converse would also be reasonable, as then it provides guidance to leaders in navigating trade-offs and clarity to stakeholders on what the enterprise stands for.
  - A purpose should be both deliberate, guided by executives, and emergent, shaped by colleagues rather than being merely executed for them. Input from external stakeholders, particularly customers, is also valuable.
- A purpose is far more than a mission statement and must live in the enterprise. It must not only be *defined*, but also *communicated* externally and *embedded* internally.
- Reporting should expand beyond financial measures of shareholder value to non-financial measures of stakeholder value, and highlight what stakeholders can do to contribute to the firm's purpose. The main value of such *integrated reporting* is to spark integrated thinking, where stakeholder concerns are integrated into all major decisions.
- Communication goes beyond reporting to a two-way in-person process. It may involve giving investors a 'say-on-purpose'. Doing so builds *investor capital*, which is far greater than investors' financial contribution to the company.
- Leaders can put purpose into practice through the firm's strategy, aligning its operating model and culture, developing an internal 'balanced scorecard' that includes relevant non-financial measures, and making purpose a priority of the board.
- An enterprise should recognise *stakeholder mutuality* – stakeholders aren't simply factors of production, but are members of the

enterprise. Applied to colleagues, this involves adopting three attitudes, each based on a tenet of Pieconomics:

○ *The attitude of empowerment* is based on the importance of errors of omission rather than just commission. It views colleagues as intrinsically motivated and intelligent. If given freedom, and guided by a clear purpose, they will generate ideas rather than shirk.

○ *The attitude of investment* is based on delivering value to stakeholders even if the link to profits is unclear. It seeks to enhance a colleague's skills and well-being because the company cares about him as a person. This involves internalising both the benefits of investment and the costs of additional work.

○ *The attitude of reward* is based on sharing the fruits of pie growth with stakeholders. It gives a colleague both financial and task ownership, so that he enjoys both the pecuniary and intrinsic gains from success.

9 INVESTORS
TURNING STEWARDSHIP FROM A POLICY INTO A PRACTICE

Chapter 6 presented the evidence that stewardship by investors, through both engagement and monitoring, grows the pie. We now discuss *how* investors can put stewardship into practice. Chapter 8's framework on implementing purpose – defining purpose, embedding it internally and communicating it externally – also applies to stewardship, and we'll draw many parallels throughout. Some of this chapter draws on my work with The Purposeful Company – in particular, numerous discussions with PwC's Tom Gosling, who co-led all of TPC's stewardship initiatives with me, including the idea of say-on-purpose in Chapter 8.

Before we start, I'll stress two points. The first is the urgency of improving stewardship. Just as purpose isn't an optional extra for companies to confine to a Corporate Social Responsibility (CSR) department, stewardship isn't an optional extra for investors to confine to a stewardship department. Most obviously, stewardship typically serves savers – investors' clients – by improving long-term returns and achieving their non-financial goals. More broadly, stewardship is important for the legitimacy of the investment management industry. Society views investors as having stewardship responsibilities and has blamed corporate collapses, such as the 2007 financial crisis, on investors failing in these responsibilities. Regulators look to investors to implement public policy objectives, by pushing companies to increase

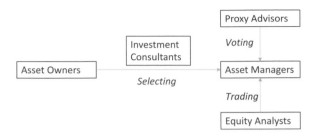

Figure 9.1 The Investment Chain

diversity or take action on climate change. Moreover, good stewardship can be a national competitive advantage. As discussed in Chapter 6, Japanese Prime Minister Shinzo Abe sees Japan's historically passive investment industry as a cause of its historically low equity returns, and is undertaking structural reforms to address this.

Given the importance of stewardship for society, several countries have introduced Stewardship Codes. While a good first step, there are widespread concerns that codes encourage statements of policy rather than actual practice. If investors don't improve stewardship by themselves, they may be faced with tougher codes or regulation. Arguments to decrease investor rights, as discussed in Chapter 6, are based on the concern that investors aren't using these rights responsibly.

The second key point is that 'investors' aren't a single entity, but consist of an entire investment chain, as shown in Figure 9.1. Chapter 6 focused on *asset managers* – investment management companies such as ValueAct and Fidelity. They run individual *funds*, such as the Fidelity Magellan active fund or the Fidelity Mid Cap Index Fund. *Investor* is a general term that can apply to both asset managers or funds.

But asset managers aren't the only link in the chain. They manage money on behalf of *asset owners* or *savers*. These may include citizens, who buy funds directly, or institutions such as a pension fund, university endowment or sovereign wealth fund. They play a critical role in holding asset managers to account for stewardship – for example, Japan's $1.5 trillion Government Pension Investment Fund uses stewardship as a major criterion in its selection and evaluation process. Institutional asset owners typically choose asset managers using *investment consultants*, such as Aon Hewitt, just as people use financial advisors. Asset managers use their own consultants – *proxy advisors* to guide voting decisions and *equity analysts* to guide trading decisions. Investment consultants and proxy advisors are collectively known as *service providers*. Regulators typically don't view equity analysts as service providers, nor see them as playing a role in stewardship. But they influence investors' trading decisions, which is a form of stewardship as discussed in Chapter 6, so we include them in this chapter.

As a result, improving stewardship requires reforming the entire investment chain, yet stewardship codes typically focus on asset managers. We'll first focus on asset managers and explain how they can *define* their stewardship policy, then *embed* this policy by turning it into a practice, and finally *communicate* outcomes externally – the same three steps we described for implementing purpose in Chapter 8. Later in this chapter, and also in the Appendix, we'll describe this process for the other links in the investment chain.

Defining Stewardship

Stewardship codes often assume a one-size-fits-all approach, for example that engagement is always more effective than monitoring and that more stewardship is always better than less. But this ignores the principle of comparative advantage. A fund may choose not to engage in stewardship. If stewardship isn't its expertise, the best way it serves society might be to provide savers with low-cost access to equity markets, so that they can share the fruits of economic growth. A clear definition of stewardship is therefore important. What matters isn't so much that a fund engages in extensive stewardship, but that it does what it says it will. This should avoid the problem of 'closet indexers', discussed in Chapter 6, who charge high fees for active management without actually practising it.

The starting point for stewardship is a fund's purpose. This purpose should explain how it aspires to serve savers and society. Its stewardship policy then follows, by outlining how it aims to use stewardship to achieve its purpose. The policy should cover not only engagement, but also monitoring – in particular, *investors should have a policy for what will cause them to sell*. This helps ensure that selling isn't a knee-jerk reaction to short-term earnings, and recognises that selling can be an effective stewardship mechanism. Some investors currently have a policy on generalised divestment, such as selling (or never buying) tobacco companies, but few have a policy on specialised divestment – long-term, intangible factors that will cause them to exit. (Note that an investor's policy might be to rarely sell, but to continue to engage even when management is intransigent.)*

For example, related purpose and stewardship statements might be:

Purpose: 'To create long-term real returns by investing in enterprises with high-quality intangible assets that are not priced by the market, and supporting enterprises in building these intangibles.'

Stewardship policy: 'We believe that prioritising short-term profit can discourage investments in intangible assets that drive long-term returns, such as marketing, human capital and innovation. We thus pay particular attention to evaluating the quality of an enterprise's intangibles, and track not just the amount of money spent, but also the output of such investment. We engage routinely with management – sometimes in collaboration with other investors – to encourage intangible asset creation, with a focus on organic rather than inorganic growth. We commit to evaluating management performance on the basis of intangible asset growth rather than short-term earnings. We will exit companies that are investing insufficiently in intangible assets and where engagement with management fails to produce change.'

Within the broad mechanisms of monitoring and engagement, there's a variety of possible approaches. Monitoring may involve ESG screens based on observable characteristics (e.g. board independence), or in-depth analysis of an enterprise's strategy and stakeholder capital. Engagement can vary by *form* – informed voting, private meetings with management or (if needed) confrontational public activism. It can also differ by *theme*. An index fund may prioritise a generalised theme – for example, State Street seeks to increase diversity in senior management. An active fund may focus on a specialised theme, such as

---

* While an asset manager will have an overall stewardship policy, individual funds may have different approaches. An index fund will undertake less specialised engagement than an active fund. But each fund should carry some traits of the general policy, just as a manufacturer's different products should all fit within its purpose. Stewardship policies (and, as we'll discuss later, stewardship performance) should be reported at the fund level, since savers buy funds, not asset managers. To minimise the reporting required, a fund can cross-reference the asset manager's general policy when defining its own approach.

improving capital allocation, which requires a deep understanding of each company.

As with purpose, stewardship must be a practice, not just a policy. For companies, we started with external communication. For asset managers, we'll start with internal embedding, to familiarise readers outside the investment industry with how it operates.

Embedding Stewardship

Recall that Chapter 6 highlighted three features of hedge funds that make them particularly effective at engagement – their portfolio concentration, financial incentives and resources. These same features also enhance monitoring. We stressed that these dimensions aren't unique to hedge funds, so the first step to embedding stewardship is to adopt these features. Starting with *portfolio concentration*, an investor that claims to be active should truly be active, holding only a small number of companies. Its default position should be not to own a stock, rather than to own it because it's part of the benchmark. Then, every company is a conviction holding, whose long-term story the investor either believes in or believes that it can turn around.

Some investors argue that a concentrated portfolio exposes their clients to too much risk. But if a client has chosen an active fund, it believes in the manager's stock selection ability and is paying for him to use it. A client that wants more diversification than what the active fund provides can simply allocate more of its portfolio to index funds. Instead, these arguments are often out of self-interest – a fund manager doesn't want to risk underperformance, as it may lead to client withdrawals or him being replaced.

The second feature is *incentives*. Just as Chapter 5 stressed that leaders should be paid like owners, the same is true for fund managers. Ajay Khorana, Henri Servaes and Lei Wedge show that when a manager owns 1% more of his fund, risk-adjusted performance rises by 3%. Chris Clifford and Laura Lindsey found that mutual funds with performance-sensitive fees lead to CEOs also receiving more performance-sensitive pay, and the companies they invest in improve profitability more in situations where engagement is likely to be effective. Ownership stakes should be locked up for the long term, since stewardship may take several years to pay off.

The third characteristic is the *resources* an investor dedicates to stewardship. One resource is the stewardship team. This is a specialist department that doesn't manage money, but focuses on engagement and monitoring. What's important isn't just the size of this team, but also its prominence. At Legal & General Investment Management (LGIM), the UK's largest institutional investor, stewardship head Sacha Sadan sits on the board and reports directly to the CEO.

Stewardship resources aren't just confined to the stewardship department. Just like the *integrated thinking* we stressed for purpose in Chapter 8, stewardship should be integrated into an asset management's investment process. Fund managers should (and sometimes do) have explicit responsibility for stewardship and be evaluated for it, and lead voting decisions and engagements jointly with stewardship departments. One asset manager requires all graduate hires to rotate through the stewardship department so that, when they become fund managers, they're able to direct stewardship efforts. However, there remains significant room for improvement in integration. A recent survey found that only 23% of investors have stewardship capabilities embedded throughout the organisation.

While a concentrated portfolio, incentives and resources lay the ground for stewardship, an investor still has to do it. The next two sections provide guidance on practising effective monitoring and engagement.

Effective Monitoring

Critics of the stock market accuse it of focusing excessively on short-term financial performance. But simply observing the astronomical valuations of tech companies, such as Facebook and Amazon, suggests that reality is more nuanced than this caricature. Their prices are several orders of magnitude higher than their current earnings, so the market must be incorporating some long-term factors.

Monitoring can only improve investor returns if it's based on long-term factors that aren't incorporated by the market. Then, when the investor trades on this information, he'll put it into the stock price and cause it to more closely reflect long-term value – a form of stewardship. There's evidence that intangible assets that directly generate profits, such as a strong brand, are incorporated in the stock price.

However, Chapter 4 showed that intangible assets that directly generate social value, such as employee satisfaction, are only partially valued. Effective monitoring thus requires investors to evaluate stocks according to how much social value they create, not how much profit – including whether companies are delivering on their stated purpose.

This requires a shift in thinking. ESG metrics should be taken seriously by all investors, even those whose only goal is financial performance. While 'socially responsible investors' use ESG metrics to pursue (and potentially trade-off) both social and financial returns, 'responsible investors' may employ such information even if they have purely financial objectives, based on the evidence of Chapter 4. Indeed, even quant funds (which use statistics to maximise purely financial returns) are starting to take stakeholder capital into account. A 2016 *Financial Times* article was entitled 'Quants are the new ethical investors'.

Not only can ESG metrics drive higher returns, but they're also increasingly available and reliable. Just as the *Fortune* list measures employee satisfaction on a consistent, comparable basis, other providers do so for different stakeholder metrics – Interbrand estimates brand value, Trucost captures environmental impact and MSCI ESG, Sustainalytics, Thomson Reuters ESG, Bloomberg ESG and Arabesque S-Ray capture a wide range of societal dimensions. *Forbes* publishes lists of the World's Most Ethical Companies and the World's Most Sustainable Companies, compiled by research firms Ethisphere and Corporate Knights, respectively. In my 2015 TEDx talk, 'The Social Responsibility of Business', I mentioned four ESG data sources, and asked the audience to put their hand up if they'd heard of all of them. Not a single person did.

And that's precisely the point. Most investors haven't heard of these measures, even though they're rigorous and objective. So they're unlikely to be priced by the stock market, and thus investors can gain a competitive advantage by using them. I've since given this talk dozens of times, including to investor audiences, but rarely see a hand.

But monitoring must go even beyond ESG metrics. As discussed in Chapter 4, some investors use them in a box-ticking manner, and screen out a company if it doesn't tick a particular box, regardless of its other qualities. But underperformance in one dimension doesn't reduce returns if the dimension is immaterial, and it may be outweighed by strong performance elsewhere. Traditional ESG measures don't capture excellence, which Chapter 8 argued is the main way a company grows the pie.

Thus, to assess whether an enterprise creates social value, an investor must move from screening to integration. It needs to consider both the firm's positive and negative effects on each member – investors and each stakeholder – and weighs them by their materiality. This is called a 'net benefit test', and it answers the question 'Does the company deliver a net benefit to society?' Doing so requires going beyond analysing data and instead visiting companies and meeting management, just as Peter Lynch did with Chrysler. The UK think tank Blueprint for Better Business has devised a list of eight questions that investors can ask to assess purpose and whether it's being put into practice.

Blueprint for Better Business questions

Blueprint for Better Business recommends the following eight questions to help investors identify whether a company is purpose-led.

1. In simple terms, what is the company in business to deliver and for whom? How does that differentiate you?
2. What does success look like and how do you measure and review it?
3. How does your pay policy link to long-term success?
4. How are your board discussions and agenda anchored to your purpose? Can you give some examples of how your purpose has changed your decisions?
5. What positive and negative impacts does your company have on society? How are you maintaining your 'licence to operate'?
6. How are your people? Can you give examples of how you have responded to specific concerns?
7. Which external relationships are most important to achieving your purpose (e.g. customer, supplier, regulatory)? What key measures do you use to assess the strength of these?
8. [For Chairs] How do you as a board know you are doing a good job?

Investors may have their own questions to add to this list – for example, 'how do you manage trade-offs between different stakeholders?' and 'how do you decide which investments in stakeholders to turn down?' Regardless of what questions they come up with, they should have a framework to evaluate whether management is truly committed to creating social value – and doing so in a way that's also consistent with long-term profitability.

A net benefit assessment is rarely simple, as we saw when discussing Amazon in Chapter 4. There's no clear answer to whether Amazon benefits society overall – it creates substantial value for some stakeholders, but arguably extracts value from others. Rather than making social criteria unattractive, this ambiguity should make them more attractive as other investors may make the wrong call. Shortly before its collapse in 2001, Enron was lauded for its CSR – it won six awards in a single year from the US Environmental Protection Agency and a corporate conscience award from the US Council on Economic Priorities. If responsible investing could be implemented simply by box-ticking, any investor could do it. Indeed, a computer would be most effective, removing the need for human fund managers. Similarly, there's no clear answer to whether a stock will be a winner based on traditional factors such as strategy and management quality – which is why conventional investors use them, hoping their assessment is more accurate than the market's.

But the ambiguity of a net benefit test also has its downsides. It means that it's almost always possible to justify a company as creating social value, because nearly every company does well on at least one stakeholder issue. A fund manager might choose a stock based on its short-term profit potential and then argue that it's pie-growing by highlighting the dimensions on which it outperforms. You can rationalise almost any investment, but in the words of psychologist Stephen Covey, you might be telling yourself 'rational lies'.

One way to reduce this risk is for the investor's stewardship policy to stipulate what will cause it to sell or prevent it from investing. Some investors may view certain issues, such as climate change or gender diversity, as 'red lines' that apply to all companies. Others will place greater weight on materiality, and so the key criteria will depend on the enterprise's industry and business model. Whatever divestment policy the investor adopts, it should ensure that it only sells companies based on this policy, not short-term profit. Equally importantly, it should indeed sell when these lines are crossed and engagement is unsuccessful, rather than being asleep at the wheel.

A second way to reduce the risk of 'rational lies' is to have an external advisory committee; I serve on one for Royal London Asset

Management (RLAM). We provide an outside opinion on whether a stock passes RLAM's net benefit test, as well as what the test criteria should be – for example, whether being in the alcohol industry or having a high CEO pay ratio should be a 'red line'. Most of these questions are nuanced and specialist, so a diversity of perspectives and expertise is valuable. The outcome of these discussions could be published in a position paper, clarifying an investor's stance to savers. To highlight the tricky nature of these issues and the potential value of outside opinions, here are examples of topics we've discussed:

- Does genetic modification create value for society? Modified seeds may escape into the wild and disrupt biodiversity, or they may discourage farming of organic or non-modified foods. But with millions of people in the world starving, is it irresponsible not to use the best technology?
- Do Chinese tech firms create value for society? They censor, but is this simply a cost of doing business in China? Is censorship even bad, if citizens are aware that it happens and so are sceptical about what's reported? In the West, there's little censorship, but some people then take news at face value.
- Do enterprises that pay low taxes create value for society? Are they splitting the pie by locating their activities in low-tax countries purely to maximise profit, or simply responding to tax incentives to invest in underdeveloped areas or undertake R&D?
- Does artificial intelligence create value for society? Might robots eliminate jobs, or instead allow colleagues to be reallocated to more fulfilling jobs? What safeguards are companies adopting to reduce the risk that robots get out of control?
- Does social media create value for society? It connects people to friends throughout the world and allows sharing of photos, stories and news. But it creates the potential for cyber-bullying, addiction, data leakage and echo chambers.
- Should evaluations of a firm's social responsibility be absolute or relative (to either its peers or itself in the past)? If a company is in a controversial industry but best-in-class, is it investible? If a company has a poor social record but is improving, is it investible?

Why should asset managers bother answering such tricky questions? First, as discussed in Chapter 4, creating societal value typically enhances returns, whereas stakeholder scandals can wreck a company. Thinking about these issues is sensible risk management.

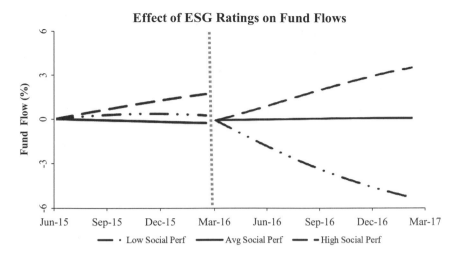

Figure 9.2

Second, savers care about more than just financial returns. To show this, we can't just point to the substantial growth in SRI funds over recent years – this growth could be due to these funds' financial rather than social performance. Sam Hartzmark and Abby Sussman were able to isolate how saver demand is affected by social performance alone, by cleverly exploiting a change to information on funds' social performance that didn't affect information on their financial returns. In March 2016, Morningstar unexpectedly published social performance rankings on more than 20,000 mutual funds, based on Sustainalytics's ESG ratings of the underlying stocks that each fund held. The impact is shown in Figure 9.2.

Before March 2016, there was only a weak relationship between social performance and fund flows. But over the next eleven months, the differences were substantial – top-ranked funds enjoyed inflows of 4% of fund size ($24 to $32 billion) and bottom-ranked funds suffered outflows of 6% ($12 to $15 billion). Strikingly, the vast majority of the 20,000 funds weren't marketed as sustainable funds – yet savers still cared about their social performance.

Effective Engagement

We'll now turn from practising effective monitoring to effective engagement. A major way in which investors engage is by voting on issues such as new directors, auditor appointments and pay. To save having to tackle each issue from scratch, most investors develop house policies – for example, to vote against director nominations that don't bring female board representation up to a given target. LGIM holds a stakeholder roundtable event each year to obtain insights from external constituencies (such as academics, consultants, asset owners and stakeholder representatives) that inform its house policies. While valuable, house policies shouldn't be automatically followed, because they may not be appropriate in every situation. Sometimes a potential director might have the ideal skill set to complement the existing board, even if he doesn't help meet a gender target.

Since analysing a director's record or pay package requires expertise, many investors use input from proxy advisors such as Institutional Shareholder Services (ISS) or Glass Lewis. Like a house policy, independent advice has value, but shouldn't be followed automatically. The best way to use it may be as a red flag – to follow a proxy advisor's recommendation if it coincides with the house policy, and focus the investor's limited time on cases where they conflict.

And engagement is far more than just voting. If an investor has voted against management, it should tell the company why, so that it can address the shortcomings. Even if the investor has voted in favour, it may not agree with every aspect of a proposal and can voice its concerns. More effective than engaging after a vote is to do so beforehand. Rather than voting against, an investor can discuss its concerns privately with management, so that it ends up making proposals that the investor is willing to support.

Just as some companies only reach out to investors in an emergency, some investors only engage when a company is in severe difficulties. But prevention is better than cure. This involves meeting with management on a regular basis even if there are no fires to be fought, and providing positive as well as negative feedback – else a company may make changes without knowing that investors support the status quo. But while engagement should be routine, investors must be careful not to micro-manage the enterprise. Leaders have far more expertise and information about day-to-day operational decisions. Instead, investors' main value-add is on long-term issues such as strategy, intangible investment and purpose – issues for which an outside perspective is particularly useful. For example, if a CEO has proposed a major investment, shareholders can evaluate whether the principles of multiplication, comparative advantage and materiality from Chapter 3 are satisfied. Similarly, while a company may be in certain businesses by historical default, investors can challenge management on whether it still has a comparative advantage in each one. Recall from Chapter 6 that selling non-core plants or patents creates value not only for the vendor, but also for society, as they're more productive under new ownership.

In addition to frequency, the theme of engagement is also important. Policymakers or citizens may pressure investors to engage on pie-splitting issues such as pay levels. But more important are pie-growing issues such as excellence and purpose. How is the enterprise ensuring continued excellence? How is it investing in innovation and its workforce, and responding to long-term challenges from technology and climate change? What is the enterprise's purpose and what has it deliberately omitted from its purpose? What steps is it taking to embed purpose internally and communicate it externally?

Resources to guide investor monitoring, mentioned in the last section, can also inform engagement. The Blueprint for Better Business questions can shape discussions on purpose; an advisory committee can highlight the priority environmental issues to engage upon, informed by both science and saver demand. Focusing Capital on the Long-Term has provided a list of questions, informed by stewardship codes and external experts, that investors can ask themselves internally to ensure that they're undertaking both monitoring and engagement effectively.

But the greatest resource may be other investors. A single investor may have too small a stake to make engagement worthwhile, and too few votes to make the enterprise take notice. Collective engagement, where several investors work together, addresses both problems. Canada's *Globe and Mail* wrote: 'It's one thing to feel the scorn of a 3% shareholder; it's another to face down 10 institutions holding half your float.' The UN Principles for Responsible Investment Collaboration Platform, the Canadian Coalition for Good Governance and the UK's Investor Forum are three frameworks for collective engagement. They are described in the Appendix, along with recent evidence of their success.

If collective engagement is effective, why don't investors work together more frequently? One reason is the pie-splitting mentality – viewing other investors as a benchmark to be beaten. Then, an investor sees his ideas on how to improve an enterprise as his own intellectual property, to be jealously guarded. But if investors don't work together, all lose from missed opportunities to grow the pie.

Another barrier is the view that different investors have different objectives, and so can't be allies. For example, activist hedge funds are allegedly short-term due to their high turnover, but index funds are long-term. Larry Fink, CEO of leading index provider BlackRock, cautioned: 'activists are trying to improve the company, in most cases, in the short term because they improve the company and then leave . . . we are not going to leave'.

But Chapter 6 showed that hedge funds make changes with long-term benefits. It pointed out the common contrast between high- and low-turnover investors is a false dichotomy, because an investor's holding period is different from its orientation. As activist Paul Singer argues, 'This divisive framing is objectively false and has done harm to the goal of generating sustainable returns for all investors.' All investors benefit from improved profitability, productivity and innovation – the pie-growing changes we saw in Chapter 6.

Since index funds have significant voting power, hedge fund engagements are much more likely to succeed if they get index funds' support. Activist investor Nelson Peltz will fly over to discuss a potential activism campaign with Sacha Sadan, the stewardship head of LGIM, which predominantly runs index funds. The need to partner with index funds helps ensure that engagement benefits all investors. Indeed, the evidence suggests that such a partnership is effective. Recall from Chapter 6 that Ian Appel, Todd Gormley and Don Keim used a regression discontinuity approach, involving Russell index inclusion, and found that index funds improve governance. A second study by these authors uses the same methodology to show that index funds allow hedge funds to run more aggressive campaigns – in particular, those in which they seek board representation – and increase campaign success. Successful engagements also increase firm value, but there's no evidence that they raise pay-outs or debt – outcomes often interpreted as being short-termist.

Communicating Stewardship

After defining an investor's stewardship policy and embedding it internally, the third step is to communicate it externally. Reporting starts with the policy itself. For monitoring, the investor should explain what factors it will pay particular attention to when deciding whether to buy, hold or sell a stock, and relatedly what will cause it to divest. It may also specify what dimensions it will choose not to monitor, if it views them as less relevant for long-term value. The engagement policy includes the *themes* the investor will prioritise and the *form* engagement will take – including the circumstances in which it will consider collaborating with other investors or escalating (and what escalation may involve). For voting, it can disclose any 'house' voting guidelines and its approach to the use of proxy advisors.

Equally important is to report outcomes – how much the policy has been put into practice. Let's start with voting. Most investors report the frequency of votes against management, broken down by theme. But of potentially more interest (and reported by some investors) is how often they vote against proxy advisor recommendations or house policy, to ensure that neither are used mechanically, as well as their voting rationale – just like companies in Chapter 8, combining numbers with narratives can be particularly telling. Turning to engagement, an investor could report how many company meetings it held and how often it discussed each theme. Since these numbers may reflect engagement frequency rather than quality, more informative might be case studies of successful engagement. Such examples may inspire savers – both institutions and citizens – by showing how the asset manager is stewarding their money.

While many investors already report on their voting and engagement, few do so for monitoring. For each major disposal, an investor could explain what caused it to sell and whether this reason is consistent with its disposal policy. Conversely, it might report cases where monitoring led to the investor buying or retaining a stake despite poor short-term financial performance. It could discuss each major holding and explain why it has continued to own it (if doing so doesn't give away proprietary information to competitors), to ensure that holding is an active rather than default decision.

Financial reporting could also be revolutionised. In addition to reporting fund performance – performance of the stocks a fund held onto – it could disclose the subsequent performance of shares it sold. This holds the investor accountable for selling prematurely, and rewards it for far-sighted divestment. Investors might also stop reporting certain traditional statistics. Just as some enterprises no longer disclose quarterly earnings, investors could report only long-term and not short-term performance.

We now turn to defining, embedding and communicating stewardship for the rest of the investment chain. For brevity, we'll explain how asset owners and investment consultants can hold asset managers accountable for stewardship in the Appendix. Instead, we'll discuss proxy advisors and equity analysts here because their stewardship roles are rather different.

Proxy Advisors

Proxy advisors give investors voting recommendations, which are highly influential. A negative ISS say-on-pay recommendation reduces voting support by 25% in the US and 10% to 15% in the UK. This evidence suggests that some investors – who are paid high fees by savers, in part to undertake stewardship – aren't actually practising it, but outsourcing it to a third-party agency. That's rational if proxy advisors have specialist expertise, but there are several potential concerns.

First, proxy advisors have to make recommendations on thousands of companies in a short space of time (typically April, when most annual general meetings take place). So there's a danger that their advice is one-size-fits-all.* Even their recommendations on generalised issues, where little tailoring is needed, may be flawed due to faulty methodologies. For example, ISS calculates pay-for-performance ignoring the incentives provided by existing shareholdings, a major omission as discussed in Chapter 5. In a rather ironic example, ISS recommended voting against the 2017 pay package of Willis Towers Watson, a leading expert on executive reward, and made basic errors when doing so.

An even more serious issue is the potential for conflicts of interest. Some proxy advisors sell not only voting recommendations to investors, but also consulting services to firms, to help them devise proposals that investors are likely to vote for. They may be biased towards consulting clients – either to thank them for the consulting

---

* A finance professor told me of a student who interned with a major proxy advisor and was surprised that they had only two full-time professionals who covered the entire Benelux region. The professionals reassured him, 'don't worry, we have tons of interns'. While anecdotal, this highlights the risk that proxy advisors have box-ticking guidelines that junior staff use to code recommendations.

business, or to show that its consulting helps design successful proposals. The Ohio Public Employees Retirement System dropped ISS's services, commenting that 'the thing that tipped us was [ISS's] actual or perceived conflicts due to the corporate consulting'.

Are these concerns valid? Let's look at the evidence. Tao Li studied potential conflicts with ISS by examining votes at 26,304 shareholder meetings. Simply showing that ISS is more likely to recommend voting 'for' consulting clients doesn't suggest bias, because it could be that consulting genuinely improved proposal quality. So Tao looked at the market entry of Glass Lewis, which provides no consulting services. Afterwards, ISS issued 'against' recommendations much more frequently – particularly for larger firms that were most likely to have been ISS clients. These findings suggest that, before Glass Lewis's entry, ISS may have been more favourable towards its consulting clients.

Also supporting a conflict explanation, Glass Lewis's entry had a greater impact on more complex votes where it's easier to be biased (e.g. on proposals related to governance and pay), rather than 'no-brainer' votes where bias might appear blatant (e.g. uncontested director elections). Importantly, any potential bias has real outcomes – it matters. To zone in on proposals where conflicts may have been pivotal, Tao compares proposals that pass by a narrow margin to those that narrowly fail. At firms with proposals that narrowly pass, executives have higher peer-adjusted pay, higher growth in pay and more cash payments – suggesting that any bias allows managers to be overpaid.

What's the remedy? The same three-step framework as for asset managers. The first step is for a proxy advisor to define its purpose and approach to stewardship. Doing so should spur it to recognise its role in promoting stewardship across the investment industry. Starting with purpose, do proxy advisors see themselves as an outsourcing service, providing asset managers with recommendations that they can automatically follow?* Or is their purpose to provide an expert outside opinion that feeds into clients' voting decisions, but is only one input? Turning to the stewardship approach, an advisor should have a clear research methodology to determine its recommendations and, if relevant, a house voting policy.

---

* Such a role can still add value, since some investors don't have in-house expertise in voting.

The next step is to put these policies into practice. Let's say a proxy advisor sees its role as providing an expert outside opinion. Then, for an issue that requires strategic judgment, it should only highlight the pros and cons and label the issue as 'For Strategic Judgment' rather than providing a recommendation. It can subject its most important screening methodologies to external review, to ensure it uses state-of-the-art techniques.

Finally, advisors should publicly disclose their research methodologies and house policies. Again, communication involves more than just reporting. Proxy advisors should explain to enterprises why they've made a particular recommendation, and consider giving the company advance notice of a negative recommendation to allow it to correct any factual inaccuracies. Sometimes a company asks to meet a proxy advisor to explain the rationale for a seemingly unusual proposal, but is turned down. It's difficult to see how such a refusal is responsible stewardship.

Equity Analysts

Equity analysts make buy and sell recommendations which substantially influence investor trading. A buy recommendation leads to stock prices increasing by 3% in the first three days and continuing to drift up 2.4% in the next month. In contrast, a sell recommendation reduces stock prices by 4.7% in the short term and 9.1% over the following six months. But stewardship codes don't consider analysts as having any role in stewardship, because they don't recognise the importance of trading for stewardship. If investors trade on short-term earnings, because they're influenced by analyst recommendations which focus on earnings, companies will focus on profits, not investment. Moreover, trading affects engagement. If shareholders don't invest in a stock due to analyst recommendations, they won't have any votes or standing to engage with it.

Existing regulation (such as the US Global Settlement) has focused on addressing analyst bias, such as an analyst being over-optimistic about clients of the bank he works for. But this isn't enough. Even if an analyst isn't biased, his recommendations may be based on short-term factors.

Analysts particularly influence trading through their earnings forecasts. Missing a forecast reduces the stock price by 3.5% and causes the CEO's bonus to fall. In Chapter 6, we discussed the survey by Graham, Harvey and Rajgopal which learned that 80% of Chief Financial Officers (CFOs) would cut investment to avoid missing an earnings benchmark. Benchmarks might be past earnings, yet the survey found that 73.5% of CFOs considered analyst forecasts an important benchmark. A separate study by Stephen Terry documented that firms that just meet analyst earnings forecasts have 2.6% lower R&D growth than those that just miss, suggesting that CEOs cut R&D to hit the forecast.

Analyst reports do go beyond forecasting earnings. They discuss long-term factors such as strategy, market outlook and management quality – but typically only those with a clear link to profits rather than stakeholder value, so they may ignore externalities such as spillovers from intangible assets. Indeed, studies find that analysts don't fully value intangible assets, particularly in R&D-intensive firms where intangibles are particularly material. As a result, when the number of analysts covering a stock falls, both the number and quality of patents rise.

Let's apply the same three-step framework used for asset managers. The first is for analysts* to define their purpose, which involves acknowledging their role in stewardship. An analyst's purpose might be to promote responsible investment by investors. If so, its approach to stewardship involves scrutinising a company's impact on society, and this assessment significantly influencing its investment recommendations.

The second step is for analysts to embed their stewardship approach internally. This involves ensuring they have adequate resources to evaluate an enterprise's stakeholder capital. While equity research departments previously had different teams covering each industry, most now also have a specialist SRI unit. Its main clients are socially responsible investors, but we've stressed that societal factors matter to all shareholders. An analyst should have processes to ensure that societal impact enters all reports, not just those by the SRI team.

The final step is external communication. The Global Settlement requires analyst reports to include a breakdown of their buy, hold and sell recommendations across all stocks, so that investors can evaluate if they're overly optimistic. Similarly, analysts could report how often they give a buy recommendation despite a pessimistic forecast of

---

* Here we use 'analyst' to refer to either an equity research department of an investment bank, or an independent equity research company.

quarterly earnings. This will allow investors to assess the extent to which analyst recommendations are driven by short-term forecasts.

The above three steps will help analysts to acknowledge and fulfil their stewardship responsibilities. But it's also important for regulators and the rest of the investment chain to acknowledge them too. Regulators should include equity analysts when contemplating stewardship reforms, and investors should consider analysts' stewardship impact when deciding which ones to particularly heed. The attitudinal shift required is substantial, since analysts are currently ignored in stewardship discussions. But it's an important one, because analyst recommendations ripple through investor trading decisions and ultimately affect firm behaviour.

In a Nutshell

- Stewardship is the responsibility of the entire investment chain – not just asset managers, but also asset owners and service providers. Improving stewardship is critical to increasing long-term returns and ensuring the legitimacy of the investment management industry.
- An investor should pursue stewardship similarly to how an enterprise pursues purpose. It starts by *defining* its stewardship policy clearly, *embedding* this policy into the investment process in an integrated manner, and *communicating* both policies and outcomes externally.
- A stewardship definition should include a divestment policy and the *form* and *themes* of engagement. The chosen approach to stewardship should follow from the asset manager's purpose and thus be based on the principle of comparative advantage.
- Embedding stewardship involves ensuring that asset managers have large stakes, long-term financial incentives and stewardship resources.
  - Effective monitoring assesses the value an enterprise creates for society – information that's likely not in the current stock price.
  - Effective voting is informed by proxy advisor recommendations and house policy, but also considers an enterprise's unique circumstances.
  - Effective engagement focuses on pie-growing (e.g. purpose and strategy) rather than pie-splitting issues (e.g. the level of pay), and may involve collective engagement with other investors and an escalation mechanism.

- Communicating stewardship involves quantitative metrics on voting behaviour and portfolio concentration. The most valuable communication may be qualitative – engagement priorities, monitoring themes and case studies of successful engagements or divestments.
- Proxy advisors' contribution to stewardship can be strengthened by ensuring adequate resourcing to provide tailored recommendations, implementing policies to address potential conflicts, subjecting their screening methodologies to external scrutiny and viewing their purpose as an advisory rather than outsourcing service.
- Equity analysts can play a key role in stewardship by basing their recommendations more on companies' intangible assets and social performance rather than short-term earnings.

10 CITIZENS
HOW INDIVIDUALS CAN ACT AND SHAPE BUSINESS, RATHER THAN BE ACTED UPON

In this chapter, we'll explore how citizens can help grow the pie. They shape business through playing the following roles:

- Members. As investors, colleagues and customers, citizens can hold enterprises to account by choosing which ones to invest in, work for and buy from.
- Policymakers. Only a few individuals directly design policy. But all citizens affect policy as voters (and, in some cases, writing to policymakers or responding to public consultations). We'll discuss the role of both hard legislation and soft codes of conduct.
- Influencers. These include the media, think-tanks and those viewed as experts. It also includes citizens who influence by the content that they share, purchase or comment on. Influencers can hold individual companies to account, and guide policy by shaping public opinion about business in general.*

This classification highlights that citizens have much more power to change business than commonly believed. A single colleague, Sherron Watkins, blew the whistle on accounting fraud in Enron,

---

* As with many taxonomies in this book, the lines are blurred. Codes of conduct can be adopted by industry participants themselves without policymaker involvement. Enterprises and investors can also be influencers.

alerting CEO Kenneth Lay to accounting irregularities and then testifying before the US House of Representatives and Senate. A single citizen, Dan O'Sullivan, started the 'Delete Uber' campaign on Twitter. When the New York Taxi Workers Alliance called a strike to protest against Donald Trump's travel ban on Muslim countries, Uber removed surge pricing, which would normally lead to higher fares. Dan and the campaign argued that Uber was trying to profit from the strike, and 500,000 customers supported it by deleting their accounts.* And citizens can even propose policies without being legislators. The Swiss referendum against rip-off salaries, mentioned in Chapter 5, was launched by Thomas Minder, an entrepreneur who made toothpaste and mouthwash for airlines. We'll call this power *agency*: people's capacity to act independently and influence their environment, rather than being acted upon. As the 14th Dalai Lama once said, 'If you think you are too small to make a difference, try sleeping with a mosquito.'

Let's first discuss how citizens can grow the pie in their role as investors, colleagues and customers.

Members

In Chapter 6, we discussed how institutional investors have two stewardship powers – monitoring (deciding which firms to own) and engagement (changing the behaviour of firms they do own). These same powers apply to individual investors, colleagues and customers.

The first source of agency is the freedom to choose which enterprises to be members of – those whose values they share. We saw in Chapter 4 how investors should select stocks in part based on their contribution to society; doing so improves not only social but also financial returns. In Chapter 9 (and the Appendix), we recommend that savers select asset managers according to their stewardship perform-ance. The UK charity ShareAction, which promotes saver engagement, ranks mutual funds on this dimension to help such selection.

Many citizens' biggest investment decision isn't a financial one, but who to work for. They have the power to turn down a job offer,

---

* Other citizens claimed that Uber cut prices to help customers, as it often does during emergencies, and so the boycott was unjustified. Regardless of whether the campaign was justified, this example shows the power of individuals to substantially affect firm value.

even if its salary and title are attractive, if the employer has a reputation for exploiting its customers and suppliers, damaging the environment or mistreating female and minority colleagues. Since employees are the key asset in nearly every company, the threat of losing talented staff to rivals is a powerful deterrent to pie-splitting behaviour.

A firm that exploits society may not only clash with an employee's own value system, but also be unsuccessful in the long run and jeopardise his job. Indeed, some company collapses were potentially predictable ahead of time by studying social performance. For example, Business Insider's October 2012 list of '13 Companies that May Be Riskier than You Think', based on ESG ratings by the data provider GMI, cautioned against Wells Fargo due to numerous governance issues. The next year, a *Los Angeles Times* article reported that 'relentless pressure to sell has battered employee morale and led to ethical breaches ... To meet quotas, employees have opened unneeded accounts for customers, ordered credit cards without customers' permission, and forged client signatures' – but little attention was paid to these revelations at the time. In September 2016, the Consumer Financial Protection Bureau announced that Wells Fargo had opened 2 million fake bank and credit card accounts. The fines and lost reputation caused the bank to announce plans to close 400 of its 6,000 branches and cut up to 10% of its workforce. Even if a worker is successful at finding a new job, he suffers a salary cut. Boris Groysberg, Eric Lin and George Serafeim found that senior managers who left firms that engaged in financial misconduct earn 4% less than their peers – even if they left before the scandal broke out. Simply having a tarnished firm on your CV harms your future earnings potential.

The same agency is enjoyed by customers. Rather than choosing products based solely on price, they can buy from enterprises that reflect what they'd like to see in the world – just as many already purchase organic or locally sourced food despite the greater cost. This need not require substantial analysis. Chapter 9 mentioned several freely available data sources on a company's social performance, which can be used by citizens in their roles as investors and colleagues. There are additional resources tailored to customers. For example, the Good Shopping Guide and Ethical Consumer websites allow you to choose a product (ranging from bananas to kettles to insurance) and then see environmental and social ratings of different brands. The Nudge for Change app lets you select which issues matter most to you, and then rates a retailer on those issues as soon as you walk into its store. With Buycott, a customer scans a product barcode and learns about its societal impact; GoodOnYou gives similar information when entering a brand name.

In addition to deciding which company to buy from, an even more powerful source of agency is the freedom not to buy at all, or to buy a different type of product. For example, choosing not to upgrade your phone, using methods of transport other than air travel and resisting 'fast fashion' purchases all have significant positive impacts on the environment. Websites such as the WWF Footprint Calculator, REAP Petite and CarbonFootprint.com allow households to calculate their carbon footprint, thus informing them on how best to reduce it.

The second source of agency is citizens' ability to engage with enterprises they're members of. As we saw in Chapter 4 with Caroline Flammer's study, investors can make shareholder proposals to embed a social orientation. Such proposals can be particularly powerful as companies often justify pie-splitting behaviour as being in investors' interest. Instead, these proposals highlight that investors want enterprises to take stakeholders seriously. Importantly, they can be made by individual as well as institutional investors. In May 2018, retail shareholder Keith Schnip asked McDonald's to issue a report on its efforts to develop substitutes for plastic straws. The proposal was defeated, but still contributed to behaviour change – the following month, McDonald's announced it would phase out plastic straws in the UK and Ireland from 2019.* Moreover, a shareholder proposal at one firm can have spillover effects on an industry or even economy. A 1973 resolution at the oil company Mobil demanded better working conditions for black employees in their South African operations. This raised awareness of apartheid and helped spark the campaign to divest from South Africa, mentioned in Chapter 6.

In addition to formal proposals, shareholders can ask questions at an annual general meeting (AGM). Every night, Abdul Durrant worked hard to clean the London offices of HSBC, including that of chair Sir John Bond. But he struggled to support his five children on his

---

* As with many decisions, it's unlikely that McDonald's decision to phase out plastic straws had a single cause. UK politicians had proposed prohibiting plastic straws earlier in 2018, but the proposal was not implemented until May 2019. Moreover, the fact that McDonald's was one of only a few companies to voluntarily take action suggests that Schnip's shareholder resolution was a contributing factor.

low wages. So Telco, an alliance of charities in East London, bought Abdul a few shares, allowing him to attend HSBC's 2003 AGM. He braved himself to speak up at the meeting and address Sir John, saying, 'I am here on behalf of all the contract staff at HSBC and the families of East London. We receive £5 per hour – a whole £5 per hour! – no pension, and a measly sick pay scheme. In our struggles our children go to school without adequate lunch. We are unable to provide necessary books for their education. School outings in particular they miss out on.' Moved by this plea, Sir John gave HSBC's cleaners a 28% pay rise. At the following year's AGM, Abdul stood up to thank Sir John: 'The cleaners at HSBC are very pleased at your decision to raise our standards and raise our money. I have come here to thank you ... I now have more time with our children and can give them quality time. In the language of the street, they say "big respect"'. This shows the power of a single employee to change the wage policy of a large multinational.

More generally, ShareAction has a team of 'citizen shareholders' that attends AGMs and asks boards to pay the Living Wage. This amount is higher than the legal minimum wage, and calculated to meet basic needs for a worker's family. When ShareAction launched its Living Wage campaign in 2011, only two FTSE 100 enterprises paid the living wage; now the number stands at thirty-seven. Even though it's shareholders who ultimately pay the higher wages, many only want to earn returns from companies whose employees are able to live a dignified life. Moreover, these higher wages typically grow the pie by improving retention and motivation, and aren't at the expense of long-run profits.

Let's now turn to customers. One way they can engage is to protest against irresponsible behaviour and walk away from unresponsive companies. Such boycotts are particularly powerful today as they can spread rapidly on social media. We've discussed the Volkswagen and Uber campaigns which seriously affected the targeted firms, but the impact of a boycott can spread to the rest of the industry. The 1990s saw many demonstrations against sweatshop conditions at Nike factories. Nike responded by acknowledging the issues, improving wages and conditions, and creating the 'Fair Labor Association' with other companies to establish independent monitoring and a code of conduct.

While customer engagement is typically thought of as involving boycotts, their agency extends much further. Customers can also support shareholder proposals. Keith Schnip's resolution came about because the consumer watchdog SumOfUs first launched a petition asking McDonald's to ban plastic straws. After collecting half a million signatures, it asked Keith (who was both a SumOfUs member and a McDonald's shareholder) to submit the resolution on SumOfUs's behalf.

Consumers can also engage by providing feedback on a company's products. This agency is higher today than it has ever been – review websites make it easy to write evaluations, and mean that these evaluations influence other customers as well as the company. Indeed, feedback on sites such as TripAdvisor, Airbnb and Amazon can cause businesses or products to live or die. Customers can also provide input to spur company innovation. After coming close to bankruptcy in 2004, Lego transformed its fortunes to become the world's largest toy company by revenue in 2015. Central to this turnaround was Lego creating the Ambassador Programme to engage with its most avid customers, gaining ideas for new products and helping it refocus current ones.

A final source of agency is customers' exclusive control of a product after purchase. As discussed in Chapter 8, Patagonia runs programmes to repair damaged clothes or resell unwanted items, but customers may not take the time to participate, instead throwing them away out of convenience. Similarly, Hewlett Packard has invested in designing their toner cartridges to be reusable, and pays return shipping. But this initiative can only work if customers take the pie-growing action of packaging and recycling the used cartridges.

As colleagues, engagement involves adopting the same pie-growing mentality that we've stressed for enterprises. Just as companies should create value for stakeholders even if there's no clear link to future profits, employees should create value for the organisation even if it's not explicitly rewarded in their evaluation system.

One example is treatment of co-workers, as discussed at the end of Chapter 8. Importantly, the attitudes of empowerment, investment and reward can be practised by all employees, not just leaders. A colleague doesn't need to accept the culture he finds himself in; he has the power to change it. Almost everyone manages someone else. Even if a worker is the lowest rank in his department, other departments may support his. A colleague can solve simple IT issues himself rather than viewing the IT department's time as freely disposable. If an IT technician has been particularly helpful, a worker can practise the attitude of reward by providing direct feedback to him, as well as finding out who his boss is and relaying it to her.

Agency extends to managing not only subordinates, but also superiors. Those on the bottom rung often believe they have little agency. In my first few months in investment banking, I operated under the assumption that my employer wanted analysts to passively do what they were told. I didn't have any evidence for this assumption; I just believed it because that's what everyone else said. My Chemicals team was next to Transport which was run by Ben, who'd become at 31 the youngest head of any industry group. He once saw me unhappy from over-work and took me to lunch, despite having no official responsibility for me – the attitude of investment. He explained the folly of my assumptions and how the analysts he – and the firm – valued were those that expressed agency, because they could contribute far more than those who just executed.

A few weeks later, I did a valuation analysis that involved fifteen comparable companies. Because one was Syngenta, an agrochemicals firm, my boss (Mark) suggested on the fly to add Monsanto, another agrochemicals firm. I explained that, with fifteen comparable companies already, a sixteenth would add little value to the client, yet require a huge number of calculations to be changed because the comparison group fed into every analysis. Mark's suggestion might appear to convey the attitude of free disposal, but he simply wasn't aware of how much extra work it would cause. In his mind, he paired Syngenta with Monsanto and suggested the latter as a reflex action. I was the only person who could make him aware, and if I didn't, I'd only have myself to blame. Mark listened open-mindedly and then quickly withdrew the suggestion. My first official evaluation, six months in, said: 'Notably for a first-year analyst, Alex has the willingness to speak up and contribute his own views, which is to be encouraged.' This said far more about Mark, and my employer more generally, than me – it showed the great value they placed on agency.

Colleagues' agency extends beyond relationships with co-workers to contributing to the enterprise, regardless of one's position. In Chapter 8, we discussed the Japanese Andon system, where factory workers have the responsibility of checking product quality and the authority to stop the production line. But it's up to them to leverage this responsibility. It's easy – and often cathartic – to complain about a problem, but harder to do something about it. But not much harder. The main barrier is simply adopting the mentality that the pie can be grown, rather than you being stuck with it; sometimes little effort is required to make a suggestion. There are numerous examples of successful innovations that came from an employee idea – both new products, such as Post-It Notes, and new processes, such as New Belgium eliminating its cardboard dividers. In Chapter 1, we discussed how Barry-Wehmiller colleagues came up with an idea not for a new product, but for how to better share the firm-wide pay reductions – some took extra unpaid leave in place of colleagues in greater need of salary.

While it's citizens' duty to use any agency they've been given, it's also an enterprise's duty to unleash it. Companies can create substantial value by harnessing the collective wisdom of their employees and customers, but sometimes don't bother. Just as Frederick Taylor viewed Schmidt as unmotivated and unintelligent, executives sometimes view consumers as being only interested in taking from a company (by buying its products) rather than giving back. Some company websites only provide forms where customers can make complaints, rather than give suggestions. They're implicitly assuming that customers have the pie-splitting mentality – they'll only bother to get in touch to demand compensation, not suggest ideas that benefit both parties.

These assumptions just aren't true. So the first step is for leaders to reset any false perception of their employees and customers as self-interested individuals and instead to see them as citizens – as creative, collaborative, empathetic members of communities. Then, the challenge is to find ways to encourage and channel their citizen energy, tapping into who they naturally are. In Chapter 9, we discussed how many companies now view their employees as partners, and some are doing so with their customers. Patagonia could have only launched the Common Threads Initiative if it trusted its customers to invest their time in repairing its products. Lego's Ambassador Programme sees its customers as an extension of its R&D department. More broadly, organisations such as the New Citizenship Project work with enterprises to unleash the citizenship potential of their customers.

We now turn to how policymakers, or voters with views on policy, can help grow the pie.

Policymakers

One way in which policymakers can support Pieconomics is through regulation. This should be viewed broadly – as any way to 'regulate', or moderate, behaviour. It includes not only legislation, but also codes of conduct, such as Stewardship Codes.

Even though regulation can play a major role in correcting market failure, it often has unintended consequences. We'll first discuss some important caveats to heed when designing regulation. Then, bearing these in mind, we'll describe several ways in which regulation can be beneficial.

The Pie-Growing Mentality

The pie-growing mentality stresses the importance of errors of omission. But regulation is most effective in punishing errors of commission – it's very difficult to fine an enterprise for not creating value. Not only does regulation fail to reduce errors of omission, but it may make them more likely. By trying not to commit an error, a company may omit to innovate.

In December 2017, upon the request of the UK government, the Investment Association (the trade body of the UK investment industry) launched a register of companies who fail to achieve 80% support in a shareholder vote, such as say-on-pay or director elections. It aims to name and shame enterprises which make proposals that investors object to. The register is colloquially referred to as the 'naughty step', given the stigma created, and so companies wish to avoid being featured.

But this 'one-strike-and-you're-out' rule deters innovation. Failure is not only a consequence of innovation (since innovation risks failure), but also a cause (since the lessons from failure can inform future innovation). If a company suggests a pay reform and 'only' gets 75% support, it can listen to the concerns of investors voting against. Indeed, the feedback loop that existed before the register seemed to be working well. Enterprises who fell below the 80% threshold for say-on-pay improved their support by an average of 17 percentage points the next year. Author Matthew Syed calls this 'open-loop thinking' (taking concerns seriously and responding to them), in contrast to 'closed-loop thinking' (assuming that investors must be wrong and pushing ahead with plans regardless).

And it's not clear what such a register aims to achieve in the first place. If there is a benefit to shaming companies, we should shame those who fail to create social value. If there's value to a register on pay, a company should be listed only if it doesn't achieve sufficient support two years in a row. This gives it one chance to respond to investor concerns and allows the feedback loop to work.

Evidence over Anecdote

Evidence can guide regulation in two ways. First, it can diagnose the extent of a problem and whether it indeed requires a solution to begin with. Regulation can sometimes be a knee-jerk reaction to a few bad apples, even if the rest of the apple cart is fresh.

In 1982, William Agee, the CEO of Bendix, received a $4.1 million 'golden parachute' (severance payment) when he was let go after his firm was taken over. The public was furious that someone could get paid for losing his job and demanded action. In response to this single case, Congress in 1984 imposed a high tax rate on golden parachutes above three times salary. This law actually increased the use of golden parachutes – it alerted CEOs to the possibility of being paid for getting fired, so they requested these parachutes. Previously rare, 41% of the largest 1,000 firms had them by 1987, increasing to 70% by 1999. Firms who used to award golden parachutes now increased them to three times salary, because the regulation implied that this is an acceptable level. Others increased salary to get around the regulation.

It might seem that these unintended consequences resulted from this particular regulation being poorly designed. But the lessons are general. There are two major problems with regulation. First, it almost always has unintended consequences. Since it focuses on tangible metrics, it's often prone to manipulation; since it usually sets a limit, it encourages companies to go right up to that limit. These outcomes are like the side effects of medical intervention. In medicine, diagnosis precedes treatment. A patient should only be subjected to invasive surgery, with all its side effects, if his condition is severe. Second, regulation is wide-ranging. Thus, we should only impose regulation, with all its side effects, if the problem is widespread across a large number of companies.

A second role for evidence is to guide the treatment of a problem, as potential solutions may have been tried in other countries. Proposing extreme reforms often gets you lauded as a revolutionary, but is very risky in the absence of evidence that they work. Indeed, research may uncover counterintuitive results that go against what hunches might suggest. When launching her 2016 campaign to become Prime Minister, Theresa May announced the intention to make annual say-on-pay votes binding rather than advisory, to give investors more power to control pay. But looking at eleven countries around the world with say-on-pay laws and comparing those with binding versus advisory votes, the evidence suggests that advisory votes are slightly more effective at both lowering pay and linking it more closely to performance. Despite appearing surprising, this result is quite logical – investors may be reluctant to vote against a pay package if a negative vote is binding and thus likely to cause greater disruption.

Indeed, the plans to make say-on-pay binding were later abandoned, due to the concerns raised during the consultation launched a few months after May became Prime Minister. This responsiveness to evidence is to be applauded. Voters often lambast politicians for doing a U-turn on a proposed policy. But listening to concerns is much better than the closed-loop thinking of ignoring contradictory evidence. If politicians can't hold consultations and subsequently abandon ideas, they may refrain from proposing ideas to begin with – an error of omission. Or they may stick dogmatically to a planned course of action regardless of whatever new evidence they learn.

Tangible Versus Intangible

It's much easier for regulators to hold enterprises to account for tangible measures because they're easier to verify. Regulators can prosecute a company for missing a measure (e.g. not paying the minimum wage) or misreporting it (e.g. fraudulently disclosing earnings).

But the focus on tangible metrics runs two major risks. The first is *quantity over quality*. Since quantity is tangible, but quality isn't, regulation may improve the former, but worsen the latter. In the US, a 2003 law made it a mutual fund's fiduciary duty to vote – but many ended up following proxy advisor recommendations rather than doing their own research. Uninformed votes are arguably worse than not voting at all.

The second is *compliance over commitment*. Regulation may lead to enterprises complying with the tangible metrics highlighted in the policy, rather than committing to its spirit. Some companies may be aware of the benefits of employee satisfaction discussed in Chapter 4.

Unregulated, they aim to improve all dimensions of satisfaction. But pay ratio disclosure may cause them to focus on pay and underweight other dimensions such as working conditions or on-the-job training. Regulation also sends the message that improving employee satisfaction is costly for companies, so you need regulation to force them to do so. This in turn may lead to firms complying to the minimum extent possible.

Ex Ante Versus Ex Post

Regulation aims to correct problems after an action has been taken. But in doing so, it may erode the incentives to take the action to begin with.

As discussed in Chapter 7, there are several influential proposals to limit share buybacks. We've already discussed how these aren't supported by the evidence, which shows that share buybacks are generally associated with higher long-term value. A further problem is the effect on ex ante incentives to issue equity. Restricting buybacks will likely discourage an enterprise from raising money from shareholders in the first place. If it no longer needs this money, it values the option to return it through a share buyback, reducing the amount of dividends it needs to pay in the future. If a law prevented the company from repaying shareholders, it might not issue shares to begin with, causing it to invest less. By analogy, a citizen values the option to repay his credit card balance in full each month, because this lowers his interest charges. If he were only allowed to make the minimum payment, he wouldn't take out the credit card to begin with and spend less.

Similarly, as discussed in Chapter 6, there are several influential proposals to lock in shareholders. Not only are they unsupported by the evidence, which shows that exit is an effective governance mechanism, but also, they ignore the effect on ex ante incentives to invest. If management destroys value and is unresponsive to an investor's engagement, he values the option to exit. Without it, he may be unwilling to invest in the first place – in particular to buy the large stake necessary for effective engagement. The UK Parliament's inquiry into the 2018 failure of outsourcing company Carillion found that investors tried to engage with management as early as 2014, but were unsuccessful due to being given misleading information by management and the board being unresponsive. Many thus sold before the collapse, saving their clients millions of pounds. Without the option to sell and avoid substantial losses, investors may not have bought shares to begin with.

System-Wide Thinking

Criticism of particular business practices sometimes ignores their role in the bigger picture. Patents allow a drug to generate substantial profits, but as Merck CEO Kenneth Frazier stressed in Chapter 3, these profits are necessary to pay for the losses from failed drug development efforts. 'Loyalty' policies hinder an investor, who's already engaged successfully in one firm, from reallocating his capital to turn around another – as ValueAct did after transforming Adobe.

System-wide thinking is also important because reforming one area may be ineffective, or even damaging, without reforming a second – particularly if the first area is a symptom and the second is the underlying problem. Poor pay design is often a symptom of ineffective investor engagement. Assume that, contrary to the 'Evidence over Anecdote' section, there was no evidence that advisory say-on-pay is more effective than binding votes. Even if so, making investor votes binding might worsen pay decisions if they vote in an uninformed manner, for instance because their stakes are too small to make it worthwhile to become informed.

One Size Rarely Fits All

A final concern is that regulation is typically one-size-fits-all. In 1993, US President Bill Clinton sought to limit pay to $1 million by making executive pay above this threshold non-deductible from corporation tax (unless it was performance-related). But what's excessive varies from firm to firm. In a large enterprise (where a talented leader can have substantial effect) in a highly competitive industry (where many firms are bidding for CEOs), $2 million might be fair. In a small enterprise in a non-competitive industry, $500,000 might be appropriate. The regulation led to pay packages being one-size-fits-all: companies that paid salaries below $1 million raised them to exactly $1 million, and those above lowered salaries to $1 million – regardless of firm size or competitive dynamics.

Rather than stipulating a one-size-fits-all level of pay, perhaps the regulator could decide how much pay would be fair in each of the 100 largest firms (just as bank regulators undertake a supervisory review for each bank). Even if the regulator had the resources to implement this idea, it might have imperfect incentives or information. First, it's unlikely to be aligned with the pie. It may be subject to lobbying by firms justifying high pay, or public pressure to crack down on pay even at the expense of value creation. (In contrast, large investors care about both the size of the pie and its division, since both affect investor returns.) Second, blockholders, directors and compensation consultants are likely to be much more informed than the regulator on the CEO labour market and pay design.

Now markets are also imperfect in both incentives and information. Compensation consultants may be conflicted, and investors may be uninformed. So there's certainly a role for regulation, but to improve the incentives and information of market participants, rather than override them. Indeed, having discussed the limitations of regulation, we now discuss how it can help grow the pie. A good principle to guide regulation is: *Is there a market failure, and can regulators improve on this market failure?* Based on this principle, we now discuss several ways regulation can help.

Information

Investors, colleagues and customers are the ultimate regulator of enterprises by walking away from a pie-splitting company. Crucially, their assessment includes intangible dimensions and can be tailored to a firm's circumstances. This requires members to be informed, and regulation can help by mandating the disclosure of relevant information. Since 1998, Norway has required companies to report their environmental impact and mitigation activities; Brazil, Denmark, Hong Kong, India, Malaysia, Singapore, Sweden and the UK are examples of other countries that stipulate or recommend the disclosure of societal impact more generally. Regulation can also help ensure that disclosure is on a comparable basis where possible – for example, that all asset managers report performance net of fees.

Instead of harmonising the reporting methodology, regulation can improve comparability by harmonising the topics being reported.

The UN's Sustainable Development Goals (SDGs) are a collection of seventeen objectives for the world to achieve by 2030. They can be pursued by governments, companies or non-profits; here, we'll discuss their relevance to companies. Importantly, the SDGs aren't prescriptive about how an enterprise should achieve a particular goal, nor do they suggest that it put equal emphasis on each goal – its priorities should depend on its purpose. Instead, the SDGs provide a common language that enterprises can use for reporting, by explaining whether and how they contribute to each objective. This in turn increases comparability to investors and stakeholders, who can see what a firm is doing to achieve the goals that matter most to them.

For example, Danone's purpose is to 'bring health through food to as many people as possible', while Vodafone's purpose is 'to connect everybody to live a better today and build a better tomorrow'. Thus, while both contribute to all goals, they emphasise different ones. One of Danone's priorities is Zero Hunger, which it supports by ensuring access to safe and nutritious food and that it's produced sustainably. While Zero Hunger is not one of Vodafone's core focuses, it still supports it by providing technology and mobile money to improve farmers' productivity. This shows how enterprises with distinctive purposes can undertake quite different activities to contribute to a common goal.

Policymakers can similarly provide a common language to harmonise other areas of reporting. For example, stewardship reporting by investors could be enhanced if regulators devised a unified set of stewardship themes, such as executive pay, capital allocation and climate change. Then, an investor could highlight which themes it prioritises and explain its unique approach to each. It might use say-on-pay-votes to improve executive pay, engage with companies on capital allocation and divest from firms that don't take action on climate change.

Note that more disclosure isn't always better. Tangible metrics may be incomplete, prone to manipulation or encourage a focus on only the disclosed measures. So one role of regulation might be to prohibit or discourage certain disclosures. From November 2015, the EU stopped requiring companies to report quarterly, but many still do. Policymakers could go further with a 'comply-or-explain' provision whereby the default is for companies not to report quarterly unless they explain the reason for doing so. In August 2018, US President Donald Trump asked the SEC to investigate abandoning the quarterly reporting requirement.

Externalities

Pie-growing firms take externalities into account. But many investors and enterprises – even enlightened ones that pursue ESV – don't practise Pieconomics, and thus sometimes ignore externalities. Regulation can address this.

The simplest – and often most effective – solution is to *prohibit* practices whose negative externalities outweigh any benefit, and *mandate* those whose positive externalities outweigh any cost. Examples include several environmental, employment and human rights laws, such as banning child labour and imposing health and safety requirements. Violation should lead to not only companies being fined, but also executives being punished. In Chapter 5, we mentioned that William McGuire had to repay UnitedHealth $468 million for inflating his pay; he was also barred from serving as an officer or director of a public company for ten years. Some Enron executives were imprisoned for fraud or concealing information on Enron's financial position. In both cases, executives extracted value from investors and were punished for doing so. Likewise, similar sanctions can be imposed for harming stakeholders. While the UK Companies Act states that a director 'must . . . have regard to' stakeholders, no director has ever been punished for failing to do so.

Other actions that create negative externalities may also have social benefits (such as air travel), so outright prohibition is unwarranted. Instead, a solution is to assign *property rights* to goods affected by externalities, so that companies take these externalities into account and weigh them up against the benefits. For example, the government can give citizens the right to clean air, or equivalently companies the right to emit pollution up to a limit. Making these rights tradable allows those with a comparative advantage in emissions reduction to sell their permits to those without. This system exists in some territories for carbon emissions.

Regulators can also cause companies to internalise negative externalities by *taxing* actions that create them. In January 2019, the *Wall Street Journal* published the largest public statement of economists in history, signed by over 3,500 US economists, including twenty-seven Nobel Laureates and four former chairs of the Federal Reserve, which advocated a tax on carbon emissions. Alternatively, they can *subsidise* activities that generate positive externalities. To encourage innovation, many countries offer R&D credits that reduce an enterprise's tax bill at the time R&D expenditures are incurred. In Chapter 6, we highlighted how the success of innovation should be measured not by its input (R&D spending), but its output (e.g. the number of patents generated). Eleven EU countries have 'patent boxes' which reduce the tax on income arising from intellectual property, thus subsidising only successful innovation.

Redistribution

We've discussed how the most harmonious outcome of pie growth is a Pareto improvement, where some members gain and none loses. But we've also stressed how Pareto improvements are rare, because most actions involve trade-offs. While pie-growing companies compensate the losers from a decision, to the extent possible, there might still be losers.

Firms are rarely able to create Pareto improvements by themselves. When Engie closed the Hazelwood power station, it participated in the Latrobe Valley Worker Transfer Scheme. But this was only possible because the government of Victoria established the scheme to begin with – subsidising other power generators in the Latrobe Valley for hiring ex-Hazelwood colleagues.

Governments have a major role to play in creating Pareto improvements by redistributing the gains and losses from pie-growing activity. One force that grows the pie, but – without remedial action – shrinks individual slices, is technology. As discussed in Chapter 8, Standard Chartered's Singapore franchise launched SkillsFuture@sc to help colleagues develop skills that will be enhanced rather than replaced by technology. This initiative was inspired by the Singapore government's own SkillsFuture programme, to provide ongoing training to its citizens at all stages of their career. Every Singaporean above 25 receives S$500 ($370), topped up periodically, to take local or online courses. SkillsFuture also offers citizens free advice, such as career guidance and personalised upskilling plans, so that they know what skills to acquire for particular roles.

Another pie-growing but potentially inequality-enhancing activity is free trade, discussed in more detail in Chapter 11. Consumers benefit from greater access to goods, and certain industries gain from cheaper inputs. But thousands of workers and firms lose from international competition, and further employees are displaced through offshoring. The US Trade Adjustment Assistance (TAA) is an example of a programme that retrains employees and helps them find new jobs. Finding causal evidence for the effect of such initiatives is usually difficult, because governments often launch them concurrently with other measures to address unemployment. In addition, only certain workers are eligible for such programmes, and they may have different skills from ineligible ones. Thus, it could be that these skill differences drive future employment outcomes.

Ben Hyman used an ingenious methodology to identify causality. A worker is eligible for TAA if he was laid off by a company whose decline in sales was due to imports or offshoring. But this eligibility assessment is subjective and depends on human judgment. Ben found that some case investigators are strict, accepting relatively few applications across the board, and others are lenient. Whether an applicant is assigned to a strict or lenient case investigator is effectively random, but has a significant effect on whether he's accepted for TAA. Ben found that TAA increases a worker's cumulative income by $50,000 over the next ten years. A third of these returns are from higher wages, with the remainder stemming from a higher likelihood of finding a job.

Two counties in Denmark used an even more random eligibility assignment when they launched a job activation programme. If a citizen became unemployed between November 2005 and March 2006 and had a birthday between the 1st and 15th of any month, he was eligible for a programme that coached him on how to find and apply for employment, monitored his job search efforts, and trained him in technical, social or language skills. Those born on or after the 16th weren't eligible and so are a control group. Since assignment to the programme depended on a worker's birth date, which has no effect on his future employability, any difference in employment outcomes between eligible and ineligible workers can be attributed to the programme. Brian Krogh Graversen and Jan van Ours found that it reduced the median duration of unemployment by 18%.

Financial Literacy

Even more effective than retraining of adults is education of the young. Most governments correctly recognise the importance of education in

STEM subjects (science, technology, engineering and mathematics) for future employability, as well as core skills such as numeracy and literacy. But financial literacy is a crucial core skill to safeguard citizens' long-term financial future. Guidance on how to budget, tax-efficient ways to save, accessing equity markets at low risk and cost through index funds, the role of interest compounding and simple rules of thumb, such as paying down credit card debt first, can have a significant effect on citizens' financial health. This in turn will tackle inequality and improve social cohesion – disparities in wealth stem from not only disparities in income, but also how people spend, borrow and save.

Moreover, financial literacy can prevent customers from being exploited by pie-splitting companies. Some credit card companies offer low 'teaser' rates which significantly jump afterwards. Financially illiterate customers may not know to look beyond the teaser rate. A study found that US credit card issuers target less-educated customers by offering lower teaser rates, but higher rates upon default, late fees and over-limit fees. Relatedly, financial literacy is key to promoting citizen engagement. If workers understand what happens to their money when they invest in a pension – how it has the power to shape and influence companies – this may galvanise them to express their non-financial goals to their pension provider and hold it accountable for pursuing them.

Competition

Competition plays several important roles in Pieconomics. By giving customers the option to switch to a rival, it ensures that firms pursue innovation and excellence, treat stakeholders responsibly and are responsive to customer feedback. In contrast, market power facilitates pie-splitting – it allows companies not only to hike prices to customers, but also to reduce payments to suppliers and workers. Indeed, Effi Benmelech, Nittai Bergman and Hyunseob Kim show that local employer concentration has a negative causal effect on wages.

The pricing distortions arising from monopoly power don't just hurt stakeholders; they also lead to misallocation of resources. Under perfect competition, an enterprise can charge no more for a good than the cost of production. Thus, the private cost to a customer equals the social cost of production. As discussed in Chapter 3, this causes the customer to take opportunity costs to society into account in his purchasing decisions. But monopoly leads to mark-ups, where prices significantly exceed production costs. Thus, even if a customer derives more value from a product than the cost of production, he may not buy it, and a pie-growing trade doesn't take place. Since policies to promote competition have been covered extensively elsewhere, I refer the reader to those sources.

Removing Distortions

Markets fail if regulations create distortions. So one way for policy-makers to create value is to remove unintended distortions from existing regulations.

We've already discussed distortions arising from disclosure requirements. A second source is the tax system. As mentioned earlier, President Clinton removed the tax deductibility of pay exceeding $1 million, except forms that Section 162(m) of the US Internal Revenue Code deemed 'performance-related'. Bizarrely, the Code didn't view restricted shares as performance-related, because the number of shares doesn't depend on performance – even though their value clearly does. But performance shares did count, skewing boards to give them despite the problems discussed in Chapter 5. Note that the distortion extends well beyond the tax implications. By labelling restricted shares as non-performance-related, the regulation discouraged boards and investors from supporting them.

In 2017, the Trump Tax Cut and Jobs Act extended Section 162(m) to *all* forms of pay exceeding $1 million. This had the beneficial, although unintended, side effect of removing the above distortions. Now, boards can choose between pay structures based on which will lead to the most long-term value creation, rather than tax implications.

Perhaps the greatest tax distortion affects an enterprise's choice of financing. In nearly every country, debt interest is deductible from corporation tax, but equity returns aren't. This asymmetric treatment makes no sense.* Evidence indicates that it skews companies to finance

---

* One explanation is that debt is costly because the founder has to pay interest, but equity isn't because she doesn't have to pay dividends. This argument is incorrect – equityholders must be compensated for the opportunity cost of being unable to invest their money elsewhere.

themselves with debt, which increases the risk of bankruptcy – an event that imposes negative externalities on colleagues who lose their jobs, suppliers who lose revenue and customers who lose after-sales support.

Now there are many benefits of debt financing. It allows both equityholders and executives to have concentrated stakes and thus strong incentives to create value.* Policymakers shouldn't discourage debt, but remove distortions that cause enterprises to choose leverage based on tax avoidance rather than pie growth. One option would be to extend the tax-deductibility of debt to equity. Belgium did so in 2006, which indeed led to firms using less debt. Another would be to remove the tax deductibility of debt, and reduce corporation tax to keep the overall tax burden roughly constant.

Best Practices

A final role for regulation is the diffusion of best practices. If market forces worked perfectly, there'd be no such role. An enterprise that employs bad practices would underperform and be driven out of the market. Members would notice bad practices, such as an ineffective board structure, and walk away. But market forces don't work perfectly. Underperforming firms can survive through market power, and members may not have the expertise to evaluate board structure.

Regulation can help the diffusion of best practices, but should recognise that even 'best' practices may not be appropriate for every firm. So they're most effectively disseminated through soft codes rather than hard legislation. *Comply-and-explain* provisions can strike the required balance and are used by several Corporate Governance Codes and Stewardship Codes throughout the world. These are guidelines that a company should follow, but can choose not to if it explains its reason. Several ideas in this book could be implemented through comply-or-explain provisions, such as rewarding leaders with restricted stock that's retained post-departure, giving investors a say-on-purpose and not reporting quarterly earnings.

---

* Consider a $100 million firm with no debt, and assume the CEO can invest $1 million of her wealth into the firm. She owns 1% of the equity. If the same firm is 50% debt financed (so it's financed by $50 million debt and $50 million equity), then the same $1 million now gives her a 2% stake.

Aside from formal codes, regulators can spread best practice simply by making it widely accessible. In November 2017, the UK launched the 'Be the Business' movement to tackle its productivity problem. It provides articles and 'quick tips' on various topics related to digitisation, employee engagement, future planning and leadership. It also establishes communities where businesses can share best practice and a national mentor programme for small business leaders.

Finally, policy involves far more than regulation, and includes other tools such as education, training and funding research. The list of policies that can grow the pie is potentially endless, and beyond the scope of this book. To give an example of these other tools, we'll discuss just one – financing small businesses. This is because small businesses play many roles in Pieconomics. They increase competition; they also invest more because growth opportunities typically decline as a firm ages. In addition, policymakers can attach conditions to the financing of small businesses to ensure that they adopt the pie-growing mentality from the get-go. Note that there are many other ways to support young enterprise, such as tax incentives and reducing red tape, which have been written about elsewhere. We focus on finance because it's a particular challenge for small businesses since they don't have the scale, tangible assets or transparency to raise substantial funds.

Governments or government agencies can finance small businesses directly – as do NRW.BANK, the state development bank of North Rhine-Westphalia in Germany, and the EU's European Investment Bank. They can also give citizens tax incentives to do so, as with the UK's Enterprise Investment Scheme, France's Madelin Provision and Germany's INVEST. Rather than funding all small businesses, a more radical solution is to reserve funding or tax incentives for 'purposeful' small businesses. This idea is compelling in theory – public support should be reserved for firms that generate strong positive externalities. The major practical challenge is that evaluating whether a business is 'purposeful' is highly subjective. As a result, companies may be tied up persuading the government that they're creating value for society (e.g. through excessive reporting) rather than actually doing so.

These challenges may not be insurmountable. Governments already need to make a subjective judgment on whether an organisation qualifies for charitable status, based on whether it serves the public interest. The awarding of purposeful status could be similar. It's critical that any reporting requirements don't go beyond what a purposeful enterprise should be doing anyway. Chapter 8 might be a useful guide – an enterprise should state its purpose, explain how it intends to embed it internally and specify the measures that it will track to verify its delivery. Then, every year, the enterprise would report these measures to the government.

Purposeful companies should already be doing this, but not all will know best practices. Far from being onerous, such a reporting requirement might be a beneficial nudge. Since the culture of a firm is difficult to change, it's especially valuable to encourage it – right from the very start – to think very seriously about what its purpose is, how to put it into practice and how to measure progress.

Influencers

We now turn to influencers' role in growing the pie. We'll discuss how the first two caveats we considered for policymakers also apply to influencers, as well as citizens who may be informed by influencers' opinion. (The other four caveats apply to influencers in the same way as they apply to policymakers.)

The Pie-Growing Mentality

Influencers can play a major role in holding companies accountable for not creating value. But it's easier to gain influence by pointing out an issue that's likely to create public outrage, so they may focus on how much profit an enterprise makes or how much a leader is paid. Given the prevalence of the pie-splitting mentality, many readers may assume that pay and profits must be at the expense of other stakeholders.

For example, the level of pay is often criticised without considering whether the leader has grown the pie – the returns earned by investors, the surplus enjoyed by customers or the number of new jobs created. Similarly, recall the Humana buyback that we discussed in Chapter 7. Some articles focused on how the buyback netted the CEO a $1.68 million bonus. They omitted the fact that it created $96 million of value for continuing investors, so the bonus wasn't at their expense.

In addition to 'naming and shaming' pie-splitters and particularly pie-shrinkers, influencers have the power to 'name and fame' pie-growers. This presents a more balanced picture of business and should reduce the public's mistrust. Influencers don't have a responsibility to reduce mistrust in business where it's deserved. But they do have a responsibility to portray business accurately so that it gets the level of trust or mistrust that's warranted.

Naming and faming pie-growers encourages citizens to invest in, buy from or work for them, and provides aspirational examples for other firms to follow. It gives leaders confidence that, by looking away from profit targets and looking up to how they can make a difference to the world, their enterprises may end up more successful.

Evidence over Anecdote

Influencers can become impactful by presenting a black-and-white view of a topic. A newspaper article that claims that buybacks are always good has a clear punchline, and will be shared and referenced by supporters of this viewpoint. A guru who argues that buybacks are always bad will become famous for this position, and be interviewed whenever a journalist wants an anti-buyback quote. Influencers can get away with presenting one-sided views because it's easy for readers to view an issue as either good or bad, a psychological tendency known as 'splitting', 'black-and-white thinking' or 'all-or-nothing thinking'. This is compounded by *confirmation bias* – the tendency to accept any evidence, no matter how flimsy, that supports one's pre-existing view on whether an issue is good or bad, and disregard evidence that contradicts it.

We've discussed the problem of policy being based on single stories. This applies to influencers also – you can always hand-pick an anecdote that illustrates a point starkly. But a single story is misleading and meaningless unless it's backed up by large-scale data. A good principle for influencers to follow is not to extrapolate from a story to make a general point, unless they also quote large-scale evidence that supports this general point.

But simply moving to evidence isn't enough. Just like with anecdotes, you can always hand-pick a study that finds a desired result. This is a major problem because there's a huge variation in the quality of studies available. Some make basic methodological mistakes, like the miscalculation of CEO incentives we saw in Chapter 5. Others claim causation when they find only correlation. So it's crucial for influencers to weight evidence by its quality and rigour, rather than because it reinforces their or the readership's opinion.

How can influencers, or consumers of influencer opinion, evaluate the quality of a study – without having to delve into the weeds and scrutinise its methodology, which would require specialist expertise and be impractically time-consuming? Three indicators, often widely overlooked, are whether a paper is published in a peer-reviewed journal, where it's published and who the authors are.

Let's start with the first. Practitioner studies have significant value. They often have better access to data than academics and are often a superior source for statistics. But academics have particular expertise in drawing relationships *between* statistics – teasing apart causation from correlation and addressing alternative explanations. Importantly, academic studies have to undergo rigorous peer review to check their scientific accuracy. This addresses not only poor execution, but also deliberate bias, such as a pharmaceuticals company releasing or funding a report on its own drugs. The very top journals have the highest standards, using the world's leading specialists to scrutinise a manuscript, and reject up to 95% of manuscripts. The 5% not rejected aren't immediately accepted either; instead, their status is 'revise-and-resubmit'. The reviewers highlight concerns that the authors need to address, and the paper can still be rejected at the next round. It's not unusual for a paper to take five years to be published after its first draft. A hard slog for the authors, but it helps ensure that the published results are correct. As discussed in the Introduction, a paper on pay ratios completely changed its conclusion after going through peer review and improving its methodology.

The second indicator is the quality of the journal in which a paper has been published. That a journal calls itself 'peer-reviewed' is far from sufficient to guarantee its rigour, since there's a vast range in the quality of reviewing standards. The analytics company Cabell's has a blacklist of 8,700 journals that claim to be peer-reviewed, but actually aren't. The top journals are most stringent about not only rigour, but also disclosure of funding sources, and have retracted articles due to a failure to disclose. Journal quality can easily be checked by looking at one of the freely available lists of the best ones, such as the *Financial Times* Top 50. One doesn't need to be an academic insider to do this.

Peer review isn't perfect – mistakes are made. Sometimes sloppy papers get accepted and good papers are rejected. But it's better to go with something checked than something unchecked. A few influencers, who don't have experience of the academic publication process, like to use the words 'publication bias' as a licence to ignore whether a paper's been published and quote whatever study they like. Their charge is that journals only publish papers that support traditional orthodoxies, such as an exclusive focus on shareholder value.

This simply isn't how the publication process works. As journal editors, we want to publish new papers that change the way people think. The main measure of journal reputation is the number of times its articles are cited. The first paper in any new area will be hugely cited, whereas the tenth in a well-established field will be relatively ignored. The 95% rejection rate is because top journals are extremely stringent about not only accuracy, but also novelty. The most common reason for rejection isn't that a paper is wrong, but that it doesn't make a novel enough contribution to knowledge – it mainly rehashes what we already know. Indeed, throughout this book, we've discussed many academic papers in top journals that support the idea of moving beyond shareholder value maximisation towards social value creation.

With these arguments, I'm not aiming to be an apologist for academia. There are many areas of the academic profession that can be improved. But journals not having incentives to publish new papers that challenge conventional wisdom just isn't one of them.

Of course, every paper starts out unpublished. How do we gauge the quality of a new paper? The third indicator is the credentials of the authors. One relevant factor is the quality of their institution, which we can compare against freely available lists of the top universities. This isn't elitism, but simply a desire to use the best evidence. We'd listen to a medical opinion from Mount Sinai more than a hospital we've never heard of. It's certainly not the case that studies by top institutions are always correct and those by others are always wrong. Thus, a second factor is the authors' track record of top-tier publications, which is easy to find as nearly all academics make their CVs available on their own website or their institution's. Indeed, we carefully scrutinise the credentials of an expert witness in a trial. Again, this doesn't mean that well-published authors are always right. Credentials are simply *one* factor to assess when evaluating evidence, just as a company's brand name is one consideration in a purchasing decision, or an undergraduate's university is one element in an entry-level hiring decision. A useful question to ask is the following: If the same study was written by the same authors, with the same credentials and had the opposite results, would we still be willing to believe it?

These three indicators help us evaluate whether one particular study is trustworthy. We'll close with tips to discern the reliability of articles or influencers' public positions, which typically cite studies in support. One tip is to go to the original source. Sometimes, a study may not actually show what the influencer claims that it shows. But, if the claim confirms what a citizen would like to be true, he might not bother checking the reference. For example, the UK House of Commons Select Committee* Report on Executive Pay stated that 'the evidence is at best ambiguous on the impact of individual CEOs on company perform-ance', with a footnote referring to the evidence submitted by 'Professor Alex Edmans' to the Executive Pay inquiry. However, nowhere did my evidence state this. My closest sentence on the 'impact of individual CEOs' was 'CEOs with high equity incentives outperform CEOs with low equity incentives by 4–10% per year, and the researchers do further tests to suggest that the results are causation rather than correlation', as discussed in Chapter 5. This suggests that CEOs do have a significant impact on firms. Since checking the original source can be cumbersome for citizens, websites such as fullfact.org do so on their behalf.

Similarly, even if an influencer correctly describes the evidence he chooses to quote, he may deliberately select only the research supporting one side of an issue. Accordingly, citizens should place more weight on balanced articles that discuss both the pros and cons of a topic. There are two sides to almost every issue in business or economics,** so those who present an extreme position may not have seriously considered the other side. Citizens thus should be particularly vigilant if they see unambiguous phrases such as 'beyond doubt' or 'clear evidence'. We saw earlier how influencers claimed that 'the outperformance of ESG strategies is beyond doubt' and 'there is clear evidence that high CEO pay is no longer strongly associated with performance', even though neither statement is true. By being wary of one-sided opinions, not only may citizens become more informed them-selves, but also discipline influencers into presenting the full picture.

For example, the Norwegian Sovereign Wealth Fund is an influencer because it's a respected investor whose lead others follow. Recall that, in April 2017, it released a position paper on CEO pay. In October 2018, it published three more on board structure. In all these

---

* This committee is an influencer in that it recommends policy rather than directly setting it.
** There are two sides to almost every issue in social sciences, because it's difficult to prove something perfectly – as discussed, evidence is not universal. However, in the physical sciences, proof is possible and so one-sided articles may be reliable.

papers, it presents not only the arguments for its position, but also those against. Including the latter strengthens the Fund's credibility, as it shows it reached its stance despite carefully considering the other side, rather than blundering into it. Acknowledging potential weaknesses in your position need not display weakness, but strength.

In a Nutshell

- Citizens enjoy agency – the power to change the way enterprises operate. Few are policymakers, but all can affect policy through their role as voters. Few are influencers, but all have influence by the views that they share and ignore. Almost all are investors, colleagues and customers.
- Like investors, colleagues and customers can *monitor* – choose companies based on the value they create for society – and *engage*. Colleagues at all levels can practise the attitudes of empowerment, investment and reward to others. They can manage up and be bold in suggesting and trialling new ideas. Customers can pressure enterprises to change behaviour through their purchasing decisions or providing product feedback.
- Regulation can address market failures such as externalities, redistribute the gains from pie growth and help spread best practices. However, it has limitations. By deterring errors of commission, it can exacerbate errors of omission by discouraging risk-taking. It's typically one-size-fits-all and not tailored to enterprises' individual circumstances. Thus, particularly effective may be 'comply-and-explain' provisions, and requiring disclosures to allow members to make informed decisions.
- Influencers can play a major role in growing the pie by drawing attention to pie-shrinking behaviour and 'naming and faming' pie-growers.
- It's much easier to gain influence by presenting only one side of an issue, and hand-picking a single story which illustrates a point starkly. But influencers' objective should be to spread truth, by only using stories to make a general point when they can be backed up with rigorous large-scale evidence.
- Consumers of influencer opinions should beware confirmation bias, the tendency to accept views that support one's own. They should place particular weight on studies published in the most stringent academic journals by researchers with strong credentials, and put more trust in influencers who present both sides of a topic.

PART IV

THE BIGGER PICTURE

11 GROWING THE PIE MORE WIDELY
WIN-WIN THINKING AT THE NATIONAL AND PERSONAL LEVELS

This chapter discusses how the core ideas of this book – the value of the pie-growing mentality; the importance of errors of omission; and the principles of multiplication, comparative advantage and materiality – can be applied to wider settings beyond the relationship between business and society. It also acknowledges the analogues between Pieconomics and ideas that others have developed in different contexts.

We'll first start with a general principle that will be relevant to many applications discussed in this chapter.

Battle of the Sexes – the Value of Cooperation

The first hobby that I remember having as a kid was playing chess. My dad taught me from an early age and I played in my first tournament when I was 5. I enjoyed the game, but the hardest part – particularly for a 5-year-old – was losing. I'd often burst into tears after losing important games. Eventually, I learned to stop crying and played for the England junior team when I was at school. But I ditched it at university for more socially acceptable pastimes.

Yet my chess background meant that my favourite topic in undergraduate economics was Game Theory. This uses games to model real-life situations where, just like in chess, different players pursue their own individual interests. Two enterprises compete within an industry, management negotiates with a trade union or country presidents engage in a trade war. These games aren't used only in academic textbooks, but also in real life – companies sometimes use war-gaming workshops to play out potential scenarios.

Perhaps the most famous Game Theory game is the Prisoners' Dilemma, often used to model industry cartels. But another well-known game, Battle of the Sexes, is more relevant for Pieconomics. Ann and Bob need to decide where to go on date night. Ann would rather go to ballet and Bob to a fight. (Yes, economics textbooks aren't known for their political correctness.) But both prefer to go to the same event rather than to be apart. Their 'pay-offs', i.e. their happiness from different choices, are given by the following table.

| | | Bob | |
		Ballet	Fight
Ann	Ballet	5, 1	0, 0
	Fight	0, 0	1, 5

Each cell contains the pay-offs first to Ann, and then to Bob. If they go to different events, both get 0. If both go to the ballet, Ann gets 5 and Bob gets 1. If they both go to the fight, Ann gets 1 and Bob gets 5.

What's the best outcome? There are two possible ones – both go either to the ballet or to the fight. The aggregate pay-off is 6, and so going to the same event grows the pie compared to going their separate ways. Even though equality is higher under the latter (both get the same – zero), few should doubt that equality is less important than creating value.

It's a no-brainer that Ann and Bob should go to the same event. The tricky question is whether this should be the ballet or the fight. They might be so caught up squabbling over how to split the pie – which event they go to – that they lose sight of the primary goal, which is to go to the same one. Perhaps as a bargaining tactic, Ann says she's already bought the ballet tickets. In Game Theory language, she *commits* to choosing 'Ballet'. The rational thing for Bob to do is also to choose 'Ballet', so that he gets 1 rather than 0 if he chooses 'Fight'.

But humans aren't always rational. Bob may view this as unfair as Ann gets a higher pay-off, so he wants to punish her by going to the fight. This punishment is successful as Ann now gets 0 – but he's also succeeded in punishing himself, and gets 0 too.

To a dispassionate outsider, Bob's behaviour seems crazy. But people choose the pie-shrinking outcome often. They're caught up in the same win-lose mentality that I had when playing chess, and so are fixated on beating the other person. By making others lose, they think they'll automatically win. But real life isn't a zero-sum game like chess. The other player isn't your opponent, but your ally. Both parties can lose and both can win, depending on whether you choose to grow the pie.

How do people actually play Battle of the Sexes? Economists have studied a richer version known as the Ultimatum Game. Here, Ann is given $10 and offers a split to Bob. If Bob agrees with the split, both keep the suggested amounts. If Bob disagrees, both get zero. It's like Battle of the Sexes except Ann can choose a whole range of options – any number from $0 to $10 – rather than only 'Ballet' or 'Fight'.

What's rational is for Bob to accept *any* split. Even if Ann proposes to give $0.01 and keep $9.99, Bob should accept it. It's unfair, but it's better than him getting zero. But this experiment has been played thousands of times, and in practice Bob rejects even $3. He's so concerned with equality that he prefers to shrink the pie, all the way to zero, to stop Ann getting more than him.

While studies have investigated how people play the Ultimatum Game, it's still an experiment. Unfortunately, people often play the same way in real-life applications of the game. It's to these settings that we now turn.

International Trade

The principle of comparative advantage in this book is based on the famous *law of comparative advantage*, pioneered by economist David Ricardo in the setting of international trade. Assume that there are two countries, Britain and America, and two goods, televisions (TVs) and personal computers (PCs). Britain has 12 workers and America has 14. The number of goods each worker can produce is shown in the table.

	TVs	PCs
Britain	3	1
America	4	3

Citizens want many types of goods. A household would rather have one TV and one PC rather than two of one and none of the other. We'll capture the need for variety in a simple way by saying that Gross National Happiness (GNH) is given by the lower of the two items produced.

Let's first assume complete autarchy – countries don't trade with each other. Then Britain would assign 3 workers to TVs and the remaining 9 to PCs. It would produce 9 of each and its GNH would be 9. America would assign 6 workers to TVs and 8 to PCs, making 24 of each for a GNH of 24. Total GNH across the two countries is 33.

Now let's allow for trade. The *law of comparative advantage* says that each country should focus on the good that it's *relatively* better at producing. The beauty of this law is that, even if a country is absolutely less productive in all goods, it will still be relatively more productive in one. Here, Britain is less productive for both items ($3 < 4$ and $1 < 3$). But it's relatively more productive for TVs. If it reallocates a worker away from PCs to TVs, it gains 3 TVs for every PC lost. If America does such a reallocation, it gains $4/3 = 1.33$ TVs for every PC lost.

So Britain should reallocate workers from PCs to TVs, where it has a comparative advantage. It switches all 12, who now make 36 TVs. America reallocates 13 workers to make 39 PCs, and keeps only one worker in the TV factory, where he makes 4. Across the two countries, there are 40 TVs and 39 PCs, and thus a combined GNH of 39. The gains from trade, in GNH terms, are 6.

Just like in Battle of the Sexes, it's not clear how to split this 6. Britain could offer America only 22 TVs in return for 14 PCs. It ends up with 14 of each item and a GNH of 14. America has 26 TVs and 25 PCs, and a GNH of 25. Britain gains 5 compared to autarchy, and America gains 1. This is like Battle of the Sexes where both go to the fight, so Bob gets 5 and Ann gets 1.

	No Trade, Production and Consumption		Trade, Production		Trade, Consumption	
	TVs	PCs	TVs	PCs	TVs	PCs
Britain	9	9	36	0	14	14
America	24	24	4	39	26	25

Or America can drive a hard bargain and demand 26 TVs from Britain, only offering 10 PCs in return. Britain ends up with 10 of each item and a GNH of 10. America has 30 TVs and 29 PCs, and thus a GNH of 29. So now America gains 5 and Britain gains 1 – like Battle of the Sexes where both go to the ballet.

Under both scenarios, the gains from trade are unequal. But just like in Battle of the Sexes, the most important point is that the pie has grown – both are better off than under autarchy. Now that's not to say that the countries should ignore how the gains are split – the division is still important. But the first priority should be for the countries to cooperate so that there are gains, and *then* to decide on the split.

In reality, countries sometimes have the pie-splitting mentality. Britain might see America as gaining 5 from trade, and think that it must be losing 5 – it doesn't realise that it's gaining 1. Or Britain might think that, by reducing America's slice of the pie by putting up trade barriers, it will increase its own slice – not recognising that both countries' slice may fall because the pie shrinks. This is often called a 'trade war'. US President Donald Trump tweeted that '[t]ariffs are working far better than anyone ever anticipated. China market has dropped 27% in last 4months [sic]', assuming that the goal of trade policy is to damage other countries. In war, it's indeed the case that making your opponent lose causes you to win. But in a trade war, making your opponent lose often causes you to lose yourself.

So far, we've considered Britain as a single entity. But what matters is the division of gains not only between Britain and America, but also between different British citizens. Who in Britain actually gains from trade?

In theory, it could be all members of society. British enterprises in aggregate generate more sales since they now focus on the product in which they have a comparative advantage. They can pay higher wages to colleagues and return greater profits to investors. The biggest gainers may be customers. Politicians often think of trade as benefiting only the elite – companies who can sell more, and thus their bosses and investors. But it also helps ordinary citizens who have access to cheaper and better goods. America is only able to export PCs because British consumers prefer them to home-made ones. The customers who benefit from trade include not only people, but also enterprises who gain from access to affordable, high-quality inputs. Tariffs put domestic companies at a competitive disadvantage to foreign firms, who have free access to these inputs.

But in practice, while investors, colleagues and customers gain at the aggregate level, not everyone gains individually – just like, for a company, the pie may grow, but an individual stakeholder may lose. PC companies can't suddenly switch to making TVs. They may go out of business, hurting investors. Their employees also lose – while new TV companies will start up, PC workers may not have the skills to manufacture TVs, or be willing to relocate to these new firms.

These redundancies, while painful and serious, aren't too different from what happens under domestic competition. If Prestige PCs, based in London, were an inefficient incumbent, and Castle Computers in Manchester entered the market and drove it out, Prestige's colleagues would be out of a job. If they're unwilling to relocate to Manchester, and they're not employable in other London firms, they'd be jobless. That Prestige lost to a domestic rather than foreign competitor doesn't make unemployment any less painful. And companies can decline through not only inefficiency, but also changes in technology, such as Kodak losing out to digital cameras.

So the job losses from international trade are an example of a more general problem. Redundancies arise when an enterprise's products are no longer in demand, because technology or preferences have changed, or there are more efficient rivals – whether domestic or foreign. Now that doesn't make the job losses any less painful. Those unemployed due to imports aren't comforted by the fact that others have become unemployed due to technology. But it does mean that governments should prioritise solutions to the general problem, rather than treating unemployment from trade as unique. While tackling unemployment is beyond the scope of this book, policies to increase workers' redeployability (such as education, apprenticeships for the young, and retraining programmes for adults) and encourage new business formation, as discussed in Chapter 10, will help all displaced colleagues – regardless of what caused their displacement.

Employment

Pie-splitting views on international trade – that there's a fixed demand for goods and so sales by foreign enterprises are at the expense of domestic ones – are similar to pie-splitting views on employment. This is often known as the 'lump of labour' fallacy: there's a fixed demand for jobs, and so giving jobs to immigrants takes jobs away from domestic citizens. But the number of jobs is not fixed. Most obviously, immigrants spend their income, which directly creates jobs, and pay taxes, which gives the government resources to do so.

More importantly, while immigrants are often seen as *substitutes* for domestic workers, taking away jobs that would otherwise have gone to them, many jobs are *complements*. Hiring an immigrant in a particular role may create several new jobs that interact with this role. An immigrant project manager allows a construction company to employ domestic construction workers; immigrant construction workers allow it to employ a domestic project manager. Both types of hire create extra demand for staff in human resources or purchasing.

This doesn't mean that immigration policies should be unfettered. Substitutability is more likely to exist in professions where there's already an abundance of domestic workers. But hiring immigrants in professions where the domestic supply is scarce – such as engineering and healthcare for the UK – is particularly likely to increase hiring in complementary jobs, as well as improve employer performance.

The 'lump of labour' fallacy applies to attitudes towards not only immigration, but also technology. A similar mentality exists – there's a fixed amount of work to be done, so any work undertaken by machines reduces the number of jobs for humans. As with immigration, there are certainly cases where technology and labour are substitutes, but they can often be complements. Leaders need to think carefully about how to redefine jobs, away from those that can be substituted by technology to those that complement it or in which humans have a *comparative advantage*, such as personal relationships. This redefinition is often tricky, but also possible.

In his 2016 TED talk, *Will Automation Take Away All Our Jobs?*, MIT economics professor David Autor notes that there were 250,000 bank tellers in the US in 1970, yet 500,000 today, with 100,000 added since 2000 – despite the proliferation of the Automated Teller Machine (ATM) from the 1970s. ATMs substitute for some tasks that tellers used to do, such as handling deposits and withdrawals. But this allows tellers to switch to more complex tasks, such as advising customers on financial products, where personal interaction and trust are important. Not only do tellers benefit from more fulfilling jobs, but the ATM also makes it cheaper for banks to open new branches. The number of bank branches in urban areas rose by 43% between 1988 and 2004, creating thousands of new jobs and offsetting the fact that fewer tellers are now needed in each branch.

Japanese Deputy Prime Minister Taro Aso similarly highlighted the importance of viewing technology as help – as a partner in growing the pie, rather than a rival: 'The Western way of thinking is "robots will steal my job," but in Japan, robots will reduce the ordinary man's load.' This help can involve technology doing tasks that were too dangerous for humans to do in the first place, such as cleaning up oil spills or firefighting at high temperatures – so there's no substitution. Even for highly skilled jobs, technology will make redefinition both necessary and feasible. Artificial intelligence will likely be able to diagnose cancer, but only humans can convey this news in a compassionate way, and discuss prognosis and treatment options.

For leaders to be able to redefine jobs, they need a flexible workforce. This in turn requires both enterprises and policymakers to train citizens in skills that can't be replaced by technology (so that it's not a substitute) and in how to use technology (so that it's a complement that makes them more productive), as in Singapore's SkillsFuture programme. This approach views technology not only as a threat to get in front of, but also an opportunity. Autor points out that tractors, and other technological advances, severely threatened US agricultural employment around the turn of the nineteenth century. The US government took the radical step of introducing compulsory schooling until age 16. The substantial investment paid off in creating a highly skilled and flexible US workforce. Many industries that are the biggest employers today couldn't have been foreseen back then. Similarly, we don't know what will be the industries of the future – but we do know that general skills will help prepare our workforce for whatever they turn out to be.

The threat posed by artificial intelligence may be of a greater scale to previous technological changes, but the challenge of responding to such changes is not new. In Autor's words, 'If you think about it, many of the great inventions of the last 200 years were designed to replace human labour.' Computers were a game-changing innovation, but they've led to jobs being redefined rather than just replaced. Moving from typewriters to word-processing software allows typists to correct mistakes, increasing their productivity and reducing demand for labour hours devoted to typing. Yet it didn't lead to typists being fired, but instead to their role being enriched to that of a secretary or executive assistant, which involves far broader responsibilities. Indeed, jobs have grown faster in industries with a high use of computers (e.g. engineering) than those without (e.g. manufacturing), suggesting that computers aren't simply a substitute for workers.

Not every employee whose job is displaced by technology will be able to be redeployed within the firm, and so the government policies mentioned at the end of the last section, to foster external reallocation, are also critical. In addition, as we discussed in Chapter 5, broad-based equity schemes can help ensure the benefits of technology are shared widely among colleagues, thus mitigating the losses to those who end up being let go, despite the firm's best efforts.

Macroeconomic Policy

The expression 'grow the pie' is sometimes used in macroeconomics to argue that growing the wealth of the nation as a whole benefits citizens, particularly less affluent ones, more than redistributing wealth. Thus, policymakers should focus primarily on economic growth.

Contrary to common belief, this doesn't mean the reliance on free markets and minimal government intervention. Instead, there remains a significant role for redistributive policies to the extent that they also support growth. Free health care or university education, or subsidising these for the poor, substantially increases the productive capacity of citizens who'd otherwise be unable to afford such investments. However, this approach to macroeconomic policy would caution against redistribution for its own sake, as doing so may reduce incentives to create wealth to begin with.

While Pieconomics stresses the importance of growing the pie, it also recognises that social welfare depends not only on the size of the pie, but also its distribution. So, in contrast to 'grow-the-pie' macroeconomic policy, Pieconomics argues that redistribution for its own sake can be desirable, even if there are disincentive effects, as long as they're not major. As we showed in Figure 2.2, a leader may prefer a smaller pie that's more evenly distributed, particularly if material stakeholders are better off.

But the most important difference is that, under 'grow-the-pie' macroeconomic policy, the pie represents wealth and a policymaker's goal is to create wealth. Under Pieconomics, the pie represents social value and a leader's responsibility is to create social value, of which profits are only one slice.

Interpersonal Dynamics

We now apply the concept of growing the pie to interactions between individuals, rather than companies or stakeholders. Perhaps the closest analogue lies in Stephen Covey's famous book, *The 7 Habits of Highly Effective People*. He talks about the *scarcity mentality* which, like the pie-splitting mentality, assumes there's a fixed amount of resources or happiness to go round. If a friend achieves personal or professional success, you feel envious – perhaps thinking that there's less happiness left for yourself. If a colleague closes a deal, you fear he'll get the next promotion, not you. As political satirist P. J. O'Rourke put it, 'In this zero-sum universe there is only so much happiness. The idea is that if we wipe the smile off the faces of people with prosperous businesses and successful careers, that will make the rest of us grin.' This is linked to the 'tall poppy syndrome', where people envy others' success (a poppy who grows taller than other poppies), even if it doesn't reduce yours.

In contrast, Covey's *abundance mentality* argues that there's an unlimited amount of resources or happiness, so there's no need for envy. But a key difference with Pieconomics is that the abundance mentality assumes there are automatically unlimited resources. The pie-growing mentality stresses that larger slices are available for all, but only through hard work and cooperation. Just as investors and stakeholders are allies in growing the pie rather than adversaries who maximise their share, colleagues are allies in ensuring the enterprise's success rather than competitors for promotion.

Let's say Ann and Bob are now heads of different divisions in the company Springbok, Inc. If Ann cooperates with Bob to close a deal for his division, that's like Ann cooperating with Bob to go to the fight in Battle of the Sexes. Bob gains the most because the deal increases his division's profits. But even though Ann gains less, she still gains. By bringing business into Springbok, she helps it thrive, which will likely give more resources for her division. Ann and Bob's primary task is to grow Springbok's pie and ensure it stays ahead of Lion, Inc., its main competitor, rather than for their division to be the best within Springbok.

In nature, a lion can't catch a springbok if it chases after it. So it waits for a herd of springboks to fight each other, and then can catch one. 'Fights' refer to actions that affect not only another division, but also the broader organisation. Bob may support a particular candidate for CEO because she's more likely to favour his division even if an alternate is of high quality. A professor may push for the hiring of a low-quality new faculty member because he's closest to her own research interest. An athlete may oppose the signing of a new team-mate because it will mean that he's no longer the star player. In all these examples, *colleagues only look at their slice. They don't look at the entire pie.*

A leader's responsibility is to design reward and evaluation systems that instead create win-win situations. It's important that, when Bob gets 5, Ann gets 1 rather than −1. The former will be the case if Ann has shares in Springbok, as advocated in Chapter 5, and if the evaluation system explicitly takes into account her support of Bob rather than comparing her performance against him. In contrast, new Harvard Law School students are allegedly told, 'Look to your left, look to your right, because one of you won't be here by the end of the year.' Such zero-sum statements engender a scarcity mentality.

The principles of Pieconomics also apply even if Ann and Bob are friends or acquaintances rather than colleagues. In *Give and Take*, social psychologist Adam Grant studies three types of people. 'Givers' help others without doing a calculation of whether they'll eventually benefit, like a pie-growing leader. 'Takers' try to exploit others as much as possible, like a pie-splitting leader. 'Matchers' help others if they can forecast a long-term benefit, like a leader who practises enlightened shareholder value. Adam shows that givers are actually more successful in the long run – even though personal success was never the motivation for their generosity. Yet he stresses how giving shouldn't be scattered and undisciplined, just as a pie-growing firm shouldn't invest in an unfettered manner.

Mindset

In addition to relationships with others (interpersonal leadership), the ideas of Pieconomics also have antecedents in prior work on your relationship with yourself (personal leadership).

Psychologist Carol Dweck, in her book *Mindset*, talks about the *fixed mindset* and the *growth mindset* as two different attitudes to personal development. The fixed mindset views a person's abilities as anchored in genetics. He's either talented at an activity or not. If he's not talented, he's predestined to fail, so there's no point working hard. If he's talented, he's predestined to succeed, so again there's no need to work hard.

In contrast, the growth mindset views abilities as expandable through effort. This mindset is similar to the pie-growing mentality, although there isn't an analogue of how a pie is split between different members. Viewing the pie as expandable gives encouragement that all parties can gain, but also the responsibility to work together to grow the pie, rather than your own slice. Viewing your abilities as expandable through the growth mindset gives encouragement, but also the responsibility to work hard to improve them.

Yet achievement through hard work is often scorned compared to achievement through talent. Kids who work hard are labelled as 'swots' or 'try-hards', as if effort is something to be ashamed of. At my secondary school, your grades had two components: attainment, which ranged from 9 (best) to 1 (worst), and effort, where the scale was from A (best) to D (worst). The most coveted grade was a 9D as it suggested that you were a natural – you'd achieved success without having to work for it.

When I was an undergraduate, I ran for student government (known as the Junior Common Room, or JCR) at Merton College, Oxford. Not surprisingly, studying Economics, the position I went for was Treasurer. In the first General Meeting after being elected, the opening motion proposed that Merton JCR's official position be to oppose tuition fees. The JCR President normally chaired all meetings, but she was proposing the motion. The chair's duty should have fallen to the Vice-President, but he was opposing the motion. (No danger of groupthink in our committee.) The Treasurer was third in command, so I was suddenly thrust into the role of chair. I never anticipated needing to do public speaking when running for Treasurer, as I'd instead looked forward to a peaceful year of signing cheques and building Excel spreadsheets.

I was a disaster. I was too shy to chair effectively, particularly in a room of opinionated, high-spirited students – often full of spirits as well as spirit. I was so bad that in the next meeting, the students proposed a motion to create a new position, called General Meeting Chairperson. That person would chair future meetings, so the student body wouldn't have to put up with my incompetence again. The motion was defeated, but there was still an easy way out for me. While it was tradition that the highest-ranked officer would chair meetings, there was nothing in the constitution that mandated this. It was tempting to have had the fixed mindset and thought that I just wasn't a public speaker, passing the duties to the fourth in command. But I decided to work at it, even though chairing meetings was uncomfortable. I took the Chair's role many more times that year when the President and Vice-President were unavailable, and ended up semi-competent.

But still only semi-competent. Knowing that I still had significant room for improvement, but also encouraged that improvement was possible, I joined the MIT Toastmasters Public Speaking Club immediately after starting graduate school. Some classmates thought Toastmasters was pointless for a native speaker because you're either born with elocution ability or you're not – only for non-natives is there growth potential. In the first meeting, I was cold-called in an exercise called 'Table Topics', where you're asked to speak on a topic on the fly. I was asked 'What's the difference between a lady and a woman?' and gave a dismal answer because I was no good at thinking on my feet. But, despite knowing that each meeting would have a 'Table Topics' and thus the risk of being cold-called, I kept coming back.

Fast-forwarding to my first year as an assistant professor at Wharton, I attended a conference jointly hosted by Duke University and the University of North Carolina. I presented one of my research papers on blockholders. Afterwards, Duke professor John Graham (whose work we've covered in this book) came up to me and said, 'That was a great presentation. You must have worked really hard on it.' I was crestfallen. I wish he'd have said, 'That was a great presentation. You must be a natural public speaker.' I wanted John to give me a 9D grade. But that would have been false, because I wasn't a natural at all. The only way I was able to give a coherent talk was because Merton JCR allowed me to keep chairing despite my initial incompetence, because the MIT Toastmasters Public Speaking Club helped develop me, and because I'd put many hours into rehearsing, recording and playing back that very talk even though I was tempted to lie to myself that I didn't need to work on it.

Embracing Failure

A recurring theme of this book is that the desire to avoid errors of commission may lead to far more serious errors of omission. In an enterprise context, such errors forgo opportunities to create social value. A company refrains from launching a new product because it fears failure, or from implementing new technology because it will lead to job losses and a media backlash. In a personal context, such errors forgo opportunities for individual development.

Growing up in England, and not having the money for foreign vacations, my main family holidays were building sandcastles on the English seaside. When I was a teenager and we had a golden retriever, we'd go to the Lake District or Yorkshire Dales, where we enjoyed long ambles. So I'd never skied before I arrived at MIT for my PhD.

Every January at MIT they have Independent Activities Period (IAP). Rather than regular classes, they put on a vast range of free lectures and workshops on extra-curricular topics. I took courses on baseball hitting and Brazilian jiu-jitsu, as well as more cerebral ones such as the Israeli–Palestinian conflict and US race relations. At the end of IAP, the Graduate Student Council runs a ski trip. I'd never skied before, but my friends were going and – buoyed by having already learned other valuable skills during IAP, such as how to put someone in a choke hold (which hopefully will never turn out to be valuable) – I decided to go. I took a beginner's class on the bunny slopes before being let loose on the rest of Smugglers' Notch, Vermont.

Being a numbers nerd, I loved to have measures of success, to see whether I was improving. The easiest measure was the number of times I fell over. I'd keep a tally of my number of falls in the morning and then have a separate tally for the afternoon. If I fell fewer times in the afternoon than in the morning, that would be improvement. If I fell fewer times on Saturday morning than Friday morning, that would also be improvement.

But I quickly devised a way to manipulate the statistics. The easiest way to avoid falling, an error of commission, was to ski on the easiest slopes – a far more serious error of omission, as it missed the opportunity to challenge myself. Even if I got around this by forcing myself to graduate from the green (easy) to blue (moderate) slopes, I'd quickly figure out what the easiest blue slopes were and ski on them. And even if I tried to do a 'controlled experiment', by skiing on the same blue slope and trying to reduce the number of times I fell on the way down, I'd simply take more turns to lower my speed and avoid falling. *The absence of 'failure' was how I defined success.* At the end of each day, when we were back in the condo enjoying a warming beverage, we'd ask each other how our days had been. While my friends talked about the thrill of trying out a new run or jump, even if they ultimately failed, I'd excitedly tell them that I'd fallen fewer times in the afternoon than the morning (of course, pro-rating the statistics to take into account the different lengths of the morning and afternoon sessions, like a good MIT student).

My goal when skiing was not to fall. But that's crazy. People don't take up skiing to avoid falling – they do it for the thrill of skiing. Just like a leader shouldn't define a good year as one in which she's avoided negative press coverage, or an enterprise shouldn't measure the success of a new product primarily by the absence of customer complaints. Fortunately, I finally figured out the true purpose of skiing with one day left on the ski trip. I decided to try Snowsnake, the hardest blue run I'd come across so far, which, despite its name, was covered with ice. I fell countless times that morning. But each fall taught me something – I tried to pinpoint what I'd done just before the fall to trigger the wipe-out. This feedback loop helped me get a little bit better each time until finally I could ski down Snowsnake unscathed.

The importance of embracing failure applies to far more important issues than how to get maximum enjoyment from a ski trip. Any major personal or professional development opportunity – trying public speaking, switching into a new career, applying for an internal promotion, entering your first 5k race – requires a willingness to fail. It's hard to keep secret that you've put yourself forward for an internal promotion. If you don't get it, your colleagues will know you weren't good enough. Some might think you were too big for your boots by applying for it. In a 5k race, someone has to come last, and some don't even finish – and the results are easily searchable on the internet. But as

J. K. Rowling said in her 2008 Harvard graduation speech, 'it is impossible to live without failing at something, unless you live so cautiously that you might as well not have lived at all – in which case, you fail by default'. That failure by default is an error of omission.

Not only is a willingness to fail valuable ex ante, but the failures themselves are valuable ex post as they allow us to learn. As discussed in Chapter 10, a negative say-on-pay vote informs an enterprise about what investors object to – just like a fall on the slopes helped me identify what error I'd just made to trigger the wipeout. Author Matthew Syed names this mindset 'Black Box Thinking', after the black boxes in aeroplanes that record the plane's movements and cockpit conversations. These boxes allow authorities to investigate the cause of a plane crash, helping to prevent future disasters.

Black box thinking is painful. Rather than taking ownership of a failure and holding yourself accountable, it's tempting to blame it on external circumstances – a behaviour known as self-attribution bias. You can blame a poor 5k time on your job suddenly becoming more hectic in the week prior. Companies like to attribute poor performance to foreign competition or 'short-term' investors.

Part of the reluctance to admit mistakes and learn from them is due to the way society views failure. We often play a game of 'gotcha' – catch others doing things wrong – and call out mistakes. As Syed argues, 'We should praise each other for trying, for experimenting … If we only ever praise each other for getting things right, for perfection, for flawlessness, we will insinuate, if only unintentionally, that it is possible to succeed without failing, to climb without falling.'

Even if there's no one else you can scapegoat and you know that failure is down to you, it's still unpleasant to open the black box. People cringe when watching videos of them public speaking, or listening to recordings of them learning to sing. But, as is well known in medicine and as stressed in Chapter 10 for regulation, diagnosis precedes treatment. Identifying your deficiencies is the only way to eradicate them.

Malcolm Gladwell's bestseller *Outliers* is often interpreted as suggesting that racking up 10,000 hours is sufficient to master a skill. But the research by Anders Ericsson and his co-authors, which the book cites, actually has a more nuanced conclusion. What matters isn't just hours spent performing the activity, but what the researchers call 'deliberate practice', which they define as an activity 'rated very high on relevance for performance, high on effort, and comparatively low on inherent enjoyment'. Deliberate practice is uncomfortable as it involves going through difficult tasks where you're likely to fail, and then reviewing your missteps. Ericsson scrutinised the diaries of violin students at a Berlin music academy, comparing the best students, who'd likely go on to join one of the top symphony orchestras in Germany, with average students who'd later become teachers. Surprisingly, there was no difference in the total amount of time spent on music across the two groups, which included activities such as group practice, playing for fun (alone or with others), taking lessons or performing. The big disparity was that the best students spent more time in solo practice. Other researchers found that chess-playing ability was strongly related to the amount of time of solitary chess study and unrelated to the amount of time playing chess games. And what you do in solo practice time matters. Another study discovered that elite figure skaters devoted more time to difficult jumps and spins they hadn't mastered; average ones preferred the comfort of routines they'd already perfected.

While I had the wrong mentality to avoiding ski falls ex ante, learning from them ex post came a bit more naturally due to my chess background. In a chess game, you keep a record of every move. So, after a game, I'd typically ally with my former adversary in learning from it. We'd replay the game and teach each other what we could have done better. When I was a kid, recording chess games was easy as you only needed pencil and paper, but recording other activities was much more difficult. We didn't have waterproof smartphones that could video your swimming stroke. Now we have the technology to record and replay our weaknesses in almost any activity, but we often lack the mentality.

Service

Throughout this book, we've stressed how enterprises should serve society – but shouldn't do so in an undisciplined manner and ignore profits. Chapter 3 introduced three principles – multiplication, comparative advantage and materiality – to guide leaders on whether to make investments in stakeholders.

The same principles can also guide a citizen in serving others. He might receive numerous requests to volunteer for non-profits, give pro bono talks or offer career advice to a friend's children. But he shouldn't ignore the impact on his own time. Just as Chapter 3 showed how these principles guide investment decisions when resources are limited, they can also guide people on how to serve effectively when time is limited.

Let's start with the analogue of the *principle of multiplication*. For enterprises, this means taking an action that creates more value for stakeholders than it costs the firm. Applied to service, this involves giving *gifts of unequal value* – taking an action that creates more value to the recipient than it costs you. We introduce a different term because thinking about service as giving gifts changes our attitude to it. Often, service is reactive. Generous people donate when their co-workers ask for sponsorship for a charity challenge, and they lend a hand when friends ask for help moving house. But it's a different mindset to serve proactively and think what gifts of unequal value we can bless others with.

One evening at university, I had an unremarkable pizza dinner. We'd ordered one too many pizzas, so my friend Stephen asked to box it up. I thought he was going to take it home and eat it cold the next day, as many students would. But he took us on a walk round Oxford, giving slices of pizza to the homeless.

Now each slice of pizza was a gift of unequal value, worth more to a homeless citizen than a student. But that's not what this story is about. Stephen didn't just give the pizza to the homeless; he talked to them. The homeless are people we often ignore – we try to avoid making eye contact, let alone talk to them, in case they're so bold as to ask us for aid. By recognising them as a fellow human, Stephen gave them a gift of unequal value. I remember the lady he gave the final slice of pizza to. He asked her name, and over twenty years later I can remember it – Janice. Even on Janice's best days, when dozens of people threw coins into her coffee cup, maybe no one would have asked her name. Stephen did.

Let's now turn to the *principle of comparative advantage*. We often think that front-line activities, where you get your hands dirty, are the ultimate form of service – such as helping in a homeless shelter. But as stressed in Chapter 8, excellence is the best form of service, and we're most likely to be excellent in activities we have a comparative advantage in. If you're skilled at bookkeeping, managing a homeless charity's accounts may be more effective than serving in the shelter.

Finally, the *principle of (intrinsic) materiality* highlights the importance of serving stakeholders that we're particularly passionate about. While this may seem obvious, it's easy to be drawn into issues due to their severity or public perception. A homeless shelter may seem more worthy than your school's charitable foundation, but the latter may be more material to you if you feel a tight bond with your school.

Applying these principles might seem formulaic for something such as service, which should be natural and from the heart. But doing so creates freedom. You have the liberty to turn down service requests without any sense of guilt, recognising that there are other people out there more talented and more passionate than you in these causes. Doing so allows you to focus on the sweet spot, where the three principles overlap and you have a profound effect in helping others in an area you care deeply about.

Career Choice

A pie-growing enterprise is driven by purpose rather than profits, yet ultimately becomes profitable by doing so. The same approach can be applied to choosing your career. By selecting a vocation that serves a purpose rather than one that's lucrative, a citizen can ultimately become not only more fulfilled, but also more financially successful. This final section is primarily aimed at readers about to start their career or contemplating a career switch. But it may also be of value to those who don't intend to change jobs, but have the flexibility to weight different priorities in their current position.

We've used Apple as an example of a pie-growing company driven by purpose. Yet arguably the most famous speech by Steve Jobs, Apple's founder, was on personal purpose. As he taught in a 2005 graduation speech at Stanford University: 'You can't connect the dots looking forward; you can only connect them looking backwards. So you have to trust that the dots will somehow connect in your future. You have to trust in something – your gut, destiny, life, karma, whatever. This approach has never let me down, and it has made all the difference in my life.'

One way to make career decisions is to reduce them to an instrumental calculation. When deciding a job after university, think about not only that job's current salary, but also how it may open the door for future positions. Taking a job in fintech may pay a lower starting salary than joining an investment bank, but the future upside could be higher. When deciding which non-profit board to join, think about which one will boost your profile the most, based on the public visibility of the non-profit and the clout of the other board members. In other words, you map out your future career – your future dots, with each one being a stepping stone to the next.

But this approach doesn't always work in practice, because it's very difficult to see where a stepping stone will lead to next. Jobs instead advocated the counterintuitive, and seemingly short-sighted approach, of stepping onto the stone that just feels right at the time. The stone may simply be beautiful to stand on, even though you don't know where it will lead.

The idea of choosing a career based on purpose is well-known, almost to the point of becoming clichéd. It also seems unrealistic and impractical. It's unrealistic because, while it preaches well from the pulpit when you're the Apple CEO and a multi-billionaire, most people have families to support and loans to repay. They can't cheerfully ignore financial motives in a carefree pursuit of purpose. But we'll show that some lucrative careers, maligned by the public, can also be deeply purposeful. Following your purpose may seem impractical because many people don't know what their purpose is. But we can turn this idea into something concrete and actionable by using the same framework we introduced in Chapter 8 for defining an enterprise's purpose.

Recall that an enterprise's purpose involves two elements – *who* it exists for, based on the principle of materiality, and *why* it exists, based on the principle of comparative advantage. These two elements also apply when discerning a citizen's purpose.

The *who* is relatively easy to decide. Business materiality doesn't have an analogue for individuals, but intrinsic materiality does – which stakeholders a citizen is particularly driven to serve. A lawyer might view refugees as more important than companies and so enter human rights rather than corporate law. Someone with a heart for the environment might work for a charity, go into politics or join a company with a material impact on the environment and change it. But the *who* still leaves many questions unanswered. Let's say you've defined the *who* as children. There are many ways of serving them: paediatrics, teaching and social work. The *why* is more complex, and what we'll focus on.

The *why* is based on the principle of comparative advantage, which involves both talent and passion. The former is relatively easy to identify, the latter far more difficult. 'Pursue your passion' seems as nebulous as 'serve a purpose' – how can you do this if you don't know what your passion is? For some careers, passion might be obvious. We can easily imagine how Roy Vagelos might have been inspired when he heard Merck chemists talk about developing drugs at his family's diner, and chosen a career in science. But for other industries such as food delivery and transport, the passion may be less obvious – even though, as discussed in Chapter 8, these industries can create substantial value for society.

Again, we can create a framework to break the idealistic advice to 'pursue your passion' into something concrete. Let's say you've decided that the *who* is to serve enterprises, because you believe they can be a force for good in society (intrinsic materiality). What's the way you'll serve them? We'll illustrate this framework using finance and consulting careers, rather than working directly for a company, because these careers are particularly viewed as non-purposeful.

This framework involves three questions. The first question is: *Where do you see yourself in ten years' time?* Now this seems as unoriginal as the idea of 'pursue your passion'. Most people think they know the answer – perhaps Managing Director of an investment bank, Partner at a consulting firm or Principal of a private equity fund. But this question doesn't ask you where you see yourself in terms of your job title. It asks what will make you tick, what will wake you up in the morning, what your days will be like. Because a career, if it's to be truly fulfilling, isn't about what you do; it's about who you are. Many people do get to the top. But many haven't taken the time to ask this question before they start out, so they reach the summit and realise they've climbed the wrong mountain.

Let's make this concrete. Say you'd like to be Managing Director of an investment bank or Partner at a consulting firm. That's your job title. Who you are is a trusted advisor. Your clients will come to you with their biggest problems. Perhaps they're in financial difficulty and ask you whether they should issue equity, raise debt, cut the dividend, sell a division or put the entire company up for sale. They trust you to give the advice that's best for them, rather than what will earn you the highest fee.

Only go into investment banking or consulting if being a trusted advisor is who you are. Perhaps you're the person who friends turn to when they need candid advice on an issue. You have a reputation for telling them what they need to hear, not what they want to hear, and keeping it confidential. And you love serving your friends in this way. Or, in a study group at university, you were the one willing to have tough conversations with other group members who weren't pulling their weight. Others find these conversations awkward, but they're second nature to you. Then you're the sort of person who should go into banking or consulting.

Or say you'd like the job title of private equity Principal. Who you are is an investor, someone who finds undervalued assets. During the day, these undervalued assets are businesses that are unloved by their current owners – so much so that they want to sell them. You see potential in them that no one else sees. You're willing to put your money where your mouth is and invest in them. And you put in more than just money, but also the time and effort to turn them around.

Outside of the office, these undervalued 'assets' might be people – the unemployed who you can invest in by funding a job-coaching programme, or local children who you can support by endowing a scholarship at a school. And you don't just throw money at them, but get your hands dirty by serving as a school governor. In an amateur sports team, you might be willing to coach a new player who doesn't immediately hit the ground running, rather than benching her or making her feel unwelcome so that she quits the team. All these investments take patience, which not everyone has – but many of the best investors, like Peter Lynch and Jeff Ubben, are willing to take long-term perspectives.

Only become a private equity investor if being an investor is who you truly are – if your passion is uncovering undervalued assets (both businesses and people) and working with them to fulfil their potential. If your passion is more finding undervalued assets than turning them around, you might be more fulfilled running a mutual fund (and exercising stewardship through monitoring).

The second question is: *What do you do in your spare time?* What you voluntarily choose to do conveys what you're passionate about. This question might seem unrealistic, since many citizens like to play sport or music, but are unlikely to become professional athletes or musicians. But pastimes are more informative than you might think.

The most common question that I get asked by students interested in finance is whether to start on the sell-side or the buy-side. To most people, the buy-side is the place to be. When I was in investment banking, the dream was to be called by a headhunter who'd move you into private equity. In sales and trading, you longed for the day when you'd be approached by a hedge fund. And the buy-side is the right place for many people. But there are far more people whose purpose is likely on the sell-side than commonly thought, because their passion is selling, and this is revealed by their pastimes.

Some business school students lead treks to their home country over the holidays, giving up the chance to explore a new land. Why? Because they love selling their country. Others captain sports teams, where they teach the activity to newcomers. Teaching has many similarities to selling – explaining complex concepts in clear language and making it engaging.

Others still might not captain sports teams, but they may play in one, or play in a band. This involves an element of 'tribalism' – being part of a small team, where you truly care about every team member, and you take your tribe on the road with you. Bruce Springsteen was once asked what continues to motivate him, as he's already sold millions of records and played Madison Square Garden countless times. He replied that it was being on stage with Clarence Clemons, his saxophonist. When Clarence plays a sax solo, he's proud simply to share the stage with him – even if Bruce is silent and getting none of the applause at that moment. As Bruce said in his eulogy of Clarence, 'Standing next to Clarence was like standing next to the baddest ass on the planet. You were proud, you were strong, you were excited and laughing with what might happen, with what together, you might be able to do.'

And that's what you get on the sell-side. Just like a band going on tour, or a sports team playing in an away game, on the sell-side you take your team – your tribe – to a client to deliver a pitch. One day you might head that team, and not give the entire pitch yourself, but choose an analyst or associate to present part of it. She nails it. You get the same pride as Bruce did when he was just passively watching Clarence play his solo.

The third question is: *What are your values?* Values are what you centre your life around, how you aim to touch the lives of others and what you'd like to be remembered by. In *The Road to Character*, David Brooks calls these 'eulogy values', since you'd like them to be read out in your eulogy – in contrast to 'resume values' that can be put on a CV. Then, having clarified what's important to you, you can find a career that roughly lines up with these values. As Harvard economist Greg Mankiw wrote, 'The secret to a happy life: find out what you like to do, and then find someone who will pay you to do it.'

Now that might seem completely unrealistic. There's a popular view that the most lucrative careers are the most valueless ones, but this is an unfair caricature as we've discussed. There are many lucrative careers which line up with several eulogy values, just as an enterprise that serves society can still be profitable.

The value 'I will always be trusted to tell the truth' lines up with an advisory vocation. One of the potential downsides of a career in banking or consulting is that it's hierarchical. But for people with the value 'I will always respect authority', this is an attraction, not a downside, as they appreciate a clear chain of command. That's why my students with military backgrounds have typically liked the hierarchical aspect of advisory careers. But others, who have the value 'I always want the freedom to be my own boss', might find this career difficult at the start.

In Stephen Covey's book *7 Habits of Highly Effective People*, Habit #2 is 'begin with the end in mind'. Covey recommends not only deciding on your purpose, but also writing it down in a personal mission statement. Oprah Winfrey's is: 'To be a teacher. And to be known for inspiring my students to be more than they thought they could be.' Virgin Group founder Sir Richard Branson's is: 'To have fun in [my] journey through life and learn from [my] mistakes.' Other mission statements, including many by ordinary people, can easily be found online for readers who'd like additional examples for inspiration.

Just like an enterprise's purpose involves trade-offs, so should a citizen's. The mission statement must be short and can't contain everything. Anything left out of the mission statement is deprioritised by default. But the more concise the mission statement, the more it helps with Covey's Habit #3, 'first things first', which is about time management and prioritisation. So personal purpose can guide not only a career switch, but also what duties to focus on in one's current position. If everything is in your mission statement, it provides no guidance on prioritisation – just like if an enterprise's purpose contained all stakeholders.

I define my professional purpose as 'to use rigorous research to influence the practice of business'. This is a commitment to disseminate as well as create knowledge, and to disseminate others' research rather than just my own. But it's also a commitment not to do certain things, such as responding to media requests for comment on general economic topics. Even if I can come up with something semi-intelligent based on broader economic intuition, and even if the media outlet is prestigious, it's precluded unless I have specific research expertise. It also means that I can't go to as many academic conferences and seminars as in the past. While I enjoy them, there just aren't enough hours in the day to be able to interact with businesses as well. My co-authors might just as effectively be able to present our joint work, and my comparative advantage might lie elsewhere.

Purpose is what binds together the members of an enterprise and inspires them to go above and beyond what's required in the contract. It encourages them to create value for society and contribute to human betterment, without doing an instrumental calculation of whether they'll ultimately benefit – but the enterprise typically ends up more profitable as a result. And purpose is what inspires a citizen to view a job as a vocation, pursued because of an intrinsic calling rather than to earn a living. Yet being fuelled by purpose ultimately leads to greater success. Purpose is aspirational, but not nebulous, and both enterprises and citizens can ask themselves concrete questions to find out what their purpose is – and then put it into practice.

In a Nutshell

- Game theory shows that, while cooperation can lead to all parties being better off, the gains from cooperation may be unequal. Concerns with equality may lead to a player rejecting cooperation and shrinking the pie, even if he is worse off as a result.
- Many real-life situations are win-win. The other player should be seen as one's ally, not one's opponent.
- The *law of comparative advantage* states that all countries can gain from international trade – even less productive ones. But concerns that the gains are split evenly can lead to countries restricting trade. Other countries reciprocate, and all countries end up worse off.

- Like trade, technology has the potential to either cause substantial job losses or grow the pie for all, including workers. Doing so requires leaders to redefine jobs away from those that are substituted by technology to those that are complemented by it, and governments to fund lifelong education.
- In interpersonal dynamics, cooperation to improve company performance typically benefits all divisions, even if some gain more than others. It's a leader's responsibility to design reward and evaluation systems that create win-win situations for colleagues and encourage the collaboration necessary for pie growth. Outside of a work setting, 'givers' who help others are more successful in the long run.
- In service, the *principle of multiplication* advocates giving *gifts of unequal value*, worth more to the recipient than it costs the giver. The *principle of comparative advantage* means that citizens need not always occupy the most front-line roles. The *principle of materiality* suggests serving on issues that matter most to the citizen rather than those seen as most worthy by the public. Together, these principles give freedom to selectively choose service activities rather than feeling pressured into accepting all requests.
- Just as the pie-growing mentality sees the pie as expandable, the *growth mindset* sees one's skill set as augmentable – but only through deliberate practice.
- Citizens should choose a career based on purpose and see financial rewards as a by-product, just like enterprises. As with enterprises, purpose depends in part on intrinsic materiality and comparative advantage, of which passion is a source.
- Passion is not a nebulous concept, but can be made concrete by asking three questions: where you see yourself in ten years' time (in terms of not what you do, but who you are), what you do in your spare time and what your values are.

CONCLUSION

We started this book by acknowledging the severe crisis that capitalism faces. In the eyes of millions of citizens, it's a rigged game. Corporations exist to line the pockets of executives and investors, paying scant attention to worker wages, customer welfare or climate change. Those lucky enough to be running businesses or investment funds see no need to change, as they're protected by market power, and can further entrench themselves by lobbying. Even worse, many see no responsibility to change, as they delude themselves that their social responsibility is to maximise profits.

That's why we have a crisis. Citizens and politicians can't just hope for the system to reform itself – many believe it's inherently broken. They argue we need a new system, and so there are serious proposals to overthrow capitalism as we know it by breaking up or nationalising large companies, regulating executive pay and share buybacks, and wresting the control of businesses away from shareholders.

But such reforms risk stifling the many positive contributions that enterprises make to society. Viewing capitalism as the enemy may be electorally popular, and mobilise voters around a common adversary, but throws away the substantial opportunities to partner with business to harness it for social good. It also ignores the crucial role that profits play, in providing ordinary citizens with a return on their savings, funding an enterprise's investment in its workers or encouraging a leader to swing for the fences on a new idea. So what we need is a solution that works for, and involves, *both* business *and* society.

That's what this book has been about. It's shown that such a solution exists – and importantly it lies within the current system, so doesn't involve taking a wild bet on the unknown. It's backed up by the rigorous evidence in the most stringent peer-reviewed journals, and complemented by concrete examples of how it can be successfully put into practice, rather than being an abstract idea. So, in the light of the major challenges that both capitalism and society face, we have genuine hope.

This solution is the pie-growing mentality. When an enterprise is run with the primary purpose of creating value for society, it isn't sacrificing profits and redistributing a fixed pie. Instead, it expands the total value that it creates, benefiting investors as well as stakeholders. Indeed, this approach typically ends up more profitable in the long term than an attempt to maximise shareholder value. So it's one that leaders should voluntarily embrace, even in the absence of regulation or public unrest. Creating social value is neither defensive nor simply 'worthy' – it's good business. The highest-quality evidence, not wishful thinking, reaches this conclusion: To reach the land of profit, follow the road of purpose.

The pie-growing mentality is freeing, as companies can make long-term investments without having to justify them by calculating their profit impact – a calculation that's often futile because this impact is hard to predict. But it's also focused, rather than a free-for-all. We've provided principles that leaders can use to discern which projects to undertake and which to rein in. Purpose isn't just a lofty mission statement, but provides a clear direction to help navigate difficult decisions. It's a commitment for leaders to follow through with action, even if it involves closing down a profitable division, and hold themselves to account by reporting on progress.

Just as a pie-growing enterprise aims to create value for all of society, so all of society has a role to play in instilling the pie-growing mentality in enterprises. Investors can play a major role through stewardship – having a deep understanding of a company's long-term value, sticking with it when others are rushing for the exit, but also not being afraid to sell or engage if it's mortgaging its future, regardless of how enticing short-term profits are. Employees have both the power and responsibility to ensure that purpose filters through to ground level and to make innovations of their own. Customers can walk away from a company, no matter how attractive its products, if they don't share its values. Citizens can influence policymakers to take an evidence-based approach to reform that considers the benefits of business as well as its costs.

Major change is already happening. Even though there are some high-profile cases of pie-splitting companies, a careful look at all the evidence shows that many others are quietly creating value for all members. Enterprises who treat their employees as colleagues, genuinely implement sustainability policies or invest in their material stakeholders end up more profitable in the long run. Those who make their leaders long-term owners deliver greater value to both shareholders and stakeholders. Investors who vote for proposals aimed at benefiting stakeholders end up themselves benefiting.

So any company or investor that embraces the pie-growing mentality isn't swimming against the tide or going it alone. They're instead riding on the tailwinds of evidence and joining a much broader movement of peers taking very seriously their responsibility to society and attempting real change. They don't need to put their trust solely in statistics and regression coefficients, but can take guidance and learn from aspirational examples. We saw how Merck – as early as the 1940s – developed penicillin to save people's lives, even though there was no clear profit stream at the time, and now donates ivermectin annually to 300 million of the world's poorest citizens suffering from river blindness. We learned how Vodafone pioneered a mobile money service to the unbanked, lifting 196,000 Kenyans households out of poverty. We observed how Barclays shut down a £1 billion revenue stream and CVS Health stopped selling a $2 billion product because they were inconsistent with their purposes.

These may seem lofty examples to follow. Not everyone has the power to develop a Nobel Prize-winning medicine, launch a new technology or close an entire business line. But pies can be grown with incremental, but continuous, sprinkles of flour. The New Belgium Brewing Company started by simply acknowledging its negative environmental impact, which inspired its colleagues to think of ways to mitigate it. Marks & Spencer reported its impact on various stakeholders and set itself targets, which united stakeholders around a common cause. The Weir Group didn't change its purpose statement or business model, but instead recognised the importance of rewarding its leaders according to the long term – and at the same time allowed all its colleagues to share in its success.

Beyond these examples, there are large and influential organisations allowing enterprises and investors to share best practice, develop frameworks to shape discussions and reforms, and collaborate on implementing change at an industry- or economy-wide level. For investors wanting to initiate dialogues with companies, we saw the eight questions that Blueprint for Better Business developed to help them discern which enterprises are genuinely embedding purpose. Conversely, for leaders wishing to engage with investors, Focusing Capital on the Long Term has established a roadmap to guide such conversations. The Purposeful Company has applied the best academic evidence to devise practical reforms to corporate governance, executive pay and stewardship. The Embankment Project for Inclusive Capitalism has brought together companies, asset managers and asset owners to develop metrics on long-term value that firms can report, with the reassurance that investors will pay serious attention to them. The UN Principles for Responsible Investment Collaboration Platform, the Canadian Coalition for Good Governance and the UK's Investor Forum help shareholders engage collectively for the common good, rather than viewing each other as a benchmark to be beaten. The New Citizenship Project works with companies to mobilise their customers as citizens. Resources are increasingly abundant and momentum is strong.

Leaders of today's companies are in a privileged position, as technology and their global reach give them more power to create social value than arguably ever before. Investors running today's funds have larger pots of capital and stronger shareholder rights than ever before, to hold companies to account for delivering both purpose and profit. And citizens have greater agency than ever before, with our ability to rally campaigns or provide public feedback on a company – or, at a personal level, to seek win-win in our interactions. It's up to all of us, together, to use this power to create a form of capitalism that works for all of society. We have the evidence to back us, the examples to inspire us and the tools to put it into practice. Let's make this vision a reality.

ACTION ITEMS

This section provides practical suggestions for acting on the ideas of this book. I've categorised them into ideas for leaders, boards, investors and citizens. Since many of the book's principles apply across several members of society, some ideas appear in more than one place, and ideas in different sections may still be relevant for a particular member.

Leaders

Define the Purpose of Your Enterprise

- Describe why your enterprise exists – its reason for being and the role it plays in the world – guided by the principle of comparative advantage. Explain who your enterprise exists for – which stakeholders are the first among equals – guided by the principle of materiality.
- Ensure that the purpose is focused and selective – that it does not try to be all things to all people, but acknowledges the inevitability of trade-offs and its role in helping navigate them. Recognise that a purpose can be powerful by what it leaves out.
- Seek input from colleagues and external stakeholders, such as customers. Once a purpose is formulated, ensure that it is clear, but not rigid, allowing it to evolve in response to changing conditions.

Communicate the Delivery of Purpose

- Formulate a broad set of metrics that track whether your company is serving its purpose. Set long-term targets for each metric and report on progress. Consciously decide not to track certain metrics if they may be manipulated or misleading.
- Use narrative reporting to add meaning and context to the numbers. For example, explain why certain metrics are off-target and the remedial actions taken; supplement headcount and turnover data by describing your company's efforts to recruit, retrain and train high-quality colleagues.
- Extend beyond impersonal, one-way reporting to personal, two-way communication. Hold meetings with investors and 'town halls' with employees and external stakeholders, so that all can keep you accountable for the delivery of purpose, as well as share their ideas.

Embed Purpose into Your Enterprise

- Scrutinise whether the enterprise's strategy is consistent with its purpose. Does every major product or service truly create value for society, and does its production cause unnecessary harm to some stakeholders? Does it still have a comparative advantage in each business or instead own them for legacy reasons?
- Align the firm's operating model and culture with its purpose. Be uncompromising about the quality of processes particularly central to the delivery of purpose. Verify that cultural fit plays an important role in hiring, promotion and retention decisions.
- Track how employees, teams and projects are performing on purpose-related dimensions. Ensure that this information enters significantly into employee evaluation and reward. Make this data available to colleagues to empower them to make better decisions.

Cultivate a Spirit of Excellence

- Ensure that the enterprise serves society not only through ancillary 'CSR' activities, but primarily through excellence in its core business. Allocate headcount, financial resources and your time to the businesses where your company has greatest comparative advantage and affects its most material stakeholders.

- Apply standards of excellence to investment decisions. Stop existing projects, and do not start new ones, if the financial and societal returns are only mediocre. Reallocate the capital to your core business or, if all good investment opportunities have been taken, pay it out to investors.
- Recognise the seriousness of errors of omission. Continually strive for improvements and take risks on untested ideas – particularly if they serve a societal need and even if the revenue stream is not yet clear. Ensure colleagues have the freedom to innovate without requiring excessive approvals or fearing failure.

View Stakeholders as Partners in the Enterprise

- Empower employees with decision-making authority and be comfortable that this may lead to errors of commission. View them as sources of ideas rather than as simply ways to execute your ideas. Mobilize the citizenship potential of customers – for example, by actively seeking their input or working with them to reduce your environmental impact.
- Invest in workers' skills and well-being. Anticipate which colleagues are likely to be displaced by technology or competition, and proactively retrain them. Monitor employees' mental and physical wellness and take pre-emptive action if needed. Create a culture where all managers, including you, internalise the effect of extra work on their team.
- Consider giving shares to all employees, so that they become financial partners in the company and enjoy the fruits of its success.

Boards

Make Leaders Long-Term Owners

- Pay executives with equity that they must hold for the long term, including after their retirement. Verify that the holding periods are appropriate given the industry cycle and the length of time it takes for a leader's actions to fully affect the stock price.

- Watch out for potential short-term behaviour – errors of omission such as the failure to launch new projects, or errors of commission such as cutting investment – in periods where the CEO has significant equity vesting.
- De-emphasise complex bonuses based on quantitative targets, and consider removing performance conditions for equity that may lead to short-termism.

Monitor the Enterprise's Delivery of Purpose

- Ensure substantial time on the meeting agenda is allocated to purpose. Evaluate major decisions, particularly those involving trade-offs, according to whether they are consistent with the firm's purpose. Consider having sub-committees for purpose-related issues (e.g. innovation, human capital); if not, ensure they are the responsibility of the full board.
- Verify the enterprise's purpose statement remains relevant today, given its current comparative advantage and the materiality of its different stakeholders, rather than being a legacy.
- Scrutinise the metrics the company is using to measure progress, and ensure these are the relevant ones. Have conversations with leaders beyond the metrics – what is behind the trends, and what dimensions they are particularly seeking to improve. Ask for examples of where purpose has caused them to make different decisions.

Engage Routinely with Investors

- Regularly meet with investors as a matter of course, not just in times of crisis. View investors as a source of ideas, rather than only a source of challenges to respond to. Ensure that some meetings take place without executives, to allow investors to express their candid opinions on leader performance.
- Hold 'Stewardship & Strategy Forums', jointly with executives, that can be attended by all large investors. Ensure these events are focused on long-term factors such as strategy, innovation and human capital development.

- Actively seek investors that align with your purpose, and consider giving investors a say-on-purpose vote. If so, ensure that this vote is only one outcome of a broader dialogue with investors on purpose.

Understand the Business at Ground Level

- Walk the 'shop floor' of an enterprise, through structured visits, to talk with employees at different levels and in different locations. Learn what inspires and frustrates them about the company.
- If the enterprise has retail customers, make unannounced visits to a retail location to understand the customer experience first-hand.
- Supplement personal visits with the insights of stakeholder panels that capture the perspectives of key stakeholders, such as customers and colleagues, more broadly. Ensure the insights learned translate into action.

Investors

Since investors, like boards, monitor enterprises, many of the action points for boards also apply to investors. In addition, since investors are enterprises themselves, many of the action points for leaders are similarly relevant. This section provides additional ideas tailored to investors.

Define Your Purpose and Approach to Stewardship

- Define your purpose – how you aim to generate long-term returns to savers – and your approach to stewardship. Recognise that more stewardship is not necessarily better; instead, ensure that your approach to stewardship is aligned with your purpose and comparative advantage.
- For engagement, clarify your key engagement priorities and how you intend to pursue them – for example, through voting, private meetings or public activism.
- For monitoring, highlight the dimensions of performance that you will particularly scrutinise. Formulate a divestment policy for what will cause you to sell a holding.

Embed Stewardship into the Investment Process

- If the fund is actively managed, ensure that every position is a conviction holding – whose long-term story you either believe in or believe you can turn around – rather than held because it's part of the benchmark.
- Pay fund managers with significant stakes in their fund, which they must hold for several years.
- Devote substantial resources to stewardship and integrate them into the investment process. Ensure that voting and engagements are jointly led by the stewardship team and fund managers rather than outsourced to the former.

Communicate the Delivery of Stewardship

- Select metrics that are relevant to your stewardship policy (e.g. voting record, including frequency of votes against house policy and proxy advisor recommendations) and report them. Consciously choose not to report certain metrics if they may be misleading, and explain why you are not doing so.
- Undertake narrative reporting – for example, how you are ensuring that stewardship is integrated into the investment process and how fund managers are incentivised. Provide case studies of engagement or divestment.
- Hold regular meetings between asset owners and asset managers to discuss stewardship performance. Ensure that asset managers understand asset owners' particular stewardship objectives and expectations.

Practice Informed Voting

- Consider formulating a house voting policy, informed by a stakeholder roundtable or advisory committee, and publish it. Anticipate the situations in which the house policy may not be applicable, and ensure that the policy is not automatically followed in these circumstances.

- Develop a policy for the use of proxy advisors. Ensure that their recommendations are only one input into the vote, particularly if strategic judgment is required. Understand proxy advisors' evaluation methodologies, to know when to be particularly cautious of their recommendations.
- View the vote as only one engagement tool and part of a broader process. Express concerns to management before a proposal is put on the table, rather than only voting against it after the fact. Communicate the reasons for your vote to management and, if appropriate, to the public.

Engage Routinely with Executives and Directors

- Regularly meet with executives and directors (either together or separately, as appropriate) as a matter of course, not just in times of crisis. Use these meetings to have a two-way dialogue on long-term factors, to both provide insights and remain informed about them. Refrain from micromanaging the enterprise.
- Involve other investors in engagements, viewing them as partners rather than a benchmark to be beaten. Consider joining a collective engagement organisation if available. Participate in industry-wide engagements – for example, to encourage all companies in a sector to report certain metrics.
- Have an escalation mechanism for when engagement fails, such as divestment or public confrontation. Ensure that it is used only as a last resort, but also that it is used when appropriate.

Monitor a Company's Long-Term Value

- Ensure that trading decisions are based not on short-term earnings, but an assessment of an enterprise's long-term value. Remain continuously informed about a company's long-term value through its public reports, third-party data sources (e.g. on ESG performance) and meetings with management.
- Ensure that retaining a stake in a company is an active, rather than a default, decision. Evaluate whether it is creating long-term value for society, and either engage or divest if it is not.

- Consider forming an external advisory committee, to help evaluate intangible factors that require specialist expertise. Use these insights to inform both investment in specific stocks and general themes, such as which sectors to overweight and avoid, and what topics to prioritise in engagement.

Citizens

As Colleagues, View Yourselves as Having Agency, Regardless of Your Position

- Empower, invest in and reward employees that report to you. Even if you are the most junior worker in your team, practise these attitudes when interacting with other departments.
- Recognise that you likely have far more agency than you may think. Resist the temptation to default to your formal job description and be bold in suggesting and trialling new ideas. Manage up: question why something is done in a particular way, and whether it can be done better or not at all. View challenging your superiors as the responsibility of a good colleague, rather than an intrusion.
- Be willing to leave (or not to join) a company that fails to match your values and is unresponsive to engagement.

As Customers, Adopt a Citizen Rather than Consumer Mindset

- Decide on your values and ensure they have a significant effect on your purchase decisions. Use values comparison websites and apps to facilitate this.
- View yourself as being a member of the enterprise and part of a customer community. Provide constructive feedback, including suggestions for improvement, to companies or customer review websites. Consider joining, or even organising, campaigns to change a company's behaviour.
- Engage in responsible ownership of a product after purchase – for example, by participating in company initiatives to recycle or repair damaged products.

Keep Informed Using the Best Available Evidence

- Evaluate a company (e.g. as a potential customer or employee) using a pie-growing, rather than pie-splitting, mindset. Consider not how much investors or executives earn, but whether these earnings are a by-product of creating value for society.
- Be mindful of confirmation bias. Recognise that there are two sides to (almost) every issue, and actively seek arguments or evidence contradicting your viewpoint. Place greater faith in balanced rather than one-sided opinions.
- Beware of the phrase 'research shows that …'. Check whether a study has been published before believing it. If so, see if the journal features on a list of the most rigorous publications or instead a blacklist. If not, examine the credentials of the authors, such as the quality of their institution and their track record.

As Regulators or Voters, Engage in Diagnosis before Treatment

- Before passing or supporting a regulation, investigate whether a problem is large-scale or confined to a few high-profile cases. Critically evaluate large-scale evidence using the above guidelines.
- Consider whether a potential policy has been implemented elsewhere, and examine the most rigorous evidence on its effects. As a voter, support politicians that take an evidence-based approach.
- Contemplate whether a regulation might lead to companies engaging in manipulation to satisfy it or refraining from innovation to avoid violating it. Assess whether the regulation would help all firms create social value or would be counterproductive for some, given their particular circumstances.

Practise the Principles of Pieconomics in Everyday Life

- Seek 'win-win' outcomes in negotiations or interpersonal dynamics. Recognise that a gain for your counterparty or acquaintance need not come at your expense.

- Be aware that your abilities are not fixed, but can be grown through intentional and uncomfortable practice. Be willing to fail ex ante, and review your failures ex post.
- In service, seek to give gifts of unequal value, which are worth significantly more to the recipient than they cost you. Have the confidence to turn down service requests that do not satisfy the principles of multiplication, comparative advantage or materiality.

APPENDIX

This appendix provides extensions to Chapter 9 on how the investment industry can put stewardship into practice.

Collective Engagement Frameworks

The UN Principles for Responsible Investment Collaboration Platform promotes collective generalised engagement on ESG issues – such as improving carbon disclosure, implementing anti-corruption policies or not sourcing minerals from conflict zones. Member investors post an issue on the platform that they want to engage with a particular company about, and invite other members to support them. This may involve signing joint letters to companies, supporting shareholder proposals or combining forces in dialogues with management. Elroy Dimson, Oğuzhan Karakaş and Xi Li studied 1,671 collective engagements and found that successful ones increased return-on-assets and sales growth. This echoes the findings of their earlier paper, discussed in Chapter 6, that environmental and social engagements by a large investor improved profits and the stock price. While the engagements in both studies aimed to create value for stakeholders, investors benefited also.

Another vehicle for collective generalised engagement is the Canadian Coalition for Good Governance (CCGG). There are two main differences with the UN platform. The CCGG focuses on governance issues (such as implementing clawback provisions or say-on-pay votes) rather than environmental or social ones. And it's the CCGG itself, rather than members, that leads the dialogue with companies. Craig Doidge, Alexander Dyck, Hamed Mahmudi and Aazam Virani found that the formation of the CCGG increased the stock prices of firms where CCGG members had large stakes and so the CCGG was most likely to engage.

The UK's Investor Forum coordinates collective specialised engagement on issues such as capital allocation, strategy and productivity. Since an investor's view of these issues depends on his private information about the company, the Investor Forum has carefully developed a framework to ensure that investors don't accidentally share private information. Similar to the CCGG, it's the Forum (rather than investors) that leads the engagement, and often investors don't know which other investors are collectively engaging with them.

For example, in July 2015, the Investor Forum represented twelve investors in the UK retailer Sports Direct, together owning 33% of the independent shares, who were concerned about its governance and employment practices. Collective engagements are usually private. But due to lack of progress, in August 2016, the Forum publicly demanded an independent review of these practices, which Sports Direct agreed to the following January. Investors were then concerned that Sports Direct's working practices might be widespread across the clothing sector, sparking an industry-wide engagement.

In addition to engagements to solve a particular problem, the Investor Forum encourages dialogues between investors and enterprises as a matter of course. Executives often lament that, in earnings calls and annual general meetings, discussions typically concern short-term profit – but they can do something about this. The Investor Forum recommends that companies hold 'Stewardship & Strategy Forums' with their large investors to discuss long-term issues; a sample meeting agenda is available on its website. For example, Rolls Royce's 2016 event discussed its research initiatives, new customer offerings and plans to reduce senior headcount. These are similar to the CEO Investor Forums discussed in Chapter 8.

Investors can also collaborate outside of formal coordination mechanisms. In May 2018, LGIM brought together sixty global asset managers and asset owners, with combined assets under management exceeding $10 trillion. This group published an open letter in the *Financial Times* demanding that the oil and gas industry do more to meet the Paris Agreement commitments on climate change.

Reforming Asset Owners and Investment Consultants

Asset Owners

Many asset owners don't recognise the value of stewardship or the role that it plays in enhancing long-term returns. A 2016 survey by the Investment Association found that over half of asset owners hadn't signed up to the Stewardship Code (compared to 3% of asset managers). The most common reason was that they weren't even aware of it, followed by other priorities taking precedence. Only 59% of them strongly agreed that they had stewardship responsibilities. Yet the power that can be unleashed if asset owners recognise the importance of stewardship is huge. Asset managers are ultimately responsible to their clients – asset owners – and so asset owners, not regulators, are best placed to hold asset managers to account for stewardship.

Let's go through the three steps for asset owners, starting with defining stewardship policy. Like an asset manager, an asset owner's policy should describe its approach to voting and engagement, if it undertakes these activities itself rather than delegating them to asset managers. More unique to an asset owner, the policy should outline how it uses stewardship to choose asset managers. At present, many look at short-term performance or tracking error – how close a fund is to its benchmark, even though such proximity discourages stewardship as discussed. Given such behaviour, it's rational for asset managers to deprioritise stewardship and become closet indexers.

The next step is to put the policy into practice. Asset owners can incorporate stewardship into three stages of the asset manager relationship. The first is *selection*. When an asset owner wishes to hire an asset manager, it puts out a Request for Proposals. This includes a detailed questionnaire asking the asset manager about its investment strategy and personnel. But there are typically few questions about stewardship, and so this analysis can be substantially expanded.

The second is *appointment*. Once an asset manager is selected, the asset owner then drafts a formal contract governing the relationship, sometimes referred to as a mandate or investment management agreement. Focusing Capital on the Long Term provides guidance for how asset owners can structure mandates to incentivise stewardship by asset managers. For example, the contract can contain stewardship expectations – Zurich Insurance's template states: 'The Investment Manager will have a process for assessing and monitoring current or potential investments in relation to . . . ESG factors. The Investment Manager will ensure that its staff receives adequate training, access to relevant data and information, and applies due care and diligence to applying this process.' The mandate can also require the asset manager to report on stewardship performance – the Environment Agency Pension Fund (EAPF) stipulates that asset managers measure the carbon footprint of their portfolio each year. In addition to lagging indicators of stewardship performance, the contract could also ask the asset manager to disclose leading indicators, such as changes to personnel or the stewardship process, and succession planning.

Third, the contract stipulates how the asset manager will be paid, which should be according to long-term performance. In April 2018, the Japanese Government Pension Investment Fund reformed its fee structure. It significantly cut its base management fee, but scrapped the previously imposed caps on the performance-based fee – recognising that high fees will only be a result of exceptional performance, and not at the expense of anyone. The majority of the fee is deferred, and the fund only awards contracts on a multi-year basis.

In Chapter 8, we stressed that the dialogue between enterprises and investors should be two-way. The same is true for the relationship between asset managers and asset owners. In addition to a contract, which states formal requirements for asset managers, some asset owners have 'covenants' which clarify the expectations that the asset manager can have of it. The EAPF's covenant states that it won't drop an asset manager based on short-term performance, will provide feedback to asset managers and will work with them to repair mandates rather than retendering them without notice.

This links to the third way to hold asset managers to account for stewardship – *monitoring* whether they've fulfilled the stewardship expectations set out in the contract. The asset owner might ask for examples of engagement, or how the asset manager incorporated societal factors into a buy or sell decision. It can also study forward-looking measures such as changes to policies, processes or personnel.

After defining and embedding stewardship, the final step is external communication. This includes disclosing the asset owner's policy – how it intends to evaluate asset managers on stewardship or engage itself. Communication of outcomes includes the voting record for asset owners who vote, changes in asset managers and the rationale for these changes.

Investment Consultants

Investment consultants advise asset owners on asset manager selection, so the guidelines largely mirror those for asset owners – in particular, assessing asset manager stewardship. They should develop a methodology to assess different stewardship approaches, and evaluate them across the varying stewardship expectations that clients may have.

More broadly, investment consultants should recognise their role in improving stewardship throughout the investment industry. They can help asset owners understand the value of stewardship in improving long-term returns, and how they can elicit it from asset managers – knowledge that the Investment Association survey found to be significantly lacking. As mentioned earlier, the legitimacy of the investment industry rests, in part, on the extent to which it's fulfilling its stewardship responsibilities. In Chapter 9, we discussed how investors can reduce the risk of being replaced by artificial intelligence by analysing qualitative information that can only be understood in the context of an enterprise's strategy. Similarly, investment consultants' client offering should expand beyond analysing financial performance and tracking error, which artificial intelligence can process in a vacuum, to evaluating an asset manager's stewardship approach, which can only be understood in the context of an asset owner's strategy.

ACKNOWLEDGEMENTS

Like any company, this book was a collaborative enterprise. I'd like to start with a big thank you to my editor Valerie Appleby at Cambridge University Press for her faith in, vision for and comments on the book. I'm also grateful to her colleagues Chris Burrows and Ellie Moriarty for their efforts with marketing and publicity and Sophie Rosinke for highly efficient copyediting.

As a first-time author, I particularly appreciate conversations with Dan Cable, Adam Grant, Lynda Gratton, Sally Holloway, Will Hutton, Freek Vermeulen and Stian Westlake on the publishing process. For the content, I'm grateful to Judith Aberg, Barend van Bergen (EY / Embankment Project for Inclusive Capitalism), Claudia Oeken (UBS) and Dorcas Oynango (Coca-Cola) for kindly granting me interviews, as well as Jon Alexander (New Citizenship Project), David Autor, Alon Brav, Emma Brown (Marks & Spencer), Andrew Curry (Kantar), Jennifer Donegan (Gallup), Caroline Flammer, Luke Fletcher, Sam Hartzmark, Catherine Howarth and Beau O'Sullivan (Share Action), Yiannis Ioannou, Wei Jiang, Hyunseob Kim, Natacha Lesellier (L'Oréal), Tao Li, Robin Nuttall, Camilla Osborne (Coca-Cola), Michael Parke, Mark Seligman, Patrick Sullivan and Garance Vidart (Danone) for ideas, facts, examples and data. London Business School generously provided funding for the research that went into this book.

The manuscript benefited enormously from the close readings, suggestions and constructive criticism from Gah-Yi Ban, Alex Berenga, Ben Clark, Dean Chaffee, Moqi Groen-Xu, Reid Hartman, Mathias Keller and Trevor Young on specific chapters and Michael Birshan,

Gaute Ulltveit-Moe and three anonymous reviewers on the whole book. Special thanks to Tim Paulin, who also contributed several important examples and 'devil's advocate' challenges, and Øyvind Bøhren, who read every word and made literally hundreds of valuable comments.

I thank Clare Chapman, Will Hutton and Dominic Rossi not only for providing direct input into the book, but also for our work together on The Purposeful Company that sparked ideas that it built on. Brady Dearden had the greatest impact on the book's exposition, reading every paragraph, in some cases several times, to make the language as crisp, fluent and accessible as possible.

It's impossible to single out one person when so many have made profound contributions to it, so I'll 'single' out two. I've been extremely lucky to work with Tom Gosling over several years on embedding the insights from academic research into practice. Many ideas in the book came from our work together on The Purposeful Company and the London Business School Centre for Corporate Governance. Tom not only read the first completed draft from start to finish, but also provided detailed comments on the initial outline, which had a major impact on its eventual direction. I'm also indebted to him for suggesting the term 'Pieconomics'.

I initially hired Marc Canal as a student researcher, but his contributions to many sections were so substantial as to be close to a co-author. Several of the real-world examples are thanks to Marc, and he was an invaluable sounding board and right-hand man for other big-picture issues such as the principles, frameworks and overall structure. Without his input, this book would be vastly inferior.

In addition to those who directly provided input into this book, many others made indirect, but no less important, contributions to it. My undergrad and doctoral academic advisors Xavier Gabaix, Dirk Jenter, Alexander Ljungqvist, Gustavo Manso, Alan Morrison and Stew Myers sparked my enthusiasm for research and desire to make it my vocation. They, plus my numerous mentors, colleagues and co-authors, made me a better researcher. I'm also grateful to the many academics I never directly worked with, yet learned tremendously from their studies, many of which are featured in this book.

Turning to practitioners, I'm grateful for conversations with Peggy Adams, Susie Balch, Amra Balic, Claudia Chapman, Ashley Hamilton Claxton, Mike Fox, Sue Garrard, Paul George, Daniel Godfrey, Andy Griffiths, Loughlin Hickey, George Littlejohn, Tonia Lovell,

Kristy Merrick, Bhakti Mirchandani, Andrew Ninian, Matt Peacock, Nicola Parker, Quintin Price, Sacha Sadan, Jen Sisson, Susan Sternglass Noble, Chris van Stolk, David Styles, Daniel Summerfield, Sarah Williamson, Charles Wookey, Ben Yeoh and especially Paul Coombes, on the challenges and opportunities associated with making responsible business a reality. I also learned significantly from academics and practitioners whose views differ from mine – including those I've debated against on conference panels or in the media. All of you have made the book a much larger pie than I could have baked myself.

ENDNOTES

Introduction

2 **10 million their homes** Jim Puzzanghera, 'A Decade after the Financial Crisis, Many Americans Are Still Struggling to Recover', *Seattle Times* (10 September 2018).

2 **poorest citizens in the world** Oxfam, '5 Shocking Facts about Extreme Global Inequality and How to Even It Up' (2019).

2 **1,200 deaths in Europe alone** Guillaume P. Chossière, Robert Malina, Akshay Ashok *et al.*, 'Public Health Impacts of Excess NO_x Emissions from Volkswagen Diesel Passenger Vehicles in Germany' (2017) 12 *Environmental Research Letters*.

2 **$4.7 trillion per year** Trucost, 'Natural Capital at Risk: The Top 100 Externalities of Business' (2013).

Chapter 1 The Pie-Growing Mentality

16 **owned less than $1,000** *Securities and Exchange Commission v. Martin Shkreli* (17 December 2015).

16 **enough money in hedge funds** Bethany McLean, 'Everything You Know about Martin Shkreli Is Wrong – Or Is It?', *Vanity Fair* (February 2016).

17 **not have the same efficacy** Andrew Pollack, 'Drug Goes from $13.50 a Tablet to $750, Overnight', *New York Times* (20 September 2015).

17 **she said to CNN** Heather Long, 'Here's What Happened to AIDS Drug that Spiked 5,000%', CNN Business (25 August 2016).

17 **'specialty' rather than regular stores** Shkreli has claimed that the closed distribution system was enacted two to three months before Turing purchased Daraprim, rather than being something that he implemented. However, Turing was already interested in Daraprim several months before the actual acquisition. Since Impax didn't have a history of closed distribution and Shkreli did, it's likely that Impax changed it due to the upcoming sale. Even if not, Turing still chose to keep the system closed post-acquisition.

19 **caused 42,000 staff to strike** Nicola Woolcock, 'University Lecturers to Strike as Students Sit Summer Exams', *The Times* (9 March 2018).

19 **petitions demanding tuition fee refunds** 'University Strike Talks Resume after Twitter Skirmishes', BBC (6 March 2018).

20 **expect me to maximise profits** Forbes Healthcare Summit, December 2015.

22 **liken myself to the robber barons** *Ibid.*

23 **(e.g. due to being self-employed)** 'Millions Are Mis-Sold Loan Cover', *Which?* (June 2008); Liz Edwards, 'PPI Mis-Sold on Credit Cards', *Which?* (10 September 2008).

23 **sometimes as much as 50%** 'Protection Racket: CAB Evidence on the Cost and Effectiveness of Payment Protection Insurance', Citizens Advice Bureau (September 2005).

23 **no work the next day** Zlata Rodionova, 'The 7 Most Shocking Testimonies from Workers at Sports Direct', *The Independent* (22 July 2016).

24 **100 million more at risk** 'A Conversation with Roy P. Vagelos', *Annual Reviews Conversations* (2011).

24 **but also in Latin America** Bonnie J. Davis and Cindy Kluger, 'Onchocerciasis and Its Control: Report of a WHO Expert Committee on Onchocerciasis Control' (1995) 89 *Geneva: World Health Organisation* 1–104.

25 **and that infected me** Ushma S. Neill, 'A Conversation with P. Roy Vagelos' (2014) 124 *Journal of Clinical Investigation* 2291–2.

25 **encouraged me to pursue chemistry** Paul Hond, 'Doctors without Debt', *Columbia Magazine* (Fall 2018).

26 **complaints from shareholders** Michael Useem, *The Leadership Moment* (New York: New Rivers Press, 1998).

26 **a career at Merck** Kimberly Collins, 'Profitable Gifts: A History of the Merck Mectizan Donation Program and Its Implications for International Health' (2004) 47 *Perspectives in Biology and Medicine* 100–9.

28 **take from other stakeholders** For example, a 28 June 2012 article by Peter Karoff in the *Stanford Social Innovation Review* is entitled 'CSR Rule #1: Do No Harm'. Google's code of conduct famously used to contain the related phrase 'Do No Evil'.

28 **prototype of the electronic camera** The Sony Mavica was electronic and filmless, but not a digital camera, since images were saved in the form of analogue scan lines, similar to a television image.

28 **than You Do in a Year** Matt Vella, 'Every 60 Seconds, Apple Makes More Money than You Do in a Year', *Time* (20 March 2014).

29 **enough to be deemed excessive** Phil Mullan, 'CSR: The Dangers of "Doing the Right Thing"', *Spiked* (31 March 2014).

30 **to earn monopoly profits** Keytruda was initially developed by Organon, which was acquired by Schering-Plough in 2007; Schering-Plough was itself bought by Merck in 2009.

30 **average cost of $2.87 billion** Joseph A. DiMasi, Henry G. Grabowski and Ronald W. Hansen, 'Innovation in the Pharmaceutical Industry: New Estimates of R&D Costs' (2016) 47 *Journal of Health Economics* 20–33. Figure is in 2013 dollars.

30 **we can't pay for losers** Adi Ignatius, 'Businesses Exist to Deliver Value to Society', *Harvard Business Review* (March–April 2018).

31 **The famous Coase theorem** Ronald H. Coase, 'The Problem of Social Cost' (1960) 3 *Journal of Law and Economics* 1–44.

31 **political scientist Vilfredo Pareto** Vilfredo Pareto, 'Il Massimo di Utilità Dato Dalla Libera Concorrenza' 9 (1894) *Giornale degli Economisti* 48–66.

33 **Finnish telecoms firm Nokia** Sandra J. Sucher and Shalene Gupta, 'Layoffs that Don't Break Your Company', *Harvard Business Review* (May–June 2018).

35 **(born between 1965 and 1979)** Kantar Futures and American Express, 'Redefining the C-Suite: Business the Millennial Way' (2017).

35 **AIESEC study of young leaders** PwC and AIESEC, 'Tomorrow's Leaders Today' (2016).

Chapter 2 Growing the Pie Doesn't Aim to Maximise Profits – But Often Does

38 **to Increase Its Profits** Milton Friedman, 'The Social Responsibility of Business Is to Increase Its Profits', *New York Times Magazine* (13 September 1970).

42 **suppliers, regulators, and communities** Michael C. Jensen, 'Value Maximization, Stakeholder Theory, and the Corporate Objective Function' (2010) 22 *Journal of Applied Corporate Finance* 32–42.

44 **increasing shareholder value** Michael C. Jensen, 'Value Maximisation, Stakeholder Theory, and the Corporate Objective Function' (2001) 7 *European Financial Management* 297–317.

45 **compared to 17% in 1975** Ocean Tomo, 'Intangible Asset Market Value Study' (2015).

46 **benefits than they should** Poterba and Summers surveyed CEOs at Fortune 1000 firms and found that they used a discount rate of 12%, higher than

the return required on either debt or equity. James Poterba and Lawrence H. Summers, 'A CEO Survey of U.S. Companies' Time Horizons and Hurdle Rates', *Sloan Management Review* (Fall 1995).

46 **led to its substantial value** Economist John Kay refers to this as the principle of 'obliquity', where goals are best pursued unintentionally. John Kay, *Obliquity: Why Our Goals Are Best Achieved Indirectly* (London: Profile Books, 2011).

47 **our people, our employees** Steven Levy, 'Inside Apple's Insanely Great (or Just Insane) New Mothership', *Wired* (16 May 2017).

48 **ends up being approved** Pharmaceutical Research and Manufacturers of America.

48 **to cover compensation costs** New City Agenda, 'The Top 10 Retail Banking Scandals: 60 Billion Reasons Why Shareholders Must Play a Greater Role in Changing Bank Culture' (11 April 2016).

48 **customer will pay 17% more** Stephanie M. Tully and Russell S. Winer, 'The Role of the Beneficiary in Willingness to Pay for Socially Responsible Products: A Meta-Analysis' (2014) 90 *Journal of Retailing* 255–274.

48 **average increase of 7,000** Rüdiger Machmann, Gabriel Ehrlich and Dimitrije Ruzic, 'Firms and Collective Reputation: The Volkswagen Emissions Scandal as a Case Study' (2017).

50 **77% between 2007 and 2016** 'U.S. Tobacco Profits Soar Despite Drop in Number of Smokers', NPR (24 April 2017).

50 **$35 billion in profit in 2016** Rob Davies, 'How Big Tobacco Has Survived Death and Taxes', *Guardian* (12 July 2017).

52 **may own stakes in suppliers** Even if a shareholder is an institution, it nearly always ultimately manages money on behalf of citizens.

53 **companies should consider both** Oliver Hart and Luigi Zingales, 'Companies Should Maximize Shareholder Welfare Not Market Value' (2017) 2 *Journal of Law, Finance, and Accounting* 247–74.

53 **as high as in 1995** The Forum for Sustainable and Responsible Investment, 'Report on US Sustainable, Responsible, and Impact Investing Trends' (2016).

53 **costing it over $250 million** Center for Climate and Energy Solutions, 'Weathering the Storm: Building Business Resilience to Climate Change' (2013).

53 **climate change of $1 trillion** Carbon Disclosure Project, 'Major Risk or Rosy Opportunity: Are Companies Ready for Climate Change?' (2019).

54 **$3.7 billion in the following year** Rüdiger Machmann, Gabriel Ehrlich and Dimitrije Ruzic, 'Firms and Collective Reputation: The Volkswagen Emissions Scandal as a Case Study' (2017).

56 **mindset change as originally intended** John Elkington, '25 Years Ago I Coined the Phrase "Triple Bottom Line". Here's Why It's Time to Rethink It', *Harvard Business Review* (25 June 2018).

Chapter 3 Growing the Pie Doesn't Mean Growing the Enterprise

59 **will produce tomorrow's drugs** Adi Ignatius, 'Businesses Exist to Deliver Value to Society', Harvard Business Review (March–April 2018).

60 **to invest in the future** Michael Kranish, 'Warren Decries Stock Buybacks, High CEO Pay', *Boston Globe* (14 June 2015).

61 **report of what they've done** Hiroko Tabuchi, 'Layoffs Taboo, Japan Workers Are Sent to the Boredom Room', *New York Times* (16 August 2013).

62 **the company as his 'baby'** Angelo Mozilo's testimony in SEC investigation, 9 November 2007.

62 **number one at 13%** Connie Bruck, 'Angelo's Ashes', *The New Yorker* (29 June 2009).

63 **redeploy its resources** Dong-Gull Lee, 'The Restructuring of Daewoo' in Stephan Haggard, Wonhyul Lim and Euysung Kim (eds), *Economic Crisis and Corporate Restructuring in Korea: Reforming the Chaebol* (Cambridge: Cambridge University Press, 2003), pp. 150–80.

64 **7,000 colleagues lost their jobs** 'Daewoo: GM's Hot New Engine', Bloomberg (29 November 2004).

64 **$240 billion through acquisitions** While part of this loss was due to overpaying for the purchased businesses (generating gains for their former owners), even subtracting these gains, the net value loss to society was $134 billion.

64 **generating on their own beforehand** Sara B. Moeller, Frederik P. Schlingemann and René M. Stulz, 'Wealth Destruction on a Massive Scale? A Study of Acquiring-Firm Returns in the Recent Merger Wave' (2005) 60 *Journal of Finance* 757–82.

69 **cause that the donor cares about** A more effective way of donating to charity may be for an enterprise to match employee donations, which helps ensure that corporate donations go to causes that employees support.

75 **16% over the next year** Australian Energy Markets Commission.

Chapter 4 Does Pieconomics Work?

78 **and its financial performance** Joshua D. Margolis and James P. Walsh, 'Misery Loves Companies: Rethinking Social Initiatives by Business' (2003) 48 *Administrative Science Quarterly* 268–305.

78 **reached the same conclusion** Marc Orlitzky, Frank L. Schmidt and Sara L. Rynes, 'Corporate Social and Financial Performance: A Meta-Analysis' (2003) 24 *Organization Studies* 403–41.

79 **twenty-six years of data** Alex Edmans, 'Does the Stock Market Fully Value Intangibles? Employee Satisfaction and Equity Prices' (2011) 101 *Journal of Financial Economics* 621–40.

79 **extended it to 2011** Alex Edmans, 'The Link between Job Satisfaction and Firm Value, with Implications for Corporate Social Responsibility' (2012) 26 *Academy of Management Perspectives* 1–19.

80 **Russell Hill and Robert Barton** Russell A. Hill and Robert A. Barton, 'Psychology: Red Enhances Human Performance in Contests' (2005) 435 *Nature* 293.

80 **Arlen Moller and Jorg Meinhardt** Andrew J. Elliot, Markus A. Maier, Arlen C. Moller and Jorg Meinhardt, 'Color and Psychological Functioning: The Effect of Red on Performance Attainment' (2007) 136 *Journal of Experimental Psychology: General* 154–68.

81 **investing on this effect** See, for example, https://youtu.be/ippgKYA5nJk by Robert Maltbie, Managing Director of Millennium Asset Management.

81 **alignment of the planets** Robert Novy-Marx, 'Predicting Anomaly Performance with Politics, the Weather, Global Warming, Sunspots, and the Stars' (2014) 112 *Journal of Financial Economics* 137–46.

82 **typically beat large stocks** Rolf W. Banz, 'The Relationship between Return and Market Value of Common Stocks' (1981) 9 *Journal of Financial Economics* 3–18; Clifford S. Asness, Andrea Frazzini, Ronen Israel *et al.*, 'Size Matters When You Control Your Junk' (2018) 129 *Journal of Financial Economics* 479–509.

84 **Take the supermarket Costco** Costco doesn't apply for inclusion in the Best Companies list, but is widely considered to be a good employer. For example, it was selected as Best Employer in the US by Forbes in 2017.

84 **for a retail sales worker** Aaron Taube, 'Why Costco Pays Its Retail Employees $20 an Hour', *Business Insider* (23 October 2014).

84 **buy a stock like that?** Amy Tsao, 'A Showdown at the Checkout for Costco', *BusinessWeek* (28 August 2003).

84 ***Wall Street Journal* article** Ann Zimmerman, 'Costco's Dilemma: Be Kind to Its Workers, or Wall Street?', *Wall Street Journal* (26 March 2004).

85 **remain with their employer** Ingrid Smithey Fulmer, Barry Gerhart and Kimberley S. Scott, 'Are the 100 Best Better? An Empirical Investigation of the Relationship between Being a "Great Place to Work" and Firm Performance' (2003) 56 *Personnel Psychology* 965–93.

85 **positive in their customer interactions** Daniel H. Simon and Jed DeVaro, 'Do the Best Companies to Work for Provide Better Customer Satisfaction?' (2006) 27 *Managerial and Decision Economics* 667–83.

85 **high- and low-tech industries** These results were not reported in the final published version of the paper given space limitations.

85 **over 1997 to 2003** Claes Fornell, Sunil Mithas, Forrest V. Morgeson III and M. S. Krishnan, 'Customer Satisfaction and Stock Prices: High Returns, Low Risk' (2006) 70 *Journal of Marketing* 3–14. The three components of the index are customer expectations, perceived quality and perceived value (quality relative to price).

86 **between 1995 and 2003** Jeroen Derwall, Nadja Guenster, Rob Bauer and Kees Koedijk, 'The Eco-Efficiency Premium Puzzle' (2005) 61 *Financial Analysts Journal* 51–63.

86 **a product of chance** Mozaffar Khan, George Serafeim and Aaron Yoon, 'Corporate Sustainability: First Evidence on Materiality' (2016) 91 *Accounting Review* 1697–724. They study changes in KLD scores after controlling for firm characteristics.

87 **4.5% over 1993 to 2010** Robert Eccles, Ioannis Ioannou and George Serafeim, 'The Impact of Corporate Sustainability on Organizational Processes and Performance' (2014) 60 *Management Science* 2835–57.

87 **issued a stakeholder report** 'From Fringe to Mainstream: Companies Integrate CSR Initiatives into Everyday Business', *Knowledge@Wharton* (23 May 2012).

87 **off their market values** Losses quoted are from the date of the event to the lowest price during the next month.

87 **with the decline exceeding 3%** Philipp Krüger, 'Corporate Goodness and Shareholder Wealth' (2015) 115 *Journal of Financial Economics* 304–29.

89 **one year to ten years** Jen Wieczner, 'How Buying Stock in the "Best Companies to Work for" Helped This Investor Crush the Market', *Fortune* (9 March 2017).

90 **different approach to nail causality** Caroline Flammer, 'Does Corporate Social Responsibility Lead to Superior Financial Performance? A Regression Discontinuity Approach' (2015) 61 *Management Science* 2549–68.

90 **social and environmental issues** Gibson Dunn, 'Shareholder Proposal Developments During the 2018 Proxy Season' (2018).

90 **made to HCC Insurance** The HCC proposal was voted on 10 May 2007; the Lear proposal was voted on 11 May 2006.

91 **insignificant after controlling for risk** Luc Renneboog, Jenke Ter Horst and Chendi Zhang, 'The Price of Ethics and Stakeholder Governance: The Performance of Socially Responsible Mutual Funds' (2008) 14 *Journal of Corporate Finance* 302–22.

91 **underperform in Europe and Asia** Luc Renneboog, Jenke Ter Horst and Chendi Zhang, 'Socially Responsible Investments: Institutional Aspects, Performance, and Investor Behavior' (2008) 32 *Journal of Banking and Finance* 1723–42.

91 **funds by 3.4% per year** Brad M. Barber, Adair Morse and Ayako Yasuda, 'Impact Investing' (2018).

92 **ESG strategies is beyond doubt** James Kynge, 'The Ethical Investment Boom', *Financial Times* (3 September 2017).

92 **governance and a sustainable future** Dina Medland, '"From Stockholder to Stakeholder" Means "No" to Short-Termism for Better Results', *Forbes* (15 September 2014).

93 **drove some employees to suicide** 'Apple "Failing to Protect Chinese Factory Workers"', BBC (18 December 2014); 'Life and Death in Apple's Forbidden City', *The Guardian* (18 June 2017).

93 **so they use bottles instead** 'Amazon Warehouse Workers Skip Bathroom Breaks to Keep Their Jobs, Says Report', *The Verge* (16 April 2018).

94 **by 3.2% per year** Harrison Hong and Marcin Kacperczyk, 'The Price of Sin: The Effects of Social Norms on Markets' (2009) 93 *Journal of Financial Economics* 15–36.

95 **America to a global setting** Alex Edmans, Lucius Li and Chendi Zhang, 'Employee Satisfaction, Labor Market Flexibility, and Stock Returns around the World' (2018).

Chapter 5 Incentives

99 **to take a lie-down** Julia Finch, 'Bart Becht's £90m Pay Packet. I Need a Lie-Down', *The Guardian* (7 April 2010).

99 **is spreading to other sectors** Jill Treanor, 'Cillit Bang Boss Bart Becht Takes Home £90m', *The Guardian* (8 April 2010).

99 **to get your head around** Finch, 'Bart Becht's £90m Pay Packet'.

100 **now faces an uncertain future** Andrew Trotman and Amy Wilson, 'Reckitt Benckiser Shares Slump after Chief Bart Becht Announces Retirement', *The Telegraph* (14 April 2011).

100 **merger with Reckitt & Colman** Paul Sonne, 'Reckitt's CEO to Step Down', *Wall Street Journal* (15 April 2011).

100 **shouldn't be in this business** Treanor, 'Cillit Bang Boss Bart Becht Takes Home £90m'.

101 **glass protector with Finish 4-in-1** Morten T. Hansen, Herminia Ibarra and Nana von Bernuth, 'Transforming Reckitt Benckiser', INSEAD case study, 04/2011-5686 (2013).

101 **running your own company** Maggie Urry, 'Reckitt's Strongly Flavoured Essence', *Financial Times* (21 January 2008).

101 **50% over the 2000s** Headcount was 18,900 in 2000 and 27,200 in 2010. In 2011, when Bart stepped down, this number had grown to 37,800.

However, the growth between 2010 and 2011 was largely due to the acquisitions of SSL International and Paras Pharmaceuticals, hence quoting the 2010 figures.

102 **unit of production by 43%** Reckitt Benckiser 2012 Annual Report.

102 **£92 million in a single year** For example, the title of a *Daily Mail* article from 8 April 2010 claims that Bart 'pocketed £90 million in one YEAR' (emphasis in the original).

102 **received as early as 1999** £74 million came from exercising share options that he'd received since 2001 and £13 million from cashing in shares awarded in 1999 and 2005.

102 **shares and options were granted** The stock price rise increased the cash-in value of options by over £74 million and stock by over £5 million (the total is £80 million when rounding). Technical note: Bart's options were initially granted 'at-the-money', which means that the stock price had to rise for them to have value. Thus, their 'intrinsic value' when granted was zero, and so it's correct to say that, if the stock price had not risen post-grant, the options would have been worth £74 million less when exercised (i.e. £0 rather than £74 million). However, the 'economic value' of the options when granted was greater than zero – they were worth something due to the possibility of the stock price rising post-grant. Thus, the increase in the economic value of the options was less than £74 million.

102 **Children and Médecins Sans Frontières** The amount that Bart donated exceeded the amount that he cashed in, since he paid money to exercise his options (i.e. to turn them into shares), and then donated the shares.

103 **any of his major shareholders** Rupert Steiner, 'Biggest Paycut in History as Cillit Bang Boss Loses £74m', *Daily Mail* (30 March 2011).

103 **when it was forty-two** AFL-CIO Executive Paywatch.

103 **earns in a whole year** 4 January is known as 'Fat Cat Wednesday', 'Fat Cat Thursday', etc. depending on which day of the week 4 January falls on.

104 **at the expense of workers** Rob Du Boff, 'What Is Just When It Comes to CEO-to-Average Worker Pay?', Forbes (10 October 2017).

104 **wealth can be created** Yaron Brook and Don Watkins, 'When It Comes to Wealth Creation, There Is No Pie', Forbes (14 June 2011).

106 **negatively correlates with performance** Chris Philp, 'Restoring Responsible Ownership: Ending the Ownerless Corporation and Controlling Executive Pay' (2016).

106 **statistically weak or non-existent** House of Commons Report on 'Executive Rewards: Paying for Success' (20 March 2019).

107 **$67 million of equity** Alex Edmans, Xavier Gabaix and Dirk Jenter, 'Executive Compensation: A Survey of Theory and Evidence' in Benjamin E. Hermalin

and Michael S. Weisbach (eds), *Handbook of the Economics of Corporate Governance* (Amsterdam: Elsevier, 2017), pp. 383–539.

107 **it doesn't make sense** PwC, 'Executive Pay in a World of Truthiness: Facts and Myths in the Pay Debate' (2017).

107 **raises in their salaries** Speech at Georgetown University (19 November 2015). Transcript at www.presidency.ucsb.edu/ws/index.php?pid=117517.

107 **over a twenty-three-year period** Ulf Von Lilienfeld-Toal and Stefan Ruenzi, 'CEO Ownership, Stock Market Performance, and Managerial Discretion' (2014) 69 *Journal of Finance* 1013–50.

109 **performance measure being rewarded** For examples of such studies, see Daniel M. Cable and Freek Vermeulen, 'Stop Paying Executives for Performance', *Harvard Business Review* (23 February 2016). For the rejoinder, see Alex Edmans, 'Performance-Based Pay for Executives Still Works', *Harvard Business Review* (23 February 2016).

109 **while hoping for B** Steven Kerr, 'On the Folly of Rewarding A, While Hoping for B' (1975) 18 *Academy of Management Journal* 769–83.

110 **what happens when CEOs die** Dirk Jenter, Egor Matveyev and Lukas Roth, 'Good and Bad CEOs' (2018).

110 **stress from the firm's troubles** Morten Bennedsen, Francisco Pérez González and Daniel Wolfenzon, 'Do CEOs Matter?' (2010).

110 **12% of its average level** Industry-adjusted profitability, measured by operating return on assets, falls by 0.7 percentage points, compared to the average of 5.63 percentage points.

110 **any increase in firm value** Edmans *et al.*, 'Executive Compensation'.

111 **relative reserves replacement ratio** This measures the amount of new oil and gas reserves discovered relative to the amount of oil and gas extracted from existing reserves.

112 **outperformed its peer group** Shell, Chevron, Exxon and Total.

115 **$250,000 a year** Sheffield Barry, '6 Steps to Hire an Effective Compensation Consultant' (2017).

115 **their goal by cutting R&D** Benjamin Bennett, J. Carr Bettis, Radhakrishnan Gopalan and Todd Milbourn, 'Compensation Goals and Firm Performance' (2017) 124 *Journal of Financial Economics* 307–30.

116 **or between great and good** Even for performance shares, the dotted line (value of shares) shows that the increase when profits exceed £6 billion is less than the decrease when profits fall below £6 billion, again discouraging good risk-taking.

116 **leader performs best on** Adair Morse, Vikram Nanda and Amit Seru, 'Are Incentive Contracts Rigged by Powerful CEOs?' (2011) 66 *Journal of Finance* 1779–821.

118 **'another rule for us'** The proportion of an employee's pay that's in shares should be lower, so that less of his wealth is at risk from poor performance.

118 **(used in place of wages)** E. Han Kim and Paige Ouimet, 'Broad-Based Employee Stock Ownership: Motives and Outcomes' (2014) 69 *Journal of Finance* 1273–319. They argue that small broad-based equity schemes (comprising fewer than 5% of shares outstanding) are more likely to be used for reward purposes, since they offer little takeover protection and few cash savings, while larger schemes are more likely to have ulterior motives.

118 **a particularly large effect** Yael V. Hochberg and Laura Lindsey, 'Incentives, Targeting, and Firm Performance: An Analysis of Non-Executive Stock Options' (2010) 23 *Review of Financial Studies* 4148–86.

119 **a lead to modest savings** Ingolf Dittmann, Ernst Maug and Oliver G. Spalt, 'Indexing Executive Compensation Contracts' (2013) 26 *Review of Financial Studies* 3182–224.

120 **'company was created in 1999'** Treanor, 'Cillit Bang Boss Bart Becht Takes Home £90m'.

121 **applied a 50% discount** The LTIP previously paid a maximum of 250% of the CEO's salary. When Weir moved to restricted stock, it gave 125% of salary in shares, hence the 50% discount. The appropriate discount will vary from case to case depending on the stringency of the performance conditions removed.

123 **'set periods of time'** House of Commons Business, Energy, and Industrial Strategy Committee, 'Corporate Governance: Third Report of Session 2016–17' (5 April 2017).

123 **'during the measurement period'** Norges Bank Investment Management, 'CEO Remuneration Position Paper' (2017).

123 **recently adopted restricted stock** Examples include Royal Bank of Scotland, The Weir Group, Pets at Home, Card Factory, Kingfisher, financial services firm Hargreaves Lansdown, and housing and social care provider Mears Group.

124 **"coherent to our shareholders"** Lynn S. Paine and Federica Gabrieli, 'The Weir Group: Reforming Executive Pay', Harvard Business School Case Study 9-319-046 (2018).

124 **nine months to August 2007** Securities and Exchange Commission, 'SEC Charges Former Countrywide Executives with Fraud' (4 June 2009).

125 **cash out before they did** Connie Bruck, 'Angelo's Ashes', *The New Yorker* (29 June 2009).

127 **(lock-ups are about to expire)** Alex Edmans, Vivian W. Fang and Katharina Lewellen, 'Equity Vesting and Investment' (2017) 30 *Review of Financial Studies* 2229–71.

128 **significantly cut investment** Tomislav Ladika and Zacharias Sautner, 'Managerial Short-Termism and Investment: Evidence from Accelerated Option Vesting', *Review of Finance* (forthcoming).

128 **increase long-term incentives** Caroline Flammer and Pratima Bansal, 'Does Long-Term Orientation Create Value? Evidence from a Regression Discontinuity' (2017) 38 *Strategic Management Journal* 1827–47. The authors include all proposals that advocate rewarding executives according to measures of long-term performance, such as through restricted stock, restricted options and long-term incentive plans. They don't report results for these different elements separately.

128 **more innovative patents** A patent's quality is measured by how many times it gets cited; innovativeness is measured by distance from the firm's existing patents.

128 **'resignation or retirement'** Norges Bank Investment Management, 'CEO Remuneration Position Paper'.

129 **not inequality, but unfairness** Christina Starmans, Mark Sheskin and Paul Bloom, 'Why People Prefer Unequal Societies' (2017) 1 *Nature Human Behavior* 0082.

130 **increases and decreases in performance** Sabrina T. Howell and J. David Brown, 'Do Firms Share Success Fairly? The Effects of a Government R&D Grant on Wages' (2019).

130 **stock returns and earnings surprises** Holger M. Mueller, Paige P. Ouimet and Elena Simintzi, 'Within-Firm Pay Inequality' (2017) 30 *Review of Financial Studies* 3605–35.

131 **risen faster than for CEOs** Steven N. Kaplan and Joshua Rauh, 'Wall Street and Main Street: What Contributes to the Rise in the Highest Incomes?' (2009) 23 *Review of Financial Studies* 1004–50.

131 **Cruyff earned in his heyday** Reuel Golden, *The Age of Innocence: Football in the 1970s* (Cologne: Taschen, 2014).

132 **you can test it** Xavier Gabaix and Augustin Landier, 'Why Has CEO Pay Increased So Much?' (2008) 123 *Quarterly Journal of Economics* 49–100.

132 **CEO pay by 28%** Xavier Gabaix, Augustin Landier and Julien Sauvagnat, 'CEO Pay and Firm Size: An Update after the Crisis' (2014) 124 *Economic Journal* 40–59.

Chapter 6 Stewardship

135 **'with 120 positions'** 'Jeffrey Ubben: The Evolution of the Active Value Investment Style', www.youtube.com/watch?v=cbFBQAm75ew.

137 **'strategy to be helpful'** Stephen Jones, 'Adobe Systems Incorporated: Adobe Signs Standstill Agreement with ValueAct Capital', *MarketScreener* (12 May 2012).

138 **end Flash for good in 2020** Brian Barrett, 'Adobe Finally Kills Flash Dead', *Wired* (25 July 2017).

138 **'eye candy for a demo'** Tekla S. Perry, 'Photoshop Creator Thomas Knoll on Subscription Software and What's Good for Engineers', *IEEE Spectrum* (30 January 2017).

138 **$202 million to $443 million** I present 2017 figures to highlight how the improvements did not reverse once ValueAct sold its stake, contrary to concerns of short-termism, and also because restructuring takes time to pay off. For 2016, revenues were $5.8 billion, headcount was 15,700 and taxes were $266 million.

138 **to buy a stake** Seagate arranged a secondary block trade, whereby an existing (undisclosed) Seagate investor sold its stake to ValueAct, rather than ValueAct buying shares on the open market (which could have happened without Seagate reaching out).

140 **'generate long-term value'** Peter Georgescu, *Capitalists, Arise!: End Economic Inequality, Grow the Middle Class, Heal the Nation* (Oakland CA: Berrett-Koehler, 2017).

140 **no long-term reversal** Alon Brav, Wei Jiang, Frank Partnoy and Randall Thomas, 'Hedge Fund Activism, Corporate Governance, and Firm Performance' (2008) 63 *Journal of Finance* 1729–75.

141 **'pump and dump'** Lucian A. Bebchuk, Alon Brav and Wei Jiang, 'The Long Term Effects of Hedge Fund Activism' (2015) 115 *Columbia Law Review* 1085–155.

141 **'long-term benefits'** Paul Singer, 'Efficient Markets Need Guys Like Me', *Wall Street Journal* (19 October 2017).

141 **tells a thousand words** Alon Brav, Wei Jiang and Hyunseob Kim, 'The Real Effects of Hedge Fund Activism: Productivity, Asset Allocation, and Labor Outcomes' (2015) 28 *Review of Financial Studies* 2723–69.

142 **look five years out** Bebchuk *et al.*, 'The Long Term Effects of Hedge Fund Activism'.

142 **plants that weren't targeted** Brav *et al.*, 'The Real Effects of Hedge Fund Activism'.

142 **output per labour hour** The authors also study a second measure of labour productivity, value added (sales minus raw material costs) per labour hour. They find similar results.

143 **reason for the productivity gains** Brav *et al.*, 'The Real Effects of Hedge Fund Activism'.

144 **outside the baking tray** Alon Brav, Wei Jiang, Song Ma and Xuan Tian, 'How Does Hedge Fund Activism Reshape Corporate Innovation?' (2018) 130 *Journal of Financial Economics* 237–64.

145 **actions to remain competitive** Hadiye Aslan and Praveen Kumar, 'The Product Market Effects of Hedge Fund Activism' (2016) 119 *Journal of Financial Economics* 226–48.

145 **taking a stake in them** Nickolay Gantchev, Oleg Gredil and Chotibhak Jotikasthira, 'Governance under the Gun: Spillover Effects of Hedge Fund Activism', *Review of Finance* (forthcoming).

145 **its variants twenty times** Martin Lipton, 'Dealing with Activist Hedge Funds' (2015).

146 **'presaged its collapse'** House of Commons Report on Carillion, 9 May 2018.

146 **'because of complacency'** Kai Ryssdal, Bridget Bodnar and Sean McHenry, 'Why Bill Ackman Sees Activist Investing as a Moral Crusade', *Marketplace* (31 October 2017).

146 **innovative investment opportunities** John Plender, 'Cash-Hoarding Companies Are Still a Problem for Japan', *Financial Times* (12 November 2017).

147 **'activism to date appears limited'** David Yermack, 'Shareholder Voting and Corporate Governance' (2010) 2 *Annual Review of Financial Economics* 103–25.

148 **classified as closet indexers** Morningstar, 'Active Share in European Equity Funds' (2016).

148 **require them to diversify** Under the Investment Company Act of 1940, a 'diversified' mutual fund can, with respect to 75% of its portfolio, have no more than 5% invested in any one security and own no more than 10% of the voting rights in one company.

148 **costs over $10 million** Nickolay Gantchev, 'The Costs of Shareholder Activism: Evidence from a Sequential Decision Model' (2013) 107 *Journal of Financial Economics* 610–31.

149 **deferred for several years** For example, the EU's Alternative Investment Fund Managers Directive requires at least 40% of variable pay (60% if variable pay is particularly high) to be deferred for at least three to five years. In addition, new hedge funds often commit to reinvest their incentive fees into the fund for the first three to five years.

149 **profits rise** Steven N. Kaplan, 'The Effects of Management Buyouts on Operating Performance and Value' (1989) 24 *Journal of Financial Economics* 217–54.

149 **total factor productivity increases** Frank R. Lichtenberg and Donald Siegel, 'The Effects of Leveraged Buyouts on Productivity and Related Aspects of Firm Behavior' (1990) 27 *Journal of Financial Economics* 165–94.

149 **new products are launched** Cesare Fracassi, Alessandro Previtero and Albert Sheen, 'Barbarians at the Store? Private Equity, Products, and Consumers' (2018).

149 **quality of patents improves** Josh Lerner, Morten Sorensen and Per Strömberg, 'Private Equity and Long-Run Investment: The Case of Innovation' (2011) 66 *Journal of Finance* 445–77.

149 **engagement achieved its goal** Marco Becht, Julian Franks, Colin Mayer and Stefano Rossi, 'Returns to Shareholder Activism: Evidence from a Clinical Study of the Hermes U.K. Focus Fund' (2008) 22 *Review of Financial Studies* 3093–129.

150 **environmental and social engagement** Elroy Dimson, Oğuzhan Karakaş and Xi Li, 'Active Ownership' (2015) 28 *Review of Financial Studies* 3225–68.

150 **shareholders in a firm** Ian R. Appel, Todd A. Gormley and Donald B. Keim, 'Passive Investors, Not Passive Owners' (2016) 121 *Journal of Financial Economics* 111–41.

151 **several improvements in governance** These improvements include: more independent directors, a higher likelihood of the firm removing a poison pill (which deters an investor from acquiring a large stake) and reducing restrictions on shareholders' ability to call special meetings, and a lower likelihood of having dual class shares.

152 **protect management from shareholder pressure** Paul Gompers, Joy Ishii and Andrew Metrick, 'Corporate Governance and Equity Prices' (2003) 118 *Quarterly Journal of Economics* 107–56.

152 **and higher profitability** Follow-up research showed that investor rights continued to be associated with higher profitability and sales growth in the 2000s. The link is much higher for five-year than one-year sales growth, suggesting that investor rights encourage long-term behaviour. However, the link with future stock returns disappeared, because the stock market now paid attention to investor rights. Companies with strong investor rights already had high stock prices at the start of the 2000s, and so didn't outperform going forwards. Lucian A. Bebchuk, Alma Cohen and Charles C. Y. Wang, 'Learning and the Disappearing Association between Governance and Returns' (2013) 108 *Journal of Financial Economics* 323–48.

152 **they reduce firm value** Lucian A. Bebchuk and Alma Cohen, 'The Costs of Entrenched Boards' (2005) 78 *Journal of Financial Economics* 409–33. Olubunmi Faleye, 'Classified Boards, Firm Value, and Managerial Entrenchment' (2007) 83 *Journal of Financial Economics* 501–29; Alma Cohen and Charles C. Y. Wang, 'How Do Staggered Boards Affect Shareholder Value? Evidence from a Natural Experiment' (2013) 110 *Journal of Financial Economics* 627–41. However, see Yakov Amihud and Stoyan Stoyanov, 'Do Staggered Boards Harm Shareholders?' (2017) 123 *Journal of Financial Economics* 432–9, who suggest that the Cohen and Wang results only apply to small stocks or stocks traded over-the-counter rather than on exchanges.

152 **decline in firm value** Paul A. Gompers, Joy Ishii and Andrew Metrick, 'Extreme Governance: An Analysis of Dual-Class Firms in the United States' (2009) 23 *Review of Financial Studies* 1051–88.

152 **allow them to empire-build** Ronald W. Masulis, Cong Wang and Fei Xie, 'Agency Problems at Dual-Class Companies' (2009) 64 *Journal of Finance* 1697–727.

152 **'based on hunches'** 'The Death of Daewoo', *The Economist* (19 August 1999).

153 **ended the year at $7.9 billion** While dual-class shares gave Mason 20% of the voting rights, the other two co-founders together held 38% of the voting rights, allowing for his departure.

153 **governance rather than social performance** Vicente Cuñat, Mireia Giné and Maria Guadalupe, 'The Vote Is Cast: The Effect of Corporate Governance on Shareholder Value' (2012) 67 *Journal of Finance* 1943–77. The governance proposals aimed to improve investor rights, board structure or voting procedures.

153 **(in July 2011)** Jonathan B. Cohn, Stuart L. Gillan and Jay C. Hartzell, 'On Enhancing Shareholder Control: A (Dodd-) Frank Assessment of Proxy Access' (2016) 71 *Journal of Finance* 1623–68.

153 **their own directors for election** Specifically, an investor (or group of investors) who has held at least 3% of the firm's shares for at least three years would be able to put its own director nominees on the firm's proxy ballot, rather than having to send them to other shareholders separately.

153 **community involvement and environmental orientation** Allen Ferrell, Hao Liang and Luc Renneboog, 'Socially Responsible Firms' (2016) 122 *Journal of Financial Economics* 585–606.

154 **few human rights violations** I. J. Alexander Dyck, Karl V. Lins, Lukas Roth and Hannes F. Wagner, 'Do Institutional Investors Drive Corporate Social Responsibility? International Evidence' (2017) 131 *Journal of Financial Economics* 693–714.

154 **an enterprise goes public** William C. Johnson, Jonathan M. Karpoff and Sangho Yi, 'The Bonding Hypothesis of Takeover Defenses: Evidence from IPO firms' (2015) 117 *Journal of Financial Economics* 307–32.

154 **above business relationships** K. J. Martijn Cremers, Lubomir P. Litov and Simone M. Sepe, 'Staggered Boards and Long-Term Firm Value, Revisited' (2017) 126 *Journal of Financial Economics* 422–44.

155 **'success of its stock'** Peter Lynch, *Beating the Street* (New York: Simon & Schuster, 2012).

157 **value of the CEO's shares** Even short-term price declines reduce the CEO's wealth if she sells a significant amount of her equity upon vesting, which occurs as discussed in Chapter 5.

157 **meet an earnings benchmark** John R. Graham, Campbell R. Harvey and Shiva Rajgopal, 'The Economic Implications of Corporate Financial Reporting' (2005) 40 *Journal of Accounting and Economics* 3–73.

158 **two days later** Note that investors' rapid rejection doesn't mean that the takeover bid was detrimental to society. Prompted by the bid, Unilever undertook a strategic review which led to it selling its margarine unit, launching a share buyback and targeting higher profit margins, all of which were positively received by investors. The share buyback was consistent with Unilever's claim that Kraft's bid undervalued it; we'll further analyse undervaluation motives for buybacks in Chapter 7.

158 **sold within two years** July 2015 speech at New York University.

158 **'running for the exits'** Keynote address at Lazard's 2015 event, 'Shareholder Expectations: The New Paradigm for Directors'.

160 **truly understand an enterprise** Alex Edmans, 'Blockholder Trading, Market Efficiency, and Managerial Myopia' (2009) 64 *Journal of Finance* 2481–513.

162 **good and invest more** See, for example, Qi Chen, Itay Goldstein and Wei Jiang, 'Price Informativeness and Investment Sensitivity to Stock Price' (2007) 20 *Review of Financial Studies* 619–50; Alex Edmans, Sudarshan Jayaraman and Jan Schneemeier, 'The Source of Information in Prices and Investment-Price Sensitivity' (2017) 126 *Journal of Financial Economics* 74–96. The idea that the stock price accumulates the views of millions of investors was pioneered by the Nobel Prize-winning economist Friedrich von Hayek.

162 **improve company decisions** Philip Bond, Alex Edmans and Itay Goldstein, 'The Real Effects of Financial Markets' (2012) 4 *Annual Review of Financial Economics* 339–60.

162 **they rarely sell** Michael E. Porter, 'Capital Disadvantage: America's Failing Capital Investment System' (1992) 70 *Harvard Business Review* 65–82.

163 **decimalisation improved firm value** Vivian W. Fang, Thomas H. Noe and Sheri Tice, 'Stock Market Liquidity and Firm Value' (2009) 94 *Journal of Financial Economics* 150–69.

163 **key driver of the gains** Sreedhar T. Bharath, Sudarshan Jayaraman and Venky Nagar, 'Exit as Governance: An Empirical Analysis' (2013) 68 *Journal of Finance* 2515–47.

163 **large stakes in the first place** Alex Edmans, Vivian W. Fang and Emanuel Zur, 'The Effect of Liquidity on Governance' (2013) 26 *Review of Financial Studies* 1443–82.

163 **large stakes in the first place** It might seem that there are two conflicting effects at work. On the one hand, higher liquidity makes it easier to sell a stock; on the other hand, it means that a given stock sale has less effect on the stock price and so provides less discipline to the CEO. However, two other effects reinforce the first one – higher liquidity encourages an

investor to monitor (he knows he can sell more if he uncovers negative information), and encourages him to buy a large stake to begin with.

163 **low-turnover investors** Xuemin (Sterling) Yan and Zhe Zhang, 'Institutional Investors and Equity Returns: Are Short-Term Institutions Better Informed?' (2009) 22 *Review of Financial Studies* 893–924.

163 **when they trade more** Lubos Pastor, Lucian A. Taylor and Robert F. Stambaugh, 'Do Funds Make More When They Trade More?' (2017) 72 *Journal of Finance* 1483–528.

163 **investors are particularly informed** Paul Brockman and Xuemin (Sterling) Yan, 'Block Ownership and Firm-Specific Information' (2009) 33 *Journal of Banking and Finance* 308–16; Brian Bushee and Theodore Goodman, 'Which Institutional Investors Trade Based on Private Information about Earnings and Returns?' (2007) 45 *Journal of Accounting Research* 289–321; Wayne Mikkelson and Megan Partch, 'Stock Price Effects and Costs of Secondary Distributions' (1985) 14 *Journal of Financial Economics* 165–94; Robert Parrino, Richard Sias and Laura T. Starks, 'Voting with Their Feet: Institutional Ownership Changes around Forced CEO Turnover' (2003) 68 *Journal of Financial Economics* 3–46; Myron Scholes, 'The Market for Securities: Substitution Versus Price Pressure and the Effects of Information on Share Prices' (1972) 45 *Journal of Business* 179–211.

163 **'subsequent firm outperformance'** David R. Gallagher, Peter A. Gardner and Peter L. Swan, 'Governance through Trading: Institutional Swing Trades and Subsequent Company Performance' (2013) 48 *Journal of Financial and Quantitative Analysis* 427–58.

163 **restate earnings less often** Patricia Dechow, Richard Sloan and Amy Sweeney, 'Causes and Consequences of Earnings Manipulation: An Analysis of Firms Subject to Enforcement Actions by the SEC' (1996) 13 *Contemporary Accounting Research* 1–36; David Farber, 'Restoring Trust after Fraud: Does Corporate Governance Matter?' (2005) 80 *Accounting Review* 539–61; Natasha Burns, Simi Kedia and Marc Lipson, 'Institutional Ownership and Monitoring: Evidence from Financial Reporting Practices' (2010) 16 *Journal of Corporate Finance* 443–55. An earnings restatement occurs when earnings have to be restated due to earlier errors.

164 **produce more patents** Barry Baysinger, Rita Kosnik and Thomas Turk, 'Effects of Board and Ownership Structure on Corporate R&D Strategy' (1991) 34 *Academy of Management Journal* 205–14; Peggy Lee, 'A Comparison of Ownership Structures and Innovations of U.S. and Japanese Firms' (2005) 26 *Managerial and Decision Economics* 39–50.

164 **investors encourage such behaviour** Brian Bushee, 'The Influence of Institutional Investors on Myopic R&D Investment Behavior' (1998) 73 *Accounting Review* 305–33.

164 **S&P 500 index** Philippe Aghion, John Van Reenen and Luigi Zingales, 'Innovation and Institutional Ownership' (2013) 103 *American Economic Review* 277–304.

164 **hold more of a stock** Some index funds have to hold the S&P 500; many active funds use it as a benchmark and thus own several of its stocks to reduce the risk of underperformance.

Chapter 7 Repurchases

166 **up two more cents to $7.51** Karen Brettell, David Gaffen and David Rohde, 'Stock Buybacks Enrich the Bosses Even When Business Sags', Reuters (10 December 2015).

167 **'higher incomes for employees'** William Lazonick, 'Profits without Prosperity', *Harvard Business Review* (September 2014).

168 **'Windfall for Patient Shareholders'** Matt Egan, 'Congress Could Give Bank Shareholders a $53 Billion Gift', CNN Money (16 April 2018). Jillian Ambrose, 'Shell Kick-Starts £19bn Windfall for Patient Shareholders', *The Telegraph* (26 July 2018).

169 **'reason to be concerned'** Chuck Schumer and Bernie Sanders, 'Schumer and Sanders: Limit Corporate Stock Buybacks', *New York Times* (3 February 2019).

169 **makes a very basic mistake** See Jesse Fried and Charles C. Y. Wang, 'Short-Termism and Capital Flows' (2019) 8 *Review of Corporate Finance Studies* 207–33, for other basic flaws in Lazonick's arguments and statistics.

170 **even other companies' shares** For example, Apple has a wholly owned subsidiary, Braeburn Capital, which manages $244 billion of cash and invests in equities and other securities. More generally, Duchin *et al.* (2012) find that S&P 500 companies own $1.6 trillion of nonoperating financial assets, of which 40% is in risky financial assets such as corporate bonds, mortgage-securities and equities. Ran Duchin, Thomas Gilbert, Jarrad Harford and Christopher Hrdlicka, 'Precautionary Savings with Risky Assets: When Cash Is Not Cash' (2012) 72 *Journal of Finance* 793–853.

175 **long-term stock return even more** David Ikenberry, Josef Lakonishok and Theo Vermaelen, 'Market Underreaction to Open Market Share Repurchases' (1995) 39 *Journal of Financial Economics* 181–208.

175 **this result generally holds worldwide** Alberto Manconi, Urs Peyer and Theo Vermaelen, 'Are Buybacks Good for Long-Term Shareholder Value? Evidence from Buybacks around the World' (2019) 54 *Journal of Financial and Quantitative Analysis* 1899–935.

175 **investors gained $96 million** $500 million shares repurchased at an average price of $146.21 equates to 3.42 million shares bought back. Applying the stock price gain of ($174.31 – $146.21) = $28.10 yields $96 million.

176 **'benefit personally from their use'** Lenore Palladino and Alex Edmans, 'Should the US Rein in Share Buybacks?', *Financial Times* (9 December 2018) (emphasis added).

176 **in place of a contentious action** I thank Professor Mathias Kronlund for suggesting this rule of thumb to me.

176 **growth opportunities are poor** Gustavo Grullon and Roni Michaely, 'The Information Content of Share Repurchase Programs' (2004) 59 *Journal of Finance* 651–80.

176 **when they have excess capital** Amy K. Dittmar, 'Why Do Firms Repurchase Stock?' (2000) 73 *Journal of Business* 331–55. Excess capital is measured by either cash holdings or cash flow in excess of investment opportunities.

176 **Cam Harvey and Roni Michaely** Alon Brav, John R. Graham, Campbell R. Harvey and Roni Michaely, 'Payout Policy in the 21st Century' (2005) 77 *Journal of Financial Economics* 483–527.

178 **own shares in public companies** Venture capital funds receive 23.2% of their financing from corporate and public pension funds, 12.6% from family offices and 30.8% from miscellaneous investors (such as endowments, insurance companies and investment banks), all of whom have significant holdings in public equity. The remainder of venture capital financing is provided by private equity funds, which themselves are held in part by other institutional investors. Andreas Kuckertz, Tobias Kollmann, Patrick Röhm and Nils Middelberg, 'The Interplay of Track Record and Trustworthiness in Venture Capital Fundraising' (2015) 4 *Journal of Business Venturing Insights* 6–13.

178 **issue equity in the future** Huaizhi Chen, 'Capital Redeployment in the Equity Market' (2018).

178 **do the opposite** Fried and Wang, 'Short-Termism and Capital Flows'.

178 **in the US in 2017** www.selectusa.gov/financial-services-industry-united-states.

179 **(or dividend payments) invest less** Joseph W. Gruber and Steven B. Kamin, 'Corporate Buybacks and Capital Investment: An International Perspective' (2017).

179 **50% over 2007 to 2016** Fried and Wang, 'Short-Termism and Capital Flows'.

179 **only $0.42 to $0.88** Amy Dittmar and Jan Mahrt-Smith, 'Corporate Governance and the Value of Cash Holdings' (2007) 83 *Journal of Financial Economics* 599–634.

180 **an average of 4%** Wei Li and Erik Lie, 'Dividend Changes and Catering Incentives' (2006) 80 *Journal of Financial Economics* 293–308.

180 **cut when profits fall** Murali Jagannathan, Clifford P. Stephens and Michael S. Weisbach, 'Financial Flexibility and the Choice between Dividends and Stock Repurchases' (2000) 57 *Journal of Financial Economics* 355–84.

181 **those who just missed** Benjamin Bennett, J. Carr Bettis, Radhakrishnan Gopalan and Todd Milbourn, 'Compensation Goals and Firm Performance' (2017) 124 *Journal of Financial Economics* 307–30.

181 **returns to these buybacks** Alex Edmans, Vivian W. Fang and Allen H. Huang, 'The Long-Term Consequences of Short-Term Incentives' (2019).

181 **SEC Commissioner Robert Jackson** 'Stock Buybacks and Corporate Cashouts', speech by Robert J. Jackson (11 June 2018).

181 **shares over the same period** The last repurchase transaction was made in May 2007.

182 **(strong buyback incentives)** Heitor Almeida, Vyacheslav Fos and Mathias Kronlund, 'The Real Effects of Share Repurchases' (2016) 119 *Journal of Financial Economics* 168–85.

Chapter 8 Enterprises

188 **send money using their phone** Unlike mobile banking, a mobile money service such as M-Pesa doesn't require you to have a bank account.

188 **'relatives and friends money'** 'M-Pesa Documentary', https://youtu.be/zQo4VoLyHeo.

188 **transformed citizens' lives** Vodafone launched M-Pesa through Safaricom, Kenya's leading mobile network, in which it held a 40% stake.

189 **out of poverty by 2014** Tavneet Suri and William Jack, 'The Long-Run Poverty and Gender Impacts of Mobile Money' (2016) 354 *Science* 1288–92.

192 **'the purpose of living'** 'The Future of Purpose-Driven Business', speech by John Kay at Blueprint for Better Business conference (30 October 2014).

192 **'not the purpose of life'** John Kay, 'Labour Party's Economic Rethink Should Focus on Good Corporations' (2015).

192 **'force for achieving them'** Larry Fink's Letter to CEOs, 2019.

193 **'the work they do is worthwhile'** PwC and AIESEC, 'Tomorrow's Leaders Today' (2016).

193 **'company's sense of purpose'** Deloitte, 'The 2016 Millennial Survey: Winning over the Next Generation of Leaders' (2016).

193 **$30 billion per year** Gallup, 'How Millennials Want to Work and Live' (2016).

193 **Merck's US subsidiary** This subsidiary then became independent of its German parent in 1917.

194 **manufacture penicillin with its rivals** Merck saw other pharmaceuticals firms as collaborators in researching penicillin production, not competitors, and had agreed with Squibb and Pfizer that the three of them would share any findings. Sharing its findings with Squibb and Pfizer was consistent with this agreement. However, other firms, upon such a major discovery, may have tried to find a loophole to back out of the agreement. In addition, Merck shared its findings with other firms not part of the original agreement, such as Abbott and Lederle.

194 **soldiers in the Second World War** www.historynet.com/penicillin-wonder-drug-world-war-ii.htm. This figure is the estimated number of soldiers treated by penicillin between D-Day and the final German surrender.

195 **Sinek's book *Start with Why*** Simon Sinek, *Start with Why* (New York: Portfolio Books, 2011).

196 **exclude all of those members** Such a statement may have been meaningful around the time that Friedman was writing, given that many believed that a company should serve only investors. Nowadays it's much more widely accepted that a company has a responsibility to stakeholders, and so a statement is only meaningful if it's specific about which stakeholders it aims to particularly serve and how it intends to serve them.

197 **'things everyone else is doing'** Craig Groeschel Leadership Podcast.

197 **value of a clear purpose** Claudia Gartenberg, Andrea Prat and George Serafeim, 'Corporate Purpose and Financial Performance' (2019) 30 *Organization Science* 1–18.

198 **clarity from management** Clarity from management is measured by the questions 'Management makes its expectations clear' and 'Management has a clear view of where the organization is going and how to get there'.

202 **potential for improvement** EY, 'Annual Reporting in 2017/18: Demonstrating Purpose, Creating Value' (September 2018).

204 **what ESG information to report** The Sustainability Accounting Standards Board provides standards for what non-financial information should be disclosed and is focused on reporting to investors. The Global Reporting

Initiative provides both principles and standards and is focused on reporting to stakeholders.

204 **report strong stakeholder performance** Laura Starks, Parth Venkat and Qifei Zhu, 'Corporate ESG Profiles and Investor Horizons' (2018).

204 **'gone through to create it'** 'Following the Footprints', *The Economist* (2 June 2011).

205 **reporting reduces investment** Ernstberger, Link, Stich and Vogler (2015) find that the EU Transparency Directive led to firms reducing investment, improving operating performance in the short term, but lowering it in the long term. Kraft, Vashishtha and Venkatachalam (2015) find that the transition from annual to semi-annual, and from semi-annual to quarterly reporting in the US led to a decline in investment. Jürgen Ernstberger, Benedikt Link, Michael Stich and Oliver Vogler, 'The Real Effects of Mandatory Quarterly Reporting' (2017) 92 *Accounting Review* 33–60; Arthur G. Kraft, Rahul Vashishtha and Mohan Venkatachalam, 'Frequent Financial Reporting and Managerial Myopia' (2018) 93 *Accounting Review* 249–75.

205 **choose to do so** The EU Transparency Directive (effective 2007) required EU companies to issue Interim Management Statements during the first and second halves of a fiscal year. They didn't need to contain a full set of financial statements, but could involve qualitative reporting – thus, from 2009, Unilever's Interim Management Statements omitted quarterly earnings. The 2013 EU Transparency Directive Amending Directive removed the requirement for Interim Management Statements from November 2015. Some countries (e.g. the UK) implemented this change earlier.

205 **$1 trillion in December 2017** Jennifer Thompson, 'Smart Beta Funds Pass $1trn in Assets', *Financial Times* (27 December 2017).

206 **maximise their effectiveness** Focusing Capital on the Long Term, 'Driving the Conversation: Long-Term Roadmaps for Long-Term Success' (2019).

207 **put it into practice** For say-on-pay, the policy vote is typically binding – enterprises can't pay leaders amounts that don't follow policy. A binding vote is feasible because it's easy to assess objectively whether actual pay follows a particular policy. For say-on-purpose, the policy vote would be advisory, as it's difficult to assess objectively whether a company has delivered on its purpose (e.g. improved colleague livelihoods by a 'sufficient' amount). The say-on-purpose vote has some similarities to Oliver Hart and Luigi Zingales's proposal that shareholders should vote on major corporate actions, so that they can express their views on the resulting externalities. I agree with the spirit of this suggestion, and indeed the idea of say-on-purpose was sparked by this proposal. However, embedding purpose involves day-to-day decisions, rather than only major corporate actions. In addition, shareholders may not have sufficient knowledge of the externalities resulting from corporate actions.

Communicating such information to investors might be time-consuming and divulge proprietary information to competitors; indeed, the process of holding the vote may allow a competitor to swoop in and take the action itself. Their model assumes that voting is costless and instantaneous. Oliver Hart and Luigi Zingales, 'Companies Should Maximize Shareholder Welfare Not Market Value' (2017) 2 *Journal of Law, Finance, and Accounting* 247–74.

208 **information around purpose** KKS Advisors and CECP, 'The Economic Significance of Long-Term Plans' (2018).

212 **sounding board for ethics queries** Employees volunteer to be considered for appointment as an ethics correspondent, alongside their regular job. They are typically quite senior, to ensure they have the trust of both leaders and colleagues, and spread across all company roles.

212 **become more widespread** Lynn S. Paine, 'Sustainability in the Boardroom', *Harvard Business Review* (July–August 2014).

212 **understand an enterprise** Financial Reporting Council, 'Corporate Culture and the Role of Boards: Report of Observations' (2016).

212 **analogous to a worker director** Unlike the director of a public company, I have no legal liability. The legal liability of worker directors would have to be carefully considered by any company contemplating voluntarily adopting them.

215 **published in 1911** Frederick W. Taylor, *The Principles of Scientific Management* (New York and London: Harper & Brothers, 1911).

215 **description of Schmidt** Schmidt's real name was Henry Noll.

216 **'it rhymed with great'** Wells Fargo 2010 Annual Report.

217 **explore and create** Daniel M. Cable, *Alive at Work: The Neuroscience of Helping Your People Love What They Do* (Cambridge, MA: Harvard Business Review Press, 2018).

218 **fuel costs and carbon emissions** Forbes, 'Why New Belgium Brewing's Employees Once Turned Down a Bonus to Invest in Wind Power Instead' (15 December 2015).

218 **performance is significantly better** Scott E. Seibert, Gang Wang and Stephen H. Courtright, 'Antecedents and Consequences of Psychological and Team Empowerment in Organizations: A Meta-Analytic Review' (2011) 96 *Journal of Applied Psychology* 981–1003.

218 **'vast and endless sea'** While widely attributed to Saint-Exupéry, this quote only appears in one American translation of his 1948 book *Citadelle*; the original French translates slightly differently.

219 **how to use its databases** Gary S. Becker, *Human Capital: A Theoretical and Empirical Analysis, with Special Reference to Education* (University of Chicago Press, 1964).

219   (e.g. Masters of Business Administration degrees) While some employ-
       ers fund Masters of Business Administration degrees, in return they
       require the worker to return to the firm for a minimum length of time
       afterwards to ensure a return on investment.

219   depressed the entire city Amy Goldstein, *Janesville: An American Story*
       (New York: Simon & Schuster, 2017).

220   reduction in absenteeism costs Katherine Baicker, David Cutler and
       Zirui Song, 'Workplace Wellness Programs Can Generate Savings'
       (2010) 29 *Health Affairs* 1–8.

221   higher insurance premiums Joel Goh, Jeffrey Pfeffer and Stefanos Zenios,
       'The Relationship between Workplace Stressors and Mortality and Health
       Costs in the United States' (2016) 62 *Management Science* 608–28.

Chapter 9 Investors

225   failing in these responsibilities The 2009 Walker Review into the UK
       financial crisis concluded that: 'The atmosphere of at least acquiescence
       in high leverage on the part of shareholders will have exacerbated critical
       problems encountered in some instances … [E]ven major fund managers
       appear to have been slow to act where issues of concern were identified in
       banks in which they were investors, and of limited effectiveness in seeking
       to address them either individually or collaboratively.'

226   introduced Stewardship Codes As of late 2017, nine countries have explicit
       national stewardship codes: in Europe (Denmark, the UK), Asia (Hong
       Kong, Japan, Malaysia, Taiwan, Thailand) and Africa (South Africa, Kenya).
       The EU Shareholder Rights Directive requires institutional investors to pub-
       licly disclose their stewardship policy or explain why they don't have one.

226–7 guide trading decisions More formally, these are known as 'sell-side
       equity analysts' as they typically work for investment banks that 'sell'
       trade ideas to investors. This contrasts with 'buy-side equity analysts'
       who are in-house analysts within an investor.

229   small number of companies An actively managed fund that instead aims
       to create value through asset allocation across sectors, or a smart-beta
       fund that aims to create value through quantitative strategies, will
       justifiably hold many stocks. However, these funds don't claim to add
       value through individual stock selection.

229   performance rises by 3% Ajay Khorana, Henri Servaes and Lei Wedge,
       'Portfolio Manager Ownership and Firm Performance' (2007) 85 *Jour-
       nal of Financial Economics* 179–204.

229 **likely to be effective** Christopher P. Clifford and Laura Lindsey, 'Blockholder Heterogeneity, CEO Compensation, and Firm Performance' (2016) 51 *Journal of Financial and Quantitative Analysis* 1491–520. They study mutual funds with 'fulcrum fees', where the annual management fee increases if fund performance exceeds a benchmark.

230 **direct stewardship efforts** Survey respondent to the UK Investment Association's 2016 Stewardship in Practice survey.

230 **embedded throughout the organisation** BNP Paribas, 'The ESG Global Survey 2019: Asset Owners and Managers Determine Their ESG Integration Strategies' (2019).

230 **incorporated in the stock price** Mary E. Barth, Michael B. Clement, George Foster and Ron Kasznik, 'Brand Values and Capital Market Valuation' (1998) 3 *Review of Accounting Studies* 41–68.

231 **'new ethical investors'** Sophie Grene, 'Quants Are the New Ethical Investors', *Financial Times* (14 January 2016).

233 **telling yourself 'rational lies'** Stephen R. Covey, *The 7 Habits of Highly Effective People* (New York: Free Press, 1989).

235 **information on their financial returns** Samuel M. Hartzmark and Abigail B. Sussman, 'Do Investors Value Sustainability? A Natural Experiment Examining Ranking and Fund Flows', *Journal of Finance* (forthcoming).

236 **it can address the shortcomings** The November 2018 'Stewardship in Practice' survey by the UK Investment Association reported that 35% of asset managers always inform management of the reason for voting against or abstaining, 60% do so sometimes and 6% never do so.

237 **monitoring and engagement effectively** Focusing Capital for the Long Term, 'Stewardship Check-List for Long-Term Success' (2019).

237 **'holding half your float'** John Lorinc, 'Stephen Jarislowsky Has Every Right to Say "I Told You So"', *Globe and Mail* (25 October 2002).

238 **'we are not going to leave'** David Benoit, 'Blackrock's Larry Fink: Typical Activists Are Too Short-Term', *Wall Street Journal* (16 January 2014).

238 **'returns for all investors'** Paul Singer, 'Efficient Markets Need Guys Like Me', *Wall Street Journal* (19 October 2017).

238 **increase campaign success** Ian R. Appel, Todd A. Gormley and Donald B. Keim, 'Standing on the Shoulders of Giants: The Effect of Passive Investors on Activism' (2019) 32 *Review of Financial Studies* 2720–74. Success is measured in a number of ways – the campaign leading to a settlement with management (and the number of board seats that the settlement gives to the activist), takeover defences being removed and the firm being sold to the activist or a third party. Prior studies showed that these outcomes increase firm value.

239 **narratives can be particularly telling** In 2016, the UK Investment Association reported that 72% of asset managers disclose votes publicly, of which 62% don't include the rationale for voting, 7% always include it and 31% include it where it voted against management, abstained or voted in favour, but the issue was controversial.

239 **not short-term performance** Naturally, savers could still calculate short-term performance themselves, using historical data or financial websites. But if marketing materials and saver updates cease to report short-term performance, it will be less salient in the minds of clients.

240 **25% in the US** Nadya Malenko and Yao Shen, 'The Role of Proxy Advisory Firms: Evidence from a Regression-Discontinuity Design' (2016) 29 *Review of Financial Studies* 3394–427. The study uses a regression discontinuity to identify causation – it's not that a flawed pay proposal leads both ISS to give a negative recommendation and also investors to vote against.

240 **15% in the UK** PwC, 'ISS: Friend or Foe to Stewardship?' (2018).

240 **as discussed in Chapter 5** The second flaw is that ISS's methodology is not size-adjusted. Small companies typically pay their CEOs less, and also typically outperform large firms, so the lack of size adjustment leads to a negative relationship between pay and performance. For further detail, see Tom Gosling, 'Shareholding Provides the Key for Linking Pay to Performance', *LinkedIn Pulse* (24 October 2017).

240 **errors when doing so** See Willis Towers Watson's Schedule 14A filing on 31 May 2017 for details of the errors.

241 **'the corporate consulting'** Dean Starkman, 'A Proxy Advisor's Two Sides: Some Question Work of ISS for Companies It Scrutinizes', *Washington Post* (23 January 2006).

241 **26,304 shareholder meetings** Tao Li, 'Outsourcing Corporate Governance: Conflicts of Interest within the Proxy Advisory Industry' (2018) 64 *Management Science* 2951–71.

241 **framework as for asset managers** The proxy advisory industry is already taking voluntary steps to address the above concerns through its Best Practice Principles for Shareholder Voting Research Providers, which stress the need for adequate resourcing and to manage conflicts of interest. However, they don't adequately recognise the role that proxy advisors play in stewardship. Even if a proxy advisor has large headcount and is free from conflicts of interest, it may use one-size-fits-all recommendations.

242 **9.1% over the following six months** Kent L. Womack, 'Do Brokerage Analysts' Recommendations Have Investment Value?' (1996) 51 *Journal of Finance* 137–67.

242   **clients of the bank he works for** The 2003 Global Analyst Research Settlement requires firewalls between the equity research and corporate finance divisions of an investment bank, and prohibits equity research analysts' pay being linked to corporate finance revenues. It aims to prevent analysts being biased towards companies who give the bank corporate finance business.

242   **reduces the stock price by 3.5%** Thomas J. Lopez and Lynn Rees, 'The Effect of Beating and Missing Analysts' Forecasts on the Information Content of Unexpected Earnings' (2002) 17 *Journal of Accounting, Auditing, and Finance* 155–84.

242–3   **causes the CEO's bonus to fall** Steven R. Matsunaga and Chul W. Park, 'The Effect of Missing a Quarterly Earnings Benchmark on the CEO's Annual Bonus' (2001) 76 *Accounting Review* 313–32.

243   **cut R&D to hit the forecast** Stephen J. Terry, 'The Macro Impact of Short-Termism' (2017).

243   **intangibles are particularly material** Eli Amir, Baruch Lev and Theodore Sougiannis, 'Do Financial Analysts Get Intangibles?' (2003) 12 *European Accounting Review* 635–59.

243   **quality of patents rise** Jie (Jack) He and Xuan Tian, 'The Dark Side of Analyst Coverage: The Case of Innovation' (2013) 109 *Journal of Financial Economics* 856–78.

243–4   **forecast of quarterly earnings** Pessimistic might be defined as being below last quarter's level, or the same quarter last year.

Chapter 10 Citizens

248   **numerous governance issues** These included a combined CEO and Chair, over-boarded directors, non-independent audit and compensation committees, and numerous CEO pay issues.

248   **revelations at the time** E. Scott Reckard, 'Wells Fargo's Pressure-Cooker Sales Culture Comes at a Cost', *Los Angeles Times* (21 December 2013).

248   **before the scandal broke out** Boris Groysberg, Eric Lin and George Serafeim, 'Does Financial Misconduct Affect the Future Compensation of Alumni Managers?' (2019).

249   **how best to reduce it** For a step-by-step guide on how an individual household can calculate its carbon footprint and take steps to reduce it, see Tom Gosling, 'Facing Up to the Truth of Our Carbon Footprint', *Linkedin Pulse* (2019).

250 **HSBC's cleaners a 28% pay rise** The cleaners were not directly employed by HSBC, but by the contract cleaning company OCS. HSBC changed the terms of its contract with OCS, allowing for this pay rise.

254 **17 percentage points the next year** Over 2013–15, UK FTSE 350 companies that garner less than 80% of votes receive an average of 71% support. One year later, the average vote for the same companies was 88%. Source: PwC, 'Executive Pay in a World of Truthiness: Facts and Myths in the Pay Debate' (2017).

254 **(pushing ahead with plans regardless)** Matthew Syed, *Black Box Thinking: The Surprising Truth about Success* (London: John Murray, 2015).

255 **this is an acceptable level** Kevin J. Murphy and Michael C. Jensen, 'The Politics of Pay: The Unintended Consequences of Regulating Executive Compensation' (2018) 3 *Journal of Law, Finance, and Accounting* 189–242.

256 **more closely to performance** Ricardo Correa and Ugur Lel, 'Say on Pay Laws, Executive Compensation, Pay Slice, and Firm Valuation around the World' (2016) 122 *Journal of Financial Economics* 500–20.

256 **May became Prime Minister** The November 2016 Green Paper on Corporate Governance asked respondents for their views on binding say-on-pay. The government's August 2017 response to the Green Paper consultation reported that only one-third of respondents supported this option.

256 **fiduciary duty to vote** This is SEC Final Rule IA-2106. It does allow investors to intentionally refrain from particular votes if they have a good reason. The example they give is 'casting a vote on a foreign security may involve additional costs such as hiring a translator or traveling to the foreign country to vote the security in person'.

257 **the board being unresponsive** The inquiry found: 'The company's shareholders suffered from an absence of reliable information and were … unable to exercise sufficient influence on the board to change its direction of travel.'

258 **raised them to exactly $1 million** Nancy L. Rose and Catherine D. Wolfram, 'Regulating Executive Pay: Using the Tax Code to Influence Chief Executive Officer Compensation' (2002) 20 *Journal of Labor Economics* 138–75.

259 **CEO labour market and pay design** Knowledge of pay design matters because the appropriate level of pay will depend on its structure. For example, if the CEO is given shorter holding periods, she should be paid less.

259 **societal impact more generally** PwC, 'Making Your Reporting More Accessible and Effective' (2015).

261   **punished for failing to do so** Currently, UK law allows a director to be barred for 'unfit conduct' such as 'allowing a company to continue trading when it can't pay its debts, not keeping proper company accounting records, not sending accounts and returns to Companies House, not paying tax owed by the company, using company money or assets for personal benefit'. However, failure to show regard to stakeholders is not classified as 'unfit conduct'.

261   **tax on carbon emissions** 'Economists' Statement on Carbon Dividends', *Wall Street Journal* (17 January 2019).

262   **all stages of their career** SkillsFuture@sc was Standard Chartered's voluntary add-on to the Singapore government's SkillsFuture programme. As a result, Standard Chartered employees could not only use the government's S$500 credit for a SkillsFuture course, but also take one of the bank-sponsored courses.

263   **helps them find new jobs** It also funds projects to improve firms' international competitiveness.

263   **methodology to identify causality** Benjamin G. Hyman, 'Can Displaced Labor Be Retrained? Evidence from Quasi-Random Assignment to Trade Adjustment Assistance' (2018).

263   **duration of unemployment by 18%** Brian Krogh Graversen and Jan C. van Ours, 'How to Help Unemployed Find Jobs Quickly: Experimental Evidence from a Mandatory Activation Program' (2008) 92 *Journal of Public Economics* 2020–35.

264   **late fees and over-limit fees** Hong Ru and Antoinette Schoar, 'Do Credit Card Companies Screen for Behavioral Biases?' (2016).

264   **negative causal effect on wages** Efraim Benmelech, Nittai Bergman and Hyunseob Kim, 'Strong Employers and Weak Employees: How Does Employer Concentration Affect Wages?' (2018).

265   **refer the reader to those sources** See the UK Competition and Markets Authority, 'Annual Plan 2017/18' (2017) and OECD, 'Competition Policy: Promoting Efficiency and Sound Markets' (2012). For an academic literature review, see Mark Armstrong and David E. M. Sappington, 'Regulation, Competition, and Liberalization' (2006) 64 *Journal of Economic Literature* 325–66.

265   **discussed in Chapter 5** Share options also counted, and have similar issues to performance shares.

265–6 **finance themselves with debt** Florian Heider and Alexander Ljungqvist, 'As Certain as Debt and Taxes: Estimating the Tax Sensitivity of Leverage from State Tax Changes' (2015) 118 *Journal of Financial Economics* 684–712.

266 **firms using less debt** Frédéric Panier, Francisco Pérez-González and Pablo Villanueva, 'Capital Structure and Taxes: What Happens When You (Also) Subsidize Equity?' (2012).

266 **Codes throughout the world** For example, the UK Corporate Governance Code requires the board to designate one of the non-executive directors as a 'senior independent director'. Sometimes a company chooses not to comply, and explains that this is because several non-executive directors have recently been appointed, and it wants to give them time to settle into their roles before choosing one.

267 **tackle its productivity problem** The genesis was UK Chancellor of the Exchequer George Osborne asking Sir Charlie Mayfield in 2015 to investigate the UK's productivity problem in depth.

267 **written about elsewhere** Examples include Steve Mariotti's *An Entrepreneur's Manifesto* (West Conshohocken, PA: Templeton Press, 2015) and David Storey's *Understanding the Small Business Sector* (Andover: Cengage Learning, 1994). See also Berger and Udell (1988) for an academic study of the challenges that small enterprises face and ways to promote their growth. Allen N. Berger and Gregory F. Udell, 'The Economics of Small Business Finance: The Roles of Private Equity and Debt Markets in the Financial Growth Cycle' (1998) 22 *Journal of Banking and Finance* 617–73.

267 **European Investment Bank** The European Investment Bank runs a European Investment Fund. It doesn't provide financing directly, but through intermediaries. For example, it invests in venture capital funds and banks, and provides loan guarantees.

Chapter 11 Growing the Pie More Widely

279 **Bob rejects even $3** Werner Güth, Rolf Schmittberger and Bernd Schwarze, 'An Experimental Analysis of Ultimatum Bargaining' (1982) 3 *Journal of Economic Behavior and Organization* 367–88.

280 **its GNH would be 9** Moving a worker to PCs would reduce the number of TVs – and thus GNH – below nine; moving a worker to TVs would have an analogous effect.

281 **'27% in last 4months [sic]'** 4 August 2018.

281 **causes you to win** Even if you win a war, it may be that you lose overall because of the resources used in doing so.

283 **healthcare for the UK** See the UK Visa Bureau's 'UK Shortage Occupations List'.

284 **now needed in each branch** James Bessen, 'Toil and Technology' (2015) 52 *Finance & Development* 16–19.

284 **'the ordinary man's load'** Nyshka Chandran, 'Japan, Unlike the West, Is Not Scared of Robots Stealing Jobs, Deputy Leader Says', CNBC (4 May 2018).

285 **substitute for workers** James Bessen, *Learning by Doing: The Real Connection between Innovation, Wages, and Wealth* (New Haven, CT: Yale University Press, 2015).

286 ***Highly Effective People*** Stephen R. Covey, *The 7 Habits of Highly Effective People* (New York: Free Press, 1989).

286 **hard work and cooperation** Covey's Habit 4, 'Think Win-Win', does stress the importance of working collaboratively to create value in negotiations.

287 **three types of people** Adam Grant, *Give and Take: A Revolutionary Approach to Success* (London: Weidenfeld & Nicolson, 2013).

292 **2008 Harvard graduation speech** 'The Fringe Benefits of Failure and the Importance of Imagination'.

292 **movements and cockpit conversations** The boxes are actually coloured orange, to aid in their recovery after a crash.

292 **a more nuanced conclusion** K. Anders Ericsson, Ralf Th. Krampe and Clemens Tesch-Romer, 'The Role of Deliberate Practice in the Acquisition of Expert Performance' (1993) 100 *Psychological Review* 363–406.

293 **time playing chess games** Neil Charness, Ralf Th. Krampe and Ulrich Mayr, 'The Role of Practice and Coaching in Entrepreneurial Skill Domains: An International Comparison of Life-Span Chess Skill Acquisition' in K. Anders Ericsson (ed.), *The Road to Excellence: The Acquisition of Expert Performance in the Arts and Sciences, Sports, and Games* (Mahwah, NJ: Erlbaum, 1996).

293 **routines they'd already perfected** Janice M. Deakin and Stephen Cobley, 'A Search for Deliberate Practice: An Examination of the Practice Environments in Figure Skating and Volleyball' in Janet L. Starkes and K. Anders Ericsson (eds), *Expert Performance in Sports: Advances in Research on Sport Expertise* (Champaign, IL: Human Kinetics, 2003).

294 **than it costs you** The idea is also similar to the concept of 'things of unequal value' in Stuart Diamond's negotiations book *Getting More*. In a negotiation, you should offer a counterparty something that's worth more to him than it costs you, so that you can ask for something in return. However, service is not about getting more from others, but giving more to others. Stuart Diamond, *Getting More: How You Can Negotiate to Succeed in Work and Life* (New York: Random House, 2012).

295 **priorities in their current position** Some elements of this section are inspired by a speech entitled 'How to Have a Successful and Meaningful Career' by Professor Andrew Metrick, one of the most celebrated professors at Wharton, in his final lecture before he left to go to Yale. It's also part of a talk called 'Fulfilling Careers and Full Lives' that I give in the final lecture of my core finance course, and available at http://bit.ly/fulfillingcareers.

299 **watching Clarence play his solo** On the buy-side, like any job at the start, there's selling involved as you have to sell your ideas to your superiors. However, once you get to the top, there are no more superiors to sell to, only occasional 'sell' meetings with investors. Someone whose passion is selling might not find as much fulfilment when she reaches the summit.

299 *The Road to Character* David Brooks, *The Road to Character* (New York: Allen Lane, 2015).

Appendix

317 **return-on-assets and sales growth** Elroy Dimson, Oğuzhan Karakaş and Xi Li, 'Coordinated Engagements' (2018).

318 **dialogue with companies** The UN Collaboration Platform does have its own team that directly leads a small number of engagements; however, most engagements are investor-led.

318 **most likely to engage** Craig Doidge, Alexander Dyck, Hamed Mahmudi and Aazam Virani, 'Collective Action and Governance Activism', *Review of Finance* (forthcoming).

320 **stewardship by asset managers** Focusing Capital on the Long Term, 'Institutional Investor Mandates: Anchors for Long-Term Performance' (2017).

320 **their portfolio each year** UN PRI, 'Appointing Equity Managers: Interview with Environment Agency Pension Fund' (2016).

321 **stewardship or engage itself** Pension Funds and Social Investment: The Government's Response (June 2018). It argues that pension funds with at least 100 members should report stewardship policies, 'including how and when trustees monitor and engage with: the firms in which they invest; people who manage the investment on their behalf; and fellow investors'.

INDEX